Referen... Rest of ...

COMPUTER BOOK SERIES FROM IDG

Are you intimidated and confused by computers? Do you find that traditional manuals are overloaded with technical details you'll never use? Do your friends and family always call you to fix simple problems on their PCs? Then the *...For Dummies®* computer book series from IDG Books Worldwide is for you.

...For Dummies books are written for those frustrated computer users who know they aren't really dumb but find that PC hardware, software, and indeed the unique vocabulary of computing make them feel helpless. *...For Dummies* books use a lighthearted approach, a down-to-earth style, and even cartoons and humorous icons to diffuse computer novices' fears and build their confidence. Lighthearted but not lightweight, these books are a perfect survival guide for anyone forced to use a computer.

"I like my copy so much I told friends; now they bought copies."

Irene C., Orwell, Ohio

"Quick, concise, nontechnical, and humorous."

Jay A., Elburn, Illinois

"Thanks, I needed this book. Now I can sleep at night."

Robin F., British Columbia, Canada

Already, hundreds of thousands of satisfied readers agree. They have made *...For Dummies* books the #1 introductory level computer book series and have written asking for more. So, if you're looking for the most fun and easy way to learn about computers, look to *...For Dummies* books to give you a helping hand.

7/96r

WordPerfect® Suite 7 For Dummies®

by Julie Adair King

IDG Books Worldwide, Inc.
An International Data Group Company

Foster City, CA ♦ Chicago, IL ♦ Indianapolis, IN ♦ Southlake, TX

WordPerfect® Suite 7 For Dummies®

Published by
IDG Books Worldwide, Inc.
An International Data Group Company
919 E. Hillsdale Blvd.
Suite 400
Foster City, CA 94404
www.idgbooks.com (IDG Books Worldwide Web Site)
http://www.dummies.com (Dummies Press Web Site)

Library of Congress Catalog Card No.: 96-75110

ISBN: 1-56884-946-X

Printed in the United States of America

10 9 8 7 6 5 4 3 2

1O/RY/QZ/ZW/IN

Distributed in the United States by IDG Books Worldwide, Inc.

Distributed by Macmillan Canada for Canada; by Contemporanea de Ediciones for Venezuela; by Distribuidora Cuspide for Argentina; by CITEC for Brazil; by Ediciones ZETA S.C.R. Ltda. for Peru; by Editorial Limusa SA for Mexico; by Transworld Publishers Limited in the United Kingdom and Europe; by Academic Bookshop for Egypt; by Levant Distributors S.A.R.L. for Lebanon; by Al Jassim for Saudi Arabia; by Simron Pty. Ltd. for South Africa; by Pustak Mahal for India; by The Computer Bookshop for India; by Toppan Company Ltd. for Japan; by Addison Wesley Publishing Company for Korea; by Longman Singapore Publishers Ltd. for Singapore, Malaysia, Thailand, and Indonesia; by Unalis Corporation for Taiwan; by WS Computer Publishing Company, Inc. for the Philippines; by WoodsLane Pty. Ltd. for Australia; by WoodsLane Enterprises Ltd. for New Zealand. Authorized Sales Agent: Anthony Rudkin Associates for the Middle East and North Africa.

For general information on IDG Books Worldwide's books in the U.S., please call our Consumer Customer Service department at 800-762-2974. For reseller information, including discounts and premium sales, please call our Reseller Customer Service department at 800-434-3422.

For information on where to purchase IDG Books Worldwide's books outside the U.S., please contact our International Sales department at 415-655-3172 or fax 415-655-3295.

For information on foreign language translations, please contact our Foreign & Subsidiary Rights department at 415-655-3021 or fax 415-655-3281.

For sales inquiries and special prices for bulk quantities, please contact our Sales department at 415-655-3200 or write to the address above.

For information on using IDG Books Worldwide's books in the classroom or for ordering examination copies, please contact our Educational Sales department at 800-434-2086 or fax 817-251-8174.

For authorization to photocopy items for corporate, personal, or educational use, please contact Copyright Clearance Center, 222 Rosewood Drive, Danvers, MA 01923, or fax 508-750-4470.

About the Author

Julie Adair King

Julie Adair King has been wrestling with computers since 1976, when she stood in line with all the other first-year geeks at Purdue University to type programming commands into now-antiquated keypunch machines. Since then, she has churned out documents using almost every type of word processor, spreadsheet, and office utility program to grace the computer-store shelves.

A long-time writer and editor, King has contributed to many computer books published by IDG Books Worldwide, including *CorelDRAW! 6 For Dummies, PerfectOffice 3 For Dummies, PageMaker 6 For Macs For Dummies,* 2nd Edition, and *PageMaker 6 For Windows For Dummies,* 2nd Edition.

When not fiddling around with computers, King writes business and career books and frequently speaks about career issues on radio and television talk shows. Her work has been published in *Cosmopolitan* and other national magazines.

ABOUT IDG BOOKS WORLDWIDE

Welcome to the world of IDG Books Worldwide.

IDG Books Worldwide, Inc., is a subsidiary of International Data Group, the world's largest publisher of computer-related information and the leading global provider of information services on information technology. IDG was founded more than 25 years ago and now employs more than 8,500 people worldwide. IDG publishes more than 270 computer publications in over 75 countries (see listing below). More than 90 million people read one or more IDG publications each month.

Launched in 1990, IDG Books Worldwide is today the #1 publisher of best-selling computer books in the United States. We are proud to have received eight awards from the Computer Press Association in recognition of editorial excellence and three from *Computer Currents*' First Annual Readers' Choice Awards. Our best-selling *...For Dummies®* series has more than 25 million copies in print with translations in 30 languages. IDG Books Worldwide, through a joint venture with IDG's Hi-Tech Beijing, became the first U.S. publisher to publish a computer book in the People's Republic of China. In record time, IDG Books Worldwide has become the first choice for millions of readers around the world who want to learn how to better manage their businesses.

Our mission is simple: Every one of our books is designed to bring extra value and skill-building instructions to the reader. Our books are written by experts who understand and care about our readers. The knowledge base of our editorial staff comes from years of experience in publishing, education, and journalism — experience which we use to produce books for the '90s. In short, we care about books, so we attract the best people. We devote special attention to details such as audience, interior design, use of icons, and illustrations. And because we use an efficient process of authoring, editing, and desktop publishing our books electronically, we can spend more time ensuring superior content and spend less time on the technicalities of making books.

You can count on our commitment to deliver high-quality books at competitive prices on topics you want to read about. At IDG Books Worldwide, we continue in the IDG tradition of delivering quality for more than 25 years. You'll find no better book on a subject than one from IDG Books Worldwide.

John Kilcullen
President and CEO
IDG Books Worldwide, Inc.

IDG Books Worldwide, Inc., is a subsidiary of International Data Group, the world's largest publisher of computer-related information and the leading global provider of information services on information technology. International Data Group publishes over 276 computer publications in over 75 countries. Ninety million people read one or more International Data Group publications each month. International Data Group's publications include: **ARGENTINA:** Annuario de Informatica, Computerworld Argentina, PC World Argentina; **AUSTRALIA:** Australian Macworld, Client/Server Journal, Computer Living, Computerworld, Computerworld 100, Digital News, IT Casebook, Network World, On-line World Australia, PC World, Publishing Essentials, Reseller, WebMaster; **AUSTRIA:** Computerwelt Osterreich, Networks Austria, PC Tip; **BELARUS:** PC World Belarus; **BELGIUM:** Data News; **BRAZIL:** Annuário de Informática, Computerworld Brazil, Connections, Super Game Power, Macworld, PC Player, PC World Brazil, Publish Brazil, Reseller News; **BULGARIA:** Computerworld Bulgaria, Networkworld/Bulgaria, PC & MacWorld Bulgaria; **CANADA:** CIO Canada, Client/Server World, ComputerWorld Canada, InfoCanada, Network World Canada; **CHILE:** Computerworld Chile, PC World Chile; **COLOMBIA:** Computerworld Colombia, PC World Colombia; **COSTA RICA:** PC World Centro America; **THE CZECH AND SLOVAK REPUBLICS:** Computerworld Czechoslovakia, Elektronika Czechoslovakia, Macworld Czech Republic, PC World Czechoslovakia; **DENMARK:** Communications World, Computerworld Danmark, Macworld Danmark, PC Privat Danmark, PC World Danmark, PC World Danmark Supplements, TECH World; **DOMINICAN REPUBLIC:** PC World Republica Dominicana; **ECUADOR:** PC World Ecuador; **EGYPT:** Computerworld Middle East, PC World Middle East; **EL SALVALDOR:** PC World Centro America; **FINLAND:** MikroPC, Tietoverkko, Tietoviikko; **FRANCE:** Distributique, Golden, Hebdo-Distributique, Info PC, Le Guide du Monde Informatique, Le Monde Informatique, Reseaux & Telecoms; **GERMANY:** Computer Partner, Computerwoche, Computerwoche Extra, Computerwoche Focus, I/M Information Management, Macwelt, PC Welt; **GREECE:** GamePro, Multimedia World; **GUATEMALA:** PC World Centro America; **HONDURAS:** PC World Centro America; **HONG KONG:** Computerworld Hong Kong, PCWorld Hong Kong, Publish in Asia; **HUNGARY:** ABCD CD-ROM, Computerworld Szamitastechnika, PC & Mac World Hungary, PC-X Magazine; **ICELAND:** Tolvuheimur/PC World Island; **INDIA:** Information Systems Computerworld, PC World India, Publish in Asia; **INDONESIA:** InfoKomputer PC World, Komputek Computerworld, Publish in Asia; **IRELAND:** ComputerScope, PC Live!; **ISRAEL:** People & Computers; **ITALY:** Computerworld Italia, Computerworld Italia Special Editions, Macworld Italia, Networking Italia, PC Shopping, PC World Italia, PC World/Walt Disney; **JAPAN:** DTP World, HP Open World Japan, Macworld Japan, Nikkei Personal Computing, Open World Japan, OS/2 World Japan, SunWorld Japan, Windows World Japan; **KENYA:** East African Computer News; **KOREA:** Hi-Tech Information/Computerworld, Macworld Korea, PC World Korea; **MACEDONIA:** PC World Macedonia; **MALAYSIA:** Computerworld Malaysia, PC World Malaysia, Publish in Asia; **MEXICO:** Computerworld Mexico, Macworld, PC World Mexico; **MYANMAR:** PC World Myanmar; **NETHERLANDS:** Computer! Totaal, LAN Magazine, LanWorld Buyers Guide, Macworld, Net Magazine, Totaal! Beurskrant; **NEW ZEALAND:** Absolute Beginner's Guide, Computer Buyer, Computer Industry Directory, Computerworld New Zealand, MTB, Network World, PC World New Zealand; **NICARAGUA:** PC World Centro America; **NIGERIA:** PC World Nigeria; **NORWAY:** Computerworld Norge, Computerworld Privat (Datamagasinet), CW Rapport Norge, IDG's KURSGUIDE, Macworld Norge, Multimediaworld, PC World Ekspress, PC World Nettverk, PC World Norge, PC World's Produktguide, Windows World Spesial; **PAKISTAN:** Computerworld Pakistan, PC World Pakistan; Panama: PC World Panama; **P. R. OF CHINA:** China Computer Users, China Computerworld, China Infoworld, China Telecom World Weekly, Computer & Communication, Electronic Design China, Electronics Today, Electronics Weekly, Game Camp, Game Soft, Network World China, PC World China, Popular Computer Weekly, Software Weekly, Software World, Telecom World; **PERU:** Computerworld Peru, PC World Profesional Peru, PC World Peru; **PHILIPPINES:** Computerworld Philippines, PC World Philippines, Publish in Asia; **POLAND:** Computerworld Poland, Computerworld Special Report, Macworld, Networld, PC World Komputer; **PORTUGAL:** Cerebro/PC World, Computerworld/Correio Informático, Dealer World Portugal, MacIn/PCIn, Multimedia World Portugal; **PUERTO RICO:** PC World Puerto Rico; **ROMANIA:** Computerworld Romania, PC World Romania, Telecom Romania; **RUSSIA:** Computerworld Russia, Mir PK, Sety; **SINGAPORE:** Computerworld Singapore, PC World Singapore, Publish in Asia; **SLOVENIA:** MONITOR; **SOUTH AFRICA:** Computing S.A., InfoWorld S.A., Network World S.A., Software World; **SPAIN:** Computerworld España, COMUNICACIONES WORLD, Dealer World, Macworld España, PC World España; **SWEDEN:** CAP&Design, Computer Sweden, Corporate Computing, MacWorld, Maxi Data, MikroDatorn, Nätverk & Kommunikation, PC/Aktiv, PC World, Windows World; **SWITZERLAND:** Computerworld Schweiz, Macworld Schweiz, PCtip; **TAIWAN:** Computerworld Taiwan, Macworld Taiwan, PC World Taiwan, Publish Taiwan, Windows World; **THAILAND:** Thai Computerworld, Publish in Asia; **TURKEY:** Computerworld Turkiye, MACWORLD Turkiye, PC WORLD Turkiye; **UKRAINE:** Computerworld Kiev, Computers & Software, Multimedia World Ukraine, PC World Ukraine; **UNITED KINGDOM:** Acorn User, Amiga Action, Amiga Computing, Appletalk, Computing, GamePro, Macworld, Network News, Parents and Computers, PC Advisor, PC Home, PSX Pro UK, The WEB; **UNITED STATES:** Cable in the Classroom, CD Review, CIO Magazine, Computerworld, Computerworld Client/Server Journal, Digital Video Magazine, DOS World, Federal Computer Week, GamePro, InfoWorld, I-Way, JavaWorld, Macworld, Multimedia World, Netscape World Online, Network World, PC Entertainment, PC World, Publish, SunWorld Online, SWATPro Magazine, Video Event, WebMaster; **URUGUAY:** PC World Uruguay; **VENEZUELA:** Computerworld Venezuela, PC World Venezuela; and **VIETNAM:** PC World Vietnam.

7/16/96

Dedication

This book is dedicated to my grandparents, George and Irene Harris, Mae King, and the late Cecil King. Thank you for a lifetime of love.

Author's Acknowledgments

Sincere thanks to project editor Jennifer Ehrlich for the insights and patience that made this book substantially better and my job significantly easier. Thanks also to copy editor Diane Smith and technical editor Sam Faulkner for their valuable input, as well as to all the people in production who work so hard to turn raw words and pictures into polished pages.

Last, but absolutely not least, I'd like to give special thanks to associate publisher Diane Graves Steele, who it has been my privilege to know these past several years. Your encouragement and support have meant more than you will ever guess.

Publisher's Acknowledgments

We're proud of this book; please send us your comments about it by using the Reader Response Card at the back of the book or by e-mailing us at `feedback/dummies@idgbooks.com`. Some of the people who helped bring this book to market include the following:

Acquisitions, Development, & Editorial

Project Editor: Jennifer Ehrlich

Assistant Acquisitions Editor: Gareth Hancock

Product Development Manager: Mary Bednarek

Copy Editors: Susan Diane Smith, Joe Jansen

Technical Reviewer: Samuel Faulkner

Editorial Manager: Mary C. Corder

Editorial Assistant: Chris H. Collins

Production

Project Coordinator: Debbie Sharpe

Layout and Graphics: E. Shawn Aylsworth, Brett Black, Elizabeth Cárdenas-Nelson, J. Tyler Connor, Cheryl Denski, Maridee V. Ennis, Julie Jordan Forey, Angela F. Hunckler, Todd Klemme, Jane Martin, Gina Scott, M. Anne Sipahimalani

Proofreaders: Joel Draper, Michael Bolinger, Nancy Price, Robert Springer

Indexer: Ty Koontz

General & Administrative

IDG Books Worldwide, Inc.: John Kilcullen, President & CEO; Steven Berkowitz, COO & Publisher

Dummies, Inc.: Milissa Koloski, Executive Vice President & Publisher

Dummies Technology Press & Dummies Editorial: Diane Graves Steele, Associate Publisher; Judith A. Taylor, Brand Manager

Dummies Trade Press: Kathleen A. Welton, Vice President & Publisher; Stacy S. Collins, Brand Manager

IDG Books Production for Dummies Press: Beth Jenkins, Production Director; Cindy L. Phipps, Supervisor of Project Coordination; Kathie S. Schutte, Supervisor of Page Layout; Shelley Lea, Supervisor of Graphics and Design; Debbie J. Gates, Production Systems Specialist

Dummies Packaging and Book Design: Patti Sandez, Packaging Assistant; Kavish+Kavish, Cover Design

♦

The publisher would like to give special thanks to Patrick J. McGovern, without whom this book would not have been possible.

♦

Contents at a Glance

Introduction 1

Part I: The Suite Life 7

Chapter 1: Browsing through the Big Box 9
Chapter 2: Basic Stuff You Need to Know 17
Chapter 3: Can I Get Some Help, Please? 29

Part II: Goodbye, Typewriter . . . Hello, WordPerfect! 37

Chapter 4: The Process of Processing Words 39
Chapter 5: Open, Close, Save, Print: Dull but Vital Basics 49
Chapter 6: Eating Your Words and Other Editing Tasks 61
Chapter 7: Making Your Text Look Pretty 73
Chapter 8: Doing the Fancy Stuff 95
Chapter 9: Tools to Save You Time (and Embarrassment) 115

Part III: Crunching Numbers like a (Quattro) Pro 131

Chapter 10: The Spreadsheet Solution 133
Chapter 11: Filling in the Blanks 147
Chapter 12: The Formula for Success 159
Chapter 13: Editing Your Spreadsheet 173
Chapter 14: Charting Your Course 191
Chapter 15: The Finishing Touches 205

Part IV: Those Other Programs 219

Chapter 16: Let's All Get Together and Put on a Show! 221
Chapter 17: Envoy: A Tree's Best Friend 251
Chapter 18: Internet Adventures 267
Chapter 19: And the Rest 281
Chapter 20: Using Everything Together 307

Part V: The Part of Tens 319

Chapter 21: Ten Cool Tricks to Try on a Slow Day 321
Chapter 22: Ten Shortcuts You Can Use All the Time 331
Chapter 23: Ten Ways to Save Time 335

Appendix: Installing WordPerfect Suite 7 341

Index 347

Reader Response Card .... *Back of Book*

Cartoons at a Glance

By Rich Tennant • Fax: 508-546-7747 • E-mail: the5wave@tiac.net

"I TELL YA I'M STILL GETTING INTERFERENCE— - COOKIE, RAGS? RAGS WANNA COOKIE? - THERE IT GOES AGAIN."

page 131

The 5th Wave By Rich Tennant

AFTER SPENDING 9 DAYS WITH 12 DIFFERENT VENDORS AND READING 26 BROCHURES, DAVE HAD AN ACUTE ATTACK OF TOXIC OPTION SYNDROME.

page 219

"YOU KNOW THAT GUY WHO BOUGHT ALL THAT SOFTWARE? HIS CHECK HAS A WARRANTY THAT SAYS IT'S TENDERED AS IS AND HAS NO FITNESS FOR ANY PARTICULAR PURPOSE INCLUDING, BUT NOT LIMITED TO, CASHING."

page 7

"IT'S NOT THAT IT DOESN'T WORK AS A COMPUTER, IT JUST WORKS BETTER AS A PAPERWEIGHT."

page 37

page 319

Table of Contents

Introduction 1

Okay, So What Will This Book Do For Me? 1
What Programs Does This Book Cover? 2
How is Stuff Organized? 3
Part I: The Suite Life 3
Part II: Goodbye, Typewriter . . . Hello, WordPerfect! 3
Part III: Crunching Numbers Like a (Quattro) Pro 4
Part IV: Those Other Programs 4
Part V: The Part of Tens 4
Appendix: Installing WordPerfect Suite 7 5
That Symbol Means Something, Doesn't It? 5
Other Conventions Used in This Book 6
What Now? 6

Part I: The Suite Life 7

Chapter 1: Browsing through the Big Box 9

What Do All These Programs Do? 10
Which Program Do I Use When? 12
Hey! These All Look Alike! 14

Chapter 2: Basic Stuff You Need to Know 17

Starting Up and Shutting Down 18
Clicking, Double-clicking, and Other Mouse Maneuvers 18
Saving Time with Keyboard Shortcuts 19
Doing Windows 20
Resizing, Moving, and Closing Windows 22
Customizing Your View 23
Using DAD 24
Digging through Dialog Boxes 24
Juggling Open Windows 26

Chapter 3: Can I Get Some Help, Please? 29

Asking an Expert 30
Using the Show Me Features 31
Using QuickTasks 32
Getting More Help 33
Navigating a Help Window 34
Using the Reference Center 35

Part II: Goodbye, Typewriter . . . Hello, WordPerfect! 37

Chapter 4: The Process of Processing Words 39

Getting Started 39
Customizing Your Workspace 41
Entering Text 44
Moving around in Your Document 46

Chapter 5: Open, Close, Save, Print: Dull but Vital Basics 49

Opening a New Document 50
  Using Experts to create common documents 51
  Using the prefab templates 51
Opening Existing Documents 52
  Figuring out the Open dialog box 52
Closing a Document 54
Saving Your Work (and Your Sanity) 54
  Saving for the very first time 54
  Saving a document with a different name or format 56
  Getting extra protection through automatic saving 57
Printing Your Pages 57

Chapter 6: Eating Your Words and Other Editing Tasks 61

Selecting Stuff You Want to Edit 62
Deleting Selected Stuff 63
Moving and Copying Text 63
  Using the Copy, Cut, and Paste commands 64
  Dragging and dropping 65
Bringing Back Lost Text 67
Undoing Changes 68
Letting WordPerfect Correct Mistakes for You 69
  Adding words to the QuickCorrect list 70
  Overruling unwanted corrections 71

Chapter 7: Making Your Text Look Pretty 73

Playing with Fonts 74
  Choosing a font 74
  Changing the type size and style 77
Choosing a Page Size and Orientation 78
Setting Page Margins 79
Setting Tabs 80
  Adding, moving, or deleting a tab stop 82
  Choosing a tab stop type 84
Indenting and Aligning Text 85
  Indenting the first line of your paragraphs 85
  Indenting entire paragraphs 86
  Justifying text 89

Spacing Things Out 91
Adjusting line spacing 92
Adjusting the space between paragraphs 92
Centering text on a page 93
Making Text Fit on a Page 93

Chapter 8: Doing the Fancy Stuff 95

Creating Bulleted and Numbered Lists 96
Adding bullets 96
Adding numbers 98
Numbering Your Pages 99
Inserting the Current Date and Time 101
Tracking Down Special Characters 102
Creating Headers and Footers 104
Putting Your Text in Columns 107
Inserting Graphics 110
Creating Borders, Fills, and Lines 112
Adding borders and fills 113
Adding lines 114

Chapter 9: Tools to Save You Time (and Embarrassment) 115

Using Styles to Speed Up Formatting Chores 115
Choosing a style type 116
Creating character and paragraph styles 117
Applying styles 118
Editing a style 119
Removing styles 120
Copying Formats with QuickFormat 122
Finding and Replacing Errant Text 123
Checking Your Spelling 127

Part III: Crunching Numbers like a (Quattro) Pro 131

Chapter 10: The Spreadsheet Solution 133

So What Can I Do with This Thing? 134
Start It Up, Shut It Down 135
Your Field Guide to a Spreadsheet 135
I Don't Like What I See Here! 137
Changing the window display 137
Changing the active page display 138
Naming Your Pages 139
Ways to Move from Here to There 139
Open Me! Close Me! Save Me! 141
Opening a new or existing notebook 141
Closing a spreadsheet 143
Saving your work 143

Chapter 11: Filling in the Blanks 147

Building a Spreadsheet 147
Entering Data 149
  Basic data entry 150
  Data entry do's and don'ts 151
QuickFilling Cells 152
Handling Basic Formatting Chores 154
  Changing the numeric format 154
  Changing the font, type size, and type style 154
  Changing text alignment 155

Chapter 12: The Formula for Success 159

Creating a Basic Formula 159
  Typing formulas for simple calculations 160
  Typing formulas using cell addresses 160
  Entering cell addresses with the mouse 162
Telling Quattro Pro What to Calculate First 163
Working with Built-in Functions 166
  Writing formulas using functions 167
  Finding the average and median values 168
  Inserting the current date 169
  Figuring out some other cool stuff 169
Adding Things Up with QuickSum 170
Fighting the ERR Message 171

Chapter 13: Editing Your Spreadsheet 173

Getting Rid of Bloopers 173
  Replacing cell contents 174
  Editing tricks and techniques 174
  Deleting versus clearing cell contents 175
Undoing Bad Moves 176
Selecting Stuff 177
Inserting and Deleting Columns and Rows 178
  Inserting an empty row or column 179
  Deleting rows and columns 179
Adding a Page 180
Resizing Columns and Rows 181
Copying Data from Here to There 183
  Dragging and dropping a copy 184
  Using Copy and Paste to copy data 184
  Getting more specific with the Copy Block command 186
Moving Data Around 187
Transposing Cells 188

Chapter 14: Charting Your Course 191

Creating a New Chart 192
Using the Chart Expert 193
Creating charts with the QuickChart tool 194
Editing a Chart 195
Changing the chart type and color scheme 197
Giving your chart a title and a border 199
Editing individual chart elements 199
Adding lines and callouts 200
Exchanging rows and columns 201
Moving, Resizing, and Deleting Charts 201
Printing a Chart without Its Spreadsheet 203

Chapter 15: The Finishing Touches 205

Using SpeedFormat 206
Adding Lines, Borders, and Colors 207
Drawing lines and borders around cells 208
Applying color to text and backgrounds 210
Inserting Page Breaks 211
Hiding a Row or Column 211
Going from Screen to Printer 212
Previewing before you print 213
Changing the page setup 215
Choosing print options 217

Part IV: Those Other Programs 219

Chapter 16: Let's All Get Together and Put on a Show! 221

Starting and Stopping 221
Building a Really Big Shew 223
Step 1: Choosing a Master 223
Step 2: Choosing a slide template 225
Step 3: Adding titles and regular text 225
Step 4: Creating additional slides 228
Adding Pretty Pictures 229
Using the QuickArt browser to add graphics 229
Creating simple graphics 231
Working with bitmap images 234
Editing graphics 234
Editing Your Slides 235
Changing the background 235
Editing the template 236
Editing and formatting text 237
Moving, deleting, resizing, and copying stuff 239
Getting Another View of Your Show 240

Adding Transitions and Other Special Effects 240
Choosing a transition 241
Choosing an advance mode 242
Adding sounds 242
Jazzing up bulleted lists 244
Animating an object 244
Playing Your Show 245
Playing Your Show on Someone Else's Computer 246
Saving Slide Shows and Drawings 248
Printing Your Masterpieces 248

Chapter 17: Envoy: A Tree's Best Friend 251

Turning a Document into an Envoy File 251
Viewing a Document in Envoy 254
Flipping through Your Pages 256
Adding Notes and Highlights 257
Highlighting important stuff 257
Adding a QuickNote 258
Adding, Deleting, and Rearranging Pages 259
Marking Your Place with a Bookmark 260
Creating and Using Hypertext 261
Sending Someone Else an Envoy File 264
Saving, Printing, and Shutting Down 265

Chapter 18: Internet Adventures 267

A Crash Course in Internet Lingo 268
Leaping onto the Net 269
Becoming a Page Jumper 271
Finding Sites that Interest You 273
Saving Online Time (and Money) 274
Sending Electronic Mail on the Internet 275
Receiving and reading your mail 275
Sending e-mail 276
Using the address book 277
Chatting in Newsgroups 278
Catching up on the latest "news" 278
Subscribing to a newsgroup 278
Posting a message to a newsgroup 280
Printing and Saving Pages and Messages 280

Chapter 19: And the Rest 281

Using Corel Address Book 282
Adding and deleting contacts 282
Searching for a long-lost loved one 284
Changing the display of information 284
Printing and inserting addresses in WordPerfect 285

Dialing for dollars 285
Keeping Tabs on Your Life with Sidekick 95 285
Using the calendar and appointment scheduler 286
Recording appointments 286
Creating a To Do list and call list 287
Using the Cardfile 288
Setting up a new cardfile 289
Selecting and marking cards 291
Editing cards and cardfile fields 291
Searching for cards 292
Changing the Card List display 292
Ringing up a contact 293
Checking out the Write view 293
Using the Viewport 295
Printing cards, calendars, and other information 295
Exploring other tools 296
Peering Over the Dashboard 297
Drawing Diagrams with CorelFLOW 300
Getting the lay of the land 300
Using Smart Libraries 301
Understanding points and pins 302
Drawing your own objects 304
Playing with objects 305
Previewing, printing, and saving 306

Chapter 20: Using Everything Together 307

Saving Time and Effort with OLE 308
Deciding Whether to Link, Embed, or Copy and Paste 309
Making Linked Copies that Update Automatically 310
Linking Copies without Automatic Updating 312
Creating an Embedded Copy 313
Embedding Objects on the Fly 314
Dragging and Dropping between Programs 315
Embedding or Linking an Entire Document 316
Editing without Leaving Home 316
Sharing Data without OLE 317

Part V: The Part of Tens 319

Chapter 21: Ten Cool Tricks to Try on a Slow Day 321

Start Off with a Drop Cap 321
Twist and Stretch Your Words 322
Add a Watermark to Your Pages 324
Display Corel Clip Art as Your Screen Saver 325
Save by Refinancing a Loan 326
Figure Out How Many Days Until 326

Play with Special Effects in Presentations 327
Send an Object into the Third Dimension 328
Make Your Documents Sing 328
Play with QuickTasks 330

Chapter 22: Ten Shortcuts You Can Use All the Time 331

Creating and Opening Documents 332
Closing the Current Document 332
Moving around Your Documents and Dialog Boxes 332
Cutting, Copying, and Pasting Data 333
Printing Documents 333
Saving Your Work 333
Undoing Mistakes 333
Making Text Bold, Underlined, or Italic 334
Getting Help 334
Quitting a Program 334

Chapter 23: Ten Ways to Save Time 335

Click Once Instead of Twice 335
Create Your Own Toolbar and Power Bar Buttons 336
Use Quick Thinking 337
Work in Style 337
Keep Automatic Backup Turned On 338
Teach Your Programs How to Share Data 338
Practice the Art of Drag and Drop 338
Seek Out Online Help 339
Don't Be Shy about Calling for Help 339
When All Else Fails 340

Appendix: Installing WordPerfect Suite 7 341

Installing over Older Versions of Suite Programs 341
Doing a Standard CD-ROM Installation 342
Performing a Custom Installation 343
Installing from Floppy Disks 344
Adding and Removing Installed Components 344

Index 347

Reader Response Card ..... Back of Book

Introduction

Whoever said "ignorance is bliss" obviously never had to use a computer. Although it's true that you're better off not knowing some things — for example, exactly *what* you just stepped in — not knowing how to use a computer program can make you decidedly unblissful, especially if someone expects you to actually do some work using that program. Even if you're lucky enough to figure out how to accomplish a certain task without any instruction — which is doubtful, given that most programs are about as self-explanatory as macroeconomics — you most certainly won't be able to do the job quickly, or well, or without a heaping dose of hair-pulling, teeth-gnashing frustration.

The problem is, working your way through the instruction manuals provided by software manufacturers takes *time* — more time than you've got. On top of that, software manuals are notoriously dull and obtuse. A few minutes with a typical manual not only strips you of any excitement you felt about getting a new program, but also leaves you more confused than you were before.

So how do you solve this dilemma — especially now that you bought WordPerfect Suite 7, which gives you not one, but eight major programs to conquer? Wait a minute . . . I think I hear . . . yes, that's definitely the sound of hoofbeats and bugles in the distance. The cavalry, in the form of *WordPerfect Suite 7 For Dummies,* has arrived to rescue you from imminent disaster. (Well, actually, you've been holding the cavalry in your hands all this time, but I didn't want to mention it earlier and spoil the dramatic build-up. Also, I was afraid you may be allergic to horses.)

Okay, So What Will This Book Do for Me?

In short, this book will get you up and running with all the major programs in WordPerfect Suite 7 in the fastest and most enjoyable way possible. You don't have to wade through pages of technobabble to find out how to do something. You don't have to waste your time reading about features you'll never use in a million years. Instead, you get quick, easy-to-understand how-to's for doing those things you need to do every day, whether you're using your computer at work, at home, or both.

Thanks to the philosophy of the . . .*For Dummies* series, you'll also have a pretty good time getting acquainted with your new software. As you probably already guessed, this series is based on the notion that you can give people the information they need and have a little fun in the process. If it's against your principles to laugh while you work, you can feel free to ignore the cartoons and other lighthearted touches throughout this book, though.

What Programs Does This Book Cover?

In its previous life, the Corel WordPerfect Suite was called Novell PerfectOffice. When Corel Corporation bought the product from Novell early in 1996, it decided to offer four versions of the suite: a standard and professional version for people using Windows 3.1 and a standard and professional version for people using Windows 95.

The standard versions of the suite include WordPerfect, Quattro Pro, Presentations, Envoy, Netscape Navigator, Sidekick, Dashboard, and CorelFLOW. The professional versions offer those programs plus a database program called Paradox, a networking tool called GroupWise, and an information manager called InfoCentral.

This book covers the Windows 95 standard version of the suite, formally known as Corel WordPerfect Suite 7. You'll find information about all the major programs in the suite, including WordPerfect 7, Quattro Pro 7, Presentations 7, Envoy 7, Netscape Navigator, Sidekick 95, Dashboard 95, and CorelFLOW 3. Of course, you can also use this book if you bought the professional version of the suite, CorelOffice Professional 7, although you won't find coverage of Paradox, GroupWise, or InfoCentral. (For help with Paradox, check out *Paradox For Dummies*, also by IDG Books.)

If you use the Windows 3.1 version of the suite, much of the content of this book applies to your suite as well. Many operations and commands are either exactly the same or very similar regardless of whether you're using the Windows 3.1 or Windows 95 suite. But because the Windows 3.1 suites include earlier versions of the suite programs — WordPerfect 6.1 instead of WordPerfect 7, for example — some features in your suite work a little differently than described in this book. And some new features included in the Windows 95 programs aren't available in your suite. The basic concepts of using most of the suite programs are similar enough, though, that you should be able to translate my Windows 95 instructions into steps that will work in Windows 3.1.

How Is Stuff Organized?

. . .*For Dummies* books are organized a little differently from other books in that they're not meant to be read cover to cover, starting with Chapter 1 and continuing in sequence through the last chapter. You can read the book in that fashion, of course, and it will make perfect sense to you. But the book is also designed to work like a reference book. When you encounter a situation or task that stumps you (or simply interests you), you look it up in the Table of Contents or Index and flip to the section that contains information on that subject. You don't have to read the entire chapter to understand what's going on in a particular section; you can find out what you need to know to tackle the problem at hand quickly and without any messy cleanup.

WordPerfect Suite 7 For Dummies is organized into several parts, with each part focusing on a different aspect of using the suite. The following paragraphs give you a little preview of what's to come.

Part I: The Suite Life

Here's where you shake hands with all your new programs and find out what each of them intends to do to justify its existence in your computer. You also discover how to do some basic things like move around inside programs, use your mouse and keyboard to make the programs actually do something, and get on-screen assistance from the suite's built in Help system. (Mind you, with this book at your side, you may never need to look up information in the Help system. But the WordPerfect Suite Help system has some tools that actually complete certain computing chores for you — which makes the Help system definitely worth checking out.)

Part II: Goodbye, Typewriter . . . Hello, WordPerfect!

Chapters in this part explain everything you need to know to create letters, memos, reports, and other documents using WordPerfect 7. You find out how to enter and edit text, change the type size and style, add graphics to your documents, check your text for spelling errors, and do all sorts of other things to produce professional-looking pages. After reading this section, you lose all respect for your typewriter.

Part III: Crunching Numbers Like a (Quattro) Pro

Part III chapters give you the lowdown on using Quattro Pro to create budgets, track sales and inventories, and do other number-crunching tasks. You also find out how to create and edit simple tables of information, such as a list of all your favorite sports teams, their win/loss records, and the amount you lost betting they could beat the other guys. And, just to help you put all your numbers in perspective, you discover how to turn your data into colorful charts and graphs.

Part IV: Those Other Programs

I probably should have rethought the title for this part, because it sounds as though the programs covered in this section of the book aren't worth much attention — which is anything but the case. Part IV explains how to use Presentations 7, a powerful tool for creating multimedia slide shows; Envoy, a program for distributing documents electronically to your friends and coworkers; and Netscape Navigator, the leading tool for browsing the Internet's World Wide Web. It also covers Sidekick 95, Dashboard 95, CorelFLOW 3.0, and the WordPerfect Address Book, which are no slouches, either.

Part IV also explains how to use all the programs in the suite together to get things done more efficiently. You find out how to create text or graphics in one program and then make copies that you can use in other documents, which is a great time-saver. You even discover how to create copies that automatically get updated when the original data changes.

Come to think of it, a better name for this part may be "Don't Miss This Part — Important Stuff Here!"

Part V: The Part of Tens

In this part, you find three top-ten lists of tricks, tips, and techniques. One list describes ten cool features that are fun to try on a day when you have some time to kill. Another lists ten shortcuts that you can use in any of the suite programs to save yourself a little time and energy. And the third offers still more ways to get more done in less time, which is what owning a computer is all about, after all.

Appendix: Installing WordPerfect Suite 7

Okay, I'll admit that this part of the book, which walks you through the steps of installing WordPerfect Suite 7 on your computer, isn't very exciting or entertaining. But seeing as how you can't use any of the programs in the suite until you install them — except as business tax write-offs, maybe — this part does contain some information you really ought to read.

That Symbol Means Something, Doesn't It?

Scattered throughout the margins in this book, you see little symbols — known as *icons* in the computer universe. The icons flag information that's especially important, interesting, or just plain useful.

A Tip icon alerts you to a secret, easy way of doing something. Well, maybe not secret, exactly, but something that you may not discover on your own.

The Remember icon marks information that you need to tuck away in a corner of your brain for future reference. Trust me, this stuff will come in handy one day.

When you see this icon, you're about to read information that may save you a big headache. Warning icons point out things you need to do to make sure that your day doesn't go horribly awry.

If you're upgrading to WordPerfect Suite 7 from an earlier version of the package, look for these icons. They signal information about features or commands that are new or work differently in this version.

This icon highlights technical or background information that you may or may not want to read. If you do take the plunge, however, you'll be better equipped to hold your own in discussions with computer geeks.

Other Conventions Used in This Book

If you flip through the pages in this book, you notice that many words have a particular letter that's underlined. As explained in Chapter 2, the underlined letters represent a keyboard shortcut for a command. You can press the Alt key in combination with the underlined letter to choose the command quickly.

When you see two words joined by a little arrow, you're looking at commands that you're to choose in sequence. For example, if I tell you to choose File⇨Print, you click on the File menu and then click on the Print command in the menu. Or, now that you're hip to keyboard shortcuts, you can also press Alt plus F and then press P.

Finally, boldface text indicates specific text that you need to type to make something work. You won't encounter boldface text too often, and you probably could have figured out what was going on all by yourself, but I didn't want to leave anything to chance.

By the way, Chapter 2 covers all this stuff (plus other tips for choosing commands quickly) in more detail.

What Now?

That's entirely up to you. You can turn the page and begin reading Chapter 1 or pick out any topic in the Index or Table of Contents that strikes your fancy and start there instead. But either way, do commit yourself to reading something, even if it's just a few paragraphs a day. I promise that you'll acquire the skills that you need to be successful with WordPerfect Suite 7 in no time — and it won't even hurt.

Remember, ignorance may be bliss in some areas of life, but when it comes to computers, knowledge is power.

Part I

The Suite Life

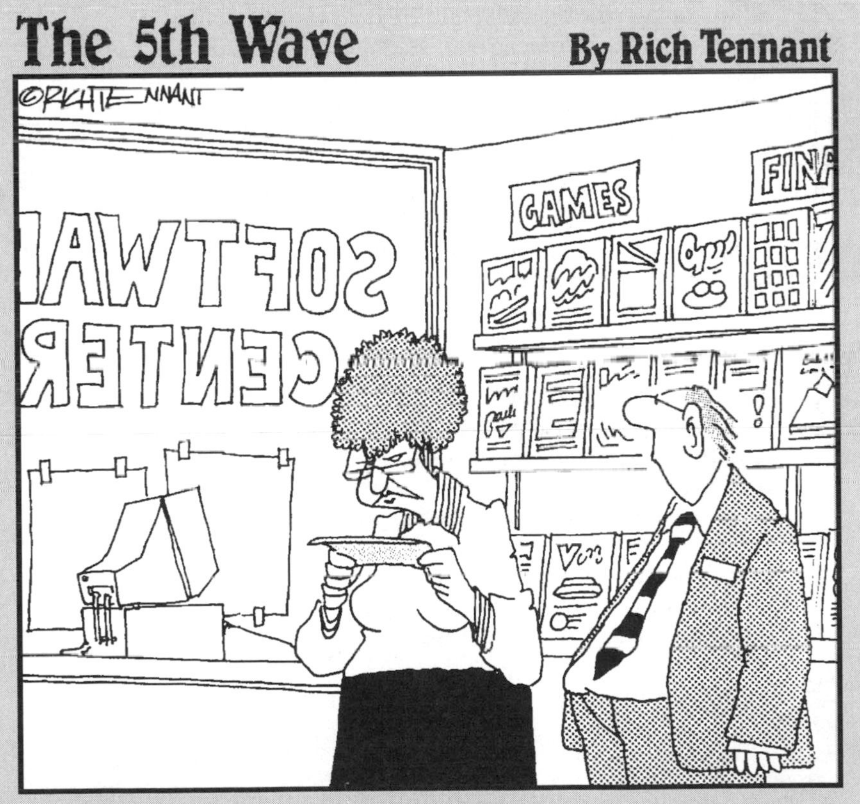

"YOU KNOW THAT GUY WHO BOUGHT ALL THAT SOFTWARE? HIS CHECK HAS A WARRANTY THAT SAYS IT'S TENDERED AS IS AND HAS NO FITNESS FOR ANY PARTICULAR PURPOSE INCLUDING, BUT NOT LIMITED TO, CASHING."

In this part . . .

If computing were an athletic event — as it sometimes is — installing WordPerfect Suite 7 would be like stuffing Michael Jordan, Monica Seles, Wayne Gretzky, and stars from several other sports into your computer. Like each of these athletic greats, each of the programs in the suite excels in a particular area.

The superstars in WordPerfect Suite 7, though, all agreed to play by the same basic set of rules to make it easier for you to figure out how things work. They also know how to play together nicely so that you can get more done in less time. On top of that, they won't hold you up for millions of dollars every time their contracts expire.

This part of the book introduces you to each of your new team members and explains which player to use in which situations. It also covers the features that work the same throughout the suite and explains how to get a program to cough up inside information when you run into trouble.

In sporting terms, this part is like spring training camp for your mind: Time spent here helps you avoid brain cramps down the road.

Chapter 1

Browsing through the Big Box

In This Chapter

- Taking a look at what you bought
- Figuring out which program to use when
- Putting the suite concept to work for you
- Using all your programs together

When I got my first apartment after leaving college, I went down to the hardware store and bought one screwdriver, one hammer, and one wrench. Not having had much exposure to tools when I was growing up, I figured that was all I needed to handle whatever household projects arose.

For years, I struggled to make those three tools work in any situation, which, of course, resulted in lots of frustration and wasted time. And then one day, confronted by a bolt I couldn't budge with any combination of screwdriver, hammer, and wrench, I splurged and bought a ratchet set. What a revelation! Suddenly, I had the power to overcome any bolt. I was so excited that I went around the house loosening and tightening everything I could find, thrilling to the little click-click-click sound of my new ratchet.

Lest you think that you've wandered into *Power Tools For Dummies* by mistake, let me interrupt this little trip down handyman lane and explain its relevance to the topic at hand: using Corel WordPerfect Suite 7. You see, that big, colorful Corel software package is like a well-equipped toolbox. It contains powerful tools to handle just about every computing chore. But as it is with hammers, wrenches, screwdrivers, and ratchets, the key to success is using the right tool for the job.

This chapter explains which of the many programs in the WordPerfect Suite you should use to accomplish various tasks. It also explains how the programs are all designed to work similarly — and work together — so that you can use several tools in tandem to complete one project.

What Do All These Programs Do?

Packing an enormous bang for the buck, WordPerfect Suite 7 includes no fewer than eight major programs. Carrying the toolbox analogy further — and, some may say, a step too far — it's as if someone gave you a Sears credit card, headed you toward the Craftsman tools aisle, and told you to go nuts.

If you're not sure exactly what each of the major programs in the suite do, the following list should provide some enlightenment. You'll probably use a few of these programs every day and start up others every now and again to handle some special project. (Note that I reserved the new icon for programs that weren't part of the suite in its previous incarnation when it was owned by Novell and called PerfectOffice. The other programs are essentially new, too, however, as they're upgrades of the versions found in PerfectOffice.)

- WordPerfect 7 is the Windows 95 incarnation of a very popular and powerful word processor. In WordPerfect, you can create any kind of text document, from a simple letter to an annual report. You can add graphics to your documents, use fancy fonts, put text into columns, and do a whole lot of other stuff that your typewriter only dreams about. Figure 1-1 shows an example of the type of documents you can create in WordPerfect. Chapters 4 through 9 explain WordPerfect's many features and commands.

Figure 1-1: In WordPerfect, you can create sophisticated, professional-looking documents such as this.

- Quattro Pro 7, the subject of Chapters 10 through 15, is the Windows 95 version of a leading spreadsheet program. With a spreadsheet program, you can handle accounting tasks from creating a budget to tracking product inventories. Quattro Pro can also crunch any numbers you throw at it, whether you want to calculate your company's annual net profits, perform cost and price analyses, or figure out whether you can save money by refinancing a loan.

  Figure 1-2 shows a spreadsheet that I created to calculate the potential profits for stocks bought and sold at various prices. When I see a stock that I'm interested in buying, I just plug in the stock price and the estimated sell price, and Quattro Pro calculates the payoff for me.

- Presentations 7 enables you to create multimedia presentations complete with graphics, sound clips, and even animation. You can create presentations that you play back on a computer as well as slides and transparencies for display on regular old projectors. For those days when you're feeling especially creative, Presentations also offers a nice selection of tools that you can use to create your own graphics and edit clip art graphics. In addition, the program provides tools for creating organizational charts and other simple charts. Chapter 16 is devoted to Presentations.

- Envoy 7 is a nifty little program that lets a group of people view and annotate (add notes to) each other's documents, regardless of what programs they have installed on their computers. For example, if you create a WordPerfect document, you can "publish" it as an Envoy document that your colleagues can view even if they don't own WordPerfect *or* Envoy.

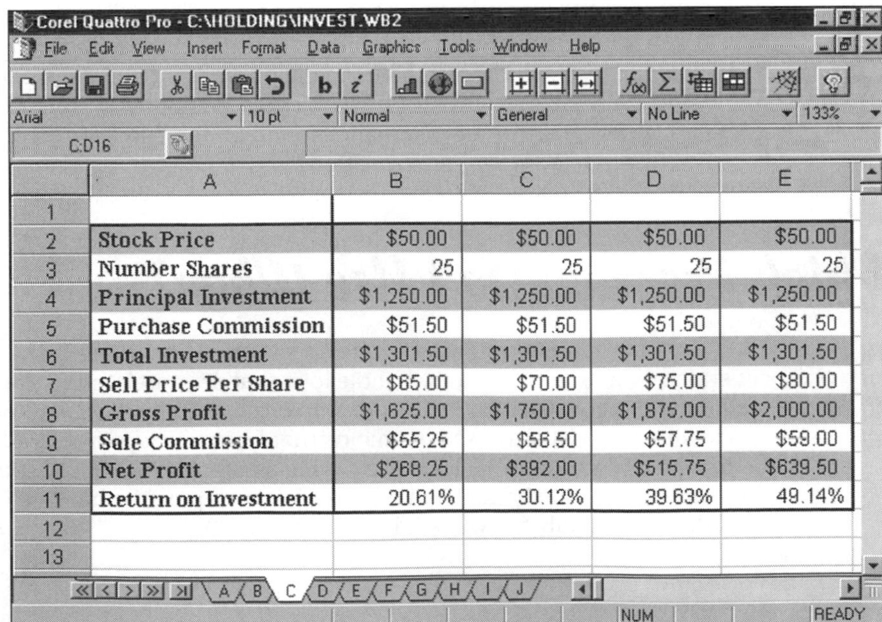

	A	B	C	D	E
1					
2	Stock Price	$50.00	$50.00	$50.00	$50.00
3	Number Shares	25	25	25	25
4	Principal Investment	$1,250.00	$1,250.00	$1,250.00	$1,250.00
5	Purchase Commission	$51.50	$51.50	$51.50	$51.50
6	Total Investment	$1,301.50	$1,301.50	$1,301.50	$1,301.50
7	Sell Price Per Share	$65.00	$70.00	$75.00	$80.00
8	Gross Profit	$1,625.00	$1,750.00	$1,875.00	$2,000.00
9	Sale Commission	$55.25	$56.50	$57.75	$59.00
10	Net Profit	$268.25	$392.00	$515.75	$639.50
11	Return on Investment	20.61%	30.12%	39.63%	49.14%
12					
13					

Figure 1-2: When you have a complex math problem to solve, don't count on your fingers — use Quattro Pro instead.

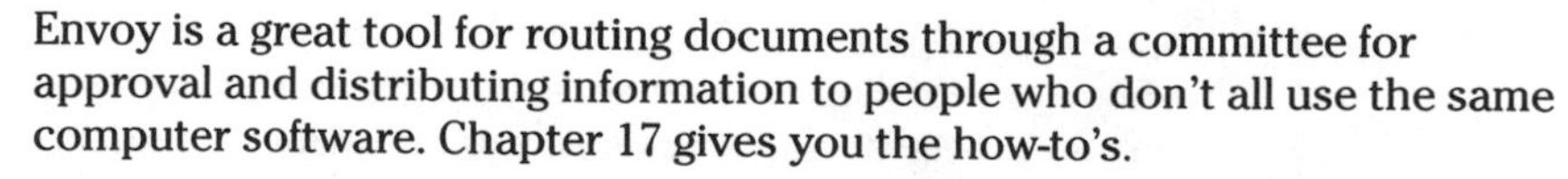
Envoy is a great tool for routing documents through a committee for approval and distributing information to people who don't all use the same computer software. Chapter 17 gives you the how-to's.

- CorelFLOW 3 is a sophisticated program for creating diagrams and charts. You can create everything from complex electrical diagrams to a family tree.

- AT&T WorldNet Service enables you to subscribe to AT&T as your Internet service provider so that you can have access to all those cool Web pages and other Internet stuff that everyone's talking about these days. More importantly, the program includes a special AT&T version of Netscape Navigator, the leading tool for browsing the World Wide Web. You can use Netscape with Internet providers other than AT&T, by the way. Chapter 18 gets you started on your Internet explorations.

- Sidekick 95, covered in Chapter 19, is the digital equivalent of a personal organizer. You can keep track of appointments, store addresses and phone numbers of important contacts, and even dial someone's e-mail or telephone number right from your computer (provided you have a modem, that is). Sidekick also has some tools that you can use to track travel expenses and create expense reports.
- WordPerfect Suite 7 also includes a small utility that gives you another way to store addresses and phone numbers, the Address Book. The Address Book doesn't have anywhere near the features that Sidekick offers, but if all you need is a simple way to keep track of contact information, it may be a good choice for you, especially if your computer's disk space is limited. See Chapter 19 for more about this program.

- Dashboard 95 gives you an alternative to running your programs from the Windows 95 desktop and Start menu. Through the Dashboard window, which is supposed to resemble the dashboard in a high-tech car of the future, you can start programs, check your computer system resources, and access many of the commands found on the Windows 95 Start menu. See Chapter 19 for more information.

Which Program Do I Use When?

Each program in the WordPerfect Suite specializes in handling certain tasks. But several programs enable you to handle jobs that are unrelated to the program's main function, too. Quattro Pro, for example, is primarily designed for creating spreadsheets, but it also has commands that let you use your spreadsheet data to create a slide show. It's a little like having a hammer that has a Swiss Army Knife attached to the handle. (Okay, okay, I'll give up on the hardware analogy now. But it was really fun while it lasted, wasn't it?)

Just because you *can* do a task in a certain program, however, doesn't mean that you *should.* Yes, you may be able to create a slide show in Quattro Pro, but you get better results if you use the tool specifically designed for creating slide shows, Presentations.

The following list offers some suggestions to help you decide which program is most appropriate for the challenge at hand. Keep in mind that you don't have to use just one program to create a document, though. As explained in the next section (as well as in Chapter 20), the programs in WordPerfect Suite 7 are designed so that you can use them all together to handle a single project.

- WordPerfect is the best choice for creating text-based documents, from letters to memos to reports. You can also use WordPerfect to create documents that contain clip art, such as advertising fliers or simple brochures.
- Use Quattro Pro for accounting projects such as creating budgets, recording sales, tracking inventories, and anything else that involves calculating data.
- Also use Quattro Pro for creating tables of data, such as an employee list showing each worker's name, phone number, address, department, and so on. You can create similar tables in WordPerfect, but Quattro Pro makes the job easier.
- To create a data chart — for example, a chart that shows your company's annual sales by region — use Quattro Pro. To create simple organizational charts, use Presentations. To create more complex diagrams or charts, such as electrical or mechanical diagrams, use CorelFLOW.
- To create slide shows — whether for display on a computer or a regular projector — use Presentations.
- If you're feeling artistic and want to create some simple graphics to enliven your documents or slide shows, use Presentations. You can also use Presentations to make minor edits to bitmap images (such as scanned photographs).
- To create text-based graphics — for example, a company logo that presents the company name in a stylized font or design — try WordPerfect's TextArt feature. You can also create fancy type in Presentations, but TextArt offers a few more bells and whistles. Figure 1-3 shows some text created using TextArt and Presentations.

- If you want to add graphics in a hurry, just use one of the many clip art drawings or bitmap images provided on the WordPerfect Suite 7 CD-ROM.
- As mentioned earlier in this chapter, you have two choices for keeping track of addresses and other contact information: the Corel Address Book or Sidekick 95. Both programs enable you to store contact information and print envelopes and mailing labels. Which one you decide to use depends on whether you just need to maintain a simple address file or need more advanced features. See Chapter 19 for the details that will help you choose.

Figure 1-3: WordPerfect TextArt enables you to bend and shape text (top); Presentations also offers some tools for creating fancy type treatments (bottom).

Hey! These All Look Alike!

If you have a sharp eye, you'll notice right away that all the programs in the WordPerfect Suite have a similar on-screen look. (Okay, so the truth is you have to be darned near asleep not to notice this fact, but you looked like you were a little intimidated by all this computer talk, so I thought I'd try to boost your self-esteem a little.) Many of the buttons you see in the program windows are the same from program to program, for example — take a look back through the figures in this chapter to see for yourself. Many of the menu commands are the same as well.

Part of this similarity has to do with the influence of Windows 95, which requires that program windows contain certain elements. But the other part is due to the fact that Corel designed the suite to make it as easy as possible to use. After you know what a particular button or command does in one program, you can apply that knowledge in all of the other programs. You don't have to memorize a different set of buttons and commands for each individual program. (Chapter 2 covers the basic elements found in all of the WordPerfect Suite programs and how to use them, by the way.)

The beauty of the WordPerfect Suite is more than skin-deep, however. As discussed in Chapter 20, the programs are also designed to interact with each other so that you can use several different programs to handle one computing project. For example, if you need to create a report that includes text, graphics, and a spreadsheet, you can create the text in WordPerfect, the graphics in Presentations, and the spreadsheet in Quattro Pro, and then combine the different elements together into one finished product. You can also create data in one document and then copy it into several other documents; you can even have the copies update automatically when you change the original data, if you want.

In many cases, you can launch another program in the suite from within the program you're currently using. You can start up Netscape Navigator and log on to the Internet by clicking on a button in WordPerfect, Presentations, and Quattro Pro, for example. And you can choose a command in WordPerfect to launch Presentations so that you can create a drawing to insert into your WordPerfect document.

The cooperative nature of your WordPerfect Suite programs gives you an important computing advantage. You not only can get up and running with all the programs quickly, you can use their combined strengths to get your work done in less time and with less effort. In fact, I *could* say that the WordPerfect Suite is a little like one of those new, many-tools-in-one power tools that are all the rage in hardware stores these days. But I swore off hardware analogies earlier in this chapter, so I won't.

Chapter 2

Basic Stuff You Need to Know

In This Chapter

- Powering up your programs
- Getting acquainted with windows
- Using the mouse and keyboard to make things happen
- Figuring out which buttons do what
- Choosing commands from menus and dialog boxes
- Moving around the screen
- Customizing your screen
- Working with two or more open windows at the same time

Life sure was simpler before computers, wasn't it? You didn't have to endure mind-numbing conversations about things like operating systems and Internet access providers. You didn't need to spend oodles of cash on the latest computer gadgets to keep up with the Joneses. And you didn't have to waste precious brain cells mastering the meaning of phrases like *logging onto the network server* and *downloading a printer driver.*

Well, like it or not, computers are here to stay, so you may as well give in and learn a few things that make it easier for you to communicate with that big, glowing box on your desk — not to mention with the kids in your life. This chapter explains the basics you need to know to get started using Corel WordPerfect Suite 7, from starting up a program to customizing your screen display.

If acquiring this information seems like a daunting (and boring) chore, take heart. First, I promise to keep it simple — I'll tell you just what you need to know to survive, and nothing more. Second, the payoff is big. After you master these basics, you'll not only find the computer a friendlier beast, you'll be able to join the legions of folks who have learned to use the computer as an excuse for goofing off. You'll acquire more and more computing lingo, and pretty soon, you, too, will be able to sound believable when you stare blankly at your boss and say, "Sorry, I can't complete that project for you today because the network server is down, and I can't download the right printer driver."

Starting Up and Shutting Down

Firing up a program in the WordPerfect Suite is a cinch. Here's the routine:

1. **Turn on your computer.**

   Okay, I really didn't need to tell you that — did I?

2. **Click on the Windows 95 Start button to display the Start menu.**
3. **Click on the Corel WordPerfect Suite 7 item in the Start menu.**
4. **Click on the name of the program you want to start.**

   To access some of the smaller programs in the suite, you have to click on the Accessories item in the WordPerfect Suite 7 menu.

You can also start some programs by using the DAD icons, as explained in the section "Using DAD."

Shutting down a program is just as easy. See that little square button in the top right corner of the program window? The one marked with an X? To put a program to bed, just click on that button. If you haven't saved your work, you'll be prompted to do so.

You can also shut down a program by choosing the Exit command from the File menu or by pressing the Alt key together with the F4 key. But those methods require two clicks or key presses rather than one. Who needs all that extra work?

Clicking, Double-clicking, and Other Mouse Maneuvers

You can get your computer to do things in two ways: by pressing the buttons on your mouse or by pressing keys on your keyboard. Sometimes, using the mouse is easiest, and other times, using the keyboard is the best option. Keyboard tricks are covered in the upcoming section "Saving Time with Keyboard Shortcuts."

If the mouse is a new entity in your world, here are some terms you need to know. (Keep in mind that this information applies to a traditional mouse. If you're using a trackball, touchpad device, or some other tool for sending signals to your computer, check its manual for instructions on how to do this stuff.)

- The *mouse cursor* is that little thing that moves around the screen when you move your mouse. Cursors take on different shapes and sizes depending on what program you're using and what you're trying to do.

- To *click* means to press and release a mouse button. It's called *clicking* because the button makes a little clicking noise when you press it, making this one of the more sensible naming decisions issued by the High Computing Council.
- If I tell you to *click on* something, move your mouse so that the cursor is pointing to that something and then click.
- To *double-click* is to press and release the mouse button twice very quickly.

- Usually, the left mouse button is the primary button — the one you use to accomplish most tasks. But some mice let you switch the buttons around so that the right button is the primary button, which is cool if you're left-handed or just like to be different. In this book, when I say to click or double-click, I mean that you should push the primary mouse button. When you need to click the secondary mouse button, I tell you to *right-click.* If you switched your mouse buttons around, remember that when I tell you to right-click, you should left-click, and vice versa. See what you get for being so contrary?
- To *drag* is to move the mouse while you hold the primary mouse button down. Dragging is a handy way to move words and objects around. When you have the item where you want it, you release the mouse button to complete the drag. Chipheads refer to this procedure as *drag and drop.*

Saving Time with Keyboard Shortcuts

Sometimes, using the mouse can be cumbersome. Luckily, you have another option. You can perform most common computing tasks without ever taking your hands off the keyboard.

Try accessing commands and options from the keyboard using these two methods:

- Press the command's or menu's *hotkey.* The hotkey is the letter that's underlined in the command or menu name. To display one of the menus at the top of a program window, press Alt plus the hotkey. Then, to choose a command from the menu, press the command's hotkey — no Alt key is necessary this time. For example, if you want to choose the Print command from WordPerfect's File menu, you press Alt+F and then press P. You can also use Alt+hotkey combos to select options in dialog boxes. (Dialog boxes are explained later, in the section "Digging through Dialog Boxes.")
- Use *keyboard shortcuts,* which enable you to choose a command by pressing one or two keys in combination. For example, if you want to open a document in WordPerfect, you can press Ctrl+O — in other words, press the Ctrl key along with the O key. The available shortcuts are listed next to the command names in the menus (and I point them out throughout this book, too). You can save a great deal of time by committing to memory the shortcuts for the commands you use regularly.

Right-clicking your way to fame and fortune

Although the left mouse button is the primary clicker, the right mouse button can be extremely useful, too. Right-clicking on an on-screen element usually displays a menu of commands or options related to that element. Some programs call these menus *context-sensitive menus;* in Corel WordPerfect Suite 7, they're called *QuickMenus.* Either way, these menus provide a convenient way to access the most commonly used commands and options. To discover what QuickMenus are available to you, just right-click your way around the screen.

When you see two commands joined by an arrow in this book, it means that you're to click on the commands in sequence. For example, Format➪Line➪Spacing means to click on the Format menu, click on the Line command in that menu, and then click on the Spacing command in the Line submenu.

Doing Windows

Figure 2-1 shows the screen — also known as a *window* — you see when you first start WordPerfect. This window looks much the same as those you see when you start other programs in the suite — or any Windows 95 program, for that matter. Here's a review of the basic window components and how you use them:

- The *title bar,* which runs across the top of the window, tells you which program you're using. The title bar is a great reference for the absent-minded.

- The *menu bar* is full of menus, appropriately enough. *Menus* contain lists of commands related to a particular function or task. To display a menu, click on it or press Alt plus the underlined letter in the menu name.

  If you choose a menu command that's followed by a little arrow, a second menu of related options, called a *submenu,* appears. Click on the option you want to select. Three dots trailing a command name indicate that if you choose the command, you'll be confronted by a dialog box full of options. For clues on how to converse with a dialog box, see the section "Digging through Dialog Boxes," later in this chapter.

  If a command is dimmed or grayed out, it's not available, either because it's not pertinent to the task you're trying to accomplish or because your system isn't set up to support the command. For example, the chart editing commands in Quattro Pro are grayed out if your document doesn't contain a chart.

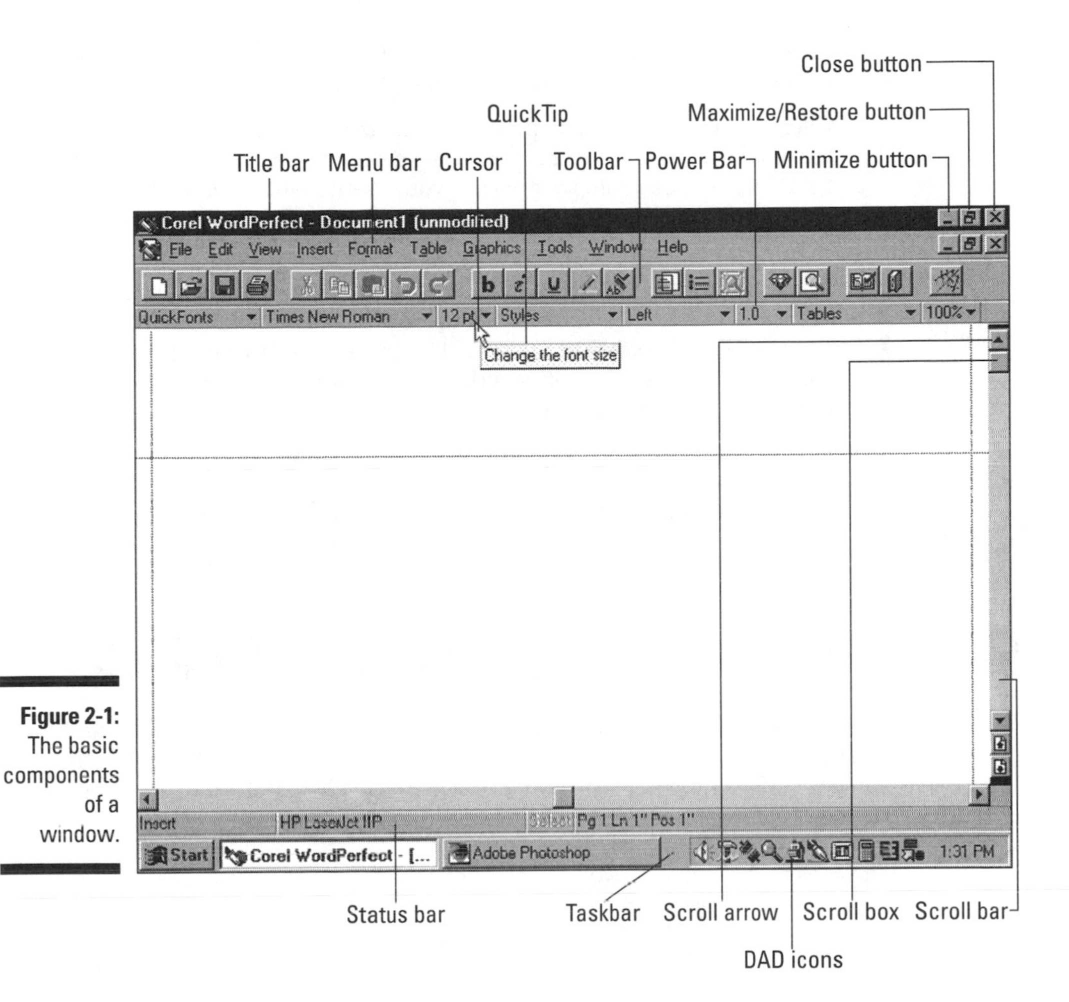

Figure 2-1: The basic components of a window.

- The *toolbar* is a strip of buttons that you can click on to choose certain commands quickly and efficiently.
- The *Power Bar,* a special feature provided in some programs in the WordPerfect Suite, is a variation on the toolbar. Like the toolbar, the Power Bar contains buttons that provide quick access to popular commands and options.
- The *status bar,* at the bottom of the window, displays pertinent information about your current document. Sometimes, clicking, double-clicking, or right-clicking on an item in the status bar enables you to perform actions or commands.
- Lurking beneath the status bar is the Windows 95 *taskbar.* You can click on the program buttons on the taskbar to switch from one running program to another. Click on the Start button to display a menu of programs and Windows 95 commands.

- On the right end of the taskbar is the WordPerfect Suite Desktop Application Director (DAD), which is explained in the section "Using DAD."
- Click on the up- and down-pointing *scroll arrows* in the *scroll bar* on the right side of the window to move the screen display slightly up or down so that you can see a different part of your document. Click on the scroll arrows at the bottom of the window to move slightly left or right. Drag the *scroll box* to scroll in bigger increments.
- In the top-right corner of the window, you find the *Minimize button,* the *Maximize/Restore button,* and the *Close button*. If you have a document open, you get two sets of buttons. The top set controls the program window; the bottom set affects the document window. These controls are covered in the section "Resizing and Moving Your Windows."

- It's not always easy to remember what all the different elements on your screen do or mean. Luckily, you can find out with just a quick move of your mouse. Just place the mouse cursor over a particular button or item, and a little flag — called a QuickTip — unfurls to give you helpful information.

Resizing, Moving, and Closing Windows

Windows 95 is nothing if not flexible. You can shrink, enlarge, reshape, and rearrange your windows until you get them just the way you like them. And if you get really annoyed, well, a quick click on the Close button wipes that smart-alecky program or document right off the monitor.

The keys to this heady power are the Minimize, Maximize/Restore, and Close buttons, labeled back in Figure 2-1. Here's how they work, moving from right to left:

- Click on the X button to close the window and the document or program it contains.
- The appearance and purpose of the Maximize/Restore button alter nates depending on the current status of the window. If the button face shows a single box, it's the Maximize button. Clicking on this button enlarges the window so that it eats up your whole screen. If the button shows two stacked boxes, it's the Restore button. Clicking on this button restores the window to its former size.
- Click on the Minimize button to hide the window temporarily. After you minimize a program window, a program button appears on the Windows 95 taskbar; click on the button to make the window reappear. After you minimize a document window, it shrinks to a tiny bar at the bottom of the program window. This bar offers both a Maximize and a Restore button; click on either one to redisplay the window.

You can resize a window by placing the cursor over an edge of a window. After the cursor becomes a two-headed arrow, drag the window to whatever size you deem appropriate. To move a window, drag its title bar.

Customizing Your View

Resizing and reshaping your windows isn't the only way to customize your view of the computer world. You can also change the way that certain other screen elements appear. Remember, you are the master of your computer (or so it would like to have you think).

- Most programs offer a Preferences command; usually, the command is found in the Edit menu. This command displays options that enable you to customize your screen. The options vary from program to program; Figure 2-2 shows the dialog box you see if you choose the command in WordPerfect. If you double-click on one of the icons in the dialog box, WordPerfect displays a second dialog box containing options related to that item.
- You can usually hide your toolbar, status bar, and, in some cases, the Power Bar. The commands that enable you to choose which bars are displayed vary from program to program, but you should find them either via a Preferences command or under the View menu. You can also sometimes right-click on the bar and choose Preferences from the QuickMenu to access the bar controls.
- Many programs offer more than one toolbar or Power Bar; you can choose which ones appear on-screen. Again, look in the View menu, right-click on the bar and choose Preferences, or look for a Preferences command in the Edit menu to hunt down the toolbar controls.
- Most programs let you customize your toolbars so that they contain buttons for the commands you use most. You'll find more information in Chapter 23, in the section "Create Your Own Toolbar and Power Bar Buttons."

- In WordPerfect 7, the default toolbar has gotten so crowded that all the buttons may not appear on-screen, depending on what screen resolution setting you're using for your monitor. To display more rows of buttons, right-click on the toolbar, choose Preferences from the QuickMenu, and then click on Options in the resulting dialog box. When the Toolbar Options dialog box appears, increase the value in the Maximum Number of Rows/Columns to Show option box.

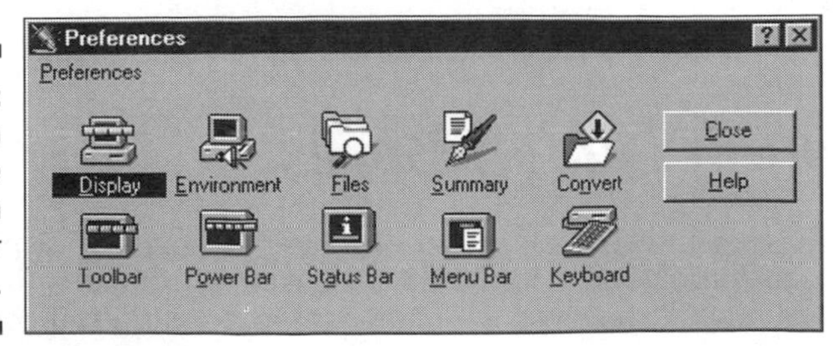

Figure 2-2: You can customize your screen to suit your taste.

- If you don't like the position of the toolbar, you can move it. Just place your cursor between one of the buttons on the toolbar and then drag the toolbar to a new home.
- You can magnify or reduce the size of your document to get a close-up view of your work or pull back to get the big picture. Some programs offer a Zoom button on the Power Bar; click on the button to display a complete menu of zoom options. Zoom options are also found under the View menu or the Zoom menu, depending on the program you're using.

Some programs in the suite, such as WordPerfect, enable you to customize many other elements of the program interface. (*Interface,* by the way, is just geekspeak for the stuff on-screen that enables you to tell your computer what to do.) Give the Preferences command a whirl and see how much havoc you can wreak.

Using DAD

The WordPerfect Suite Desktop Application Director — DAD for short — places icons for certain programs and features in the suite along the bottom of your Windows 95 taskbar. You can click on an icon to launch the program or feature, which is usually quicker than wading through the Windows 95 Start menus. To see a QuickTip explaining what a particular icon does, pause your mouse cursor over the icon for a few seconds.

If you don't see the DAD icons on your screen, click on the Windows 95 Start button and then choose Corel WordPerfect Suite 7⇨Accessories⇨Corel Desktop Application Director.

If you want to remove an icon from the taskbar, right-click on any DAD icon and choose Properties from the QuickMenu that appears. When the DAD Properties dialog box appears, click on the name of the icon you want to remove from the taskbar. To add an icon, click next to the icon name to place a check mark in the option box. Click on OK to close the dialog box.

To turn off the DAD icons altogether, right-click on any icon and then choose Exit DAD from the QuickMenu.

Digging through Dialog Boxes

When you choose some commands, your computer responds by displaying a *dialog box* like the one shown in Figure 2-3. By making selections in the dialog box, you tell the program how you want it to carry out a particular command.

The components of a dialog box work like this:

- To change a value in an *option box,* first double-click on the box or press the option's hotkey (the underlined letter in the option name). Then enter a new value from the keyboard. In some cases, you can change the value by clicking on the little up and down arrows next to the option box.
- To display the contents of a *drop-down list* — sometimes called *pop-up menus* or *pick lists,* depending on which computer dialect is spoken in your neck of the woods — click on the little down-pointing arrow. Then click on the option you want to use.
- To turn a *radio button* on or off, just click on the button. The option is turned on if a black dot appears in the middle of the button. You can turn on only one radio button in a group.
- To turn a *check box* on or off, click on the check box. An X or checkmark in the box means that the option is turned on. You can turn on as many check boxes in a group as you want.
- Clicking on the rectangular *buttons* initiates a command or displays a menu or second dialog box of related options.

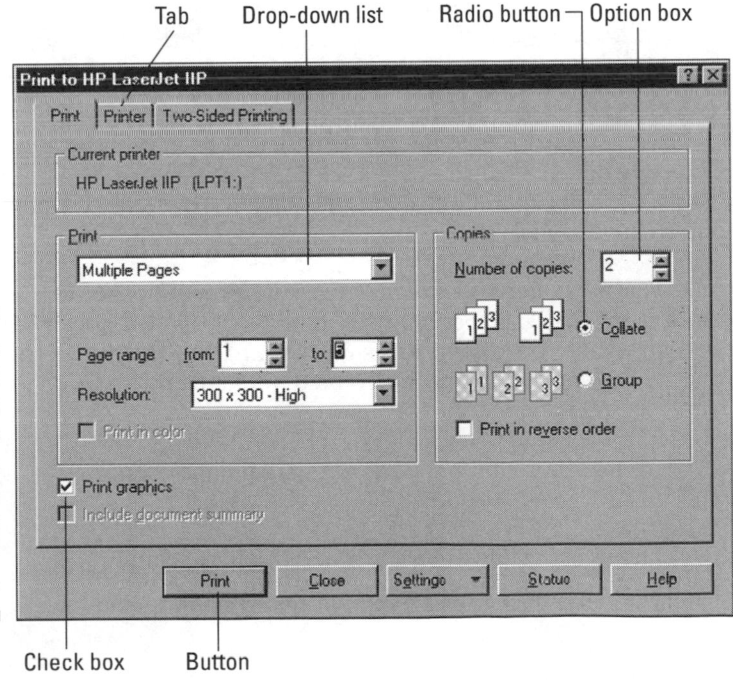

Figure 2-3: Dialog boxes give you a way to specify how you want to apply a particular command.

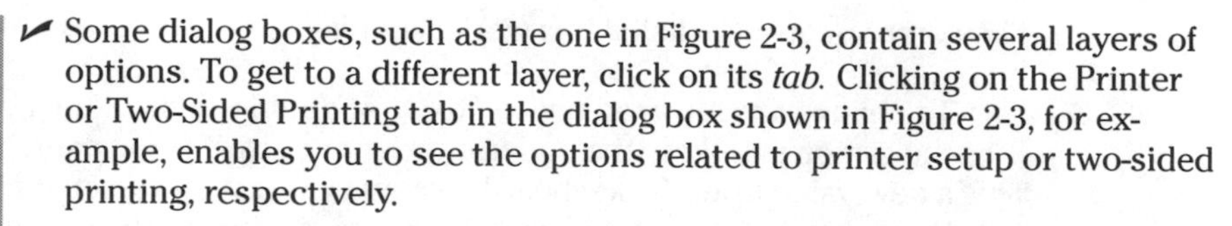

- Some dialog boxes, such as the one in Figure 2-3, contain several layers of options. To get to a different layer, click on its *tab.* Clicking on the Printer or Two-Sided Printing tab in the dialog box shown in Figure 2-3, for example, enables you to see the options related to printer setup or two-sided printing, respectively.

- If you get tired of clicking your way through dialog boxes, you can move from option to option by pressing the Tab key. To move to the previous option, press Shift+Tab. You can also select a button or option by pressing Alt plus the appropriate hotkey.
- Options that are grayed out (dimmed) are unavailable, either because they're not relevant to your document or because your system doesn't support them.
- To close a dialog box and return to your document, you usually click on the OK or Close button. Like program and document windows, dialog boxes also have a Close button in the upper-right corner (it looks like a little X). You can also click on this button to close the dialog box.
- As explained in Chapter 3, some dialog boxes (such as the one in Figure 2-3) contain a question mark button. Click on this button and then click on an option in the dialog box to get more information about how the option works.

Juggling Open Windows

One of the big benefits of using Windows 95 is that you can run several programs at once. You can open as many program and document windows as your computer's memory allows.

Only one window is active at any one time, however — that is, any keyboard strokes or mouse clicks affect only the contents of that window. The other windows are said to be *running in the background.* The title bar of the program that's active appears highlighted or colored, while the title bars of programs that are inactive are dimmed.

To send an active program to the background and make another program active:

- Click anywhere inside the background program window.
- Or click on the background program's button in the Windows 95 taskbar.

To switch between one or more open document windows within the same program:

- Click inside the window you want to make active.
- Or choose the name of the window from the Window menu.

Almost everything discussed in this chapter is applicable to most Windows 95 programs, not just to those in the WordPerfect Suite. That means that you now have a head start when you need to learn any new program. Don't you feel smarter than the rest of the class already?

Chapter 3

Can I Get Some Help, Please?

In This Chapter

- Quizzing the PerfectExpert
- Letting the program do the job for you
- Viewing on-screen demonstrations
- Getting step-by-step advice
- Navigating a Help window
- Using the Reference Center

Are you the sort who hates to ask for help from anyone? Do you prefer driving around in hopeless circles to stopping at a gas station for directions, for example? Is your VCR still blinking "12:00" because you refuse to let your ten-year-old show you how to set the clock?

If so, you probably want to skip this chapter. On the other hand, if you believe that there's nothing shameful about asking for help — and that doing so can save you time and headaches — you'll find the information on the next few pages invaluable.

This chapter explains the various tools offered by the WordPerfect Suite Help system. You discover where to click to get information about a particular topic, how to display step-by-step on-screen instructions for completing a task, and how to use tools that automatically create common documents with hardly a keystroke or deep thought on your part required.

In the past, I've found on-screen Help systems to be more of a nuisance than a blessing. For one thing, they didn't provide any more information than you could find in the program manual. For another, you had to keep switching back and forth between the Help window and the task at hand — hardly as convenient as reading instructions from a manual on your desk. These drawbacks still exist to some extent in the Help system in the WordPerfect Suite. But the Help system now offers some pretty cool goodies, such as multimedia demonstrations, that are worth trying. So if you haven't had much success with older Help systems, don't be too quick to dismiss the ones in this version of the WordPerfect Suite.

Not all programs in the WordPerfect Suite offer all the advanced Help features covered in this chapter. And some use slightly different command names or hotkeys than the ones mentioned here. But the basic aspects of the Help systems work the same way, and even the most simple Help systems should be able to provide some guidance if you get stuck.

Asking an Expert

One of the easiest ways to get help is to use the PerfectExpert. Available in WordPerfect, Quattro Pro, and Presentations, the PerfectExpert is sort of like having a software service representative built into your computer (only better, because you don't have to wade through a snarl of voicemail commands or cool your heels on hold for 30 minutes before you get your question answered).

To access the PerfectExpert, follow these steps:

1. **Choose Help⇨Ask the PerfectExpert.**

   Or click on the PerfectExpert toolbar button — it's the one that looks like a yellow light bulb with a question mark in it. Either way, the top half of the dialog box shown in Figure 3-1 appears.

Figure 3-1: The PerfectExpert is like having your own personal computer guru.

2. **Type your question in the What Do You Want to Know? box.**

   You can use plain English — geekspeak isn't required. Also, you can type your question in all lowercase if you like — the PerfectExpert isn't particular.

3. **Click on the Search button.**

   The dialog box expands to give you a list of choices, as in Figure 3-1.

4. **Click on the topic that matches your interest and then click on the Display button.**

   Up pops a Help window containing the information you requested, as shown in Figure 3-2. The intricacies of the Help window are explained later in this chapter, in the section "Navigating a Help Window."

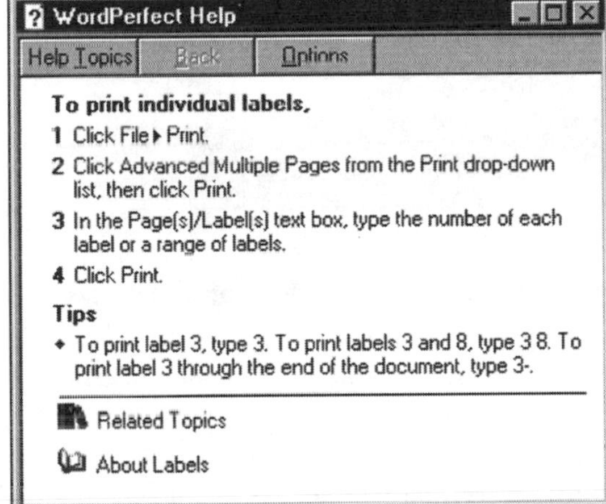

Figure 3-2: Information about your requested topic appears in a Help window.

Using the Show Me Features

Ask the PerfectExpert is just the tip of the Help iceberg. The Help system in WordPerfect and Presentations also has a Show Me feature that can play on-screen demonstrations of a particular feature, guide you through the steps involved in completing a task, and even complete the task for you.

To use the Show Me features:

1. **Choose Help⇨Help Topics or press F1 to display the dialog box shown in Figure 3-3.**

   If the Show Me tab isn't at the front of the dialog box, click on it to make it active.

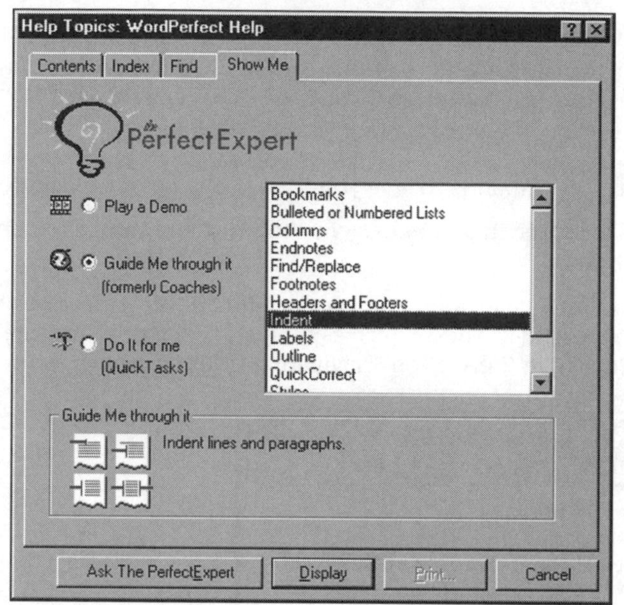

Figure 3-3: You can view demonstrations of features, get step-by-step coaching through a task, and even have the program perform a task for you.

2. **Choose the radio button that matches the feature you want to use.**
   - Play a Demo displays an audio-visual tutorial that explains how to perform a task or use a feature. You need to put your Suite CD in your CD-ROM drive to play the demos.
   - Guide Me Through It walks you through the process of completing a task. (This feature was formerly known as Coaches.)
   - Do It for Me does just that — performs a task for you. This feature is also called QuickTasks. (For more about QuickTasks, see the next section in this chapter.)
3. **Click on a topic or task in the list box.**

   Use the scroll arrows to scroll the list of topics if necessary.
4. **Click on the Display button.**

Using QuickTasks

QuickTasks are little jobs that the WordPerfect Suite can do for you almost automatically. The suite offers QuickTasks to help you create mailing labels, an expense report, a household budget, and much more.

You can access the QuickTasks in WordPerfect and Presentations by choosing the Do It for Me option on the Show Me tab of the Help Topics dialog box, as explained in the preceding section. Or you can access QuickTasks via the Windows 95 Start menu. Click on the Start button and then choose Corel WordPerfect Suite 7⇨Accessories⇨QuickTasks to display the QuickTasks dialog box. Click on the QuickTask you want to use and then click on Run. In many cases, you're prompted to enter some information that enables the QuickTask to complete the job for you.

Getting More Help

Here are still more ways to dig up information about a subject that's troubling you:

- Choose Help⇨Help Topics or press F1 to display a dialog box similar to the one shown back in Figure 3-3. Then click on the Index tab to display the screen shown in Figure 3-4. Enter a topic in the first option box or use the scroll bar and arrows to locate the topic in the list box. Click on the topic in the list box and then click on the Display button.
- Click on the Find tab in the Help Topics dialog box to search the Help files for any mention of a particular word or words.

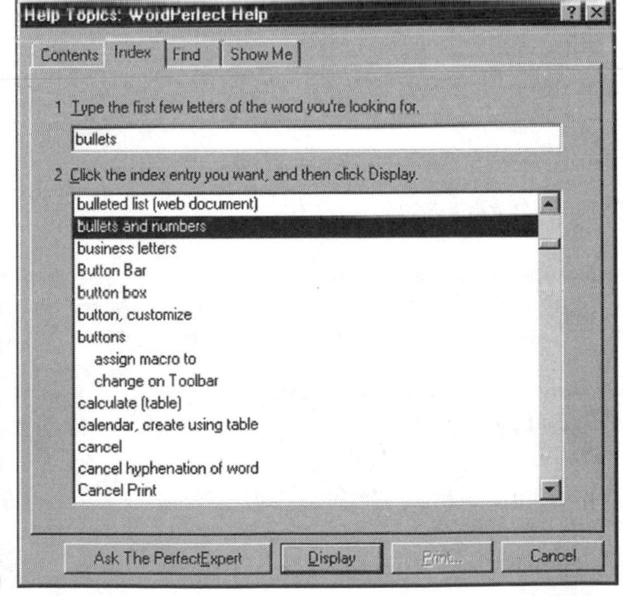

Figure 3-4: You can search the Help index to find out about a particular topic.

- On the Contents tab in the Help Topics dialog box, Help information is organized by task. Double-click on one of the book icons to display a list of "page icons" for different tasks. Double-click on a page icon to display the Help information for that task.
- Double-click on the Examples option on the Contents tab to display sample documents that use certain program features. Click on an example you want to inspect and then click on the colored triangles in the example to find out about the different features.
- WordPerfect and Presentations offer a help command that's useful if you're upgrading from an earlier version of a program or if you're switching from a competitor's program. Choose Help⇨Upgrade Help (or select the Upgrade Help option from the Contents tab of the Help Topics dialog box). Then select the name of the program that you formerly used and select the name of the feature you need help with. Click on the Guide Me button to have the Help system walk you through the steps involved in using the feature. Click on Find It to have the program locate the feature or command for you. Or click on Do It to have the program use the feature in your document. (Quattro Pro also offers limited upgrade help information.)
- Some dialog boxes have a little question mark button, usually at the top of the dialog box. For information about a dialog box option, click on the question mark icon and then click on the option to display a pop-up information box. Click again to get rid of the information box.

- If you have a modem and are hooked into the Internet, you can get online help by choosing Help⇨Help Online.
- As mentioned in Chapter 2, placing your mouse cursor over a button or other on-screen element displays a QuickTip box with hints about what that button or element does.

Navigating a Help Window

Figure 3-5 shows a typical Help window that appears when you display information about a particular command or task. Here are a few tips for making your way around the Help window and performing some other useful tricks:

- Click on underlined words or phrases to jump to information about that topic. Clicking on a word or phrase that's adorned with little icons or gray squares also jumps you to that topic.
- If you click on a term that's underlined with dots, an explanation of the term pops up.
- Click on the Back button to return to the previous screen.
- Click on the Help Topics button to display the Help Topics dialog box.

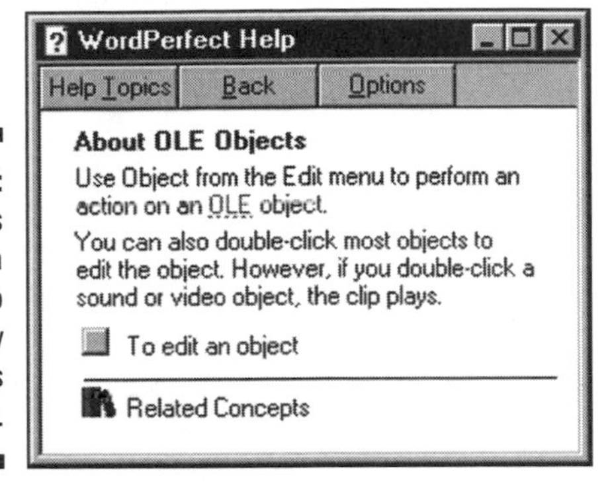

Figure 3-5: There's more to a Help window than meets the eye.

- To print a Help screen, choose Options⇨Print Topic.
- If you want to keep the Help window displayed as you work in the program, choose Options⇨Keep Help on Top⇨On Top. You can resize the Help window as you would any window — just drag on an edge or corner of the window.

Using the Reference Center

The WordPerfect Suite comes with its own digital library of reference manuals for many of the programs in the suite. Called the Reference Center, the library is stored on the Suite CD-ROM and isn't installed on your hard drive. To open the Reference Center, put the CD into your CD drive. Then click on the Windows 95 Start button, click on the Corel WordPerfect Suite 7 item in the Start menu, choose Accessories, and then choose Reference Center. When the Reference Center screen appears, click on the icon for the manual you want to see. After a few seconds, the manual opens in an Envoy window. You can find out more about viewing documents in Envoy in Chapter 17.

If you want assistance with advanced topics not covered in this book, don't forget to check out the *...For Dummies* titles on the individual programs in the WordPerfect Suite. They're excellent, easy-to-digest references that provide more in-depth coverage on the programs than can be included in this book.

Part II

Goodbye, Typewriter . . . Hello, WordPerfect!

"IT'S NOT THAT IT DOESN'T WORK AS A COMPUTER, IT JUST WORKS BETTER AS A PAPERWEIGHT."

In this part . . .

Back in the old days (you know, before Bill Gates took over the world), producing reports, letters, and other text documents was no easy feat. Even if you had a really good typewriter, turning out professional-looking, error-free pages often required hours and hours of tedious labor — not to mention gallons of correction fluid.

Thanks to the advent of the word processor, you can now produce flawless pages of text and graphics in minutes. Okay, maybe not minutes, but certainly in a heck of a lot less time than it took using the old Smith-Corona. What's more, you can easily rearrange sentences and paragraphs, fancy up your pages with all sorts of fonts and pictures, and even get the computer to check your spelling.

WordPerfect 7 is one of the most powerful word processors on the market. In fact, it offers so many features that you'll probably never use them all. This part introduces you to the features you'll use every day to create basic documents — as well as a few fun tricks for producing not-so-basic documents.

Chapter 4

The Process of Processing Words

In This Chapter

- Firing up WordPerfect
- Customizing your screen
- Entering text
- Moving around in your text

If you're old enough to remember the days before there was a personal computer on every desk — well, then, let's face it, your best years may be behind you. But that's beside the point. If you were alive in the precomputing era, when the typewriter was the primary mechanism for producing text, you'll have a special appreciation for WordPerfect. No longer do you have to type and retype the same page over and over again until you get it just right. No longer do you have to spend hours dabbing at mistakes with correction fluid. And no longer do you have to hurl that heavy typewriter at your boss when he or she informs you that you must add three paragraphs to the beginning of that 20-page report that took you days to complete.

WordPerfect gives you the power to churn out page after page of great-looking (and properly spelled) text in no time. This chapter gets you started on your word processing adventure by explaining what's what on the WordPerfect screen, giving you basic how-to's for entering text and moving around the screen, and describing ways to make the WordPerfect interface behave just the way you want.

Getting Started

To start WordPerfect, click on the WordPerfect DAD icon on the taskbar or click on Corel Windows 95 Start button, click on the WordPerfect Suite 7 button at the top of the Start menu, and then click on the WordPerfect 7 menu item. After some gurgling and wheezing by your computer, you see a screen that looks something like the one shown in Figure 4-1. The middle of your screen won't have the text you see in the figure — WordPerfect foolishly declined my offer to use my poetry in the opening screen.

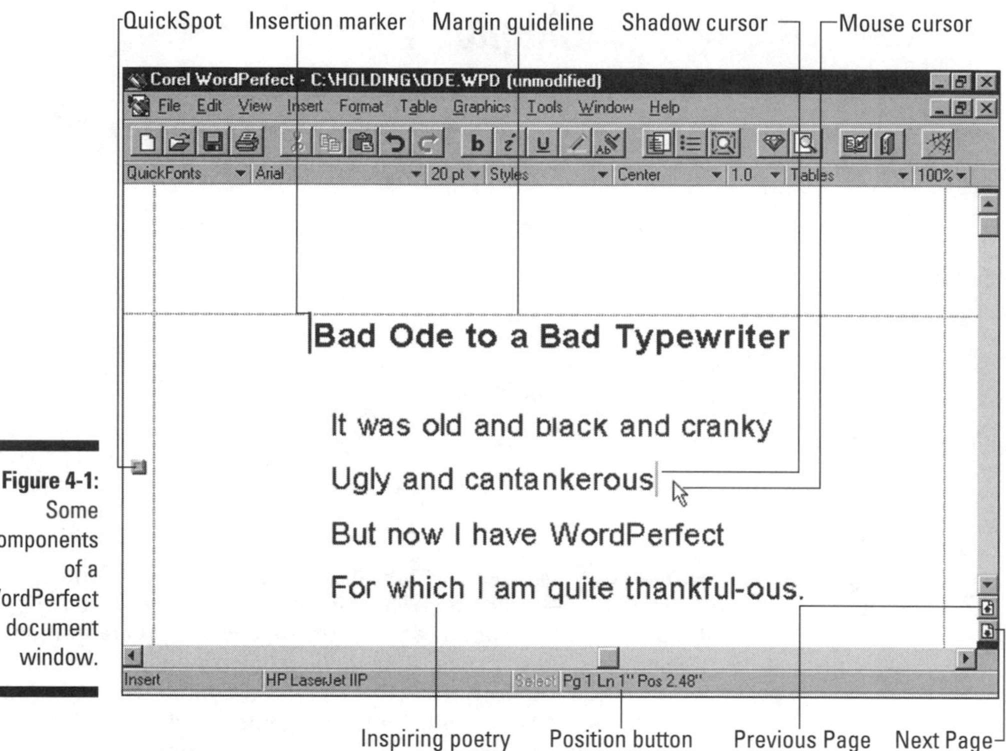

Figure 4-1: Some components of a WordPerfect document window.

Most elements of the WordPerfect window are the same as you find in any Windows 95 window, covered in Chapter 2, in the section "Doing Windows." But a few elements require some explanation:

- The blinking black bar is the *insertion marker*. The marker indicates where the next character you type will appear. To position the insertion marker, place the mouse cursor at the spot where you want to type and click.

- The nonblinking gray bar is the *shadow cursor*. It follows your mouse cursor and shows you where the insertion marker will appear if you click. (In this book, "cursor" refers to the mouse cursor rather than the shadow cursor unless I specifically say otherwise.)

- The dotted blue horizontal and vertical lines indicate the page margins. To move a margin, just place your mouse cursor over the margin guideline until the cursor changes into a two-headed arrow. Then drag the line. (Chapter 7 provides more information about margins.)

- The little gray button in the left margin is called a *QuickSpot.* The QuickSpot appears when you pass your cursor over a paragraph. You can click on the QuickSpot to display a dialog box of options that change the look of a paragraph. You can find more information about these options in Chapter 7.
- Click on the *page icons* at the bottom of the vertical scroll bar for a quick way to move from page to page in your document.
- The *Position button* on the status bar gives you information about the current location of your cursor. It displays the page number, line number, and distance from the left edge of the page.

Customizing Your Workspace

You can control many things about the WordPerfect *environment* (a fancy term for how the program looks and behaves). The key to making most of these changes lies in the Preferences command of the Edit menu. After you choose the command, WordPerfect displays the Preferences dialog box, shown in Figure 4-2.

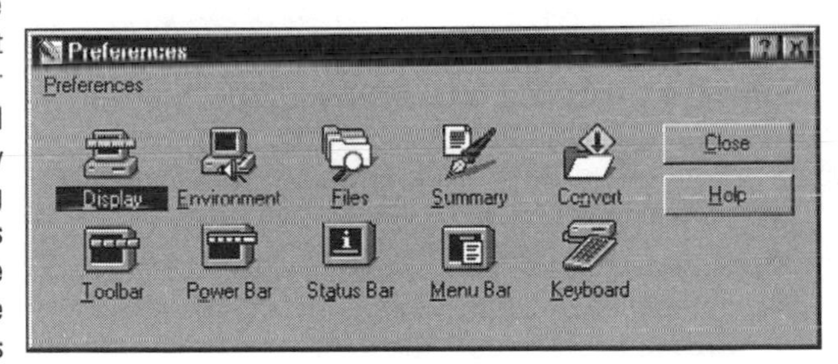

Figure 4-2: Make WordPerfect bow to your personal whims by changing settings available through the Preferences dialog box.

Double-clicking on the Display icon in the Preferences dialog box brings up the Display Preferences dialog box, shown in Figure 4-3. Note that the Display icon is available only when no text is selected (highlighted). Here's a sampling of the preferences you can set in this dialog box:

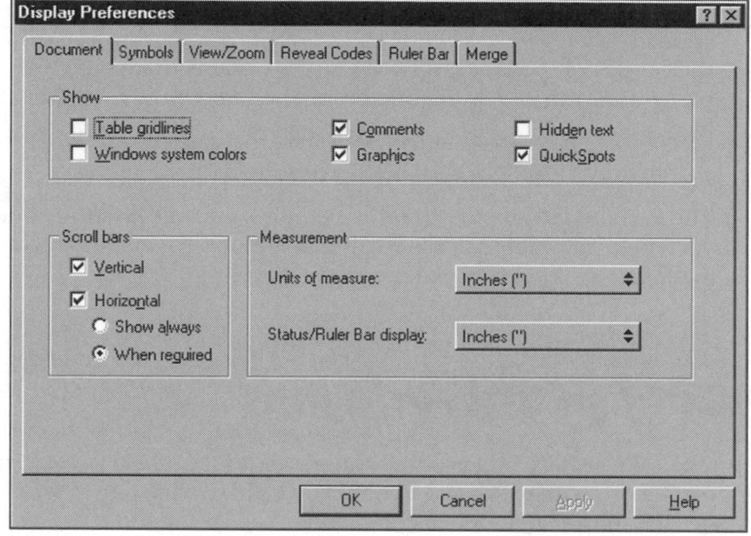

Figure 4-3: You can control how certain screen elements are displayed through this dialog box.

- On the Document tab, you can select the elements that you want to display on-screen, change the unit of measure used on the ruler bar (described shortly), and specify when and if you want the scroll bars to appcar.
- Options on the Symbols tab determine whether so-called *hidden symbols* display. Hidden symbols are little symbols that show you where spaces, paragraph breaks (also known as *hard returns*), tabs, indents, and other formatting instructions are placed throughout your text. Figure 4-4 shows some hidden symbols scattered throughout a famous ode. You can also turn hidden symbols on and off by choosing View⇨Show ¶ or pressing Ctrl+Shift+F3.
- On the View/Zoom tab, you can choose the default zoom size (magnification) and view mode for your document display. Page view mode displays your document as it will appear when printed; Two Page view is similar except that you see two pages side by side. Draft mode displays your document close to its printed appearance, but without certain formatting features such as headers and footers (covered in Chapter 8). Hiding these features speeds up screen display somewhat. You can also access zoom and view mode options via the View menu and the Zoom button on the Power Bar (labeled in Figure 4-4).

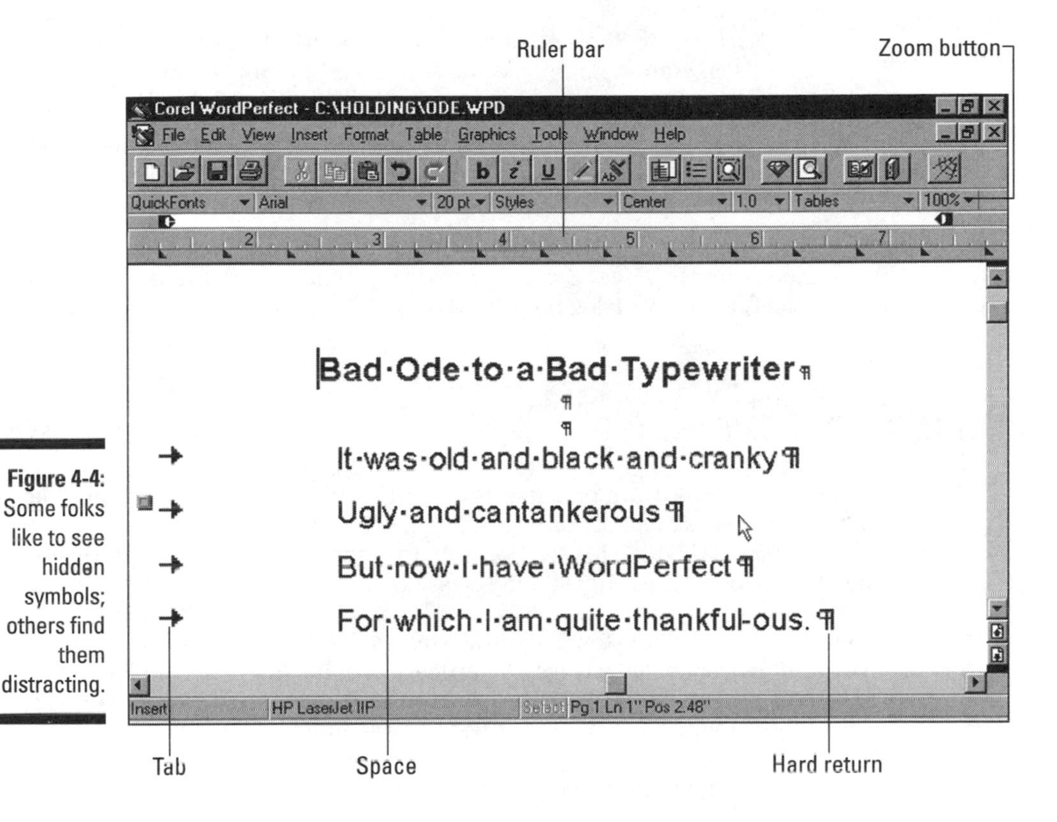

Figure 4-4: Some folks like to see hidden symbols; others find them distracting.

Other choices in the Preferences dialog box enable you to customize your toolbar, Power Bar, status bar, menu bar, keyboard, and other screen elements. Play around with these options to see what's available and what setups best suit your needs.

The Preferences dialog box isn't the only vehicle for custom-tailoring the WordPerfect interface, however. Check out these other options, too:

- Choose View⇨Toolbars/Ruler to display or hide the toolbar, Power Bar, status bar, or ruler bar. (The ruler bar, shown in Figure 4-4, is used for setting tabs and indents, as explained in Chapter 7.)
- You can also access preference settings by right-clicking on the status bar, ruler bar, or toolbar and choosing Preferences from the QuickMenu. Right-click on the Power Bar and choose Options from the QuickMenu to access Power Bar options.
- You can control how many rows of buttons appear in your toolbar. Right-click on the toolbar, choose Preferences from the QuickMenu to display the Toolbar Preferences dialog box, and then click on the Options button. In the dialog box that appears next, change the Maximum Number of

Rows/Columns to Show setting. The number of buttons that fit on a a row depends on your monitor size and screen resolution; you may get more or fewer buttons per row than you see in the figures in this book.

- WordPerfect also lets you add, remove, and rearrange toolbar and Power Bar buttons. For how-to's, see "Create Your Own Toolbar and Power Bar buttons" in Chapter 23.
- To hide or display margin guides, column guides, and other non-printing guides, choose View⇨Guidelines and select the guides you want to display in the Guidelines dialog box.

Entering Text

Putting your words down on paper is easy in WordPerfect. Just bang those keys, and WordPerfect slaps the corresponding letters onto your page. Go ahead, try it: Type "Now is the time for all good men to come to the aid of the party," or one of those other hysterical typing-class goodies.

In a lot of ways, creating text in WordPerfect is the same as typing on a typewriter. But in just as many ways, the process is quite different. And if you try to rely on the same techniques that worked so well on your typewriter, not only will you botch things up, you won't be taking advantage of the power that WordPerfect offers. So unless you want your computer to serve as a $2,000 typewriter, you need to remember the following things as you enter text:

- If you type a character or characters and then decide better of it, press the Backspace key (sometimes labeled with a left-pointing arrow or Bksp) or the Delete key to wipe out your mistake. The Backspace key gets rid of letters to the left of the insertion marker; the Delete key zaps characters to the right of the insertion marker. For a host of other editing options, see Chapter 6.
- Don't press the Enter or the Return key when you get to the right edge of your page. WordPerfect automatically wraps the text to the next line when needed. Pressing Enter or Return creates a paragraph break. This rule is important because of the way that WordPerfect applies paragraph formatting such as line spacing, indents, and so on, as explained in Chapter 7.
- When you get to the end of a page, WordPerfect creates a new page for you and wraps the text to the new page. If you want to create a page break manually, press Ctrl+Enter or choose Insert⇨Page Break.

- Don't use spaces to indent paragraphs or lines of text. If you do, you waste a lot of time and you don't get consistent spacing, as illustrated in Figure 4-5. Instead, use the indent and tab controls explained in Chapter 7.

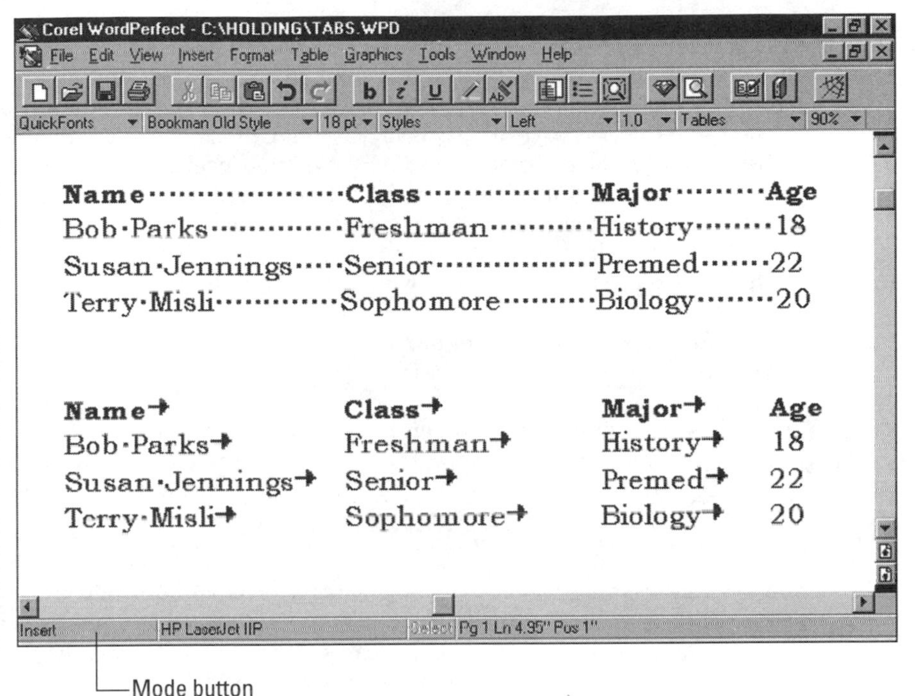

Figure 4-5: With spaces between column entries, text doesn't align exactly. If tabs are used, everything lines up neat and tidy-like.

- You can work in either of two text-entry modes. If you work in Insert mode, whatever you type is inserted between existing text. For example, if you type *Bob,* click between the *B* and the *o,* and press *l,* you get *Blob.* If you work in Typeover mode, whatever you type replaces existing type. In the preceding example, the *o* is replaced by the *l,* and you get *Blb.* To switch between text-entry modes, double-click on the Mode button at the left end of the status bar (labeled in Figure 4-5).

A little red, striped line underneath a word you typed is WordPerfect's way of letting you know you may have a spelling problem on your hands. This feature is called Spell-As-You-Go, and you turn it on and off by choosing Tools⇨Spell-As-You-Go or pressing Ctrl+Alt+F1. For more info, see Chapter 9.

- If WordPerfect changes the text you type or overrules your formatting instructions, the program's QuickCorrect feature is probably enabled. For information about QuickCorrect, see Chapters 6 and 8.

- Don't forget that the *insertion marker,* and not the mouse cursor or shadow cursor, controls where your next text will appear. Before you type, make sure that the blinking black insertion marker is where you want to place the text. If not, you can move the insertion marker by clicking at the spot where you want to add the text.

Moving around in Your Document

Sophisticated programs like WordPerfect give you lots of different ways to do the same thing. That flexibility is nice, but it can also be overwhelming. Such is the case with the topic of *navigation* — which is geekspeak for moving the cursor around in your document. WordPerfect gives you about a zillion ways to move the insertion marker and view different portions of your document. Don't be intimidated by the variety of options, though — just pick the ones that make the most sense for the way you work and forget about the others.

Here are some of the ways to move the insertion point to a different spot in your document:

- Use the scroll arrows or scroll box, explained in Chapter 2, to scroll the document so that you can see the page where you want to place the insertion marker. Alternatively, click on the Previous Page or Next Page icons, labeled back in Figure 4-1, to move to the page. Then click at the spot where you want the insertion mark to appear.
- Your keyboard should have either one or two groups of keys that have little arrows on them. You can press an arrow key to move the insertion marker in the direction of the arrow. Note that if an arrow key also has a number on it, it is a dual-purpose key. If the Num Lock key on your keyboard is on, the arrow key types a number. If the Num Lock key is off, the arrow key moves the cursor.
- If you double-click on the Position button in the status bar (refer back to Figure 4-1), WordPerfect displays the Go To box, not to be confused with the go-to guy on your favorite basketball team. One takes you to a new place in the document, the other takes you to the playoffs. Anyway, in the dialog box (see Figure 4-6), you can enter a specific page number or choose from a number of position options. Click on OK, and WordPerfect scoots the cursor to that page or position.

  Just for good measure, WordPerfect gives you three — that's right, three — other ways to access the Go To box: choose Edit⇨Go To, press Ctrl+G, or right-click on the scroll bar and choose Go To from the QuickMenu.

Believe it or not, these options are just the tip of the navigation iceberg. You also have all the navigation keys and keyboard shortcuts listed in Table 4-1 at your disposal. The first four items are really worth committing to memory, as you'll need them a lot. The usefulness of the others is a matter of personal preference — personally, I don't use them because I find it easier to simply click or use the arrow keys to move the insertion point short distances. But you may disagree, depending on your disposition and ability to remember scads of keyboard shortcuts.

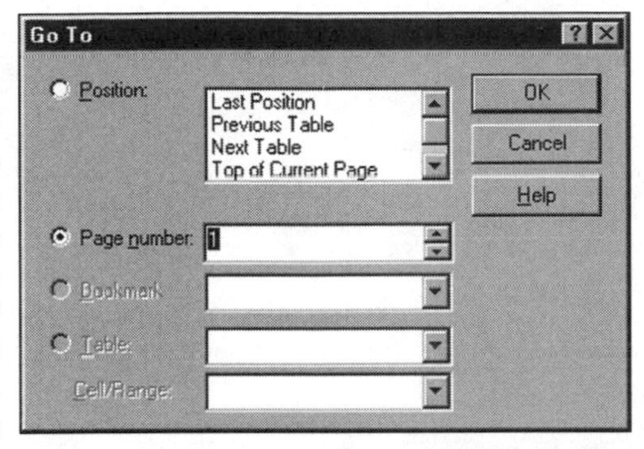

Figure 4-6: The Go To box enables you to move to a new place in the document.

Table 4-1 Keyboard Navigation Shortcuts

Press This Key	*To Do This*
Home	Move to the beginning of the current line
End	Move to the end of the current line
Ctrl+Home	Move to the beginning of the document
Ctrl+End	Move to the end of the document
Page Up (PgUp)	Move up one screen
Page Down (PgDn)	Move down one screen
Alt+PgUp	Move up one page
Alt+PgDn	Move down one page
Ctrl+up arrow	Move to the beginning of the current paragraph, or if you're at the beginning, to the beginning of the preceding paragraph
Ctrl+down arrow	Move to the beginning of the next paragraph
Ctrl+left arrow	Move left one word
Ctrl+right arrow	Move right one word

These keyboard shortcuts can really speed up navigation time. What's more, you can use them to navigate documents in most Windows programs, not just in WordPerfect. So it really pays to dump some of the more useless pieces of information in your brain's memory banks — for example, maybe you don't really need to remember the theme song from *Gilligan's Island* anymore — to make room for these shortcuts.

Chapter 5

Open, Close, Save, Print: Dull but Vital Basics

In This Chapter

- Opening new and existing documents
- Saving time by using WordPerfect templates and Experts
- Getting familiar with filenames, folders, and other document storage terms
- Putting documents away
- Saving your work
- Making your printer spit out pages of text

Some chapters in this book are a lot of fun to explore. You find out about all sorts of cool things you can do by clicking here, clicking there, and otherwise messing around with on-screen gizmos and gadgets. Other chapters — like this one, I'm sad to say — are less action-packed but vital to getting your money's worth out of your software investment.

This chapter focuses on some of the dull but very necessary aspects of word processing: how to open and close documents, save documents to your computer's hard drive or a floppy disk, and print out your finished masterpiece. It's not the kind of stuff you can use to titillate your friends and relatives (unless you have really geeky friends and relatives), but the information is important if you want to stop fooling around and actually produce something in WordPerfect.

The good news is that after you muddle through these yawner topics, you won't have to repeat the process for every program you want to use. Although this chapter explains concepts in terms specific to WordPerfect, you use virtually the same procedures to open, close, save, and print documents in all programs in the WordPerfect Suite and in most other Windows programs as well.

Opening a New Document

Before you can type on a typewriter, you need to put a piece of paper in the machine. And before you can do anything in WordPerfect, you need a *document,* sometimes also referred to as a *file.* When you first start WordPerfect, as explained in Chapter 4, it presents you with a new blank document. If you need a second blank document, you can get one in four ways:

- Choose File⇨New.
- Press Ctrl+Shift+N.
- Click on the New Document from Template button, which is labeled in the upcoming Figure 5-2.
- Click on the New Blank Document button on the far left end of the toolbar — the one that looks like a blank sheet of paper.

If you use either of the first three methods to open a new document, WordPerfect displays the Select New Document dialog box shown in Figure 5-1. In this dialog box, you select a *template* for the document. Providing the basic framework for your document, the template contains such basic formatting instructions as the size of the page, margin settings, and tab settings.

By default, WordPerfect chooses the Create a Blank Document option in the dialog box, which is normally the template you want. But you can also use templates and Experts that make it easy to create resumes, message pads, and other common documents, as explained in the next two sections. To choose a template or Expert, click on it. Then press Enter or click on the Select button.

If you use the New Blank Document toolbar button to create a document, the Select New Document dialog box doesn't appear; WordPerfect automatically selects the Create a Blank Document template for you.

Figure 5-1: WordPerfect offers several prefab templates that you can use to create different types of documents quickly.

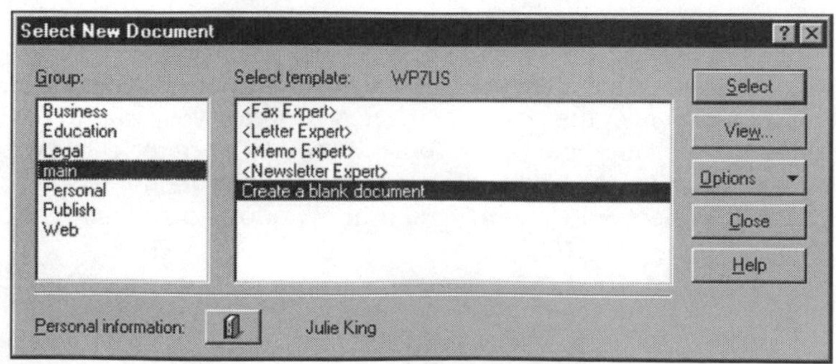

Using Experts to create common documents

WordPerfect offers several *Experts* that you can use to create some common documents, such as fax cover sheets and memos. To discover the available Experts, click on the different categories in the Group list box in the Select New Document dialog box. Click on the Expert you want to use in the Select Template list box, and then click on Select. WordPerfect ponders your request for a few seconds and then displays a document containing some preformatted text.

The Expert may ask you to enter some information, which it places in the document for you. For example, the Memo Expert asks you to enter your name, the name of the memo recipient, and other pertinent information you normally find at the top of a memo. After WordPerfect creates the basic structure of your document, you can add any additional information to the page and edit any existing text.

If your company requires that all corporate documents follow a certain structure or design, documents created by the Experts probably won't meet your needs. But if you just want to create a piece of casual correspondence and you don't care much about the design, give the Experts a whirl.

Using the prefab templates

In addition to Experts, WordPerfect offers some templates that can be useful when you're in a hurry to produce certain types of documents. Like Experts, the templates provide you with documents that contain preformatted text and graphics. To see what templates are all about, take these steps:

1. **Choose File⇨New or press Ctrl+Shift+N.**

   Or click on the New Document from Template button, labeled in Figure 5-2. The Select a New Document dialog box appears, as shown back in Figure 5-1.

2. **Choose a template category from the Group list box.**

   For templates that create everyday business documents, for example, choose the Business category.

3. **Click on a template in the Select Template list box and then click on Select or press Enter.**

   WordPerfect prompts you for some information from which it creates the document. You can edit the document as necessary. Figure 5-2 shows the document created by using the Telephone Message Pad template in the Business group.

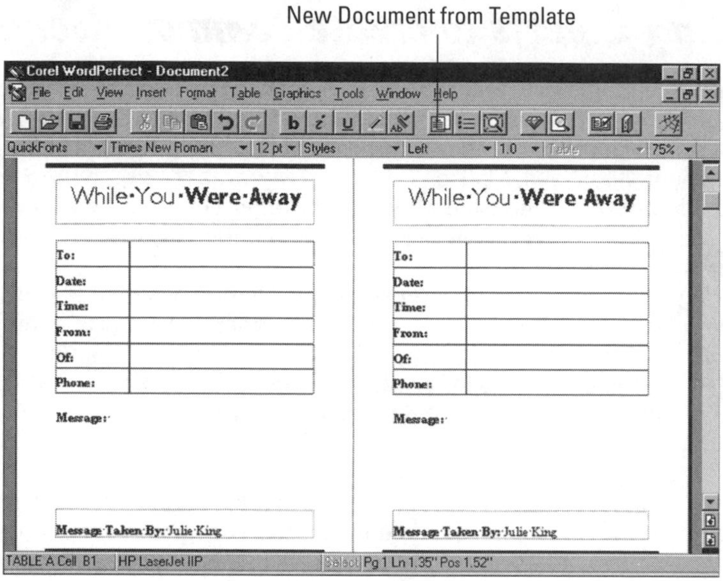

New Document from Template

Figure 5-2: A telephone message pad created by a template — fast, easy, and painless!

Opening Existing Documents

To open an existing document, you have three options:

- Choose File⇨Open.
- Press Ctrl+O.
- Click on the Open toolbar button. (It looks like an open manila file folder and is a neighbor to the New Blank Document button, on the far left end of the toolbar.)

Figuring out the Open dialog box

Whichever method of opening a document you choose, you're greeted by the imposing Open dialog box, shown in Figure 5-3. If you're familiar with using Open dialog boxes in other Windows 95 programs, you can skip the rest of this section; the WordPerfect Open dialog box works pretty much the same as every other Open dialog box. If you're new to the game, however, here's what you need to know:

- To open a document, just double-click on its name in the document list box, labeled in Figure 5-3. Or click once on the document name and then click on Open or press Enter.

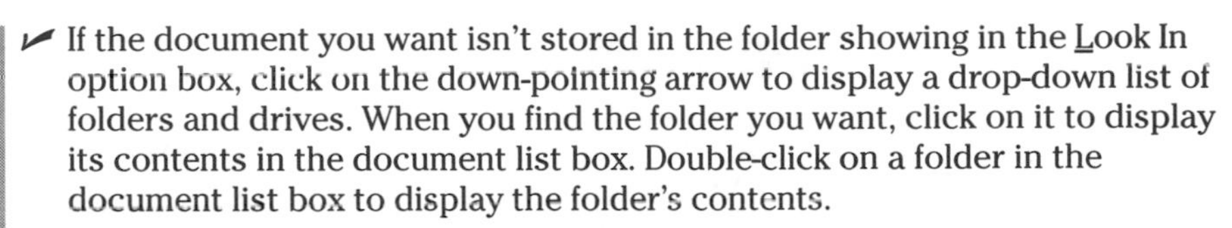

- If the document you want isn't stored in the folder showing in the Look In option box, click on the down-pointing arrow to display a drop-down list of folders and drives. When you find the folder you want, click on it to display its contents in the document list box. Double-click on a folder in the document list box to display the folder's contents.

- *Folders* are little storage compartments on your computer's hard disk. You use them just as you would use hanging files or file folders in your file cabinet — to store groups of related documents together. Before Windows 95, folders were called *directories.* Many programs still use the old term, but the meaning is the same. You can create a new folder in the Open dialog box by choosing File⇨New⇨Folder.
- If you still don't see the file you want, you may need to change the file type shown in the For Type option box. If you want to see all types of files, select All Files. If you only want to see WordPerfect documents, select the WP Documents (.wpd) option.

- Notice the Details button at the top of the dialog box, labeled in 5-3. If you select this button, you can see detailed information about each file, including the date it was last modified and its size.
- If you click on the Open as Copy button rather than the Open button when opening a document, WordPerfect opens a copy of your original document. This option gives you a way to fool around with a document secure in the knowledge that if you screw it up, you still have the original available.

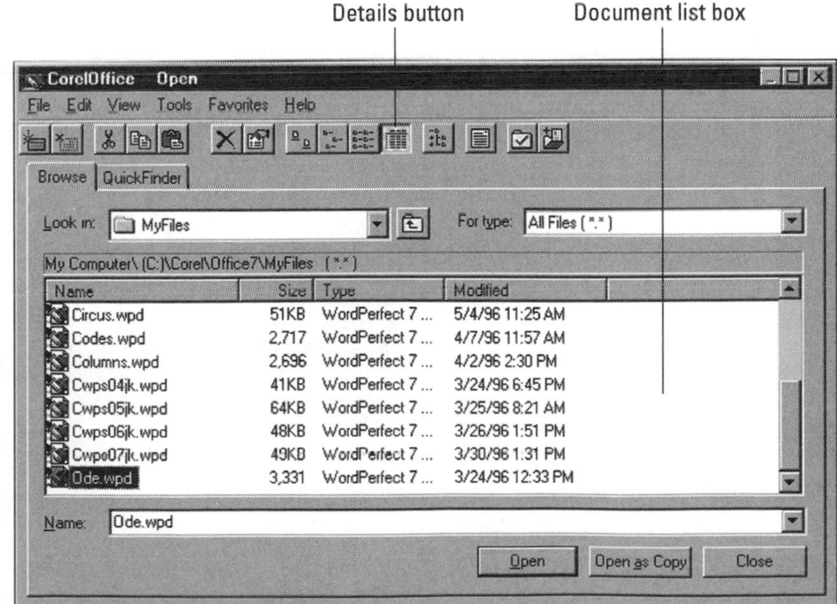

Figure 5-3: The imposing Open dialog box isn't as complicated as it looks.

Closing a Document

When you're sick and tired of looking at a document, click on the document window's Close button — it's the one marked with an X, at the far right end of the menu bar. (Be sure to click on the Close button on the menu bar, and not the one on the title bar, which closes the WordPerfect program.) Alternatively, you can choose File⇨Close or press Ctrl+F4.

If you haven't saved your document to disk yet, WordPerfect prompts you to do so. For specifics on saving, see the next section.

Saving Your Work (and Your Sanity)

Here's a little saying to remember when you're working in WordPerfect or in any other computer program: Save your work, save your mind.

Until you choose the Save command, everything you do in a document is temporary. If WordPerfect shuts down for any reason — the computer crashes, you have a power failure, or you close the program so you'll have enough computer memory to play Myst — you zap your document into the electronic abyss, and all your hard work is gone forever. So learn to save early and save often.

Saving for the very first time

To save a document for the first time, follow these steps:

1. **Choose File⇨Save or press Ctrl+S.**

   Alternatively, you can click on the Save button on the toolbar (it's the third button from the left — the one that looks like a little floppy disk). The Save As dialog box, shown in Figure 5-4, appears *unless* some text is selected in your document (as explained in Chapter 6). If text is selected, you see a dialog box that gives you the option of saving either just the selected text or the entire file. Click on the option you want and then click on OK or press Enter to get to the Save As dialog box.

2. **Choose a storage location for your document.**

   Tell WordPerfect where you want to store the document by choosing a drive (hard drive or floppy drive) and folder from the Save In drop-down menu.

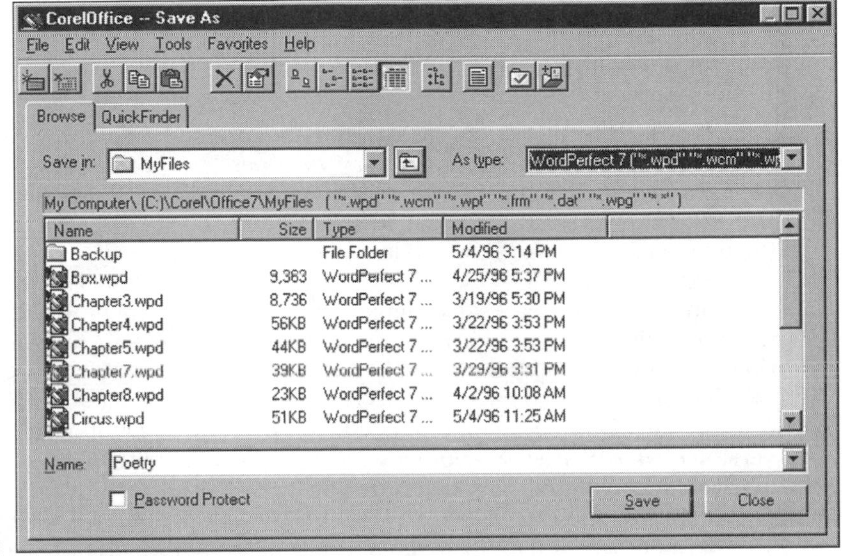

Figure 5-4: Get familiar with this dialog box to avoid torture, torment, and teeth-gnashing.

3. **Enter a document name in the Name option box.**

   For tips on choosing a filename, see the upcoming sidebar "What's in a (Windows 95) filename?" Note that you don't have to enter the three letter file extension (such as .WPD for WordPerfect documents); WordPerfect takes care of that business for you.

4. **Choose a file type.**

   The As Type drop-down list lets you choose from many different file formats, including those used by other programs. By default, WordPerfect saves your document in its native (own) format; usually, this is the choice you want. But if you want to save the document for use in some other program, choose that program's file format from the As Type drop-down list.

5. **Click on the Save button.**

That's it! You're protected — for now. But if you make any changes to your document after you save it once, those changes aren't protected until you resave the document. So it's important to save often during your computing sessions and also before you close a document. (WordPerfect prompts you to do this.) To resave the document, just issue the Save command again. WordPerfect saves your document, this time without bothering you with the Save As dialog box.

Saving a document with a different name or format

Sometimes, you may want to save a document under a different name than you saved it the first time. For example, say you open Document A and make some changes to it. You're not sure whether your client will like the changes or prefer the original version. By using the Save As command, you can save the changed document as Document B, which leaves Document A intact.

You can also use the Save As command to save the document to a different folder or drive than you originally saved it — for example, if you stored the document on your hard drive and now want to save a copy on a floppy disk. Another use for the command is to save a document in a different file *format* (type of file). If you're giving your document to a coworker who uses an earlier version of WordPerfect or another word processor, for example, you can save it in a format compatible with that program.

To save a document under a new name, in a different format, or to a new destination, choose File⇨Save As to open the Save As dialog box (shown back in Figure 5-4). Choose a folder and hard drive from the Save In drop-down menu, choose a file format from the As Type drop-down menu, and enter a name in the Name option box. Then click on the Save button or press Enter.

What's in a (Windows 95) filename?

In the past, Windows insisted that you follow strict rules when naming files. A proper file name consisted of an eight-character document name, followed by a period, followed by a three-letter file extension. (The extension indicated the type of document — WPD for WordPerfect documents, TIF for a graphics file saved in the TIFF format, and so on.)

Windows 95 changes the naming rules somewhat. You can now have filenames up to 255 characters long, although why you'd want such a long name is beyond me. Filenames still have three-letter file extensions, but you usually don't have to add the extension when you're saving a file — the extension is added automatically for you. If for some reason you want to specify the extension, of course, you can.

One file-naming rule from the old days does still apply: Spaces and special characters such as ampersands, parentheses, and brackets are verboten. To be absolutely safe, use only regular alphabetical and numerical characters in your filenames. Also, if you want to share a document with a coworker who doesn't use Windows 95 or Windows 95 programs, stick with the old eight-character, three-letter extension naming conventions.

Getting extra protection through automatic saving

With all the other things you have to remember during a workday — your manager's favorite flavor of latté, the names of all the really important people in the office, the date of your next salary review — it can be difficult to remember to save your documents on a regular basis. Fortunately, WordPerfect offers an option that saves your document automatically at specified intervals.

To use this feature, make sure no text is selected, and then choose Edit⇨Preferences to display the Preferences dialog box, and then double-click on the Files item in the dialog box. The Files Preferences dialog box appears, as shown in Figure 5-5. If you don't see a checkmark in the Timed Document Backup check box as spotlighted in the figure, click on the box to turn the option on. By default, WordPerfect automatically saves your document every 10 minutes; this value is usually a safe bet, but you can raise or lower it according to your individual tolerance for risk.

Printing Your Pages

Usually, printing is a pretty straightforward process — if your printer and your computer are properly connected and configured to work together. If they're not, well, let's just say that it can be easier to print your documents by hand, using a calligraphy pen and ink.

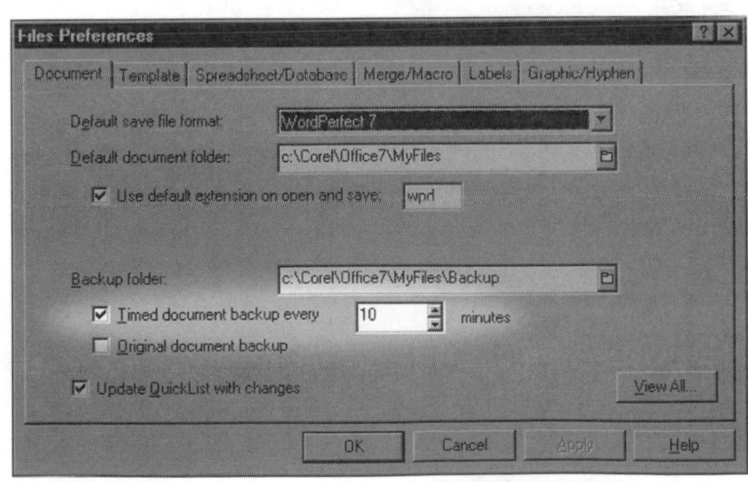

Figure 5-5: To protect yourself against unnecessary document losses, make sure that the Timed Document Backup option is turned on.

Because different printers and computer systems require different configurations — and because I'm not sure which printer or system you're using today — I can't give you specific instructions for setting up your printer. So the following steps assume that your printer and computer are on speaking terms and willing to cooperate in the printing process. If you have trouble, find your local printer guru (look for the person with toner-stained sleeves) and ask for help.

Having expertly dodged that responsibility, I'll move on to basic printing steps. Here's how you print an open document:

1. **Choose File➪Print or click on the Print button on the toolbar.**

   The Print button looks like a printer with paper coming out of it (in a crude, minimalist sort of way, that is). The Print dialog box, shown in Figure 5-6, zooms into view.

2. **Specify how many copies you want to print.**

   Enter the number of copies in the Number of Copies option box (there's a surprise). If you print more than one copy, the Group and Collate options become available. If you choose Group, the printer prints all copies of page 1, and then prints all copies of page 2, and so on. If you choose Collate, the printer prints the entire document once, prints the second copy of the document, and so on — in other words, it collates the pages for you.

   The Print in Reverse Order option prints your pages in the opposite order than they normally print. For example, if your printer usually prints the first page in the document first, checking this option prints the last page in the document first.

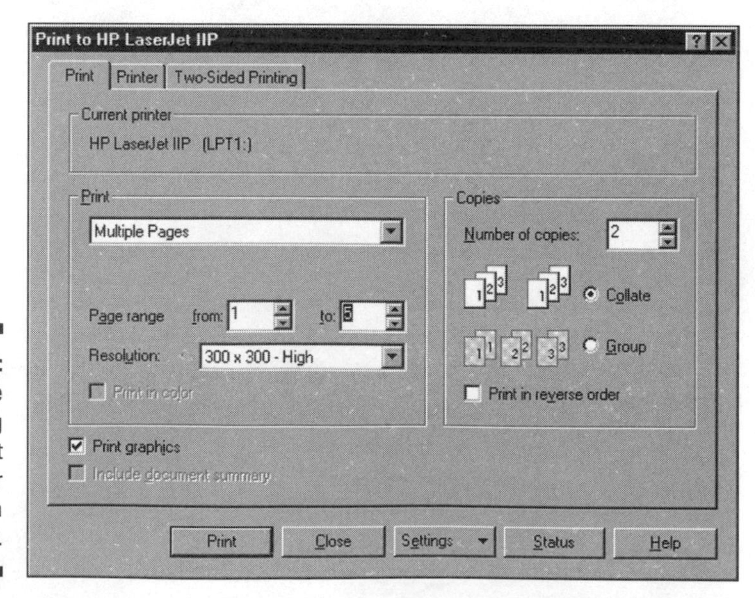

Figure 5-6: You use the Print dialog box to select options for printing a document.

3. Specify which pages you want to print.

You do this by making choices in the Print drop-down list and the Page Range option boxes.

- To print your entire document, choose Full Document from the Print drop-down list.
- To print just the current page (the page on which the insertion marker is located), choose Current Page from the Print drop-down list.
- To print several pages that fall together (for example, pages 1 through 5), choose Multiple Pages in the Print drop-down list and then enter the first page number and last page number in the Page Range option boxes, as in Figure 5-6.
- To print several pages that don't fall in sequence — say, pages 1, 4, and 5 — choose Advanced Multiple Pages from the Print drop-down list and then click on the Edit button that appears. The Advanced Multiple Pages dialog box appears, as shown in Figure 5-7. Enter the numbers of the pages you want to print in the Page(s)/label(s) option box and ignore the other options in the dialog box. Click on OK after you enter the page numbers.

You can enter page numbers in several ways. You can enter each page number, separated by a comma or space, as in Figure 5-7. Or you can indicate a range of pages by entering the first page in the range, a hyphen, and then the last number in the range. You can also combine the two approaches, entering *1,4-5*, for example.

4. Click on the Print button.

Your pages should start shooting out of your printer momentarily. Well, maybe not shooting, exactly — they actually sort of crawl out, if you have a printer like mine. May as well go get that cup of latté for your boss while you're waiting.

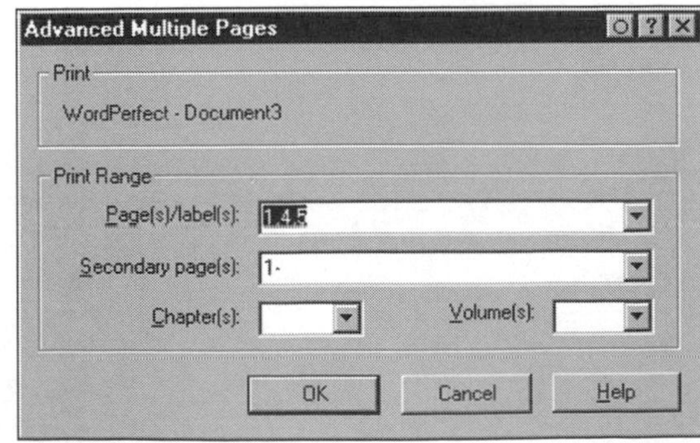

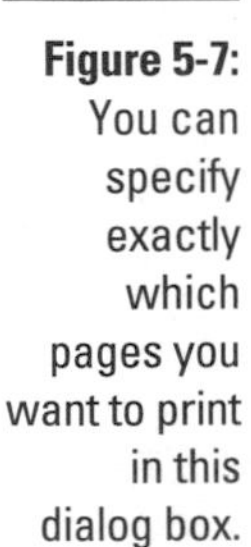
Figure 5-7: You can specify exactly which pages you want to print in this dialog box.

If you want to print a document without opening it, choose File⇨Print, enter the number of copies, select the Document on Disk option from the Print drop-down list, and click on the Edit button that appears. After the Document on Disk dialog box appears, enter the name of the file in the Document Name option box. You need to enter the entire pathname (see the discussion on pathnames in the following sidebar "What's a pathname, anyway?"). If you don't know the pathname, click on the little white button at the right end of the Document Name option box to display the Open dialog box, locate the file there, and then click on OK to put the pathname in the Document Name option box. Enter the page numbers or range of pages you want to print in the Page(s)/label(s) box. Click on OK and then click on Print to express your document to the printer.

Printing graphics sometimes takes a lot of time and printer memory. If you're short on either or both and are just printing a rough draft of your document, you can print your document without graphics by deselecting the Print Graphics check box in the Print dialog box.

Another option for printing graphics when time or printer memory is limited is to lower the Resolution setting in the Print dialog box. Your printed piece won't look as good as it would if printed at a high resolution, but the output may be okay for a draft copy.

What's a pathname, anyway?

Every now and then, a program will demand that you enter a file's *pathname.* The pathname gives your computer all the information it needs to locate a particular file: the name of the file plus the name of the hard drive, main folder, and subfolders that hold the document. For example, if you stored a file named File1.wpd inside a folder called Subfolder1, which is itself stored inside a folder called Folder1, which is stored on your C: drive, the pathname would be C:\Folder1\Subfolder1\File1.wpd.

Chapter 6

Eating Your Words and Other Editing Tasks

In This Chapter

- Selecting stuff you want to change
- Getting rid of unsavory characters
- Cutting, pasting, and copying text
- Dragging and dropping
- Undoing the past
- Letting QuickCorrect fix things automatically

This chapter shows you the basics of editing in WordPerfect. You find out how to delete unwanted text, how to copy and move words, sentences, and entire paragraphs, and how to use the QuickCorrect feature to automatically correct mistakes as you type.

After you get familiar with editing in a word processor, you're forever ruined as far as using a traditional typewriter. Not only will you find the limitations of a typewriter unbearable, but your typing accuracy will go to pot as well. WordPerfect makes it so easy to fix mistakes that you'll soon find yourself typing with far less regard for hitting the right keys than you used to have. You can type as fast as your thoughts can take you, knowing that you can come back and quickly clean up any typos, bloopers, or blunders later.

Don't mourn the loss of your typing accuracy, though. Look at it from the positive side: When the computer's down and someone asks you to just type that letter or memo on a typewriter, you can honestly say, "Gee, I'd like to, but now that I'm a word processing expert, I'm just no good on the typewriter. We pay a heavy price for this advancing technology, don't we?"

Be sure to walk away quickly, before the other party has a chance to get over the shock and question your sincerity.

Selecting Stuff You Want to Edit

Before you can edit text, you must first *select* the characters or paragraphs you want to change. Figure 6-1 shows an example of what selected text looks like on-screen. You can select text — also known as *highlighting* text — in countless ways. Here are just a few:

- Drag the cursor over the text you want to select.
- To select a single word, double-click on it. To select a sentence, triple-click on it.
- To select a paragraph, quadruple-click on it. Yikes! Who thought up that one? If this maneuver is beyond you, try this instead: Move the mouse pointer to the left margin of the paragraph until you see it become a right-pointing arrow. Then double-click.
- Click anywhere in the word, sentence, or paragraph you want to select. Move the mouse pointer to the left margin until it becomes a right-pointing arrow and then right-click to display the QuickMenu shown in Figure 6-1. Then choose the selection option you want from the menu.
- You can access the same selection commands found on the QuickMenu by choosing Edit⇨Select. If you ask me, this is the hard way to do things, but you may like doing things the hard way.
- To select everything in a document, press Ctrl+A (*A* for *all*).

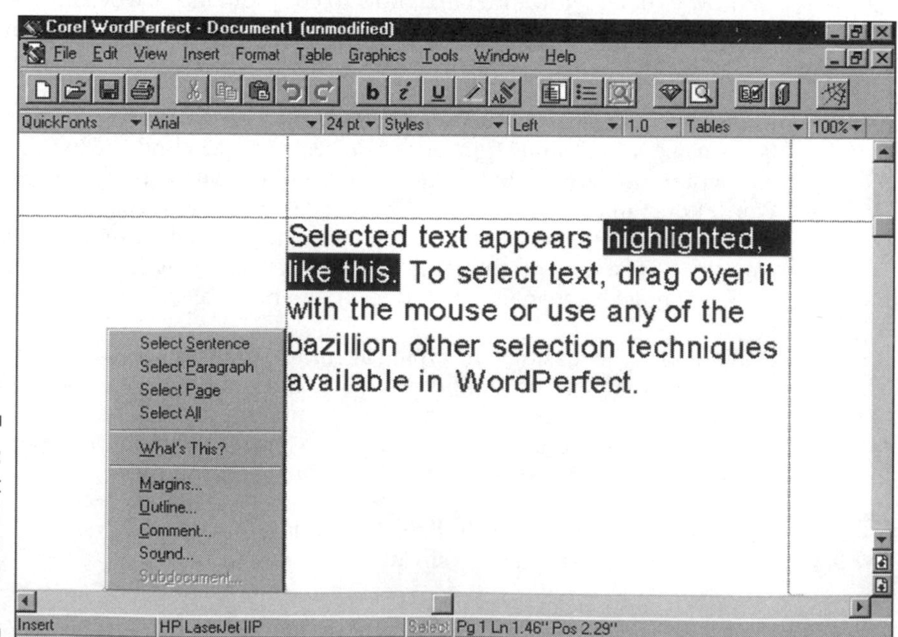

Figure 6-1: A look at selected text and the selection QuickMenu.

- Here's one of my favorites: Place the insertion marker at the beginning of the text you want to select. Press Shift and then use the arrow keys and other cursor movement keys covered in Chapter 4 (End, Home, and so on) to extend the selection over the rest of the text you want to select. For example, click and then press Shift+End to select everything from the insertion marker to the end of the current line.

- If you select something and then decide you want to add to the selection or subtract from it, just hold down the Shift key and use the arrow keys to move the end of the selection. Or press Shift and click to set the new end of the selection.

After you select text, you can wreak all kinds of havoc on it. You can copy it, delete it, move it, and replace it, as covered throughout the rest of this chapter. And, as discussed in Chapters 7 and 8, you can make it bold or italic, change the font and type size, change the line spacing and paragraph spacing, indent it, capitalize it, number it, and make it do a little clogging dance to "Rocky Top." Oh, sorry, got a little carried away — in Windows 95, text clogs only to "Orange Blossom Special."

If you begin typing while text is selected, the selected text is replaced by the new text you type.

Deleting Selected Stuff

To get rid of unwanted text, select it and press the Delete key or the Backspace key. Or right-click to display an editing QuickMenu and choose Delete from the menu.

As covered in Chapter 4, you can also use Delete and Backspace to get rid of unselected text. Delete erases characters to the right of the insertion marker; Backspace erases characters to the left.

If you zap something into oblivion and then realize that you didn't want to get rid of it after all, don't panic. You can usually get it back by using the Undo or Undelete commands explained later in this chapter.

Moving and Copying Text

Being able to erase unwanted text with a click of the mouse or press of a single key is pretty cool. But it's nothing compared with the editing power you gain when you discover how to cut, copy, and paste text. With these techniques, you can quickly move and copy text from one place to another.

The cut, copy, and paste techniques described in this section work similarly in all Windows programs. You can use them to copy and move graphics as well as text. (More about editing graphics in WordPerfect in Chapter 8.) Be sure to also check out Chapter 20, which discusses some special ways to move and copy data between documents and programs.

Because of the way WordPerfect handles formatted text, you can easily screw up your text formatting when you rearrange text. That's why you're better off doing the bulk of your editing before you apply formatting commands such as boldface, paragraph styles, and so on. For more information, see the upcoming sidebar, "Help! Everything got screwy when I moved stuff around!"

Using the Copy, Cut, and Paste commands

You can copy a piece of text and place the copy in a new location using two methods. You can drag and drop the text, as explained in the upcoming section, "Dragging and dropping," or you can use the Copy and Paste commands, as outlined in this section.

Which method is best depends on your dexterity with the mouse and the type of copying or moving you're doing. If you're copying a large block of text or copying from one document to another, using the Cut, Copy, and Paste commands is often easier. For small bits of text, dragging and dropping is more convenient.

To copy text using the Copy command:

1. **Select the text you want to copy.**

   Use any of the selection techniques discussed earlier in this chapter.

2. **Choose Edit⇨Copy or press Ctrl+C.**

   If you're a toolbar fan, click on the Copy button instead. The Copy button is in the second group of buttons from the left, and it looks like two identical sheets of paper. Or right-click to display a QuickMenu that sports the Copy command.

   WordPerfect sends a copy of your text to the Windows Clipboard, which is a temporary storage shed for copied and cut text.

3. **Click the spot where you want to place the copy.**

   You can put the copy in your current document or in another open document. You can even put the copy in a document you created in another program.

4. **Choose Edit⇨Paste or press Ctrl+V.**

   An alternative method is to click on the Paste toolbar button, which is right next to the Copy button and looks like a clipboard with a piece of paper attached. You can also right-click and choose the command from the resulting QuickMenu.

   Whichever method you pick, WordPerfect places your copy at the new location.

The process for moving selected text is the same as for copying text except that you use the Cut command rather than the Copy command. You can choose the command from the Edit menu or from the QuickMenu, click on the Cut button on the toolbar (it's the button with the scissors on it), or press the command keyboard shortcut, Ctrl+X.

After you cut or copy something to the Clipboard, it stays there until you cut or copy something else. So you can paste the cut or copied text as many times as needed in your document. Just keep pressing Ctrl+V.

Cutting, copying, and pasting is something you do a lot, whether you're working in WordPerfect, Quattro Pro, or any other program where you enter and edit text or data. If you commit to memory the keyboard shortcuts for these commands — Ctrl+X, Ctrl+C, and Ctrl+V, respectively — you'll save yourself lots of needless clicking and menu-opening.

Note that the three shortcut keys, X, C, and V, lie right next to each other on your keyboard (go ahead, take a peek). Why these keys? Well, maybe because the X sort of looks like a pair of scissors (for Cut), the C is the first letter in *Copy,* and the V . . . well, maybe it's supposed to bring to mind the word *Viscid,* which means *sticky* (like paste). Then again, maybe not.

Dragging and dropping

If you're handy with a mouse — and who isn't, these days? — dragging and dropping provides a quick, menuless way to cut and copy text. Try using this technique to move a piece of text:

1. **Select the text you want to move.**
2. **Place the mouse pointer on the selected text.**
3. **Press and hold down the left mouse button as you drag the text to its new home.**

   As you drag, you should see a little box attached to the mouse pointer. The box indicates that you're moving the selected text. The insertion marker moves in tandem with your mouse and indicates where the text will appear when you drop it.

Help! Everything got screwy when I moved stuff around!

If everything goes kablooey when you rearrange text — for example, all your plain text suddenly becomes bold and vice versa — you've messed up WordPerfect's hidden codes. You see, any time you give WordPerfect a formatting instruction, whether you want to set a tab, make text bold, or change a paragraph indent, the program inserts little hidden codes into your text to remind it what to do. And if you accidentally grab a code when you select a piece of text — or you don't grab a code that should be moved along with that text — WordPerfect gets all perplexed and cranky.

If this happens, you have a couple of options. One, you can reformat the text as needed. In some cases, you may need to remove all formatting from a paragraph and then reapply the formatting you want. Two, you can choose View➪Reveal Codes or press Alt+F3 to display the Reveal Codes window, shown in the following figure. In this window, you can see and edit the hidden formatting codes.

The problem with editing codes is that the process is confusing, complicated, and often darned frustrating. If you like puzzle-solving, though, and you want to become a code-cracker, check out *WordPerfect For Windows For Dummies*, which dedicates an entire chapter to the subject.

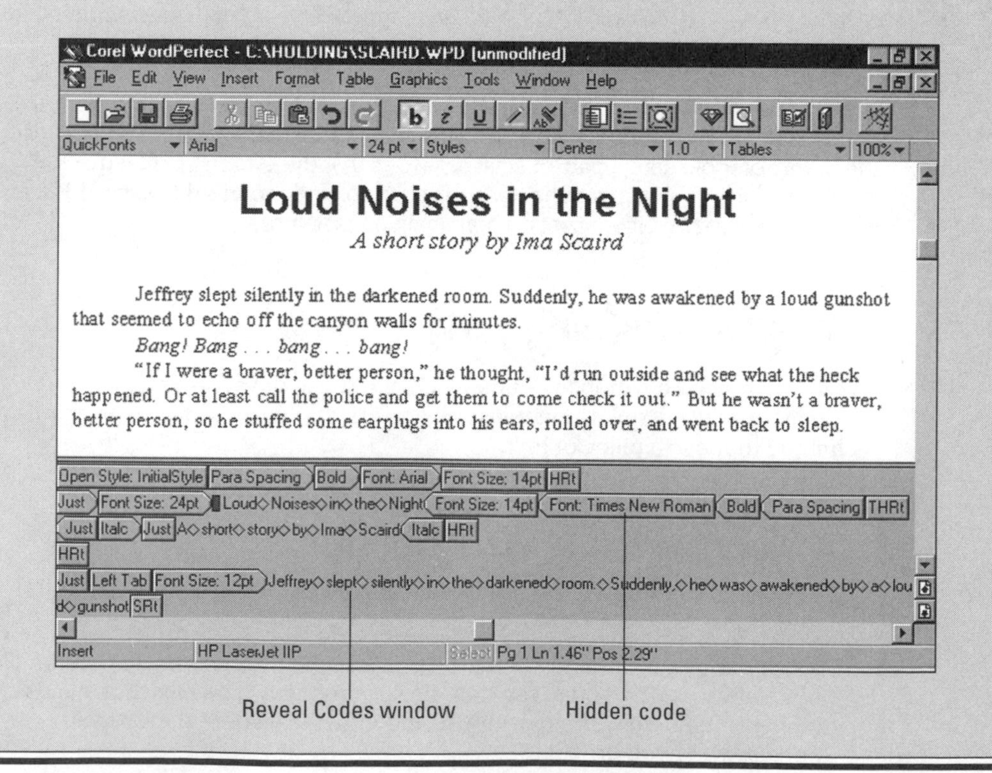

4. **When you have the text where you want it, release the mouse button.**

   If you want to copy a piece of text rather than move it, press Ctrl anytime before you release the mouse button. A plus sign appears next to the cursor to tell you that you're copying rather than cutting the selected text.

You can drag and drop text between two open WordPerfect documents or between two different programs. The following steps explain how to drag and drop between programs:

1. **Open the document that contains the text you want to move.**

   This document is sometimes called the *source.*

2. **Open the document where you want to move or copy the text.**

   This document is sometimes referred to as the *destination.*

3. **Select the text and then drag it to the taskbar button of the destination program.**

   Don't let up on the mouse button when you get to the taskbar; keep the button pressed until the window for the destination program appears. Then drag to the position where you want to place the text and release the mouse button.

As an alternative method, you can arrange the source and destination windows so that they appear side-by-side and just drag from one window to the other. Use this method to drag between documents in the same program. (Choose Window⇨Tile Side by Side to arrange the document windows.)

Whichever method you choose, dragging text cuts it from the source document and pastes it into the desintation document. To copy the text, press Ctrl before you release the mouse button.

Dragging and dropping between programs is possible through the magic of *Object Linking and Embedding,* otherwise known as OLE (pronounced *olé,* like at a bullfight). You can do lots of interesting things with OLE, so be sure to check out Chapter 20, which covers the subject in excruciating detail.

Bringing Back Lost Text

Sooner or later, it happens: You delete some text and then realize with horror that you wiped out the wrong thing. The thing it will take you hours to re-create. The thing that your boss wants to see on her desk in 30 minutes. Don't panic. WordPerfect has a built-in safety net just for situations like this. It's called the Undelete command, and you find it under the Edit menu. With this command, you can undelete the last three pieces of text you deleted.

When you choose the Undelete command or press its shortcut, Ctrl+Shift+Z, WordPerfect displays the Undelete dialog box, shown in Figure 6-2, and places the last text you deleted at the insertion marker. The text is highlighted to make it easy to spot. (You may need to move the dialog box out of the way. To do so, just drag it by the title bar.) Click on Previous to see the two previous deletions you made; click on Next to cycle back through the three deletions. Click on Restore if you see one you want to undelete.

Undelete only brings back text you erase using the Delete key or QuickMenu Delete command. If you used the Cut command, use Undo to reverse your mistake. The Undo command is explained in the next section.

Figure 6-2: You can undelete your last three deletions.

Undoing Changes

Undelete is a handy tool, but it pales in comparison to the restorative powers of the Undo command. Like Undelete, Undo reverses changes that you decide you really shouldn't have made. But Undo can reverse almost any editing action, not just deletions made with the Delete key or command. And whereas Undelete restores text at the insertion marker, Undo puts it back in its original location. What's more, it can reverse up to your last 300 editing moves.

- To undo the last editing change you made, choose Edit⇨Undo, click on the Undo button on the toolbar (it looks like a curving, left-pointing arrow), or press either of two available shortcuts: Ctrl+Z or Alt+Backspace.
- Change your mind about that undo? Choose Edit⇨Redo, click on the Redo toolbar button (it's right next to the Undo button), or press Ctrl+Shift+R to put things back the way they were before you chose the Undo command.

- You must choose the Redo command immediately after choosing the Undo command. If you click a mouse button, type new text, or make any other changes to your document, the Redo command becomes unavailable.
- If you want to go further back in time than your last editing action, choose Edit⇨Undo/Redo History to display the Undo/Redo History dialog box, which is shown in Figure 6-3. The Undo list box shows your recent editing changes — albeit in rather cryptic terms. Choose the action you want to undo in the Undo list box and then click on Undo.

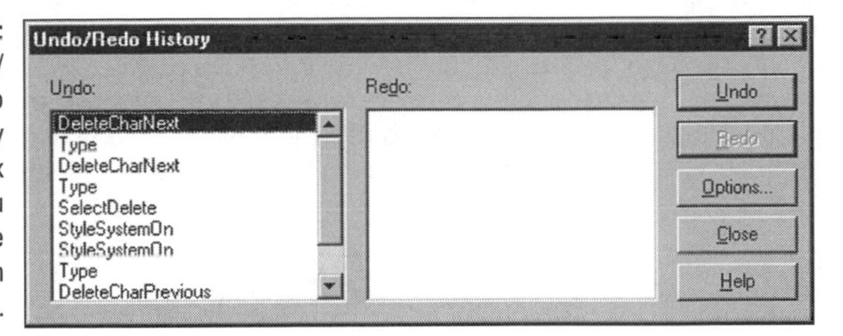

Figure 6-3: The Undo/Redo History dialog box takes you back in time so you can undo edits.

- Note that when you select an action in the list box, all the actions above it are automatically selected and will also be undone. You can't select the third action in the list, for example, without undoing the first and second actions as well.
- After you click on Undo, the actions you reversed appear in the Redo list box. WordPerfect makes the changes in your document, but nothing's set in stone until you close the dialog box. If you change your mind and want to restore an action, select it in the Redo list box and click on the Redo button.
- By default, WordPerfect enables you to undo your last 10 editing changes. But if you click on the Options button in the Undo/Redo History dialog box, you can raise or lower the number by adjusting the value in the Number of Undo/Redo Items option box. Keep in mind that the higher the number of undos you specify, the more you tax your computer's memory banks.
- When you're done undoing stuff, click on Close or click on the Close button in the top right corner of the dialog box to return to your document.

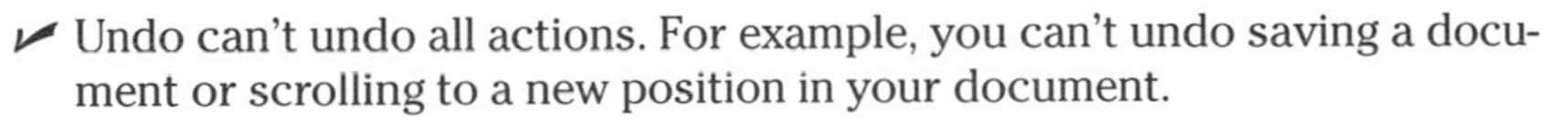

- Undo can't undo all actions. For example, you can't undo saving a document or scrolling to a new position in your document.

Letting WordPerfect Correct Mistakes for You

Wouldn't it be nice to have a servant that trailed around after you all the time, picking up stuff you drop, wiping up drinks you spill, and otherwise cleaning up your messes for you? What — you say you're a mom, and *you're* the servant? Well, now's your chance to be the mess-maker and let someone else — namely WordPerfect — pick up after you.

WordPerfect's QuickCorrect feature provides as-you-type error correction. Type a word incorrectly, and WordPerfect automatically corrects it for you as soon as you hit the spacebar. For example, try typing *teh* and pressing the spacebar. WordPerfect assumes that what you really meant to type was *the,* so it automatically changes *teh* to *the.* It doesn't even bother you with a dialog box, beep, or other whiny complaint — it just goes quietly about its cleanup business.

Adding words to the QuickCorrect list

To determine which words need correcting, WordPerfect consults an internal list of commonly misspelled and mistyped words. You can add words to the list by choosing Tools⇨QuickCorrect or pressing Ctrl+Shift+F1 to display the QuickCorrect dialog box, shown in Figure 6-4.

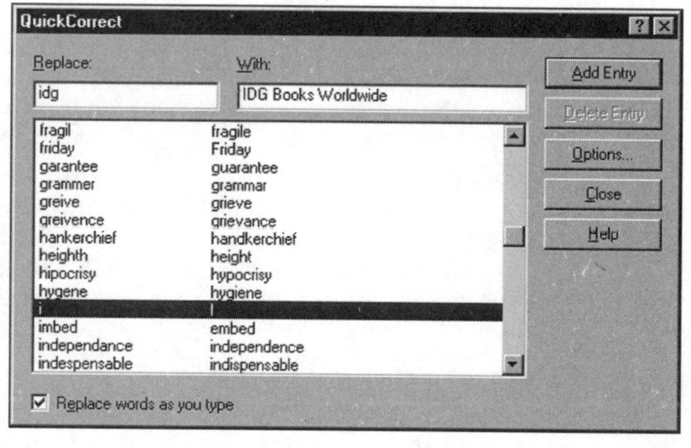

Figure 6-4: You can add or delete words from WordPerfect's QuickCorrect list.

To add a word to the QuickCorrect list, type the misspelled version into the Replace option box and enter the correct word into the With option box. Click on Add Entry to make your addition official and make sure that the Replace Words as You Type check box is selected. Click on Close or hit the dialog box Close button to return to your document.

You can use QuickCorrect to automatically replace abbreviations with the full word or phrase. For example, the entries made in Figure 6-4 tell WordPerfect that when I type the letters *idg,* I want it to substitute the words *IDG Books Worldwide.*

In addition to fixing spelling and typing errors, QuickCorrect can make several corrections related to sentences. It can make sure that the first letter in a sentence is capitalized, change two uppercase letters in a row into an uppercase letter followed by a lowercase letter (changing *THe* to *The,* for example), eliminate double spaces between words, and convert two spaces at the end of a sentence to a single space.

To turn these features on and off, click on the Options button in the QuickCorrect dialog box to open the dialog box shown in Figure 6-5. The sentence correction options are at the top of the dialog box (they're spotlighted in Figure 6-5). Other QuickCorrect options automatically apply certain formatting commands and features, as discussed in Chapter 8.

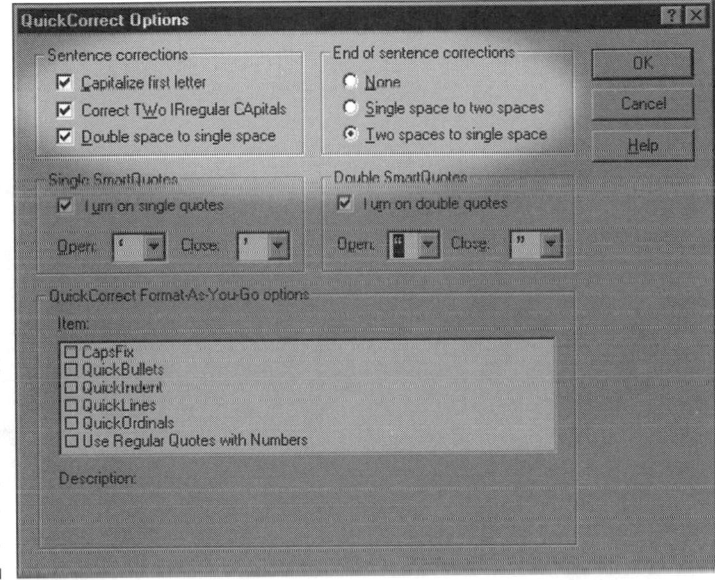

Figure 6-5: WordPerfect can also make automatic corrections to sentences.

Overruling unwanted corrections

As helpful as QuickCorrect can be, it can also get in the way sometimes. Suppose that you want to use the word *august* in its adverbial sense rather than referring to the month — as in, "The king had an august nature." WordPerfect plows right ahead and changes your lowercase *august* to *August*.

You can overrule WordPerfect by deleting the word it's correcting from the QuickCorrect list. Choose Tools⇨QuickCorrect (or press Ctrl+Shift+F1) to display the QuickCorrect dialog box, select the word in the list box, and click on the Delete Entry button.

If you want WordPerfect to substitute different text when you type a particular word or set of characters, select the original word in the list box, enter the new replacement text in the With option box, and click on the Replace Entry button (the button becomes available when you click in the With box). Click on Close or on the dialog box Close button to make your wish the law of the land.

Chapter 7

Making Your Text Look Pretty

In This Chapter

- Changing the font, size, and style of your text
- Choosing a page size and orientation
- Setting margins, tabs, and indents
- Justifying text
- Changing the spacing between lines and paragraphs
- Making text fit the available space

Creating professional-looking text is an artistic endeavor. And it involves more than just turning a fancy phrase. You also need to think about things like type style and size, the amount of spacing between words and letters, and how much to indent lines and paragraphs from the margins, if at all.

These design considerations — known collectively as *formatting* — play a significant role in whether people will take the time to read your documents. Eye-catching, easy-to-read pages draw in readers and make them more receptive to your message. Poorly designed, difficult-to-read pages become receptacles for used chewing gum (or worse).

This chapter shows you the ins and outs of getting your text ready for public consumption. You find out how to make characters bold and italic, how to control text spacing, and how to perform other feats of formatting magic. In other words, it's a chance to explore your artistic side.

If you want to feel like a real artist, be sure to dress in weird clothes (all black is good) and drink tons of espresso as you work. You should also start describing your page designs in complex psychological and sociological terms that make sense only to you. Don't forget to look scornfully at anyone who doesn't pretend to understand what you're saying.

After you get a block of text formatted just the way you like it, you can use the QuickFormat command and paragraph styles, discussed in Chapter 9, to have WordPerfect automatically copy the formatting to other text.

Playing with Fonts

One of the most noticeable ways to dress up your text is by changing the font, type style, and type size.

The *font* — sometimes called *typeface* — determines the shape and design of the characters. Each font has a distinct name, such as Times New Roman, Helvetica, and so on. Figure 7-1 shows a few different fonts for your amusement.

Type style refers to any special formatting attributes applied to the text — boldface, italics, underline, and so on. The *type size* determines, uh, well, how big the characters are. Sorry to insult you.

The following sections explain how to deal with each of these character formatting issues.

Choosing a font

The WordPerfect Suite comes with a bunch of fonts, and you may have other fonts installed on your system, too. By default, WordPerfect uses the Times New Roman font, a time-honored and traditional serif font.

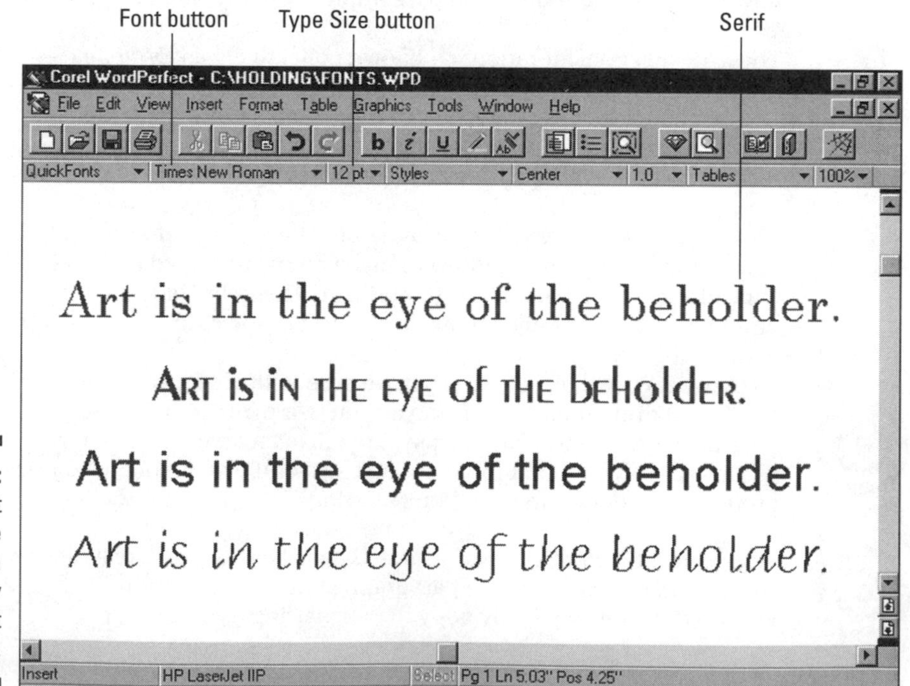

Figure 7-1: Different fonts give your text a decidedly different feel.

Why won't WordPerfect do what I tell it to?

If you can't get a particular formatting command to work the way it's supposed to — or applying a formatting command gives you unexpected results — it's probably because you've messed up the hidden codes that WordPerfect inserts in your text as you apply formatting. Moving text around, deleting text, and removing and reapplying formatting can wreak havoc on formatting codes — and on your document.

If things get screwy, one solution is to open the Reveal Codes window (press Alt+F3 or choose View⇨Reveal Codes). (If you flip back to Chapter 6, you can get a look at the Reveal Codes window in the sidebar "Hey, everything got screwy when I moved stuff around!") If you're familiar with WordPerfect's codes, you can take a stab at sorting out the formatting codes to figure out what went wrong. If you want to become a hidden code guru, check out *WordPerfect For Windows For Dummies* (IDG Books Worldwide, Inc.), which offers an in-depth explanation of the subject.

If playing in the Reveal Codes Amusement Park makes you queasy, however, simply try selecting the text you want to format and reissuing the formatting command. If you still don't get the results you want, check the style applied to the text (styles are explained in Chapter 9). Try applying the None style and then applying your formatting again. If things still don't work right, you need a WordPerfect guru to help you clean up your hidden codes.

A *serif* font is one that has serifs — little lines decorating the upper and lower ends of the strokes of the letters. A sans serif font has no serifs (*sans serif* means "without serifs" in French). The top example in Figure 7-1 is a serif font; the other three are sans serif fonts.

For long blocks of text, use a serif font, which is easier to read. Sans serif fonts are best used for headlines, subheads, and other short blocks of text.

Before you dig into the methods for changing fonts, you need to understand a bit about how WordPerfect applies your changes. If you select a piece of text before choosing a font, the font is applied to the selected text only. If you don't select any text, the font is applied to all text from the insertion marker forward, up to the point where you previously applied a font change.

With that little tidbit of information under your belt, you're now ready to start playing with your fonts. To choose a new font, you can use any of the following tactics:

- Click on the Font button (labeled in Figure 7-1) on the Power Bar to display a list of fonts installed in your system. Click on the font you want to use.
- Choose Format⇨Font, press F9, or right-click anywhere on the document window and choose the Font command from the resulting QuickMenu. The Font dialog box, shown in Figure 7-2, appears. Click on the font you want in

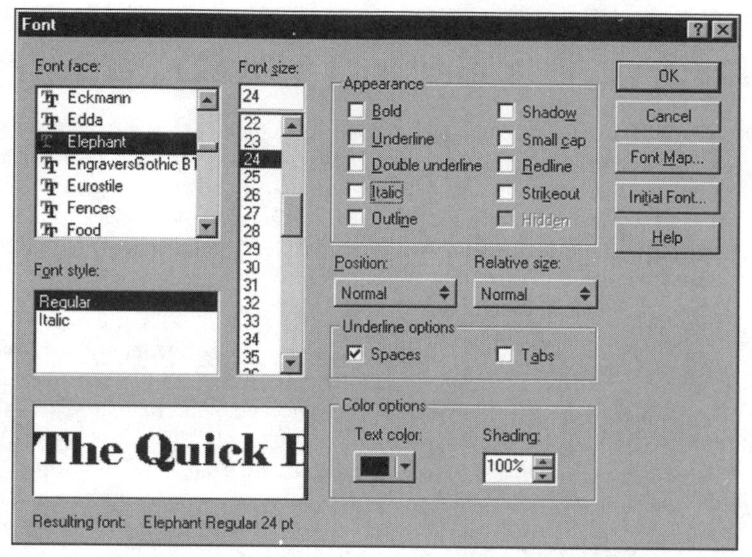

Figure 7-2: The Font dialog box gives you a way to set several type options at once.

the Font Face list box. When you select a font, a preview box in the bottom left corner of the dialog box shows you what the font looks like. If the font seems okay to you, click on OK or press Enter to apply your changes.

Using the Font dialog box can be a convenient option if you want to set a number of character formatting attributes at the same time. You can choose type size, style, color, and shading for selected text in the dialog box.

- Click on the QuickFonts button on the Power Bar to display a drop-down list of the 20 most recent font combinations (font, size, and style) you've used. Using the QuickFonts button is usually quicker than using the Font button because you don't have to scroll through the entire list of installed fonts.

If you want to change the default font that WordPerfect uses, make sure that no text is selected, open the Font dialog box (pressing F9 is the speediest method), and click on the Initial Font button. You get a miniature version of the Font dialog box in which you can specify the default font, size, and style. If you select the Set as Printer Initial Font check box, WordPerfect uses the font as the default for the current document and for any new documents you create. If you don't select the check box, the default font is used for the current document only. Either way, WordPerfect applies the font to any text that used the default font. If you previously applied a font, size, or style to a piece of text, WordPerfect leaves that formatting intact.

Changing the type size and style

As with font changes, changes to type size and style affect any text from the insertion marker forward *except* for text you previously formatted. If you want to change the size or style for a specific portion of text only, select the text and then apply your formatting changes.

The quickest way to change the type size is to click on the Type Size button (labeled back in Figure 7-1) on the Power Bar and click on the size you want. If you don't see the size you want — for example, if you want to use 12.5 point type — open the Font dialog box by pressing F9, choosing Format⇨Font, or right-clicking in the document window and choosing Font from the QuickMenu that appears. Then double-click on the Font Size option box and enter the size you want in the option box. Click on OK or press Enter to exit the dialog box.

Fonts are measured in *points*. A point is roughly equivalent to 1/72 inch. If you want people to be able to read your text easily, don't use type smaller than 10 points.

Three type style options — boldface, italics, and underline — are available on the toolbar. The **b** button makes text bold, the *i* button makes it italic, and the u button underlines it. The toolbar buttons toggle the styles on and off — click on the button once to turn the style on; click on it again to turn the style off. You can also use the shortcut keys for these styles: Ctrl+B, Ctrl+I, and Ctrl+U, respectively. Pressing the shortcut once turns the style on; pressing it a second time turns the style off.

For other style attributes, go to the Font dialog box (press F9 for speedy results). In the right half of the dialog box, you can tweak your text style in a variety of ways:

- The Appearance attributes apply special effects to your type. In addition to bold, italic, and underlined type, you can create shadowed type, outline type, double-underlined type, and more. You can apply as many attributes to a piece of text as your conscience allows. (Hint: Unless you want people to run away screaming after taking one look at your text, use these effects *very* sparingly.)
- You may have noticed that italic and bold options are also sometimes available in the Font Style option box on the left side of the dialog box. What gives? Well, some fonts have a style already built in. The font Elephant, for example, is available on my system in both Regular (plain) style and Italic. So I can choose the Regular style and apply italics through the Appearance settings or just choose the Italic style in the Font Style list box and be done with it.
- The Position drop-down list offers superscript and subscript options. Leave the setting on Normal for normal text (did you guess that one already?).

- You can use the Relative Size option to make your text proportionally larger or smaller than the current font size. The option stays in effect until you change the font back to Normal. You probably won't have much use for this option.
- The Underline options tell WordPerfect whether you want to underline the spaces in your text. If you choose the Spaces option, the space between words is underlined. If you choose the Tabs option, WordPerfect underlines across tabs as well.
- The Color options let you add color and shading to text. Remember that the colors won't print unless you have a color printer. They can look fun on-screen, though, and can be useful if you share documents with others. You can put notes to each other in color to distinguish them from the regular document text.

The last 20 font combinations you used are available on the QuickFonts drop-down menu on the Power Bar. Click on the QuickFonts button to access them.

Choosing a Page Size and Orientation

When you start a standard new document, WordPerfect gives you an $8^1/_2 \times 11$-inch page size, with text oriented in portrait position — that is, with text running parallel to the short edge of the paper. It's called *portrait,* by the way, because portraits normally use this same orientation. If you choose one of the special templates or Experts discussed in Chapter 4 to create your document, WordPerfect selects a page size that's appropriate for the document.

You can change the page size and/or orientation at whim, however. Here's how:

- To change the page size, make sure that no text is selected and then choose Format⇨Page⇨Page Size. The Page Size dialog box opens, as shown in Figure 7-3. Choose a page size and orientation (known collectively as a *page definition*) by making a selection from the Name drop-down list box. The Orientation icon reflects the orientation of the page you select. Click on OK or press Enter to choose the size.
- If one of the preset page definitions won't do, you can choose New to create a new page definition or choose Edit to edit an existing page definition.

The page definition takes effect from the insertion marker through the end of your document or to the point where you previously set a new page definition.

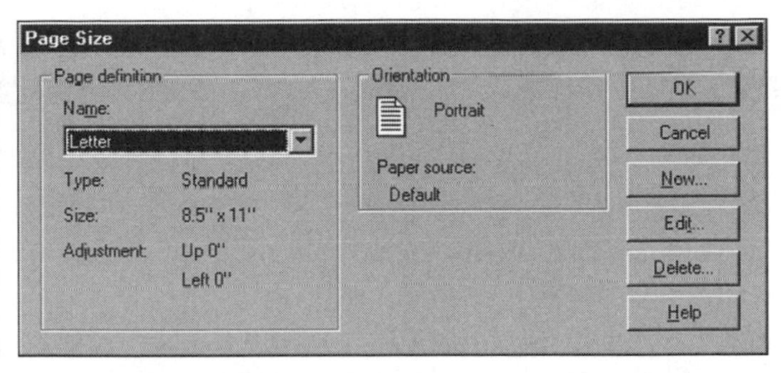

Figure 7-3: Choose the page size and orientation using the Page Size dialog box.

Your printer may or may not be capable of printing the page sizes you define. In addition, the printer may have difficulty applying two or more different page definitions in the same document. The types of pages available through the Page Size dialog box also depend on the capabilities of your printer. Check the instructions that came with your printer to find out how much flexibility you have. If you're on an office network and have several printers at your beck and call, go tug on the sleeve of your network administrator and ask for the inside scoop on your printing options.

Setting Page Margins

WordPerfect 7 provides a speedy way to set the top, bottom, left, and right margins of your pages. See those dotted blue lines running across the top, bottom, left, and right sides of your page? Those are margin guidelines. (If the guidelines aren't displayed on your screen, choose View⇨Guidelines to open the Guidelines dialog box, turn on the Margins check box, and click on OK or press Enter.) To change margins, just move your mouse cursor over a margin guideline until the cursor becomes a two-headed arrow, as shown in Figure 7-4. Then drag the guide to a new position. As you move the guideline, a little box (called a QuickStatus box) pops up to show you the cursor's exact distance from the edge of the page.

If you prefer, you can use these methods for setting margins instead:

- Choose Format⇨Margins or press Ctrl+F8 and make your settings in the resulting Margins dialog box.
- To change the left and right margins, display the ruler bar by choosing View⇨Toolbars/Ruler and turning on the Ruler Bar check box. Then drag the left and right margin controls, labeled in Figure 7-4. Be sure that you drag the margin controls — the left- and right-most black thingies on the ruler bar — and not just the diamonds beside the margin controls, which set margins for individual paragraphs. A vertical dotted line appears to show you where the margin will be set when you release the mouse button.

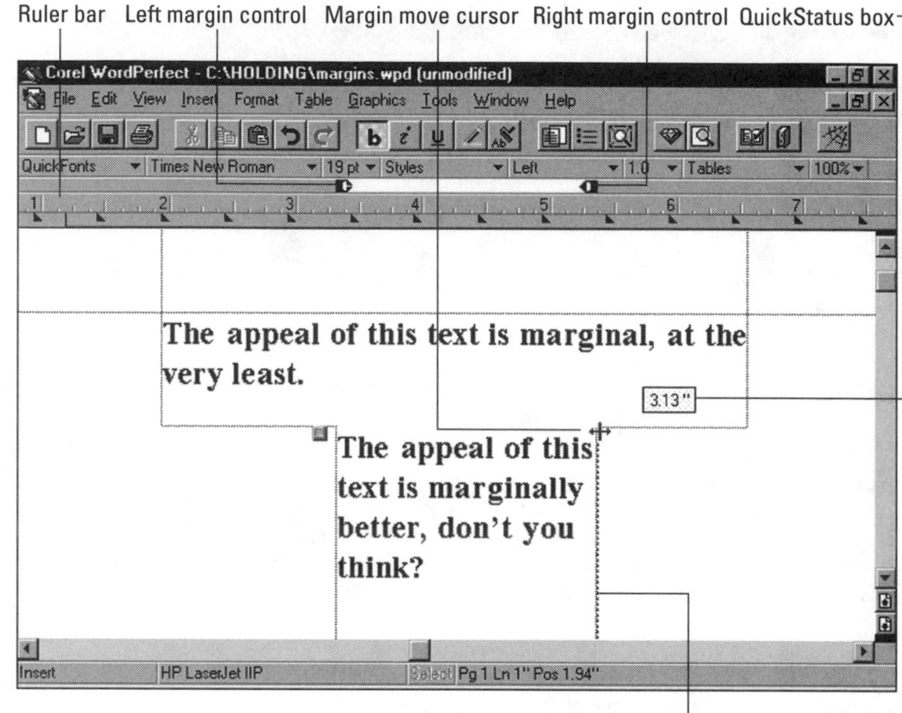

Figure 7-4: WordPerfect gives you a cornucopia of ways to set page margins.

You can change the margins as many times as you want in a document. Left and right margin settings affect text from the point of the insertion marker forward and remain in effect until WordPerfect encounters another margin setting that you previously established. Top and bottom margin settings affect the current page and any subsequent pages up to the point where you previously changed the margins. If you want, you can also apply margin settings to selected text only.

Most desktop printers can't print all the way to the edges of a page. Being the protective sort that it is, WordPerfect won't let you set margins that are smaller than your printer can handle.

Setting Tabs

Please place your left hand on your computer monitor — on the top, not the screen, please (fingerprints, you know) — and repeat this pledge: "I hereby swear to always use tabs instead of spaces to line things up in columns." Why? Well, for one thing, it's a heck of a lot easier to press the Tab key once instead of hitting the spacebar a zillion times to shove text across the page. But more importantly, your text may not line up properly if you use spaces, as shown in Chapter 4, in Figure 4-5 (go ahead, flip back and take a look).

This alignment problem happens because many fonts on your computer aren't fixed-width fonts — in other words, different characters vary in width. So if you type *Mary,* for example, and then press the spacebar four times, you won't end up at the same spot as you do if you type *Jill* and press the spacebar four times. In addition, the width of a space varies depending upon the font you're using. Tabs, on the other hand, move the insertion marker to a specific spot on the page, so everything lines up as it should.

Don't use tabs to indent the first line of a paragraph, however. Instead, use the First Line Indent option explained in the upcoming section "Indenting the first line of your paragraphs."

If you're new to tabs, here's how they work: Each time you press the Tab key, WordPerfect moves the insertion marker to the next available tab stop to the right. Press Shift+Tab, and you move the insertion marker to the previous tab stop — a procedure known in WordPerfect clubs as *back tabbing.*

By default, WordPerfect gives you a tab stop every half inch across the page. That setup is okay for some uses, but in many cases you'll want to override these default tab stops and set your own custom tab stops. The following sections tell you what you need to know.

When should I take a paragraph break?

When you're entering text, don't press the Enter key (labeled the Return key on some keyboards) when you get to the end of a line as you do on a typewriter. WordPerfect automatically wraps your text to the next line for you. Pressing Enter inserts a *hard return.*

A hard return tells WordPerfect when one paragraph ends and another begins. When you select a paragraph, WordPerfect grabs everything from the paragraph break preceding the insertion marker to the next paragraph mark after the insertion marker. WordPerfect also relies on the hard returns to tell it which text to change when you apply certain paragraph-level formatting, such as line spacing and paragraph spacing.

The moral of the story: Press Enter at the end of a line of text *only* if you want to end the paragraph. If you want to break text at the end of a line but don't want to start a new paragraph, press Ctrl+Shift+L.

Adding, moving, or deleting a tab stop

If you add, move, or delete a tab stop, the new setting takes effect from the current paragraph forward up to the point where you previously changed tab settings. If you select a paragraph before changing a tab stop, the change affects the selected paragraph only.

The easiest way to set a tab is to use the ruler bar. (If the ruler bar isn't displayed, choose View⇨Toolbars/Ruler Bar and turn on the Ruler Bar item in the Toolbars dialog box.) The little black triangles at the bottom of the ruler bar represent the tab stops. To set a standard left tab, just click on the ruler bar. (The next section explains how to set other types of tabs, such as decimal tabs.) To move a tab stop, drag it. To delete a tab stop, drag it down off the ruler bar.

You can also set tab stops in the Tab Set dialog box, shown in Figure 7-5. To display the dialog box, choose Format⇨Line⇨Tab Set or right-click on the bottom of the ruler bar and choose Tab Set from the resulting QuickMenu. In the dialog box, enter the tab stop position in the Position option box and click on Set. Click on OK to close the dialog box.

Figure 7-5: The Tab Set dialog box lets you get specific about how you want tabbed text to appear.

Here's some more stuff you need to know about changing your tab stops:

- You can choose from eight different tab types, each of which aligns and formats tabbed text differently. These tab types are explained in the next section.
- Normally, WordPerfect measures tab stops from the left margin of your page. But you can tell it to measure them from the left edge of the page if you prefer. WordPerfect calls tabs measured from the left margin of the page *relative tabs;* tabs measured from the edge of the page are called *absolute tabs.* You can specify which option you want by selecting one of the Position From radio buttons in the Tab Set dialog box.

- After you add, delete, or move a tab stop, WordPerfect displays an icon in the left margin (see Figure 7-6). You may need to scroll the screen display left to see the icon. If you click on the icon, you get a *tab bar,* which is a miniature version of the ruler bar. You can change the tab settings for the paragraph just as you do on the ruler bar. Click outside the tab bar to hide it again.
- If you see a little balloon with quotation marks instead of the normal tab set icon, you have inserted more than one formatting instruction or other element, such as a sound clip (as explained in Chapter 21). Click on the icon to display the individual formatting icons and then click on the tab icon to display the tab bar.

- You can tell WordPerfect to space tabs at a specified increment evenly across the page — for example, if you want a tab stop every 3 inches. To do this, set the position of the first tab in the Position option box of the Tab Set dialog box, check the Repeat Every check box, and specify the distance between tabs in the adjacent option box.
- To clear all tab stops, right-click on a tab stop on the ruler bar and then choose Clear All Tabs. Or choose the Clear All button in the Tab Set dialog box.
- To return to the default tab stops — a left tab every half inch across the page — choose Default Tab Settings from the QuickMenu or choose the Default button in the Tab Set dialog box.

- If you display hidden symbols on-screen (as described in Chapter 4), you may notice that WordPerfect sometimes gives you an indent character instead of a tab when you press the Tab key. This weirdness is a result of the QuickCorrect feature. WordPerfect assumes that when you're using tabs to indent multiple lines of text, you really want to use indents instead. In some cases, this intrusion can be helpful, but at other times it can be a nuisance. You can turn the feature off by choosing Tools⇨QuickCorrect to open the QuickCorrect dialog box, clicking on the Options button to open the QuickCorrect Options dialog box, and deselecting the QuickIndent item in the list at the bottom of the dialog box. Alternatively, you can override an individual indent by backspacing to delete the indent and then pressing Tab to reinsert the tab.

- The Tab key functions differently in Typeover mode than it does in Insert mode (see Chapter 4 for an explanation of these editing modes). In Typeover mode, pressing Tab moves the insertion marker across a line of text from one tab stop to the next but doesn't insert a tab. If there is no text, pressing Tab does insert a tab.
- By default, you can position a tab stop on a tick mark on the ruler or exactly between two tick marks. If you want to position a tab somewhere else, you have two options. You can set the tab by entering a specific

position in the Position option box of the Tab Set dialog box, or you can change the way the ruler works. Right-click on the ruler bar and choose Preferences from the QuickMenu to open the Ruler Bar tab of the Display Preferences dialog box. Deselect the Tabs Snap to Ruler Bar Grid item and click on OK to exit the dialog box.

Choosing a tab stop type

WordPerfect gives you eight different types of tab stops, which you choose either from the Type drop-down list in the Tab Set dialog box or right-clicking on the ruler bar, choosing a tab type from the resulting QuickMenu, and then clicking on the tab stop you want to change. Your options, illustrated in Figure 7-6, are

- **Left:** Text aligns to the right of the tab stop. The default tab stops are all left tabs. A left tab on the ruler bar looks like this: ◣.
- **Right:** Text aligns to the left of the tab stop. A right tab stop looks like this: ◢.
- **Center:** Text is centered on the tab stop. A center tab stop appears like this: ▲.

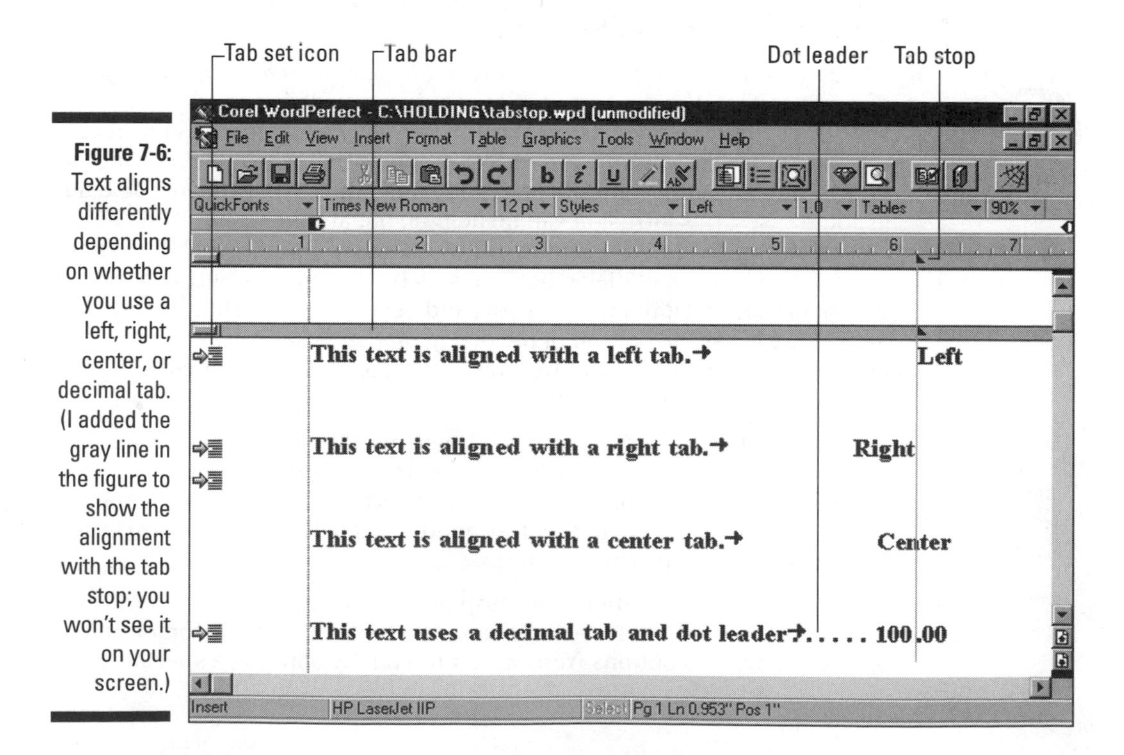

Figure 7-6: Text aligns differently depending on whether you use a left, right, center, or decimal tab. (I added the gray line in the figure to show the alignment with the tab stop; you won't see it on your screen.)

- **Decimal:** The decimal point lines up with the tab stop. This setting is normally used to align columns of numbers. It looks like this on the ruler bar: ▲.

By default, decimal tabs align text by the decimal point (period). But you can change the character on which text aligns by entering a new one in the Character option box in the Tab Set dialog box. For example, if you have a column of numbers that incorporate commas but no decimal points — such as $95,000 — you can set the align character to a comma.

- You can put a *dot leader* into your tabbed text by choosing the Dot Left, Dot Right, Dot Center, or Dot Decimal options from the Type drop-down list. (On the QuickMenu, these options appear as ...Decimal, ...Right, and so on.) Dot leaders help guide the reader's eye across columns of text, as shown in Figure 7-6. You can change the character used for the dot leader by entering a new one in the Dot Leader Character option box in the Tab Set dialog box. You can also vary the amount of space between each dot leader by changing the Spaces Between Characters value.

Indenting and Aligning Text

Pressing the Tab key isn't the only way to shove your text across the page. You can also use WordPerfect's indent and justification options to change the way that text fits between the left and right margins of your page.

Indenting the first line of your paragraphs

If you want to indent the first line of each paragraph in your document — a common formatting choice — use indents instead of tabs. Why? Well, suppose that you use a tab to indent every paragraph in a long document. Then you decide that you don't want to indent those paragraphs after all. If you use tabs, you have to remove the tab from every paragraph. If you use indents, on the other hand, all you need to do is change the indent setting to zero.

Revealing the mysterious hidden symbols

When you're formatting text, you may find it very helpful to display WordPerfect's hidden symbols. (Hidden symbols, hidden codes — all this cloak-and-dagger stuff makes you wonder a little, doesn't it?) If you display hidden symbols (choose View➪Show ¶ or press Ctrl+Shift+F3), you can see the exact location of tabs, indents, and hard returns (paragraph breaks), which makes it easier to edit and reformat your text.

If you travel back to Chapter 4, to the section "Customizing Your Workspace," you can get a glimpse of what hidden codes look like and find out how to specify which symbols appear on-screen.

If you apply a first-line indent without any text selected, WordPerfect indents the first line of every paragraph after the insertion marker, up to the point at which you previously indented a paragraph. If you select text before applying a first-line indent, only the selected paragraphs are affected.

1. **Choose Format⇨Paragraph⇨Format.**

   WordPerfect displays the Paragraph Format dialog box, shown in Figure 7-7.

Figure 7-7: Decide on paragraph style options with the Paragraph Format dialog box.

2. **Enter the amount of the indent you want in the First Line Indent option box.**
3. **Click on OK or press Enter.**

If you later want to remove the first line indents, select the paragraphs, open the Paragraph Format dialog box, and change the First Line Indent value to zero.

The Back Tab indent option, explained in the next section, offers a variation on the First Line option. The Back Tab option shoves the first line of a paragraph one tab stop to the *left* instead of one tab stop to the right.

Indenting entire paragraphs

You can also indent the entire paragraph from the left margin, indent the paragraph from both the right and left margins (called a *double indent*), or indent all but the first line of a paragraph (called a *hanging indent*). Double indents are often used to offset long quotations in a document, and hanging indents are used to create bulleted and numbered lists, such as the ones in this book.

Here's how to apply these indents:

1. **Select the paragraphs you want to indent.**

   If you want to indent just one paragraph, click on the beginning of the paragraph. To indent all the paragraphs in your document, press Ctrl+A to select the entire document.

2. **Click on the QuickSpot button.**

   The QuickSpot, as explained in Chapter 4, is that little gray button that appears in the left margin when you pass your cursor over a paragraph. The Paragraph dialog box shown in Figure 7-8 appears after you click on the button.

3. **Choose an indent option from the Indent drop-down list.**

   Table 7-1 explains your options; Figure 7-9 offers some examples.

4. **Click on the dialog box Close button.**

You can also set indents by using the keyboard shortcuts listed in Table 7-1 or by selecting Format⇨Paragraph and choosing the indent option you want from the Paragraph submenu. To create a standard indent, you can just select the paragraph and press Tab. And if those aren't enough options for you, you can drag the paragraph indent controls on the ruler bar (labeled in Figure 7-9).

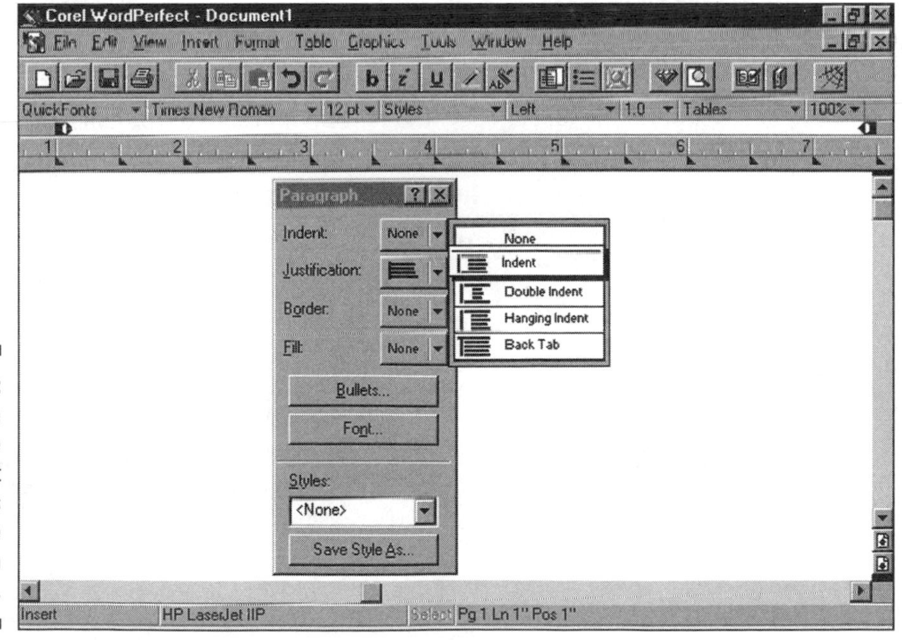

Figure 7-8: You can choose indent options using the Paragraph dialog box.

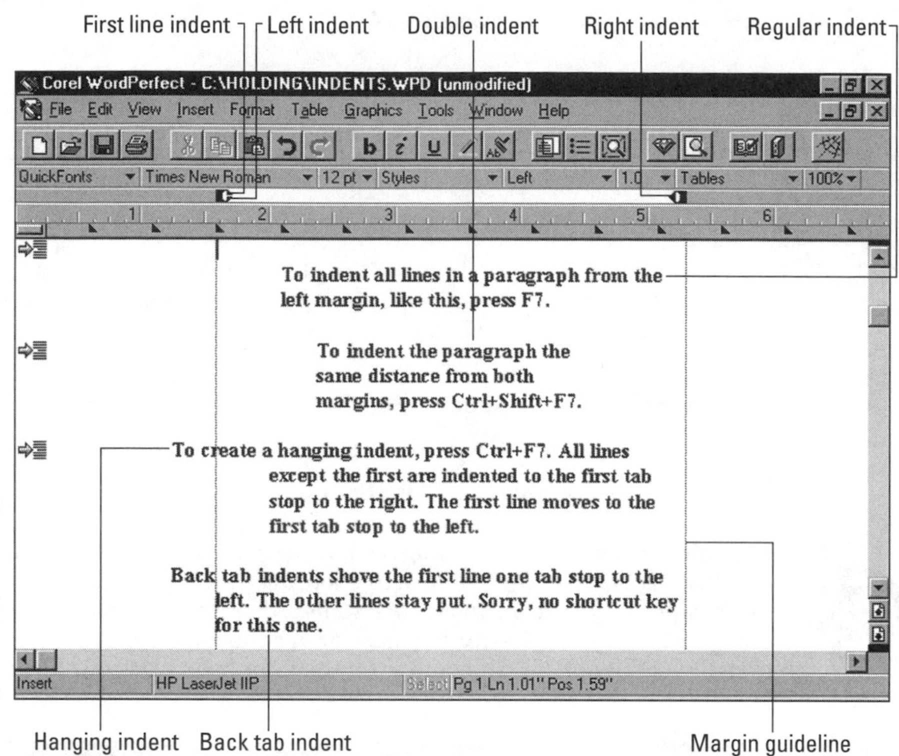

Figure 7-9: Examples of different kinds of indents.

To remove an indent from a selected paragraph or paragraphs, click on the QuickSpot button and choose the None option from the Indent drop-down list.

Table 7-1 Indent Options and Shortcuts

Indent Type	*Shortcut*	*What It Does*
First Line Indent	None	Indents the first line of a paragraph; available only in the Paragraph Format dialog box (Format➪Paragraph➪Format)
Indent	F7	Indents all lines of a paragraph one tab stop to the right
Double Indent	Ctrl+Shift+F7	Moves all lines of a paragraph inward one tab stop from the left margin and an equal distance from the right margin

Indent Type	Shortcut	What It Does
Hanging Indent	Ctrl+F7	Indents all lines of a paragraph except the first line one tab stop to the right. The first line is shoved leftward, to the first tab stop to the left
Back Tab	None	Moves the first line of a paragraph one tab stop to the left

With the exception of the first line indents, WordPerfect indents your text according to the tab stops you set. To change the amount of indent, you have to change the tab stops as explained earlier in this chapter.

Justifying text

Another way to change the amount of space between the edges of a paragraph and the left and right margins is to change the *justification,* sometimes referred to as *alignment.* Figure 7-10 shows the five available alignment options: Left, Right, Center, Full, and All.

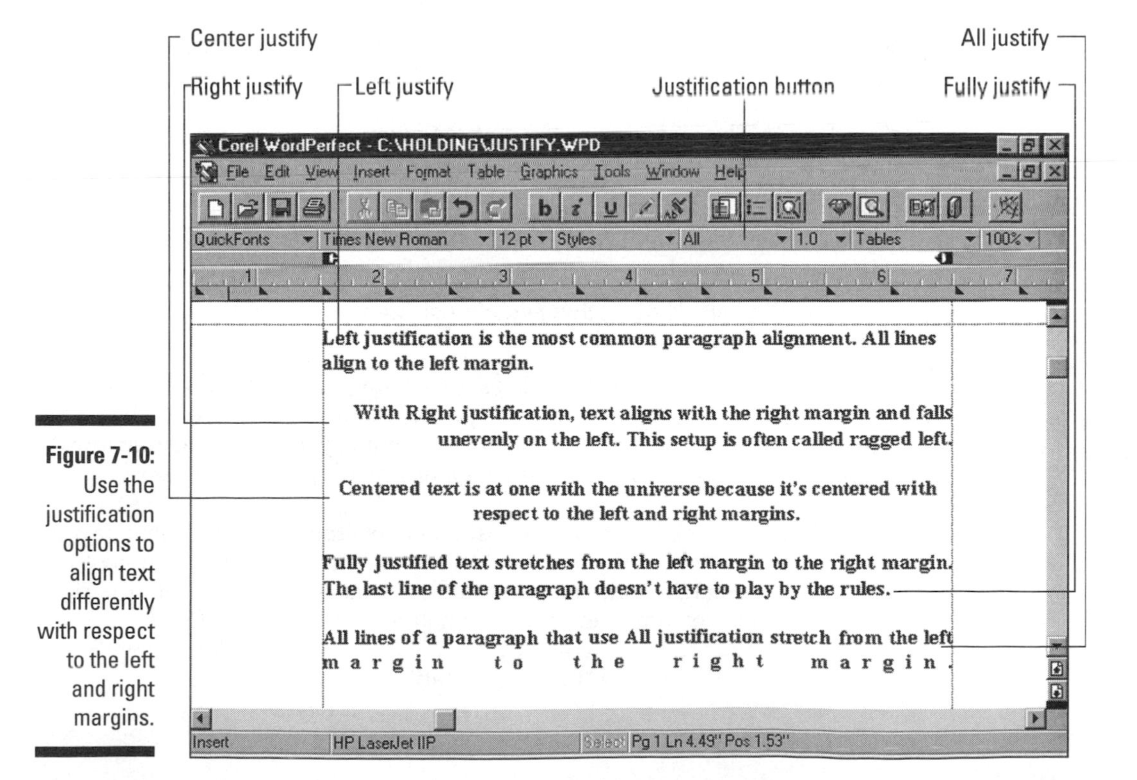

Figure 7-10: Use the justification options to align text differently with respect to the left and right margins.

- Left justification aligns all lines in a paragraph to the left margin. This alignment is sometimes called *ragged right* because the right edge of the paragraph has an uneven look. It's the most commonly used justification.
- Right justification aligns the paragraph to the right margin and is sometimes known as *ragged left* because of the appearance of the left edge of the paragraph.
- Center justification centers each line between the left and right margins.
- Full justification spaces the text so that all lines align perfectly with both the left and the right margin — *except* for the last line of the paragraph, which simply aligns with the left margin. Sometimes, WordPerfect has to add spaces throughout the text in a line to justify it; sometimes it has to cram the text closer together.
- All justification is the same as Full justification except that the last line of the paragraph is fully justified along with all the other lines. As you can see in Figure 7-10, this option can result in awkwardly spaced text.

As with other formatting commands, justification affects all paragraphs from the insertion marker forward through the rest of the document, up to the point where you previously changed the justification. If you select text before applying a justification command, the justification affects the selected paragraph only.

That said, here's a rundown of the various and sundry ways to change the justification:

- Click on the Justification button on the Power Bar (labeled in Figure 7-10) and select an option from the drop-down list.
- Click on the paragraph's QuickSpot button to display the Paragraph dialog box (it's shown back in Figure 7-8) and select an option from the Justification drop-down list.
- Choose Format⇨Justification and choose an option from the Justification submenu.
- Press the justification shortcut keys: Ctrl+L for Left justification; Ctrl+R for Right justification; Ctrl+E for Center justification; and Ctrl+J for Full justification. The fact that there is no shortcut key for the All justification option should be a clue that this isn't a terrific option in most cases.

WordPerfect also enables you to right-justify and center just a single line or part of a line of text. For example, you may want to have the name of a document align with the left margin of the page and have the day's date align with the right margin. To do this, you type the document name, issue the Flush Right command, and then type the day's date. If you want, you can place dot leaders (explained back in the section "Choosing a tab stop type") before the right-justified line.

- To right-justify a line, place the insertion marker at the beginning of the line and choose Format⇨Line⇨Flush Right or press Alt+F7.
- To right-justify part of a line, place the insertion marker before the text you want to justify and then choose the Flush Right command.
- To add dot leaders before the justified text, choose Format⇨Line⇨Flush Right with Dot Leaders.
- To center a line, choose Format⇨Line⇨Center or press Shift+F7.
- You can also right-click anywhere in the document window to display a QuickMenu that contains the Center and Flush Right commands.

Spacing Things Out

The amount of space between lines and paragraphs in your text has a dramatic impact on how readable and attractive your document is. Text that's all crammed together is difficult to read and looks intimidating — just take a look at any legal document. On the other hand, text that's too spaced out is also difficult to read because the reader's eye has to work too hard to get from one character to the next. Examples of some too-tight text, too-loose text, and just-right text are shown in Figure 7-11.

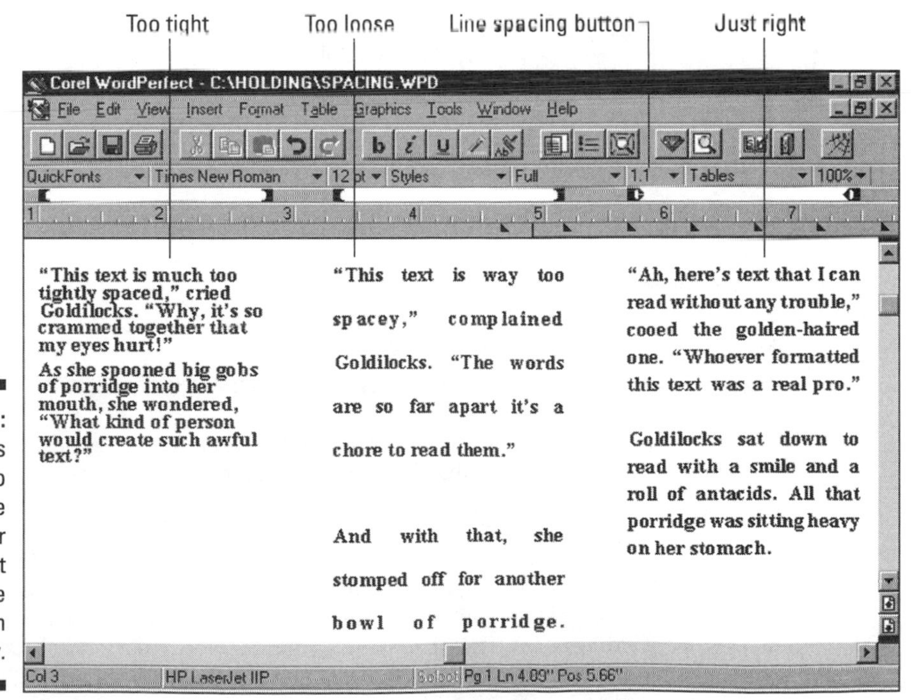

Figure 7-11: Text that's spaced too close together or too far apart can make readers turn away.

Adjusting line spacing

The quickest way to change the space between lines in paragraphs — known in typesetting circles as *leading* — is via the Line Spacing button on the Power Bar, labeled in Figure 7-11. Click at the point where you want the line spacing to change or select the paragraph you want to format. Then click on the Line Spacing button and select a spacing value from the drop-down list.

If you select any text in a paragraph before adjusting line spacing, your changes affect that paragraph only. Otherwise, the new spacing is applied to any text from the insertion marker forward, up to the point where you previously changed the line spacing.

The drop-down list gives you the option of using single, one-and-a-half, or double spacing between lines. If you want to use some other spacing value, click on the Other item in the list to open the Line Spacing dialog box, shown in Figure 7-12. This dialog box offers only one option: Spacing. Enter the value you want to use in the option box and click on OK or press Enter.

Figure 7-12: You can set precise line spacing in this delightfully simple dialog box.

You can also choose Format⇨Line⇨Spacing to open the Line Spacing dialog box. But I'm not sure why you'd want to, as you would have to click three times instead of twice.

Adjusting the space between paragraphs

While line spacing sets the amount of space between lines in a paragraph, paragraph spacing sets the amount of space between paragraphs. Sorry, I probably didn't need to explain that to you, did I?

Well, anyhow, paragraph spacing works just like line spacing in that if you select a paragraph before adjusting the spacing, your changes affect only that paragraph. If you don't select anything, your changes apply from the insertion marker forward, up to the point at which you inserted any previous paragraph spacing changes.

After you finish pondering that bit of news, here's how to move forward to adjust the paragraph spacing:

1. **Choose Format⇨Paragraph⇨Format.**

   The Paragraph Format dialog box opens. You probably remember this dialog box from Figure 7-7.

2. **Enter a value in the Spacing Between Paragraphs option.**
3. **Click on OK or press Enter.**

Centering text on a page

If you want your document text to be perfectly centered between the top and bottom margins on your page — you perfectionist, you — move the insertion marker to the beginning of the text you want to center. Choose Format⇨Page⇨Center to display the Center Page(s) dialog box, and specify whether you want to center the current page of text or the current page and any subsequent pages. Click on OK or press Enter to scoot your text smack dab in the vertical center of the page.

If you later want to remove the centering, choose the Center command again and select the No Centering option in the Center Page(s) dialog box.

Making Text Fit on a Page

WordPerfect has a nifty little feature called Make It Fit that automatically adjusts your margins, font sizes, and line spacing so that your text fits neatly on the page. To try it out, choose Format⇨Make It Fit or click on the Make It Fit button on the toolbar — it looks like a magnifying glass encircled by three little arrows. (Note that this command isn't available if you have any text selected.) The Make It Fit dialog box, shown in Figure 7-13, appears.

In the dialog box, specify how many pages you want the text to consume and which formatting items WordPerfect can play with when laying out the pages. Click on the Make It Fit button to see what WordPerfect can do. If you don't like the results, click on the Undo button or press Ctrl+Z to put things back the way they were.

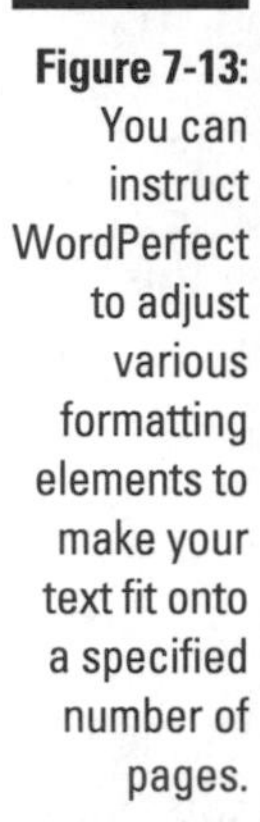

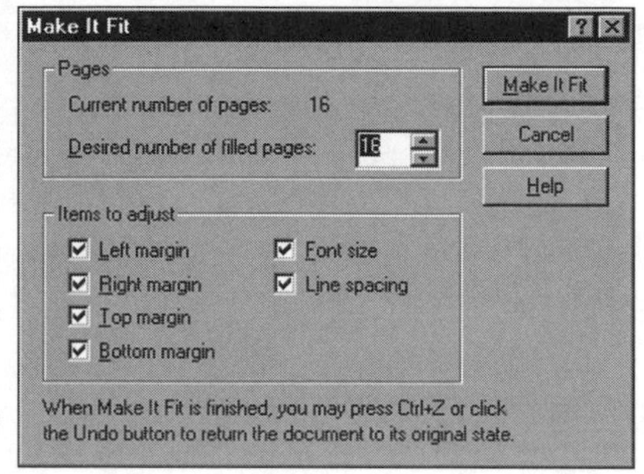

Figure 7-13: You can instruct WordPerfect to adjust various formatting elements to make your text fit onto a specified number of pages.

Chapter 8

Doing the Fancy Stuff

In This Chapter

- Creating bulleted and numbered lists
- Inserting page numbers, dates, and special characters
- Adding headers and footers
- Putting text into columns
- Inserting graphics
- Creating lines, borders, and fills

In their earliest incarnations, word processors did little more than, well, process words. You could cut, copy, and paste text, make words italic or bold, and play with margins and paragraph indents — but that was about it. If you wanted to do anything more complicated — say, add a graphic to a page or put your text in columns — you turned the work over to the publishing department or sent it out to a printing company.

Today, WordPerfect and other high-end word processors give you the power to handle many page layout and design tasks right at your desk. As you find out in this chapter, you can create bulleted and numbered lists with ease, add headers and footers, and even get WordPerfect to number your pages automatically. And if you need even fancier pages, you can insert graphics, put text in columns, and add borders and backgrounds to elements on the page.

If you're going to be creating a lot of sophisticated documents, such as newsletters, ads, or annual reports, you really should invest in a professional page layout program such as PageMaker, QuarkXPress, or Microsoft Publisher. Although WordPerfect is adequate for handling simple page layout tasks, it's no match for the speed and power you get with a true page layout program.

Creating Bulleted and Numbered Lists

One of the most common design devices used in everyday documents is the bulleted or numbered list. WordPerfect gives you several ways to create these lists easily.

Adding bullets

To add bullets before paragraphs that you've already typed, follow these steps:

1. **Select the paragraphs you want to bullet.**
2. **Choose Insert⇨Bullets & Numbers.**

   The Bullets & Numbers dialog box, shown in Figure 8-1, appears.
3. **Choose a bullet style from the Styles list.**
4. **Click on OK.**

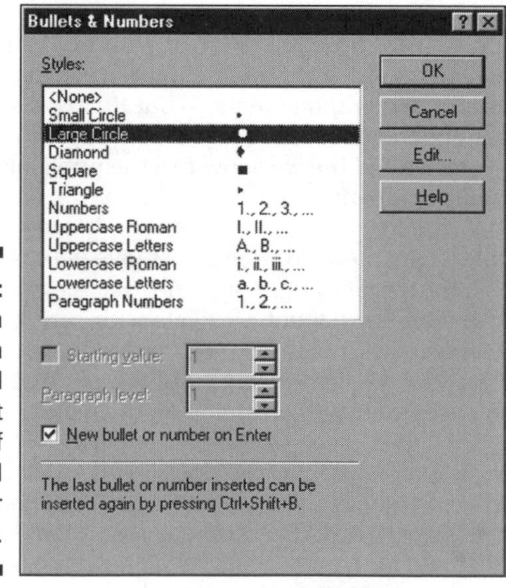

Figure 8-1: You can select from several different styles of bullets and numbers for your lists.

To create a bulleted list on the fly, press Ctrl+Shift+B. WordPerfect inserts the bullet that's currently selected in the Bullets & Numbers dialog box and then creates a hanging indent for the bulleted text (hanging indents are explained in Chapter 7). Type the text for the first bulleted item and then press Enter to create the next bullet. After you type the last item in the bulleted list, press Enter and then press Backspace to discontinue the bullets.

Here are some other tips for using bullets:

- When the New Bullet or Number on Enter option in the Bullets & Numbers dialog box is turned on (as it is by default), WordPerfect gives you a new bullet every time you press Enter as you create a bulleted list. To discontinue the bullets, press Enter and then Backspace. If the option is turned off, you don't get the automatic bullet when you press Enter.
- WordPerfect's QuickCorrect feature automatically inserts a bullet and formats the paragraph for a bulleted list if you type any of the following characters and then press Tab: asterisk (*), the letter O, plus (+), minus (-), right-angle bracket (>), or caret (^). If you don't want this automatic replacement, turn off the QuickBullets option in the QuickCorrect Options dialog box, as explained in the upcoming section "Tracking Down Special Characters."
- You can also create bullets by choosing the Insert Bullet button on the toolbar (it's the one that looks like a bulleted list). The button applies bullets according to the current settings in the Bullets & Numbers dialog box.
- To delete bullets from text, select the bulleted paragraphs, choose Insert⇨Bullets & Numbers, and choose the None option in the Bullets & Numbers dialog box.
- By default, WordPerfect places the bullet character at the left margin and indents the bulleted text to the first tab stop to the right. To change the amount of space between the bullet and the text, move the tab stop. To indent the entire paragraph *without* changing the amount of space between the bullet and the text, choose Format⇨Paragraph⇨Format and change the First Line Indent setting. Or drag the first-line indent marker on the ruler bar, as described in Chapter 7.
- If an item in the list is more than one paragraph long, press Ctrl+Shift+L to separate the paragraphs instead of pressing Enter. Otherwise, you get a bullet at the start of each paragraph.

Adding numbers

The steps for getting WordPerfect to number the items in a list are pretty much the same as for adding bullets to a list.

To apply numbers to existing text, follow these steps:

1. **Select the paragraphs you want to number.**
2. **Choose Insert➪Bullets & Numbers.**

   The Bullets & Numbers dialog box shown back in Figure 8-1 appears.
3. **Choose a numbering style from the Styles list box.**

   The one style you don't want to use is Paragraph Numbers. This option is for creating outlines with WordPerfect's Outline command, which is one of those advanced topics that page space prevents me from covering in this book.
4. **Specify a starting number.**

   By default, WordPerfect starts your list with the number 1. If you want to start at some other number, select the Starting Value check box and enter a number in the adjacent option box.
5. **Click on OK.**

To create a numbered list on the fly, simply type the first number and a period and then press Tab. You can type letters (*a, b, c*) or Roman numerals (*I, ii*) instead of regular numbers if you prefer. WordPerfect automatically formats your paragraph for a numbered list. After you type the first item in the list, press Enter, and WordPerfect presents you with the next number. After you type the last item in the list, press Enter and then press Backspace to delete the extra number and return to regular paragraph formatting.

For WordPerfect's automatic numbering to work, the QuickBullets option must be turned on in the QuickCorrect Options dialog box, which is covered in the upcoming section "Tracking Down Special Characters." The option is turned on by default.

- If you later need to add or delete an item in the list, WordPerfect renumbers the list automatically, providing that the New Bullet or Number on Enter check box is selected in the Bullets & Numbers dialog box and/or the QuickBullets item is turned on in the QuickCorrect Options dialog box. To add an item, click just before the paragraph break for the preceding item and press Enter to get the number for the new item. To delete a numbered item, just delete the paragraph as you normally would.

- To delete numbers from a numbered list, select the paragraphs, choose Insert⇨Bullets & Numbers, and choose the None option.
- If an item in your list has two paragraphs, use a line break (Ctrl+Shift+L) to separate the paragraphs instead of pressing Enter. Otherwise, WordPerfect assigns a number to both paragraphs.
- By default, the number appears at the left margin, and the item text is indented to the first tab stop to the right. To indent the entire paragraph — number and all — change the first-line indent of the paragraph, as explained in Chapter 7. To change the amount of space between the number and the text, change the position of the tab stop.

Numbering Your Pages

WordPerfect can automatically number the pages in your document — and renumber them if you add or delete pages. To turn on automatic page numbering for a document, walk this way:

1. **Make sure that no text is selected.**
2. **Click anywhere on the page where you want the page numbering to begin.**

   If your document has a title page, for example, and you want the numbering to begin on page 2, click on page 2.
3. **Choose Format⇨Page Numbering⇨Select.**

   The dialog box shown in Figure 8-2 appears.
4. **Select the placement and format of the page numbers.**

   Choose the placement from the Position drop-down list and the format from the Page Numbering Format list box. The preview at the bottom of the dialog box shows you how and where the page numbers appear.
5. **Choose the font and size for your page numbers.**

   Page numbers normally appear in the same font as the initial document font. If you want to use a different font, click on the Font button to open the standard Font dialog box, discussed in Chapter 7. After you specify the font, size, style, and other font attributes, click on OK.

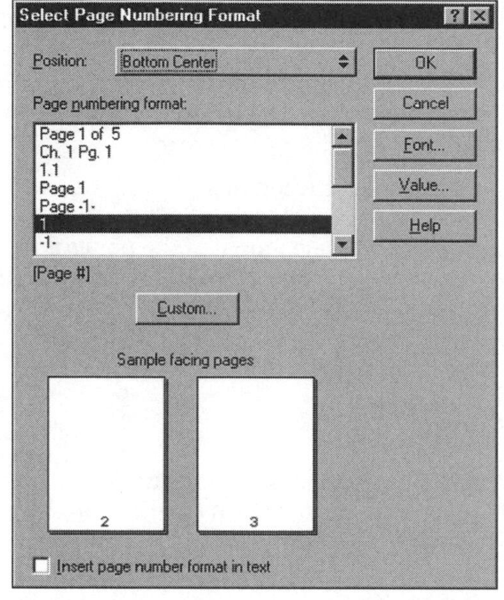

Figure 8-2: Don't number your pages manually — tell WordPerfect to do it for you.

6. **Set the starting page number.**

   Normally, WordPerfect numbers pages according to their position in your document. Suppose that in Step 1, you click on the third page of your document to tell WordPerfect that you want page numbering to begin on that page — maybe pages one and two are your title page and table of contents. If you want that third page to be numbered Page 1, you need to click on the Value button to display the dialog box shown in Figure 8-3. Enter the starting page number in the Set Page Number option box, ignore the rest of the options, and click on OK.

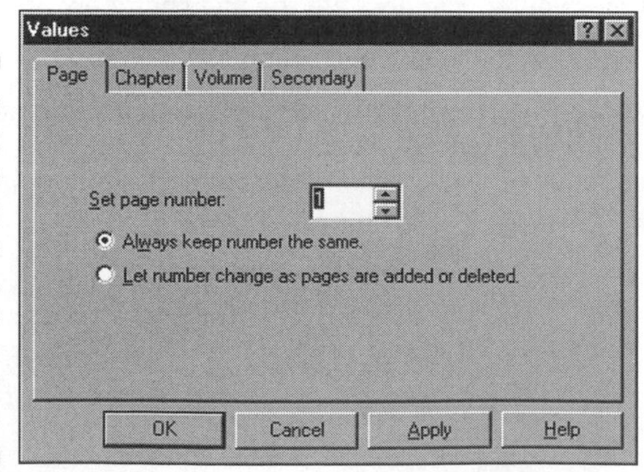

Figure 8-3: If you want to change the starting page number, change the Set Page Number value.

If you later want to reset the starting page number, you can get to the Values dialog box quickly by choosing Format⇨Page Numbering⇨Value/Adjust.

7. **Click on OK.**

   The page numbers appear as you requested. (You must be working in Page view or Two Page view to see them.) If you add or delete pages, WordPerfect renumbers the pages as needed.

To remove page numbers, click on the first numbered page, choose Format⇨Page Numbering⇨Select, and choose No Page Numbering from the Position drop-down list in the Select Page Numbering Format dialog box.

If you want to prevent a page number from printing on a particular page, click on that page, choose Format⇨Page⇨Suppress, and turn on the check box for the Page Numbering item.

Inserting the Current Date and Time

Here's a tool you'll love if you're never sure what day it is, let alone what time it is. WordPerfect can automatically insert the current date and/or time into your text and even update the information each time you open or print the document. You may want to use this feature to add the date to form letters that you use frequently, for example.

1. **Place the insertion marker at the spot where you want to insert the date/time.**
2. **Choose Insert⇨Date⇨Date Format.**

   WordPerfect opens a dialog box that asks you to choose the format for the date and time information. You can select from a wide range of formats, from the traditional month/date/year style (for example, *August 30, 1996*) to the downright odd (*31Jan97*). You can also choose to insert just the date, just the current time, or the date and time together. After you choose the format, click on OK to close the dialog box. WordPerfect uses the selected format any time you insert the date or time in your current document until you change the settings in the dialog box.

3. **Choose Insert⇨Date⇨Date Text or Insert⇨Date⇨Date Code.**

   If you choose the Date Text command, WordPerfect inserts the current date/time only. If you choose the Date Code command, WordPerfect inserts the current date/time *and* updates the date/time every time you open or save the document.

The keyboard shortcut for the Date Text command is Ctrl+D; the shortcut for the Date Code command is Ctrl+Shift+D.

WordPerfect inserts the date and time according to your computer's system clock. If the date or time is incorrect, update it via the Windows 95 Control panel.

Tracking Down Special Characters

You're gleefully typing up your annual holiday letter to friends and relatives, bragging about your two-week vacation in France, and you realize with horror that your computer keyboard doesn't have any of those little accent marks you need to type foreign words. However will you tell that hilarious story about that quaint café in Chalôns, let alone mention your upcoming second honeymoon in Curaçao?

Relax — all those foreign accent marks and other special typographical symbols are yours for the taking. You just need to know where to find them.

One major hunting ground for special symbols is the WordPerfect Characters dialog box, shown in Figure 8-4.

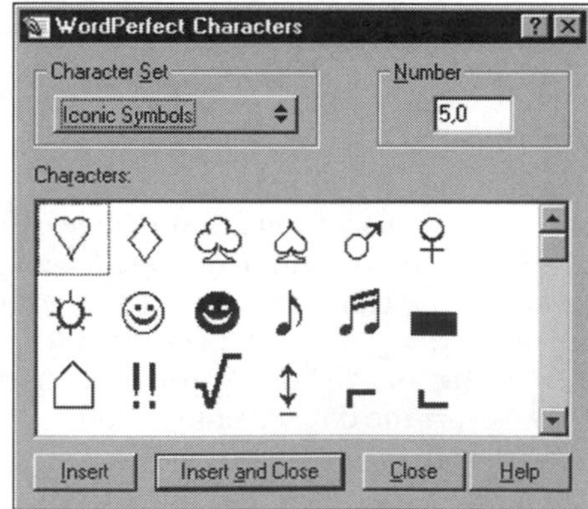

Figure 8-4: If you feel compelled to add a smiley face, musical note, or other special symbol in your document, WordPerfect obliges.

To grab a symbol and put it in your document, follow these steps:

1. **Position your insertion marker where you want the symbol to appear.**
2. **Choose Insert⇨Character or press Ctrl+W to open the WordPerfect Characters dialog box.**
3. **Locate the character you want to insert.**

   Each of the symbol sets in the Character Set drop-down menu offers a different selection of special characters. (Hint: For foreign characters, choose the Multinational option.) Use the scroll arrows alongside the Characters list box to hunt through the available characters in the current character set. After you find the one you want, click on it.
4. **Click on Insert.**

   Or just double-click on the character. WordPerfect inserts the character in your document.

You can leave the WordPerfect Characters dialog box on-screen for as long as you need it. The dialog box operates like any other open window — click on it to make it the active window; click on your document to make the document the active window. After you're finished inserting your special characters, click on the Close button.

You can insert some commonly used symbols, such as em dashes (—) and the registered trademark symbol (®), without hassling with the Insert⇨Character command. WordPerfect's QuickCorrect feature is set up to automatically translate certain keystrokes into special symbols. A list of the available shortcuts appears in Table 8-1. (For these keystrokes to work, the Replace Words as You Type option box must be checked in the QuickCorrect dialog box. Press Ctrl+Shift+F1 to open the dialog box and turn on the option.) Remember that WordPerfect doesn't change your keystrokes into the corresponding symbol until you press the spacebar.

By default, QuickCorrect also automatically replaces so-called *straight quotes* (") and *straight single quotes* (') — otherwise known as apostrophes — with *curly quotes* (“”) and *curly single quotes* (‘’). This is a good thing — straight quotes are considered gauche in professional typesetting circles. But if you're typing measurements, such as 9'5", you *need* those straight quotes. No worries — when you type a number, WordPerfect uses the straight quotes instead.

All this quotation mark substituting depends, however, on the settings in the QuickCorrect Options dialog box. Press Ctrl+Shift+F1 to open the QuickCorrect dialog box, click on the Options button, and make sure that these three options are turned on: Turn On Single Quotes, Turn on Double Quotes, and Use Regular Quotes with Numbers.

If you use a special symbol frequently and WordPerfect doesn't offer a QuickCorrect shortcut for it, you can create your own. Here's how: In the Replace option box of the QuickCorrect dialog box, enter the shortcut you want to use — for example, you may want to use the shortcut *tm* for a trademark symbol. Then, click in the With option box and press Ctrl+W to open the WordPerfect Characters dialog box. Find the symbol you want and click on Insert and Close to put the symbol in the With option box. Click on Add Entry and then click on Close.

Table 8-1 Shortcuts to Common Symbols

Symbol	*Shortcut*
©	(c or (c)
®	(r
—	- - (hyphen hyphen) or m- (m, hyphen)
–	n- (n, hyphen)

Creating Headers and Footers

Headers and footers provide a quick and convenient way to create text that repeats on every page (or almost every page) in your document. A *header* contains text that appears at the top of every page — for example, the document title or chapter title. A *footer* contains text that appears at the bottom of your pages — the current date and the page number are two common footer elements.

The advantage of using headers and footers is that you don't have to retype the same text, page after page. You create the text once and use the Header/Footer command to place it automatically on every page.

Before you create a header or footer, be sure that you're working in Page view (choose View⇨Page or press Alt+F5) so that you can see what you're doing on-screen. Then follow these steps:

1. **Click at the top of the first page where you want the header/footer to appear.**
2. **Choose Format⇨Header/Footer to open the dialog box shown in Figure 8-5.**

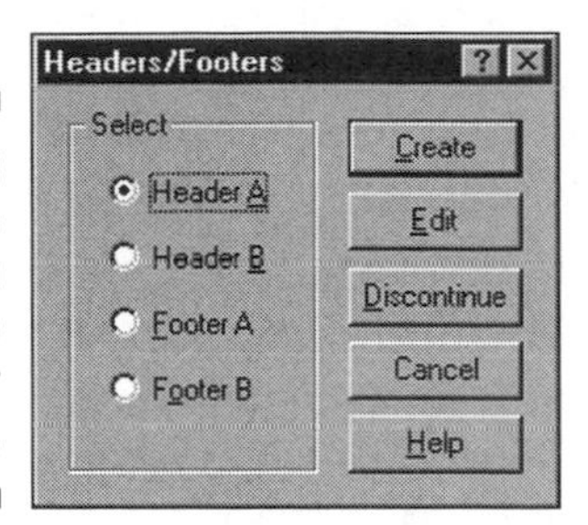

Figure 8-5: Choose the header you want to create or edit.

3. Select the header/footer you want to create.

If you need only one header/footer for your document, use Header A or Footer A. If you need two different sets of headers/footers — as you would if you want a different header/footer for your left-hand pages than you do for your right-hand pages — choose either A or B.

4. Click on Create.

WordPerfect inserts what looks like a blank line at the top of your page and displays the Header/Footer bar, as shown in Figure 8-6. More about what those buttons do in a moment. You can tell that you're working in the Header/Footer zone by looking at the title of the document window; the title now includes the name of the current Header/Footer.

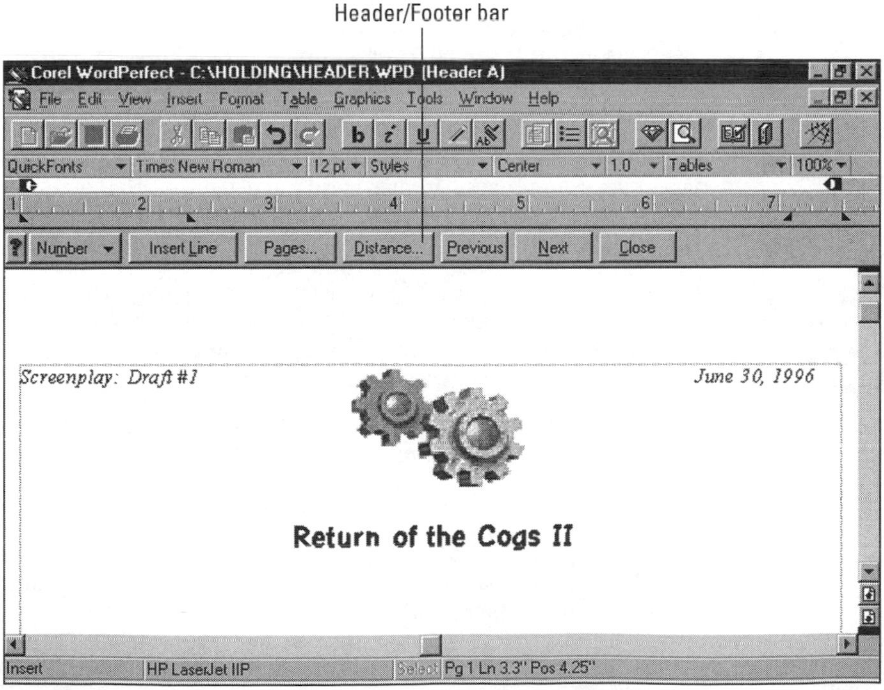

Header/Footer bar

Figure 8-6: This header text appears at the top of every page in my sreenplay.

5. **Create your text.**

   You can enter as much text as you want and even add graphics (as explained later in this chapter). Figure 8-6 shows the header text I created for my next blockbuster screenplay.

6. **Click on the Close button on the Header/Footer bar.**

   Or, if you want to keep the Header/Footer bar displayed for future editing purposes, just click anywhere in your main document. WordPerfect displays the header/footer on the page, adjusting your text to make room for the header/footer.

Here's some additional info you need to know about headers and footers:

- You can edit a header/footer by simply clicking on it on any page on which it appears. The title bar of the document window should change to show that you're working on the header/footer. Click outside the header/footer to return to your main document.
- If you closed the Header/Footer bar and you want to redisplay it to do some editing, choose Format⇨Header/Footer, select the header/footer you want to edit, and then click on Edit. After you finish editing, click on the Close button to close the Header/Footer bar and return to the main document or, if you want to leave the bar displayed, just click in the main document text.

- If you want to include the page number on pages that have a header/footer, it's best to insert them in the header/footer instead of using the Format⇨Page Numbering command explained earlier in this chapter. Otherwise, your header/footer text may overprint your page numbers. To insert the page number in a header/footer, click on the Number button in the Header/Footer bar and choose Page Number.
- You can specify whether you want a header/footer to appear on every page, every even page, or every odd page. Choose the Pages button on the Header/Footer bar, click on the radio button for the option you want to use, and click on OK or press Enter.

- If you don't want a header/footer to print on a particular page, you can *suppress* it. Put the insertion marker on the page, choose Format⇨Page⇨Suppress to open the Suppress dialog box, and check the option box for the header or footer that you want to suppress.
- If you want to discontinue the header/footer after a certain page, put the insertion marker on that page, choose Format⇨Header/Footer to open the Headers/Footers dialog box, choose the header/footer that you want to discontinue, and click on the Discontinue button.
- To control the distance between the header/footer and the main document text, click on the Distance button on the Header/Footer bar and set the distance value in the resulting dialog box.

- Another way to get rid of a header/footer is to delete its hidden code. Put the insertion marker at the very beginning of the main document text on the first page that uses the header/footer. Press Alt+F3 to open the frightening Reveal Codes window. If you positioned the insertion marker correctly, you should see a little button-like thing labeled *Header A* or *Footer A* (or whatever the letter of the header/footer you're trying to delete) in the Reveal Codes window, as in Figure 8-7. Drag that little button out of the Reveal Codes window to get rid of the header/footer.

Putting Your Text in Columns

WordPerfect makes it possible to divide your pages into columns — as you may want to do when creating a newsletter article, for example. Here are the steps:

1. **Put the insertion marker at the point where you want the columns to begin.**

   If you want to format just certain paragraphs in columns, select the paragraphs instead. If you don't select text, the column formatting continues until the end of the document or until the spot where you insert the Columns⇨Off command (as described a little later).

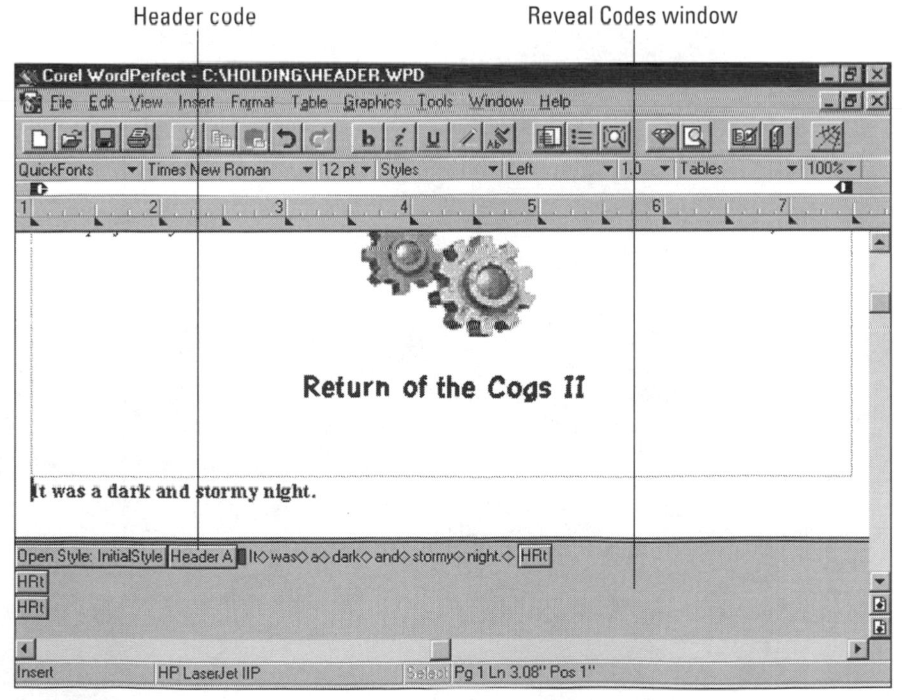

Figure 8-7: To delete a header or footer from your document, drag the header/footer code out of the Reveal Codes window.

2. **Choose Format⇨Columns⇨Define.**

   The dialog box shown in Figure 8-8 appears.

3. **Specify the number of columns you want in the Columns option box.**
4. **Choose a column format by clicking on one of the Type radio buttons.**

   Here are your options:

   - Newspaper fills the first column on the left all the way to the bottom of the page, fills the next column to the bottom of the page, and so on, until all the text is placed in columns.
   - Balanced Newspaper fills the columns in the same way as Newspaper, except that WordPerfect attempts to make all the columns the same length.
   - Parallel groups text across the page in rows, similar to what you find in a table. You may want to use this option if you're creating a script, for example, in which you want the video portion of the scene to run down the left side of the page and the audio to appear on the right side, as in Figure 8-9.
   - Parallel w/Block Protect works the same way as Parallel, except that WordPerfect makes sure that no row of text is split across two pages. If the text in one column in the row is too long to fit on the page, the entire row moves to the next page.

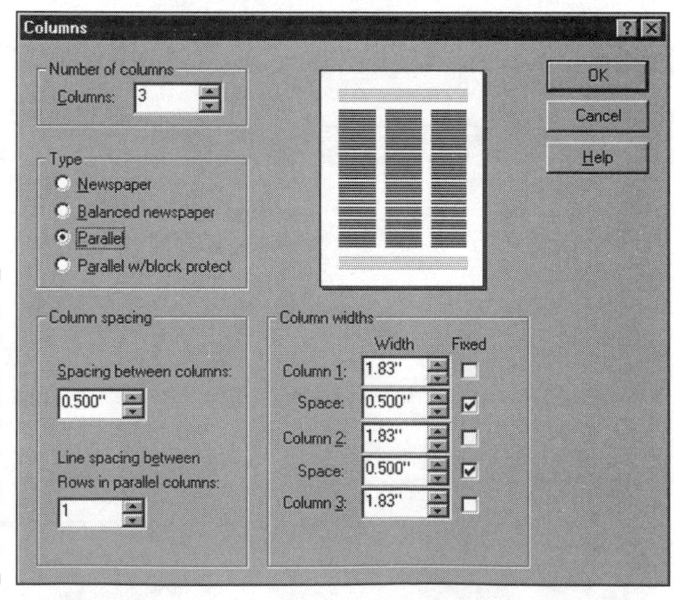

Figure 8-8: You specify the number, type, and spacing of your columns in this dialog box.

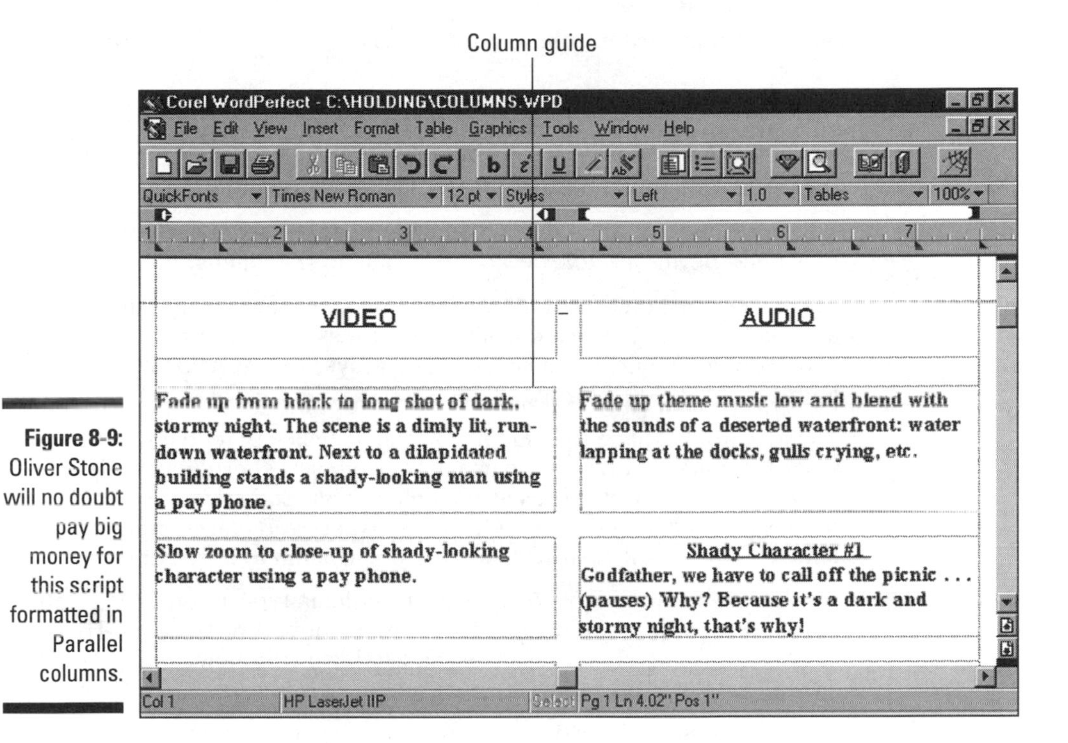

Figure 8-9: Oliver Stone will no doubt pay big money for this script formatted in Parallel columns.

As you make your choices, the preview pages in the dialog box change to show you how your columns will appear.

5. **If necessary, adjust the column width and spacing.**

   By default, WordPerfect spaces your columns evenly across the page and puts a half-inch of space between each column. If you want some other spacing, change the values in the Column Spacing and Column Width option boxes. If you're not sure what spacing or width values you want, don't sweat it; you can easily change the values later.

6. **Click on OK or press Enter to close the dialog box and create your columns.**

As you can see in Figure 8-9, WordPerfect displays dotted guidelines to indicate the boundaries of each column. (If you don't see the guidelines on-screen, choose View➪Guidelines and turn on the Columns option in the resulting dialog box.)

You can resize your columns by dragging the guidelines or by dragging the space between columns (in publishing terms, that space is called a *gutter*).

Entering and editing text in columns involves a few special techniques:

- When you're typing text in a Newspaper column, WordPerfect automatically moves the insertion marker to the next column when you fill up the current column. But if you want to break the column before that point, just press Ctrl+Enter or choose Format⇨Columns⇨Column Break.
- When you're editing text in a Balanced Newspaper column, pressing Ctrl+Enter begins a whole new block of balanced columns.
- In Parallel and Parallel with Block Protect columns, Ctrl+Enter moves you across the row to the next column. If you press Ctrl+Enter at the end of a row, WordPerfect creates a new row and moves the insertion marker to the leftmost column in that row.
- To move from column to column, you can just click to reposition the insertion marker. You can also use these keyboard shortcuts: Alt+Home moves you to the top of the current column; Alt+End moves you to the end of the current column; Alt+← (left arrow) takes you one column to the left; and Alt+→ (right arrow) takes you one column to the right.
- To change the number of columns or the column type, put the insertion marker where you want the different column formatting to begin. Then choose Format⇨Columns⇨Define and establish your new column settings as outlined in the preceding steps.
- To turn off column formatting and return to regular text layout, put the insertion marker at the point where you want to get rid of the column formatting and choose Format⇨Columns⇨Off.

Inserting Graphics

Ah, here's the really fun part: adding pictures to your pages. The WordPerfect Suite comes with a bunch of clip art — pictures, borders, and other graphic elements — that you can use to add zest and power to your next document.

To place a graphic on a page:

1. **Position the insertion marker at the spot where you want to put the graphic.**
2. **Click on the toolbar button that looks like a big green diamond.**

   Officially, this button is known as the Image button. If you hate toolbars, choose Graphics⇨Image instead. (You can't access the command or the icon if you have any text selected in your document.) WordPerfect opens up the Insert Image dialog box, which looks suspiciously like the regular Open dialog box discussed back in Chapter 5 — and works just like it, too.

If you don't get the Insert Image dialog box but instead get a little hand cursor, you have the Drag to Create option in the Graphics menu turned on. Click on the option to turn it off.

The graphics that come with the WordPerfect Suite are stored in the Graphics folder, which should appear in the Look In option box by default. In this folder, you can find several subfolders containing borders and pictures. Scout around until you find a graphic file that looks interesting.

If you choose View➪Preview➪Page View or View➪Preview➪Content in the Insert Image dialog box, WordPerfect displays a preview of the graphic in the dialog box.

You aren't limited to the pictures that came with the WordPerfect Suite, however. You can use any graphics saved in any format that WordPerfect can handle. Check the For Type drop-down list to see the different graphics formats WordPerfect accepts.

3. **Double-click on the graphic you want to use.**

   WordPerfect plops the graphic onto your page. When you first place a graphic on a page, it's surrounded by little black boxes, as shown in Figure 8-10. These boxes are called *selection handles,* and they indicate that the graphic is selected and ready to be moved or edited.

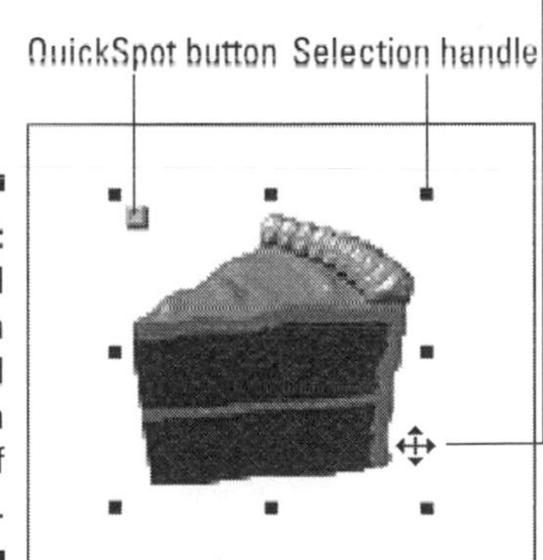

Figure 8-10: Moving and resizing a selected graphic is a piece of cake.

WordPerfect offers a whole slew of graphics editing possibilities, but the truth is, if you want to do very much editing to a graphic, you should use Presentations instead. In fact, if you right-click on a graphic and choose Edit Image from the QuickMenu, the Presentations window opens inside WordPerfect so that you can use the Presentations drawing tools on your graphic. (For more about using Presentations, see Chapter 16. Also check out Chapter 20, which explains how this program within a program stuff works.) But here are some of the simple editing tricks you can try in WordPerfect:

- To resize the graphic, drag one of its handles. Or right-click on the graphic, choose Size from the resulting QuickMenu, and enter new height and width values in the Box Size dialog box.

- It's easy to distort a graphic when you're resizing it with the mouse. To prevent this from happening, right-click on the graphic, choose Content from the resulting QuickMenu, and then turn on the Preserve Image Width/ Height Ratio.
- To move a graphic, click on it to select it, place the cursor on the graphic until you see a four-way arrow, and then drag the graphic to the new position.
- To draw a border around the graphic, right-click on it and choose Border/ Fill from the QuickMenu. WordPerfect displays a dialog box that enables you to choose from various borders. To preview a border, click on the Apply button. If you like what you see, click on OK or press Enter. If not, choose another border and click on Apply again. If you want to get rid of the border, click on the Off button.
- WordPerfect *wraps* text around graphics — that is, it shoves lines of text out of the way to make room for the image. You can change the amount of space between the text and graphic by right-clicking on the graphic and choosing the Wrap command from the QuickMenu. You get a dialog box full of wrap options; play around with different settings until you find one that works for your document.

- You can also access the graphic editing commands by clicking on the graphic's QuickSpot button.
- To delete a graphic, click on it to select it (you should see the black handles). Then just press Delete. That graphic's outta here.

If you want to create your own custom graphics, take a gander at Chapter 16 for information on the drawing tools offered in Presentations. You can create a graphic in Presentations and then insert it into your WordPerfect document, as explained in Chapter 20.

Creating Borders, Fills, and Lines

Another way to jazz up your pages is to add borders, lines, and fills to selected text. *Fill* by the way, is a computer-art term that means "background" — loosely translated, of course.

Adding borders and fills

You can put a border around a page, paragraph, or column. To do so, select the text you want to border-ize. Or, if you want to put a border on all your pages, paragraphs, or columns, don't select any text. Then choose Format⇨Border/Fill and choose either Paragraph, Page, or Column, depending on what you want to put a border around. You get a dialog box that looks something like the one in Figure 8-11.

Click on a border style and then play around with the Color, Line Style, and Drop Shadow options until you create an acceptable border. When applying a border to a page, choose the Line option from the Border Type menu to access these options. As you mess with the options, the preview box shows you what your border will look like. Click on Apply to preview the border on your actual text. If you want to apply the border to more than the current paragraph/page/column, make sure that the check box at the bottom of the Border tab isn't selected. When you're satisfied, click on OK.

To remove a border from selected text, choose the Format⇨Border/Fill command and click on the Off button in the Border/Fill dialog box.

You can also apply borders and fills to paragraphs by clicking on the QuickSpot for the paragraph and choosing the Border and Fill options.

The procedure for adding a fill (background) behind paragraphs, pages, and columns is the same, except that you choose a fill on the Fill tab of the Border/Fill dialog box. (When applying fills to pages, you must choose the Line option from the Border Type menu to access fill options.) If you want to delete a fill, though, you choose the blank (white) fill instead of using the Off button.

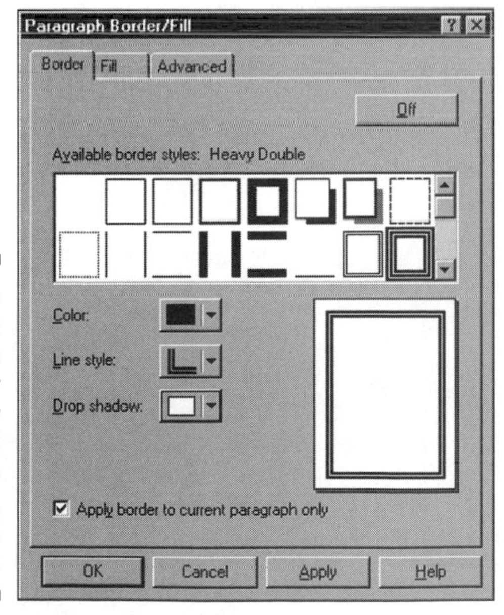

Figure 8-11: You can apply a border and/or background to paragraphs, pages, and columns.

Adding lines

To draw a straight line from the left margin to the right margin, click at the spot where you want the line to appear and choose Graphics⇨Horizontal Line or press Ctrl+F11. You can also type three hyphens or three equal signs and then press Enter to create a single or double horizontal line, respectively. (The QuickLines option in the QuickCorrect Options dialog box must be checked. Choose Tools⇨QuickCorrect and click on Options to open the dialog box.)

To create a vertical line from the top margin to the right margin, click on the spot where you want to position the line and then choose Graphics⇨Vertical Line or press Ctrl+Shift+F11.

To move a line, click on it to display its selection handles (little black squares) and then drag it to the new position. To resize the line, drag on its handles. Depending on which handle you drag, you can make the line fatter, skinnier, longer, or shorter. To delete a line, click on it to display the selection handles and then press Delete.

Chapter 9

Tools to Save You Time (and Embarrassment)

In This Chapter

- Using styles to speed up formatting
- Copying character and paragraph formatting
- Finding and replacing words and phrases
- Checking your spelling

Have you heard the expression, "The hurrieder I go, the behinder I get"? No? Well, my Grandma King says it all the time, and she's nobody's fool. Loosely translated, this time-honored saying means that if you rush to get a job done, you make mistakes that put you even further behind schedule than if you had taken a slow, methodical approach. At least, I think that's what it means.

At any rate, going slow isn't always possible in our speed-it-up, get-it-done-yesterday world. Your boss wants that report done *now,* your client wants that project done *yesterday,* and the IRS wants all your money *this very minute* — with a hefty interest penalty for any delay whatsoever. (Sorry about that last part; April 15 looms as I write this.)

Fortunately, WordPerfect has some tools that not only help you work faster but also help make sure that your documents don't contain any embarrassing spelling or formatting mistakes. This chapter shows you how to use these tools so that you can go hurrieder without getting any behinder.

Using Styles to Speed Up Formatting Chores

Without a doubt, one of the best ways to save time is to use *styles.* Styles are like templates that you can use to quickly apply character and paragraph formatting to your text.

Here's how it works. You create a style that contains all the formatting instructions for a specific text element. For example, you may want to create a headline style that uses 14-point, bold, Helvetica type, centered alignment, and double paragraph spacing. Then, to format your headlines, you just select the headline text and choose the headline style from the Styles drop-down list on the Power Bar. WordPerfect applies the right font, type size, alignment, and paragraph spacing in one fell swoop.

Using styles not only saves you time, it ensures that your formatting is consistent throughout your document. You don't have to worry about what font, type size, or spacing you're supposed to use each time you create a new headline — all the formatting information is contained in the style. And if you want to change the formatting of your headlines (for example, if you decide to use 13-point type instead of 14-point type), you don't have to search through your document looking for headlines and changing them manually. You just edit the style, and WordPerfect automatically applies the new formatting to any paragraphs that use the style.

Creating and using styles in WordPerfect is a much bigger topic than I have room to cover in this book. In the following sections, I show you the basics of using styles. If you want to explore more advanced ways to create, edit, and use styles, I heartily recommend that you take a look at *WordPerfect 6.1 For Windows For Dummies,* 2nd Edition, by Margaret Levine Young and David C. Kay (published by IDG Books Worldwide, Inc.).

Choosing a style type

You can create three types of styles in WordPerfect:

- **Character styles:** These styles can contain formatting related to individual characters of text — font, type size, type style, and so on. They can't contain paragraph-level formatting such as indents and line spacing. If you apply a character style, it affects selected text only.
- **Paragraph styles:** These styles contain paragraph-level formatting *plus* character-level formatting. If you apply a paragraph style, it affects all text in the current paragraph or in all selected paragraphs.
- **Document styles:** These styles can contain paragraph-level formatting, character-level formatting, plus document-level formatting such as page size. I don't cover this option because frankly, creating and editing document styles is complicated (it involves that yucky Reveal Codes window) and you probably won't have much reason to use them anyhow.

WordPerfect assigns a standard document style, called InitialStyle, to every document you create. You can't delete this style, although you can edit it if you're a WordPerfect hidden codes aficionado (or know someone who is), as explained later in this chapter, in the section "Editing a style." However, you really shouldn't need to delete or edit the InitialStyle style, because any formatting you do inside the document overrides the InitialStyle formatting instructions.

Creating character and paragraph styles

WordPerfect comes with some prefab styles that you can see if you click on the Styles button on the Power Bar. But you probably want to define your own styles, as the prefab styles aren't likely to meet your specific formatting needs.

You can create styles from scratch, but it's easier to create some text, apply the formatting you want to use, and then use the QuickStyle command to create a style based on your formatted text.

To create a character or paragraph style using the QuickStyle command, just step this way:

1. **Format and select the text you want to use as the basis for the style.**
2. **Click on the Styles button on the Power Bar and choose the QuickStyle command.**

   The QuickStyle dialog box, shown in Figure 9-1, appears.

QuickStyle
Create a style based on the formatting in effect at the insertion point.
Style name: Bylines
Description: Author bylines
Style type
Paragraph (auto)
Character
OK
Cancel
Help

Figure 9-1: Use the QuickStyle command to create a style based on formatted text.

3. **Give your style a name and description.**

   Enter the name into the Style Name option box. Note that you can't use a style name that already exists. In the Description box, enter some descriptive text that will remind you what sort of text you plan to format with the style.

4. **Choose a style type.**

   Click on Paragraph (auto) to create a paragraph style; click on Character to create a character style. The differences between the style types are explained in the preceding section, "Choosing a style type."

5. **Click on OK or press Enter.**

   You should see your new style on the Styles button on the Power Bar.

You can reuse styles from document to document. Press Alt+F8 or choose Format⇨Styles to open the Style List dialog box, shown in Figure 9-2. Click on Options and choose Retrieve from the drop-down list. In the next dialog box that appears, enter the pathname of the document containing the styles you want to use (pathnames are covered in the sidebars in Chapter 5). Or click on the white box next to the Filename box and select the document from the dialog box that appears. Click on the User Styles radio button and click on OK. WordPerfect may ask your permission to override any styles in the current document that have the same names as the ones you're bringing in from the other document. Click on Yes to give your okay. Click on Close to wrap things up.

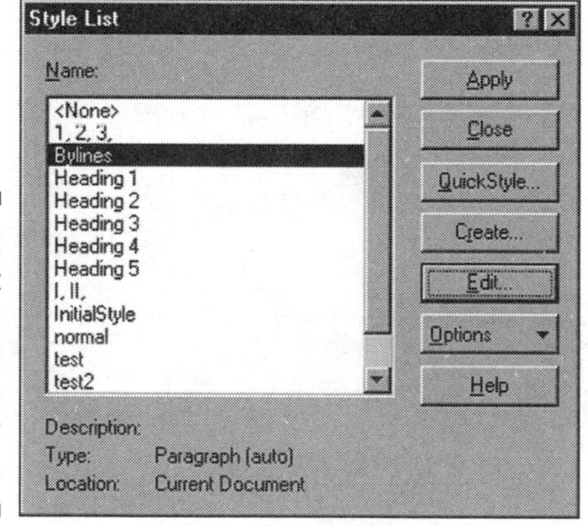

Figure 9-2: WordPerfect lets you reuse styles created in other documents.

Applying styles

Applying styles to your text is easy. To apply a character style, select the text you want to format and then select the style from the Styles drop-down list on the Power Bar. To apply a paragraph style, click in the paragraph you want to format and select the style from the Styles drop-down list. To apply a style to several paragraphs, select the paragraphs before selecting the style.

If you're not sure what style you applied to a particular paragraph, click in the paragraph and take a look at the Styles button on the Power Bar. It should show the name of the current style. If no style is applied, the button just reads *Styles.*

Editing a style

Here's the messy part about using styles in WordPerfect. You can edit styles and remove styles from text, but doing so sometimes involves playing around with hidden codes in the Reveal Codes window — which, if I haven't stated it often enough yet, can be something of a headache. But don't despair; depending on what formatting you want to change, the process may not be too awful.

Suppose that you create a paragraph style named Byline to use for all the author bylines in your monthly newsletter. You originally specify that you want all the bylines to be boldfaced. Now, you decide that you want them to be italicized instead. All you need to do is click on one of the bylines, click on the **b** button on the toolbar to remove the boldface, and click on the *i* button to make the text italic. WordPerfect automatically makes the same change to all text using the Byline style.

If you want to turn off this automatic updating for a paragraph style, follow the upcoming steps and change the Type setting in the Styles Editor dialog box from Paragraph (paired-auto) to Paragraph (paired).

To edit a character style, you have to dive into the Styles Editor. You can also use this method if you want to make a change to all paragraphs that use a certain style, but you turned off automatic updating for that style.

Here's how to make your edits:

1. **Choose Format⇨Styles or press Alt+F8 to open the Style List dialog box.**
2. **Select the name of the style you want to edit and click on the Edit button.**

   WordPerfect displays the Styles Editor dialog box, shown in Figure 9-3.
3. **Make your edits.**

   The Styles Editor dialog box has a menu bar that offers many of the same commands as the regular WordPerfect menu bar. If you want to *add* a formatting attribute, you just choose the appropriate command from the menu bar, as you would when you normally format text. To make the Byline text bold *and* italic, for example, you would choose Format⇨Font and turn on the italic attribute in the Font dialog box.

   If you want to *delete* a formatting attribute, you have to drag its code out of the Contents window at the bottom of the Styles Editor dialog box. For example, to get rid of the bold attribute in the Byline style, you would drag the Bold code (it's at the end of the Contents line in Figure 9-3) out of the window. If your style isn't overly complicated, you may be able to figure out which codes to remove. But if the style contains a lot of formatting, you may need a WordPerfect hidden codes guru by your side.

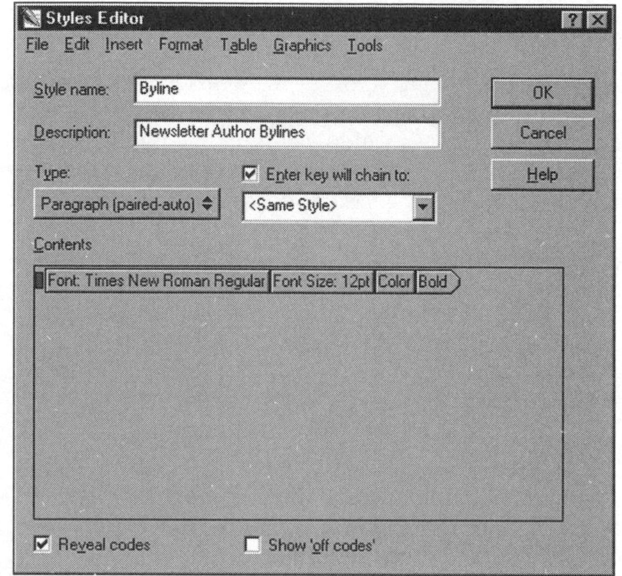

Figure 9-3: You can make changes to a style by using the Styles Editor.

If you want to *replace* a formatting attribute — say, to substitute 10-point type for 12-point type — drag the old code out of the window before you use the menu commands to set the new attribute.

4. **Click on OK or press Enter.**
5. **Click on the Close button.**

   WordPerfect closes the Style List dialog box and applies the updated formatting to any text that uses the style.

Removing styles

If you want to remove a style from a paragraph, click inside the paragraph and choose <None> from the Styles drop-down list on the Power Bar.

Removing character styles is dicier — it requires deleting hidden codes in the Reveal Codes window. Take a big breath and follow me:

1. **Click on the space to the left of the first character in the text that you want to "destyle."**
2. **Press Alt+F3 to open the Reveal Codes window.**

   In the window, you can see your document text along with all the hidden formatting codes. At the left of the first character in the text you want to unformat, you should see a code that begins with *Char Style* (the character style code), as shown in Figure 9-4. A similar character style code appears at the end of the text that uses the style.

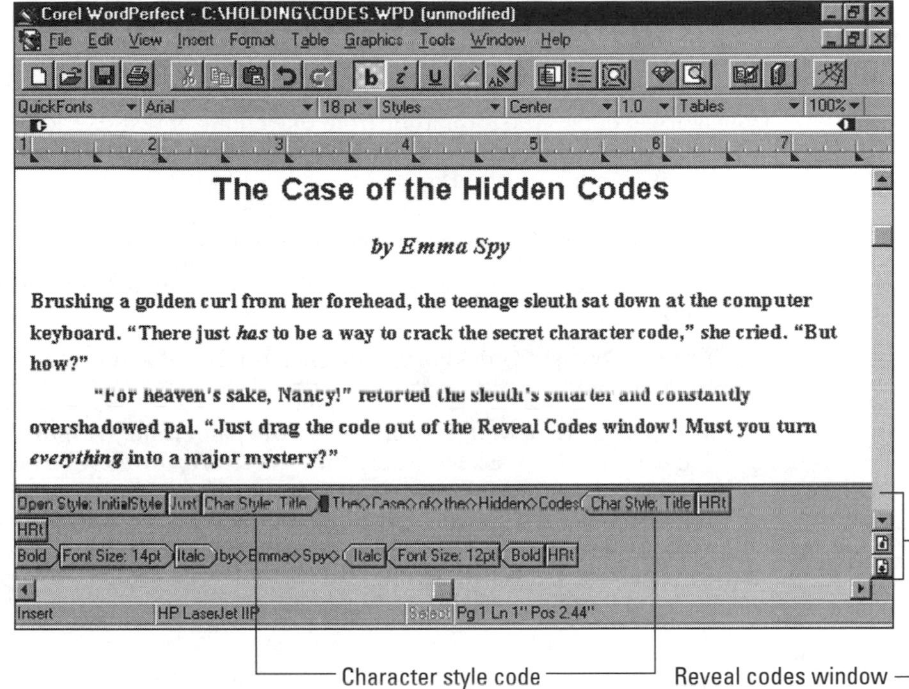

Figure 9-4: To remove a character style, drag either of the Char Style codes out of the Reveal Codes window.

3. **Drag either of the codes out of the Reveal Codes window.**

   Deleting one code deletes both.

   If things don't look right after you remove the style code, press Ctrl+Z to undo your edit. Then go make nice with the WordPerfect guru in your office to get some help sorting out your codes.

To completely remove a style from the document, follow these steps:

1. **Press Alt+F8 or choose Format⇨Styles to display the Style List dialog box (shown in Figure 9-2).**
2. **Select the style name to remove, click on the Options button, and select Delete from the drop-down list.**

   WordPerfect presents a dialog box asking whether you want to keep all the formatting codes contained in the style. In other words, do you want to delete the style but leave the formatting it applies intact?

3. **If you want to keep the formatting, choose the Leave Codes option.**
4. **If you want to erase both the formatting and the styles, choose Include Codes.**
5. **To complete your mission, click on OK and then click on the Close button.**

Copying Formats with QuickFormat

WordPerfect offers another tool to speed up your formatting life: QuickFormat. QuickFormat copies the formatting from one chunk of text to another. You can copy the formatting of a selected word, a selected block of text, or an entire paragraph. Here's how it works:

1. **Select the text that has the formatting you want to copy.**

   If you want to copy paragraph formatting, you can just click inside the paragraph.

2. **Choose Format⇨QuickFormat or click on the QuickFormat button on the toolbar.**

   The QuickFormat button looks like a little paint roller with the letters *Ab* in the corner. (Don't ask me where they got the *Ab* — *apply boldly,* maybe?) If you don't care for toolbar buttons, another alternative is to right-click in the document and choose QuickFormat from the resulting QuickMenu. Whichever route you choose, the QuickFormat dialog box, shown in Figure 9-5, appears.

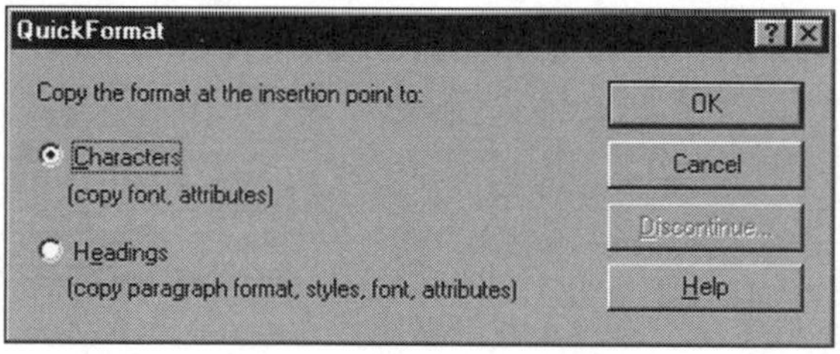

Figure 9-5: You can copy character or paragraph formatting from one spot to another.

3. **Choose a copy option.**

   If you select the Characters radio button, you copy the formatting of the selected characters only — font, type size, type style, and so on. If you choose the Headings button, you copy both the text formatting and the paragraph formatting (styles, indents, borders, and so on).

4. **Click on OK or press Enter.**

   If you chose the Characters option in Step 3, your cursor changes to a little paint brush. If you chose the Headings option, the cursor changes to an I-beam with a paint roller attached. Very clever.

5. **Drag over the text you want to format.**

   Or, if you're copying paragraph formatting to a single paragraph, you can just click inside the paragraph. The paint roller/paint brush icon remains visible, and you can keep "painting" the formatting onto as much other text as you want.

6. **After you finish painting, turn off QuickFormat.**

   For the fastest results, just click again on the QuickFormat button or right-click and choose QuickFormat from the QuickMenu.

When you copy paragraph formatting, WordPerfect creates a QuickFormat paragraph style (styles are explained in the preceding section in this chapter). The style appears on the Styles drop-down list in the Power Bar, just like a regular style. The first QuickFormat style you create is called QuickFormat 1, the second one is called QuickFormat 2, and so on.

If you want to copy the paragraph formatting to a new paragraph, you don't have to go through the trouble of using the QuickFormat painting tools; you can just apply the QuickFormat style from the Styles list. If you want, you can rename the style by changing its name in the Styles Editor dialog box, as explained earlier in this chapter, in the section "Editing a style."

If you change the formatting in one paragraph that uses the QuickFormat style, WordPerfect automatically makes the same change to any other paragraphs using the style. If you want to turn this feature off, click inside the paragraph you want to change. Then click on the QuickFormat toolbar button (or choose the QuickFormat command from the QuickMenu) and click on the Discontinue button in the QuickFormat dialog box. If you choose the Current Heading option, automatic updating is turned off for the current paragraph only. If you choose the All Associated Headings option, WordPerfect turns off automatic updating for all paragraphs that use the QuickFormat style.

Finding and Replacing Errant Text

People seem to have a hard time making up their minds these days. You no sooner type in the text for your company's 100-page annual report, and the board of directors replaces all the top management. You create a catalog touting your client's new product, and just before you send the thing to the printer, the client decides that it would be cool to spell the product *ConsumerScam* instead of *Consumer Scam.*

When these sorts of unavoidable changes happen, you could scroll through your text, hunt down all instances of outdated or incorrect information, and make the changes manually. Or you could do the smart thing and let the WordPerfect Find and Replace feature do the job for you.

Here's how to go on your search and destroy mission:

1. **Click at the spot where you want to begin searching for the incorrect text.**
2. **Choose Edit⇨Find and Replace or press Ctrl+F.**

   The Find and Replace dialog box appears, as shown in Figure 9-6.

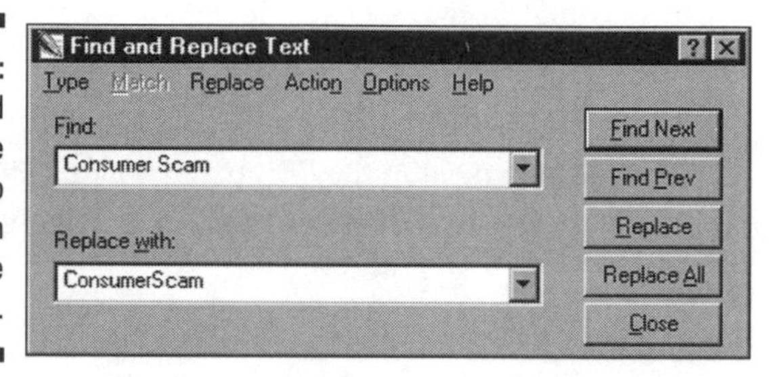

Figure 9-6: Use the Find and Replace command to track down and replace errant text.

3. **Turn on the Text option from the Type menu.**

   If you see a checkmark next to the option, it's turned on. Turn off the other options in the menu, if they happen to be checked. (More about what you can do with those options in a bit.)
4. **Type the word or phrase you want to replace in the Find option box.**

   Or click on the arrow at the end of the box to select text for which you recently searched and replaced.
5. **Type the replacement word or phrase in the Replace With option box.**

   Or click on the arrow at the end of the box to select replacement text that you recently used.
6. **Click on the Find Next or Find Prev button.**

   Find Next finds the first occurrence of the incorrect text *after* the insertion marker. Find Prev searches for the first occurrence of the incorrect text *before* the insertion marker.

   After WordPerfect finds the incorrect text, it highlights it in your document. If you click on Replace, WordPerfect replaces that text and moves on to find the next occurrence. If you click on Find Next or Find Prev, it leaves the current text alone and starts hunting for another occurrence of the text.

   If you click on Replace All, WordPerfect replaces every occurrence of the text from the insertion marker through the end of the document. (You can change the extent of the search by changing the settings in the Options menu, described in the upcoming bulleted list.)

If you want to edit the found text instead of replacing it, just click in your document and edit away. When you want to begin searching again, click inside the Find and Replace dialog box to make it active.

If WordPerfect can't find any more occurrences of the incorrect text, an alert box appears to tell you so. Click on OK to get rid of the box.

7. **Click on Close to shut the Find and Replace dialog box.**

   Or, if you prefer, you can leave the dialog box open and available for future searches.

WordPerfect's Find and Replace feature doesn't have an Undo function. If you replace a word by mistake, click inside the main document immediately and press Ctrl+Z or click on the Undo button to undo the replacement.

If you want to delete every occurrence of a word or phrase, leave the Replace With option box empty. WordPerfect then replaces each occurrence of the incorrect text with, uh, nothing, which is the same as deleting it. Nifty, huh?

Now that you know the basic steps involved in the Find and Replace dance, try out a few variations. The Find and Replace dialog box offers all sorts of options that enable you to customize your search:

- If you turn on the Word Forms option in the Type menu, you can search and replace all forms of a word. For example, if you type *fish* in the Find box, WordPerfect finds the words *fish, fishing,* and *fishes.* It also alters the Replace With text to match the form of the word it found — for example, if you originally used *hare* as the Replace With text, and the search found the word *fishes,* the Replace With text changes to *hares.* Sometimes, WordPerfect gives you a drop-down list offering several choices of Replace With text.
- Normally, WordPerfect finds any word that contains the characters you type in the Find box. For example, if you tell it to search for *bee,* it finds any words that contain those three letters, including *been, beer, beet,* and so on. If you choose the Whole Word option in the Match menu, it finds only the word *bee.* This option isn't available if you have the Word Forms option selected in the Type menu.
- Turn on the Case option in the Match menu to limit the search to text that uses the same case (uppercase or lowercase letters) as the text you type in the Find box.
- The Font option in the Match menu enables you to search for text that uses a specific font, type size, and type style. Type the text you want to find in the Find box and then choose the Font option. WordPerfect displays a Match Font dialog box in which you can specify the specific font characteristics you want to use in the search.

- You can also replace just the font or case of the found text. For example, if you want to make *ConsumerScam* boldface as well as italicized, you can enter ConsumerScam in both the Find option box and the Replace With option box, choose the Font command from the Replace menu, and turn on the bold and italic attributes in the resulting Replace Font dialog box. You can use the Replace and Match options together to find text with certain attributes and replace those attributes with other attributes — for example, to find all instances where *ConsumerScam* is italicized and make it boldface instead.
- Note that the Replace menu only becomes available if the Replace With option box is active; the Match menu is available only if the Find option box is active.

- The menu options stay active until you turn them off. If you turn on font matching for one search, for example, it's automatically turned on for the next search you do. So be sure to check the options before you start each search to make sure that everything's the way you want it.
- The options on the Action menu tell WordPerfect to select the text it finds or to position the insertion marker before or after the text. For example, if you turn on Select Match, WordPerfect selects the first text it finds. You can then edit, delete, format, or move the text without having to select it first. Just click in the document window to make it active; when you finish editing and are ready to continue your search, click inside the Find and Rcplacc dialog box again.
- The commands on the Options menu control the direction and extent of the search. The first option on the menu tells WordPerfect to begin searching at the top of the document; the second option tells it to search from the insertion marker to the end of the document and then search from the beginning of the document to the insertion marker. If you don't turn on either option, WordPerfect searches from the insertion marker forward to the end of the document and then stops.
- The Limit Find Within Selection option searches selected text only; the Include Headers, Footers, etc. in Find option searches the main body of the document as well as in headers, footers, text boxes, and so on.
- The Limit Number of Changes option in the Options menu controls how many replacements WordPerfect makes when you choose the Replace All button. If you specify 3 changes, for example, WordPerfect replaces only the first three occurrences of the text that it finds. If you specify 0 as the limit, WordPerfect replaces all occurrences of the found text.

You can use the Find and Replace command to simply find text as well as to find and replace text. For example, when I open up a long document to do some editing, I often use the command to find the particular passage I want to edit. To find your place in this way, enter the text that you want to locate in the Find box and use the Find Next and Find Prev buttons until you locate it. Then close the dialog box or just click inside your document to resume editing.

Checking Your Spelling

Remember that kid in grade school who won all the class spelling bees and other vocabulary contests? Well, WordPerfect makes that kid's brain cells available to you through its Spell Checker. You can ask the Spell Checker — also known as Mr. Smarty Pants — to look over your document and point out any misspelled or duplicated words.

The Spell Checker only knows whether the words you use are spelled correctly — it doesn't know whether you used the wrong word or the wrong form of a word. For example, the Spell Checker won't notify you that you typed *your* when you meant to say *you're*. The moral of the story: Just like Mr. Smarty Pants in grade school, the Spell Checker isn't nearly as smart as you may have been led to believe. And running the Spell Checker is no substitute for proofreading your document.

Even so, running the Spell Checker before you print or save your finished copy is always a good idea. WordPerfect will likely turn up some typos or misspellings that you missed.

If you want to be notified of incorrect spellings as you type, turn on the Spell-As-You-Go feature (choose Tools⇨Spell-As-You-Go). WordPerfect underscores any misspelled word with a red, striped line after you type it. You can fix the word on the spot or correct it later. Right-click on the word to display a QuickMenu of suggested spellings. Personally, I find the feature distracting, but you may like it.

Here's how to give your document the spelling test:

1. **Make sure that no text is selected.**

   If you have text selected, WordPerfect checks only the selected text.

   If you want to check only a portion of your document, of course, select it first. Alternatively, after you start the spell checker, you can choose one of the Check options in the Spell Checker dialog box, shown in the upcoming Figure 9-7. Your choices include checking the entire document, checking from the insertion marker to the end of the document, checking a single page, a range of pages, a paragraph, or a sentence.

2. **Press Ctrl+F1 or click on the Spell Checker toolbar button.**

   The button is near the right end of the toolbar and looks like an open book with an *S* and a checkmark on it. Get it — *S*-check? You can also start the Spell Checker by choosing Tools⇨Spell Check.

   However you choose the command, the Spell Checker window opens, as shown in Figure 9-7. WordPerfect finds and highlights the first misspelled or duplicated word and places it in the Not Found box of the Spell Checker window. The Replace With box shows WordPerfect's suggested correction, and the Replacements list offers other possible corrections.

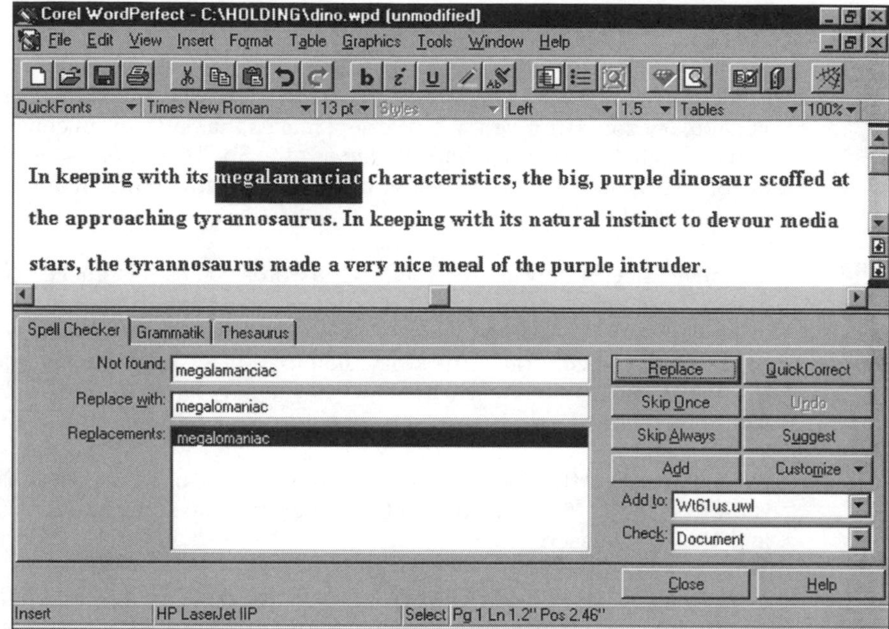

Figure 9-7: WordPerfect's Spell Checker happily points out any incorrectly spelled or duplicated words and even suggests possible corrections.

3. **Tell WordPerfect to replace, ignore, or add the word.**

   - To replace the misspelled word with the word in the Replace With box, click on the Replace button. If you want to replace the misspelled word with some other word, type it into the Replace With box or choose it from the Replacements list box. To see whether WordPerfect has any additional suggestions for a replacement word, click on the Suggest button.
   - Alternatively, you can click inside your document to make it active again and edit the word yourself. Click inside the Spell Checker window and click on Resume when you're ready to start checking more words.
   - WordPerfect only knows the words that have been included in its internal dictionary — which means that Spell Checker will mark as incorrect many words that are really okay. To tell WordPerfect to ignore this particular word and move on to the next misspelled word, click on Skip Once. To tell it to ignore this word throughout the rest of the document, click on Skip Always. To add the word to the WordPerfect dictionary, click on Add.

   - By default, WordPerfect checks words that contain numbers, checks for duplicate words, and checks for incorrect capitalization. If you don't want it to do any or all of these things, click on the Customize button and turn off the options in the resulting drop-down list.

After WordPerfect finishes grading your spelling, it asks whether you want to close the Spell Checker window. Click on Yes to close the window or No to leave it open and available for your next spelling session. If you leave the window open, click on the Start button to check more text.

You can resize the window by dragging its top edge up or down. You can also move it to another position on the screen by placing the cursor near the top of the window until the cursor becomes a little hand. When you see the hand, you can drag the window.

Part III
Crunching Numbers like a (Quattro) Pro

"I TELL YA I'M STILL GETTING INTERFERENCE—
- COOKIE, RAGS? RAGS WANNA COOKIE? -
THERE IT GOES AGAIN."

In this part . . .

In the interest of keeping everyone thoroughly confused, computer industry bigwigs like to give things obscure, meaningless names. Take Quattro Pro, for example. Loosely translated, *quattro* means *four* in some long-forgotten language. So it follows that Quattro Pro makes you a professional at . . . four?

The real story behind Quattro Pro's name has to do with a marketing ploy to unseat a rival program, Lotus 1-2-3. (Get it — four is one better than 3?) Well, at least that's the rumored reason, and it seems as plausible as any.

As you dive into this part of the book, I recommend that you don't waste another minute worrying about why Quattro Pro was given such a name. Concentrate instead on what this terrific program can do for you: build tables, do mathematical calculations, turn ordinary numbers into impressive charts, and generally help you keep track of and calculate any kind of data, from your annual sales figures to your household budget. Come to think of it, that's *four* things that Quattro Pro does well . . . hmm.

Chapter 10

The Spreadsheet Solution

In This Chapter

- Avoiding math by using spreadsheets
- Starting and closing Quattro Pro
- Getting familiar with the spreadsheet window
- Moving around in your spreadsheet
- Customizing the on-screen display
- Creating, opening, and closing spreadsheets
- Saving your work

I *hate* math. If you want me to add, multiply, subtract, or divide, you darn well better give me a good reason — and a calculator. Numbers and I just don't get along — never have, never will.

If you share my aversion to things mathematical, you'll love Quattro Pro. "But," you ask, "isn't math one of the main things you *do* with Quattro Pro?" Yep. Sure is. And that's why I appreciate this program so much. Any time a project involving lots of calculations rears its ugly head, I just crank up Quattro Pro. I get the answers I need in no time, without having to tax my numerically-challenged brain.

Of course, if you're the sort who gets all giddy when presented with a fresh column of numbers to add — you sicko — you'll like Quattro Pro even more. One of the top spreadsheet programs on the market, Quattro Pro gives you advanced mathematical features you've only dreamed about until now.

This chapter gets you started on the road to spreadsheet heaven by explaining the basics of the Quattro Pro spreadsheet window and showing you how to open, close, and save your work.

So What Can I Do with This Thing?

As mentioned in Chapter 1, Quattro Pro is a whiz at figuring out the answers to any problem that involves numbers. This program is also a handy financial record-keeping tool. Here are some of the different types of projects you can manage with Quattro Pro:

- **Keep a household or business budget.** You can record your monthly expenses by category — rent, gas, utilities, and so on. You can then have Quattro Pro calculate your total monthly expenses, quarterly expenses, year-to-date expenses, and your actual expenses versus your annual budget forecast.
- **Perform a profit and loss analysis.** You can determine the net return on your company's latest product given various pricing and manufacturing scenarios. You can easily try out different price points, for example, to determine which pricing structure will net you the most profit considering your production, marketing, and distribution costs.
- **Track business sales and inventories.** You can record the monthly sales for each item you sell and then calculate the totals of all items in a certain category, figure out your net profit on different items, keep track of your remaining inventory, and even determine the top salesperson in your store for a particular month or quarter.
- **Create tables of information.** You can create a list of vendor names, phone numbers, addresses, and products. Quattro Pro makes it easy to enter and format table data.
- **Create charts to present financial information.** After you create an income and expense spreadsheet, for example, you can create a pie chart showing expenses by category, so you can easily see where your money goes each month. You can print your charts from Quattro Pro or put them in a WordPerfect document or Presentations slide show.

In other words, if your project involves many different pieces of data or lots of calculations, Quattro Pro can help you get the job done with less effort and in less time than if you were to attempt your calculations with a piece of paper and a desktop calculator. Quattro Pro also gives you a painless way to turn on-screen spreadsheets into professional-looking printed reports. You'll look for all the world like you really know what you're doing.

Don't get confused over the various terms used for *spreadsheet.* Quattro Pro calls spreadsheets *notebooks,* but they're spreadsheets just the same. You may also hear a spreadsheet referred to as a *worksheet, sheet, document,* or *file.*

Start It Up, Shut It Down

Starting Quattro Pro is just like starting any other program in the WordPerfect Suite: Click on the Quattro Pro DAD icon or click on the Windows 95 Start button, click on the WordPerfect Suite 7 item, and then choose Quattro Pro from the Suite submenu. The Quattro Pro opening screen, shown in the upcoming Figure 10-1, comes to life. (The next section details the various bells and whistles of the Quattro Pro screen.)

To call it a day and send Quattro Pro packing, click on the program window's Close button (it's that little button with the X, in the top-right corner of the screen) or choose File⇨Exit. If you haven't saved your work yet, Quattro Pro prompts you to do so. (Saving is explained later in this chapter, in the section "Open Me! Close Me! Save Me!")

You can switch back and forth between Quattro Pro and other open programs by using the buttons on the Windows 95 taskbar. For more info on switching between open programs, see Chapter 2.

Your Field Guide to a Spreadsheet

When you first start Quattro Pro, you get a brand new spreadsheet, contained in its very own spreadsheet window, as shown in Figure 10-1. Most elements in the Quattro Pro program window and the spreadsheet window are standard Windows elements. (You can find more information about Windows elements in Chapter 2, in the section "Doing Windows.") But a few elements are unique to Quattro Pro and call for some explanation:

- Like WordPerfect, Quattro Pro offers a *Power Bar* that enables you to quickly select some popular formatting options, such as font, type size, and text alignment.
- You can zoom in or out on your work by choosing a zoom percentage from the *Zoom Factor* drop-down list on the far-right end of the Power Bar.

  If you want to focus on a particular area of your spreadsheet, select that area first and choose the Selection option. Quattro Pro enlarges or reduces the selected cells to fill the available screen space.

- That big, white, grid-like thing that consumes most of the window is a *notebook page*. Each spreadsheet you create contains 256 notebook pages, which are actually 256 individual spreadsheets. You'll probably never use all 256 pages, but it sure is nice to know you can if you want to, isn't it?
- After the 256 notebook pages comes the *Objects* page, which is a special page used for charts and other special objects you can create but probably won't (such as custom dialog boxes). The Objects page is discussed more fully in Chapter 14, in the section "Editing a Chart."

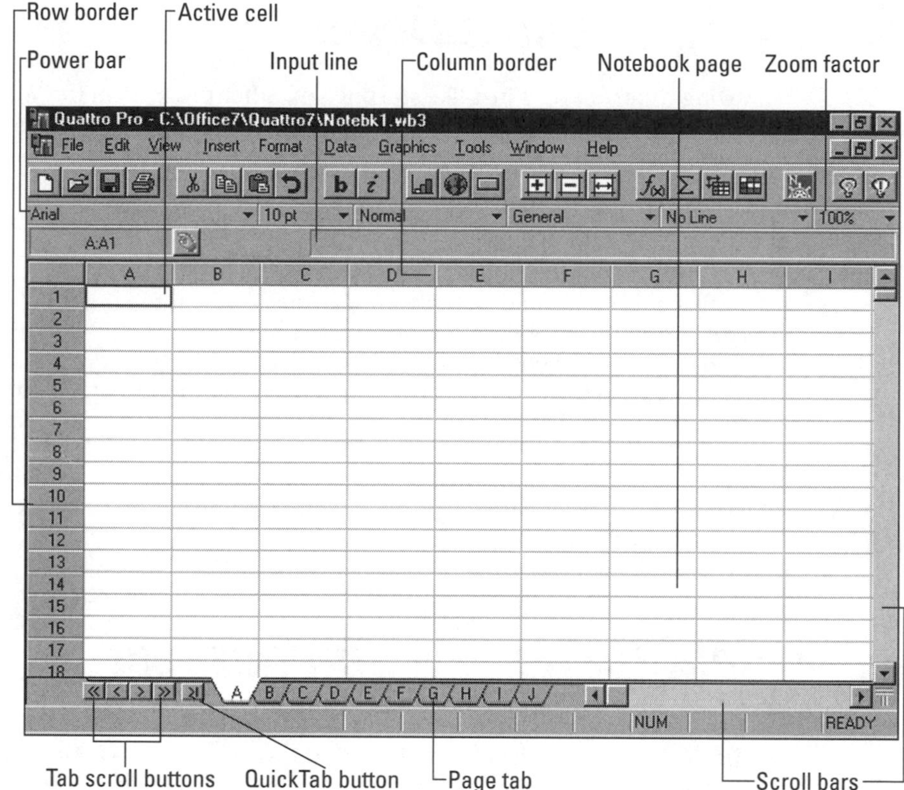

Figure 10-1: The Quattro Pro window is packed with tools to make an accountant's heart soar.

- A notebook page is divided into *columns* and *rows.* Columns are identified by the letters on the *Column border,* and rows are identified by the numbers on the *Row border.* Each notebook page has an incredible 8,192 rows and 256 columns. But you needn't feel compelled to use them all (and if you do feel so compelled, please seek psychiatric help immediately).
- The little boxes created by the intersection of a column and a row are called *cells.* You enter your spreadsheet data into the cells.
- Each cell has a unique *cell address* (name) that includes its notebook page followed by its column letter and row number. For example, the cell in the top-left corner of the notebook in Figure 10-1 is cell A:A1.
- The black border around a cell indicates the *active cell* — where the next piece of data you enter will appear. The active cell in Figure 10-1 is cell A:A1.
- Just beneath the Power Bar is the *Input line*. The Input line shows the data in the active cell. You can enter and edit data either in the Input line or directly in a cell. The address of the active cell is displayed at the far-left end of the Input line.

- To move from page to page in your notebook, you can click on the *page tabs* or use the *tab scroll buttons.* From left to right, the buttons are: Go back several pages; move backward one page; move forward one page; and move forward several pages.
- The *QuickTab button* takes you to the Objects page. Click on the button again to return to the last active spreadsheet page.
- The scroll bars on the right and bottom sides of the window scroll your view of the current notebook page. If you drag the scroll box on the vertical scroll bar, a little box displays row numbers as you move to let you know how far you're going. If you drag the horizontal scroll box, Quattro Pro displays column letters as you scroll.

If you can't remember what a particular button does, just pause your mouse cursor on it for a few seconds. A little flag called a *QuickTip* appears to give you some helpful hints about what the button does.

I Don't Like What I See Here!

You can alter some aspects of the Quattro Pro display to suit your preferences. See the section "Customizing Your View" in Chapter 2 for more information on fiddling with your screens. Some settings affect the display of the overall Quattro Pro window, and others affect the way certain elements of the current notebook page appear.

Changing the window display

Choose View⇨Display Options to open the Display dialog box, shown in Figure 10-2.

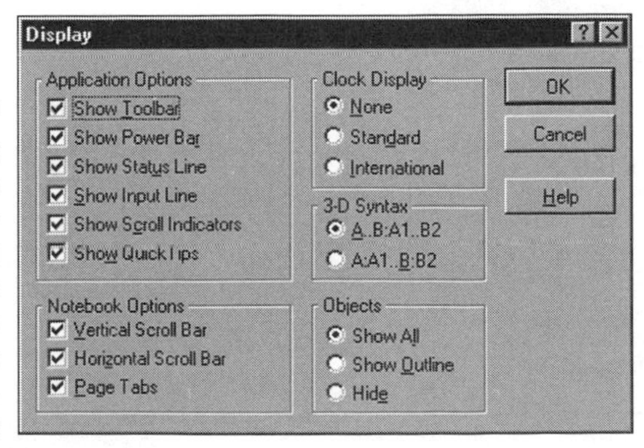

Figure 10-2: You can control how certain parts of the Quattro Pro screen appear.

The dialog box is full of preference settings that enable you to do the following:

- Customize the clock display.
- Hide or display the scroll bars and page tabs.
- Hide or display the toolbar, Power Bar, Status line, Input line, scroll indicators, and QuickTips.
- Control the display of objects such as charts and graphs. If you choose Show All, these objects display in their entirety. If you choose Show Outline, you see only the outline of the object — this option can speed up screen display if you use very complex objects. The Hide option, none too surprisingly, hides objects from view.

You can also change the 3-D Syntax, but don't. The default setting (the first radio button) is fine.

You can access some of these same settings by choosing Edit⇨Preferences to open the Application dialog box, and then clicking on the Display tab. You can get to some of the other preference settings by choosing Format⇨Notebook and clicking on the Display tab. Quattro Pro believes in giving you plenty of ways to do the same thing just in case you get bored with the routine.

Changing the active page display

If you choose Format⇨Page or right-click on the page tab, you can open the Active Page dialog box, shown in Figure 10-3. On the Display tab of the dialog box, you can control how certain parts of your spreadsheet appear.

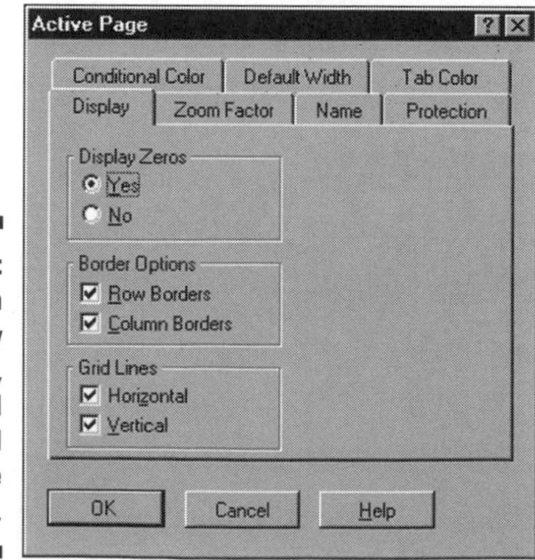

Figure 10-3: You can control how zeros, borders, grid lines, and even page tabs appear.

- The Display Zeros options determine whether Quattro Pro displays a zero in a cell that has a value of zero or simply leaves the cell blank.
- You can turn row and column borders on and off by using the Border Options. If an option is checked, it's turned on.
- You can hide or display the horizontal and vertical grid lines that separate the cells in your spreadsheet.

Want to add a little color to your view? You can change the color of a page tab by right-clicking on it and clicking on the Tab Color tab of the Active Page dialog box. Then uncheck the Use System Color option box and click on the drop-down list directly beneath the option box to display a palette of available colors. Click on the color you want to use and then click on OK.

Naming Your Pages

When you first open a new spreadsheet, Quattro Pro assigns a letter to each page in the notebook. The first page is page A, the second is page B, and so on. The page tabs at the bottom of the spreadsheet window reflect the page names.

However, you can give a page a different name if you want. For example, if you put your June sales data on page 1, you can name that page June (or something more inventive, if you're in the mood). Naming your pages makes it a little easier to remember what sort of data you're keeping on each page.

To name (or rename) a spreadsheet page, simply double-click on the page tab, type the name, and press Enter. Or right-click on the page tab to display the Active Page dialog box, click on the Name tab of the dialog box, enter the new page name in the Page Name option box, and click on OK or press Enter.

If you rename your pages, remember to use the new name in your cell addresses when entering formulas, as discussed in Chapter 12, in the section, "Typing formulas using cell addresses."

Ways to Move from Here to There

You can navigate your spreadsheet in numerous ways:

- To make a cell active (so that you can enter data into it), just click on the cell.
- To scroll the screen display so that you can view another portion of the current notebook page, use the horizontal or vertical scroll bars. If you drag the scroll boxes, a box appears to indicate your position in the spreadsheet as you scroll.

My spreadsheet's in 3-D? Cool!

You may hear Quattro Pro and other advanced spreadsheet programs referred to as *3-D spreadsheets.* But this kind of 3-D is different from the kind you get when you wear those funky 3-D glasses at the movies.

Each spreadsheet you create in Quattro Pro is really 256 separate spreadsheets stacked like pages in a notebook. On any page, you can calculate in two dimensions — that is, you can calculate data in horizontal rows and in vertical columns. But you can also calculate in a third dimension, which in this case happens to be up and down through the stack of notebook pages.

Confused? Don't be. This 3-D business simply means that in addition to calculating data you enter in one notebook page, you can calculate data entered in many different notebook pages. For example, say that page A of your notebook contains your monthly sales activity for January: how many units you sold of each item, the price of each item, your cost for each item, the date of the sale, and the total sales for the month. Page B contains the same information for February, and page C contains the data for March. With Quattro Pro, you can create a fourth page that takes the data from pages A, B, and C, and calculates all the sales information on a quarterly basis.

Before the days of 3-D spreadsheets, you could only calculate data contained in a single spreadsheet page, which meant that spreadsheets could quickly become very large and cumbersome. The real benefit of a 3-D spreadsheet is that you can segment your spreadsheet into more easily managed, easily updated, and easily viewed chunks of data.

And you don't even have to wear special glasses to see your results.

- To move from page to page, use the page tabs or the tab scroll buttons, as discussed in the section "Your Field Guide to a Spreadsheet," earlier in this chapter.
- To move to a specific cell, press Ctrl+G or choose Edit⇨Go To. Quattro Pro displays the Go To dialog box shown in Figure 10-4. Enter the cell address in the Reference option box and press Enter or click on OK. Type the cell address in this order: notebook page, colon, column number, and cell number — as in A:F238. You probably won't want to use this method of moving to a cell unless you need to find a cell that's buried deep in your spreadsheet or is way off-screen; otherwise, it's quicker to use the mouse and the scroll arrows.
- You can also navigate your spreadsheet by using the handy-dandy keyboard shortcuts outlined in Table 10-1.

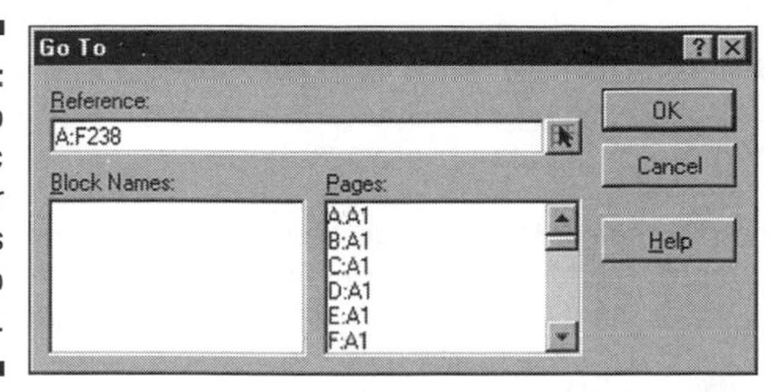

Figure 10-4: To move to a specific cell, enter its address in the Go To dialog box.

Table 10-1 Keys That Really Move You

Press This	*To Do This*
↑ (Up arrow)	Move up one cell
↓ (Down arrow)	Move down one cell
→ (Right arrow) or Tab	Move right one cell
← (Left arrow) or Shift+Tab	Move left one cell
Home	Go to the first cell on the current notebook page
Ctrl+Home	Go to the first cell on the first page of the notebook
Ctrl+← (left arrow)	Scroll left one screen
Ctrl+→ (right arrow)	Scroll right one screen
PgDn	Scroll one screen down
PgUp	Scroll one screen up

Open Me! Close Me! Save Me!

Opening, closing, and saving files in Quattro Pro is handled pretty much the same way as in any Windows 95 program. But here's the skinny on each job, just in case you need a refresher.

Opening a new or existing notebook

To create a new notebook, choose File⇨New, press Ctrl+N, or click on the New Notebook toolbar button (it's the one that looks like a blank sheet of paper, on the far-left end of the toolbar). If you click on the toolbar button, Quattro Pro gives you a new blank notebook. If you choose File⇨New or press Ctrl+N, Quattro Pro gives you the option to create a blank notebook or to create a notebook based on one of its QuickTemplates.

QuickTemplates produce spreadsheets that already contain some formatting and data used to handle some common tasks, such as household budgets and business forms. Quattro Pro even offers a QuickTemplate for tracking your fitness regime and another for planning your vacation.

To create a blank notebook, select the Plain Notebook radio button. To use a template, click on the From QuickTemplate radio button and then select a template in the QuickTemplates list. Click on OK to create your new spreadsheet.

To open an existing notebook, choose File⇨Open, press Ctrl+O, or click on the Open Notebook toolbar button (it's right next to the New button and looks like an opening file folder). Quattro Pro answers your command by displaying the Open File dialog box, shown in Figure 10-5.

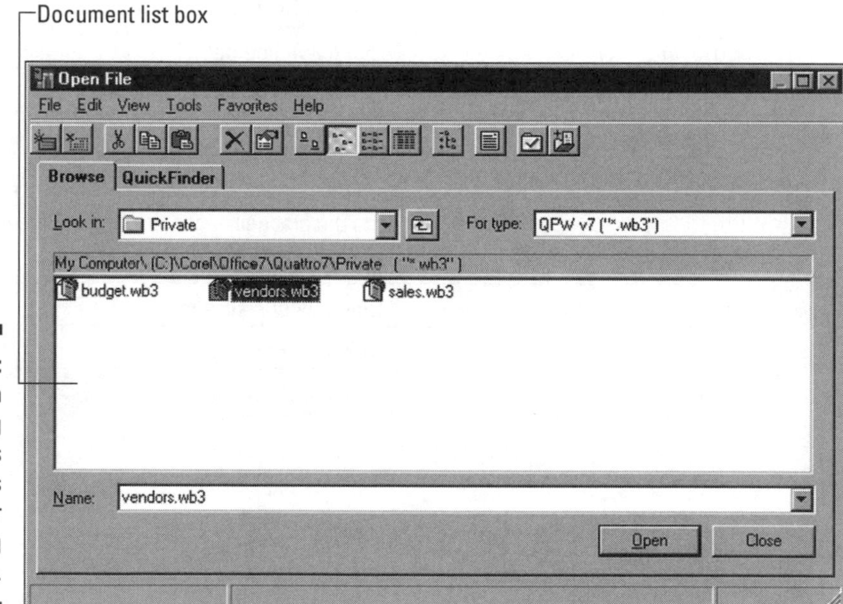

Figure 10-5: The Open File dialog box gives you access to all your existing spreadsheets.

The Open File dialog box looks and works the same as the WordPerfect Open dialog box discussed in Chapter 5. Here's a recap:

- Enter the name of the notebook you want to open in the Name option box and click on Open or double-click on the name in the document list box.
- If you don't see the notebook you want in the scrolling file list, hunt through the various folders and drives using the Look In drop-down list. For more information on how folders work, see the section "Figuring out the Open dialog box" in Chapter 5.

- If you still don't see the file you want, you may need to change the file type in the For Type option box. Files that you create and save in Quattro Pro 7 end with the letters WB3. If you want to open a file that you created in an earlier version of Quattro Pro or in another spreadsheet program, select that program's file type from the drop-down list. Quattro Pro can open many different types of files, including spreadsheets created in Microsoft Excel, and Lotus 1-2-3, as well as database files created in Paradox and dBASE.

Closing a spreadsheet

To close a spreadsheet, click on the spreadsheet window's Close button (it's the little button with an X at the far-right end of the menu bar). Or choose File⇨Close or press Ctrl+W. (You can also use the standard Windows shortcut, Ctrl+F4.) Quattro Pro gives you a gentle reminder to save your work if you haven't done so yet. Saving is the subject of the very next section.

Saving your work

Saving early — and saving often — is essential to keeping your sanity. If you don't save your work, your efforts can go up in electronic smoke when you shut down Quattro Pro, if the power goes out for some reason, or if your computer crashes just to see what kind of response it can get from you.

To save your spreadsheet for the first time, choose File⇨Save, press Ctrl+S, or click on the Save Notebook toolbar button (it looks like a little floppy disk). Quattro Pro leaps to attention and shows you the Save File dialog box, shown in Figure 10-6.

If the Save command is dimmed, click anywhere on your spreadsheet page and then try again.

Here's the step-by-step procedure for saving a spreadsheet for the first time:

1. **Choose the folder where you want to store the spreadsheet.**

   If you want to store the spreadsheet to a drive or folder other than the one that appears in the Save In option box, choose your preferred drive or folder from the Save In drop-down list.

2. **Enter a name for the spreadsheet in the Name option box.**

   For the inside track on file naming rules, see the sidebar "What's in a (Windows 95) filename?" in Chapter 5.

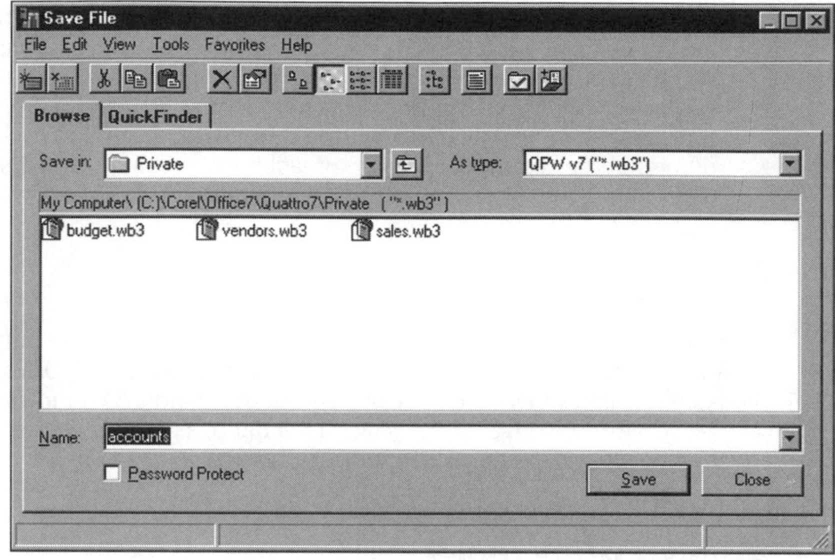

Figure 10-6: Unless you want all your work to disappear when you shut down your computer, don't forget to save your spreadsheet.

If you try to give your spreadsheet a name that's already in use, Quattro Pro alerts you and asks whether you really want to proceed with that name. If you say yes, Quattro Pro replaces the spreadsheet you previously saved under that name with your new spreadsheet.

3. **Choose a file type from the As Type drop-down list.**

   If you created the file in Quattro Pro 7 and you want to save it as a Quattro Pro 7 file, choose the QPW v7 ("*.wb3") option. If you want to save the file in some other format, such as one used by an earlier version of Quattro Pro or another spreadsheet program (such as Excel or Lotus 1-2-3), choose that file format from the drop-down list.

   If you save to a file format used by another spreadsheet program, be aware that you may be able to save only the current page of your spreadsheet. Quattro Pro alerts you if the file format can't save multiple-page spreadsheets.

4. **Click on Save or press Enter.**

Saving a document once doesn't protect you forever. If you make any changes to your spreadsheet, those changes aren't saved until you choose the File⇨Save command again. To resave your work, just choose the Save command from the File menu, press Ctrl+S, or click on the Save Notebook toolbar button. Quattro Pro quickly resaves the spreadsheet without bothering you with the Save File dialog box.

If you want to save your spreadsheet under a different name, to a different folder or drive, or in a different file format, choose the File⇨Save As command instead of the regular Save command. Quattro Pro gives you the Save File dialog box, where you can choose a new name, folder, drive, or format. Note that when you're finished, you'll have two copies of your spreadsheet — one saved with the old name, drive, folder, and so on, and one saved with the new. If you don't have any more need for the first spreadsheet you saved, delete that original spreadsheet in order to avoid possible confusion later.

To protect yourself even further, turn on Quattro Pro's automatic save feature. Choose Edit⇨Preferences to display the Application dialog box and click on the File Options tab. Specify an interval for the Auto-backup Time option and check the Activate option box, as shown in Figure 10-7. From now on, Quattro Pro will automatically save your document at the interval you specified. If your computer crashes or some other unexpected event causes your system to shut down, Quattro Pro can recover most of what you were working on at the time of the crash. When you restart the program, it asks you for permission to recover the open files; by all means, give your okay.

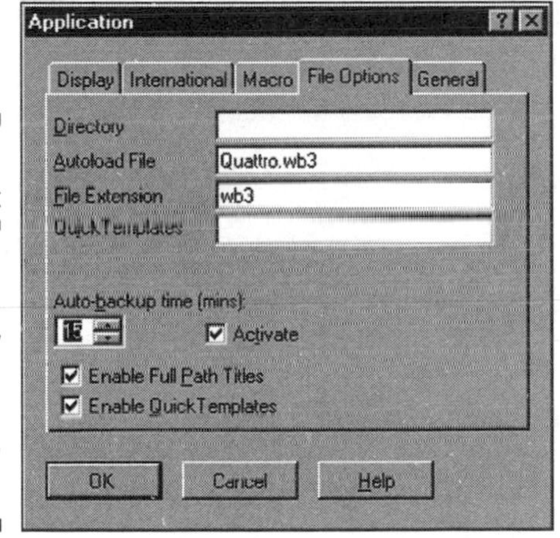

Figure 10-7: Protect yourself from unexpected crashes by turning on the Auto-backup feature.

Chapter 11
Filling in the Blanks

In This Chapter

- Taking the spreadsheet plunge
- Entering values and labels — and knowing which is which
- Learning Quattro Pro data-entry rules
- Letting QuickFill enter data for you
- Applying basic formatting

When you first start Quattro Pro, it graciously presents you with a sparkling new notebook filled with 256 pristine spreadsheet pages. What Quattro Pro doesn't do is give you any hints about what to do next. Where do you start? How do you get from these rows and rows of empty cells to a spreadsheet that actually does something?

Well, try this: Press your forehead up to your computer screen, close your eyes, and chant "Spreadsheet, spreadsheet, spreadsheet" in a loud falsetto voice. Rumor has it that if you do this long and hard enough, Quattro Pro will divine your problem and build your spreadsheet for you.

Didn't work? Hmm, guess that rumor was off the mark. Fortunately, though, this chapter tells you everything you need to know to start turning that blank notebook page into a working spreadsheet.

Building a Spreadsheet

Before you get into the nitty-gritty of entering data into your spreadsheet, you need a basic understanding of the process of building a spreadsheet.

Take a look at Figure 11-1. It shows a spreadsheet that calculates the total sales and profits for one day — June 15, as indicated on the page tab. The approach I used to create this spreadsheet is the same approach you use to create any spreadsheet:

Formula for cell G2

Cell G2

Quattro Pro - C:\Office7\Quattro7\Notebk6.wb3

File Edit View Insert Format Data Graphics Tools Window Help

Arial | 10 pt | Currency | General | No Line | 121%

June 15:G2 | +E2-F2

	A	B	C	D	E	F	G
1		Units Sold	Unit Price	Unit Cost	Total Revenue	Total Cost	Net Profit
2	Jackets	4	$34.99	$16.99	$139.96	$67.96	$72.00
3	Shorts	20	$9.95	$4.55	$199.00	$91.00	$108.00
4	Socks	12	$4.99	$1.99	$59.88	$23.88	$36.00
5	Sweatbands	15	$3.99	$1.15	$59.85	$17.25	$42.60
6	T-Shirts	14	$14.95	$8.25	$209.30	$115.50	$93.80
7	Totals	65	$68.87	$32.93	$667.99	$315.59	$352.40
8							
9							
10							
11							
12							
13							

June 15 B C D E F G H I

NUM READY

Figure 11-1: Quattro Pro makes it easy to calculate the day's total sales and profits.

1. **Enter the column and row labels.**

   I'm referring to the category names found at the top of each column and the beginning of each row. In Figure 11-1, the column labels are Units Sold, Unit Price, and so on, and the row labels are Jackets, Shorts, Socks, and so on.

2. **Enter the known values.**

   Next, enter the known data — that is, the data that already exists and doesn't require any calculating by Quattro Pro. In Figure 11-1, for example, the known values are the units sold, the unit price, and the unit cost.

3. **Enter the formulas for the values you want Quattro Pro to find.**

   In Chapter 10, I say that you don't need to do any math to use Quattro Pro. Well, that's not completely true. You don't need to do the actual calculations — the addition, the multiplication, and so on — but you do need to enter the basic mathematical formulas that you want Quattro Pro to solve. But cheer up — if I can do it, you can, too. Really. Just ask my accountant.

In Figure 11-1, I entered three different formulas: one to calculate the total revenue received from each item (Units Sold multiplied by Unit Price); one to calculate the total cost of each item (Units Sold multiplied by Unit Cost); and one to calculate the total profit of the day's sales (Total Revenue minus Total Cost). In Figure 11-1, the Input line shows the actual formula used to calculate the value in cell G2. (Chapter 12 explains how to write and enter formulas, by the way.)

4. **Edit and format your data.**

   After you enter your initial data, you'll no doubt find things that you want to fix. Chapter 13 shows you how to edit your data.

   You find out how to do basic formatting, such as making your data boldface or italic, at the end of this chapter. Chapters 14 and 15 explain how to add graphs and put the finishing formatting touches on your data. Chapter 15 also shows you how to print your spreadsheet.

In reality, you won't always perform these steps in this order. You may find it easier to format your data as you enter it, for example. But the basic steps involved remain the same whether you're creating a simple spreadsheet like the one in Figure 11-1 or developing some mondo-complex thing that would turn Albert Einstein green with envy.

Entering Data

As explained in Chapter 10, spreadsheet data goes into *cells* — those little squares created by the intersection of a row and a column. You can enter two types of data in Quattro Pro:

- A *label* is a text entry, such as a column title and a row title. Labels can actually contain numbers as well as letters (as in the label *1st Quarter,* for example).
- A *value* is a number or a formula.

I bring up this techno-nerd issue only because Quattro Pro treats labels a little differently from values, as you discover at the end of this section.

Basic data entry

To enter data — whether it's a label or a value — into a cell, just do this:

1. **Click on the cell where you want to put the data.**

   You enter data into the *active cell,* which is the one surrounded by the little black box. Clicking on a cell makes it active.

2. **Type the value or label.**

   When you begin typing, Quattro Pro displays an insertion marker that indicates where the next character you type will appear, as shown in Figure 11-2. The mouse cursor also changes to the I-beam cursor. The data you type appears both in the cell and in the Input line, as shown in the figure.

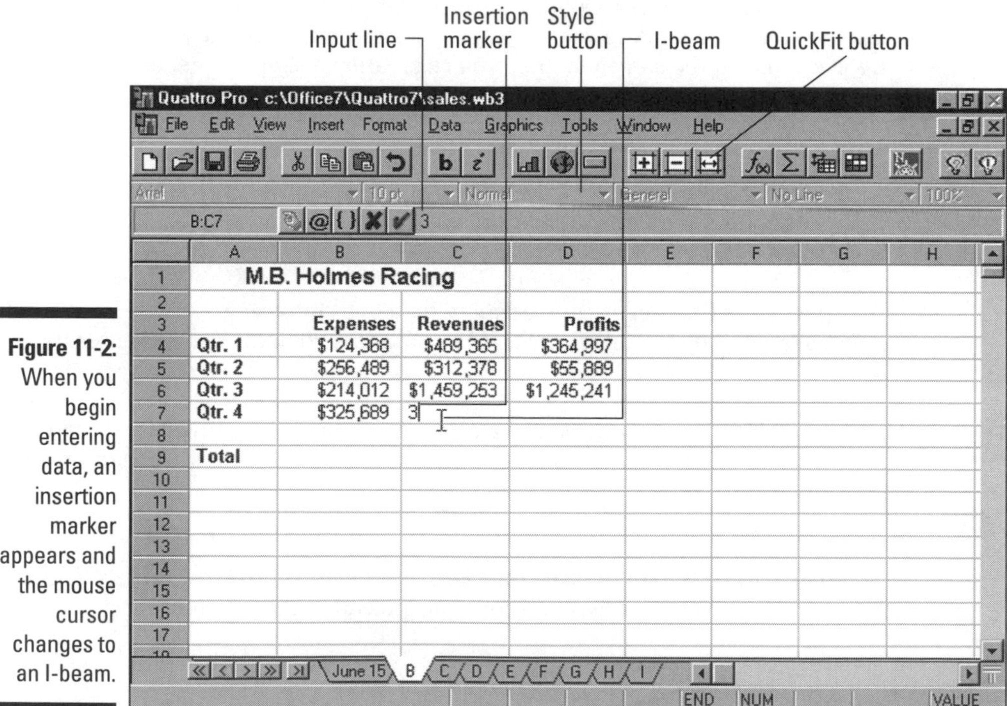

Figure 11-2: When you begin entering data, an insertion marker appears and the mouse cursor changes to an I-beam.

If you make a mistake as you type, press the Backspace key to erase characters to the left of the insertion marker. Or use any of the other editing techniques discussed in Chapter 13. (The specifics of entering formulas are covered in Chapter 12.)

3. Press Enter or make another cell active.

To complete your data entry, press the Enter key. Or move to another cell by clicking on it or using one of the other navigation keys listed in Table 10-1 (in Chapter 10).

If you enter a formula, as covered in Chapter 12, Quattro Pro displays the results of its calculations in the cell and not the formula itself. The formula appears in the Input line.

Basically, that's all there is to entering data. But a few things may trip you up:

- If you see a row of asterisks or some other weird characters in the cell after you press Enter, the cell is too small to hold the value you entered. Chapter 13 explains how to precisely resize cells, columns, and rows. But for a quick fix, click on the cell and click on the QuickFit button on the toolbar (labeled in Figure 11-2).
- If a label is too long to fit in a cell, it spills over into the neighboring cell. But if that neighboring cell contains an entry, Quattro Pro hides the part of the label that won't fit. The data's still in there — but it won't display or print properly until you fix things. Again, you can use the editing approaches explained in Chapter 13 or just click on the QuickFit button.
- When you enter a value or label, Quattro Pro automatically formats it according to the current style, which is displayed on the Style button on the Power Bar — labeled back in Figure 11-2. (The button is grayed out in the figure because the option is unavailable when you're entering data.) In some cases, the style can change what you enter into the cell. If the Normal style is active and you enter **9.00**, for example, Quattro Pro automatically changes your entry to just **9**, which complies with the numeric formatting used by the Normal style. For information on how to change the style or numeric formatting, see the section "Handling Basic Formatting Chores," later in this chapter.

Data entry do's and don'ts

When you begin entering data into a cell, Quattro Pro furrows its brow and tries to determine whether you're entering a label or a value. Quattro Pro bases its guess on such things as whether you start the entry with a number and whether the entry contains any text.

If Quattro Pro guesses wrong, it may not do what you want with the data you entered. So if things seem wacky, enter the data again. But this time, take a look at the right end of the status bar before you press Enter. As shown back in Figure 11-2, the status bar displays the word LABEL or VALUE, depending on what Quattro Pro thinks you're entering. If the status bar doesn't match what you had in mind, check to see whether you broke any of the following taboos:

- If you type numbers *and* text in the same cell, Quattro Pro deems the entry a label. So don't make the mistake of trying to use the *O* (*oh*) key to enter a zero or press the letter *l* when you really want to enter a one.
- Don't use any spaces, commas, or currency symbols when you're entering values. If you do, Quattro Pro treats the data like a label rather than a value. (The exception is the dollar sign, which you can use without problems.)
- By Quattro Pro decree, labels can't start with the following punctuation marks: the plus sign (+), minus sign (-), dollar sign ($), left parentheses (( ), ampersand (&), period (.), pound sign (#), or equals sign (=). If you really, really want to start a label with one of these characters, you have to enter one of the following *label-prefix* characters at the start of the label: apostrophe ('), quotation mark ("), or caret (^). The apostrophe aligns the label with the left edge of the cell; the quotation mark aligns it with the right edge of the cell, and the caret centers the label in the cell. (Because these three punctuation marks serve as label-prefix characters, you shouldn't start a label with one of them, either.)

- If you're not a fanatic about whether your stuff lines up perfectly in your spreadsheet, you can just enter a space before your label text instead of trying to remember that apostrophe, quotation mark, and caret stuff.

- If the first character in the cell is a backslash (\), Quattro Pro repeats the characters that follow over and over to fill up the cell. In other words, if you enter \Hey!, Quattro Pro fills your cell with Hey!Hey!Hey! I'm not sure when or if you may find this feature helpful, but I thought you ought to know. (If you don't want the characters to repeat, enter a space before the backslash.)

QuickFilling Cells

Quattro Pro offers a neat feature called QuickFill that can speed up the entry of labels and values that fall in a sequence. Suppose that you want to fill the first 30 rows of Column A with the numbers 1 through 30 – to label the rows with the days of the month, for example. Instead of typing in each number, you can use the following technique and let Quattro Pro fill in the cells for you.

1. **Type the first label or value in the first cell you want to fill and press Enter.**
2. **Click and drag from the first cell over the rest of the cells you want to fill.**

   The cells should become highlighted (selected) as you drag, as shown in Column G of Figure 11-3. (If you see a little hand cursor rather than the highlighted cells, you're moving the cell contents rather than selecting the cells. Try again. This time, begin dragging a little quicker after you click on the first cell.)

QuickFill button

Quattro Pro - C:\Office7\Quattro7\Notebk2.wb3

A:G1 1996

	A	B	C	D	E	F	G
1	Client 1247	January	Monday	06/01	$10	Red	1996
2	Client 1248	February	Tuesday	06/02	$11	Green	
3	Client 1249	March	Wednesday	06/03	$12	Blue	
4	Client 1250	April	Thursday	06/04	$13	Yellow	
5	Client 1251	May	Friday	06/05	$14	Red	
6	Client 1252	June	Saturday	06/06	$15	Green	
7	Client 1253	July	Sunday	06/07	$16	Blue	
8	Client 1254	August	Monday	06/08	$17	Yellow	
9	Client 1255	September	Tuesday	06/09	$18	Red	
10	Client 1256	October	Wednesday	06/10	$19	Green	
11	Client 1257	November	Thursday	06/11	$20	Blue	
12	Client 1258	December	Friday	06/12	$21	Yellow	
13	Client 1259	January	Saturday	06/13	$22	Red	
14	Client 1260	February	Sunday	06/14	$23	Green	
15	Client 1261	March	Monday	06/15	$24	Blue	
16	Client 1262	April	Tuesday	06/16	$25	Yellow	
17	Client 1263	May	Wednesday	06/17	$26	Red	

Figure 11-3: QuickFill can automate the entry of values and labels that fall in sequence.

Note that the cell you filled in Step 1 should still be the active cell — that is, the one surrounded by the black outline box.

3. **Click on the QuickFill button (labeled in Figure 11-3).**

   Alternatively, you can right-click on the selected cells and choose QuickFill from the resulting QuickMenu. Either way, Quattro Pro fills your rows with the remaining numbers or words in the sequence.

Figure 11-3 shows several rows and columns that I filled using QuickFill. As you can see, you can QuickFill dates, months, and even a mixture of text and numbers.

You can create your own series, as I did in Column F in Figure 11-3, by typing all the elements of the series once. (In Column F, for example, I entered Red, Green, Blue, and Yellow in the first four cells.) After typing in the series once, click on the first cell in the series, drag from that cell to the last cell you want to fill, and click on the QuickFill button. Quattro Pro repeats the series as many times as necessary to fill the selected cells.

Another way to quickly fill cells is to copy the contents of one cell and paste the contents into other cells, as explained in Chapter 13.

Handling Basic Formatting Chores

Like WordPerfect, Quattro Pro uses *styles,* which apply certain basic formatting attributes, such as font, type size, and numeric format, to your data. The default style is Normal, which uses 10-point Arial type and the General numeric format. If you click on the Style button on the Power Bar (labeled back in Figure 11-2), you display a drop-down list of other styles that you can apply to selected cells.

You can override the Normal style — or any style — by applying different formatting to selected cells. The following sections tell you how to change the font, type size, type style, alignment, and numeric format of your data.

Before you can apply formatting to data in a cell, you must *select* the cell. To select a single cell, just click on it; to select a block of cells, drag over the cells or use one of the other techniques outlined in "Selecting Stuff" in Chapter 13.

Changing the numeric format

Many of the styles available by clicking on the Style button on the Power Bar affect the numeric format used for a cell — including the Currency, Currency0, and Percent styles. If the formatting applied by one of these styles doesn't suit your fancy, click on the cell you want to format (or select a range of cells) and press F12, choose Format⇨Block, or right-click and choose Block Properties from the resulting QuickMenu.

Quattro Pro leaps to attention and displays the Active Block dialog box, shown in Figure 11-4. The Numeric Format panel of the dialog box offers a variety of formatting options for numbers, dates, and times. When you click on some of the formatting radio buttons, options that enable you to get even more specific about the format appear. If you select the Currency option, for example, you can specify how many decimal places you want to include and select which country's currency standards you want to use. The little preview box in the bottom-right corner of the dialog box shows you how your data will look in the chosen format.

When you're satisfied with your choices, click on OK or press Enter to apply the format.

Changing the font, type size, and type style

By default, Quattro Pro uses 10-point Arial type for all your data. To change the font, select the data you want to format, click on the Font button on the Power Bar (it's at the far left end of the bar), and select a font from the drop-down list. To change the type size of selected data, click on the Size button, which hangs out right next door to the Font button, and select a size from the drop-down list.

Figure 11-4: You can specify exactly how you want Quattro Pro to format your numbers.

To change the type style of selected data —that is, to make it bold or italic — click on the **b** button (for bold) or the *i* button (for italic) on the toolbar. To remove boldface or italics from selected data, click on the button again.

You can also access the font, type size, and type style formatting attributes by choosing the Format⇨Block command (F12) to open the Active Block dialog box (shown in Figure 11-4) and then clicking on the Font tab. You may notice that you can apply two additional style attributes, underline and strikethrough, through this dialog box. But underlining data in a spreadsheet usually isn't a good idea, because the underlines can bump into the line you may use to separate your rows and columns of data (as explained in Chapter 15). Strikethrough is usually used to let people reviewing your spreadsheet know that you plan to delete certain data later — in other words, you probably won't have much call for this attribute, either.

Changing text alignment

One of the many formatting attributes contained in the Normal style is the horizontal alignment of data within the cell. The Normal style uses the General alignment option, which aligns labels with the left edge of the cell and aligns numbers, formulas, and dates to the right edge of the cell.

The Align button on the Power Bar displays a drop-down list offering five horizontal alignment options: General, Left, Right, Center, and Center Across. Figure 11-5 shows how labels and values are aligned using each option.

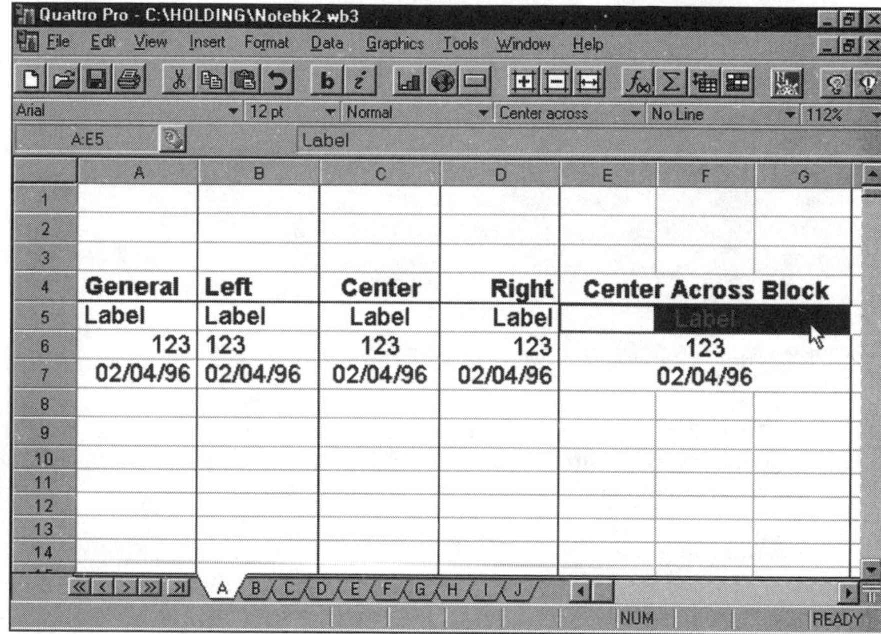

Figure 11-5: You can align data within a cell or center it across a block of cells.

To apply the General, Left, Right, or Center option, just select the cell or cells you want to format and then select the option from the drop-down list. The Center Across option, which centers the value or label within a specified number of cells, works a little differently. First, you need to enter the data in the leftmost cell of the block of cells you want to center the data across. In the highlighted example in Figure 11-5, I entered the data in cell E5. Next, select the cell that contains the data along with the rest of the block you want to center the data across. In Figure 11-5, I selected cells E5 through G5. Then select the Center Across option from the drop-down list.

To uncover still more alignment options, select the cell or cells you want to format and then press F12, choose the Format⇨Block command, or right-click and choose the Block Properties option from the resulting QuickMenu. When the Active Block dialog box appears, click on the Alignment tab to display the alignment options, as shown in Figure 11-6.

The Alignment tab contains the same horizontal alignment options found on the Align drop-down list on the Power Bar, plus the following options:

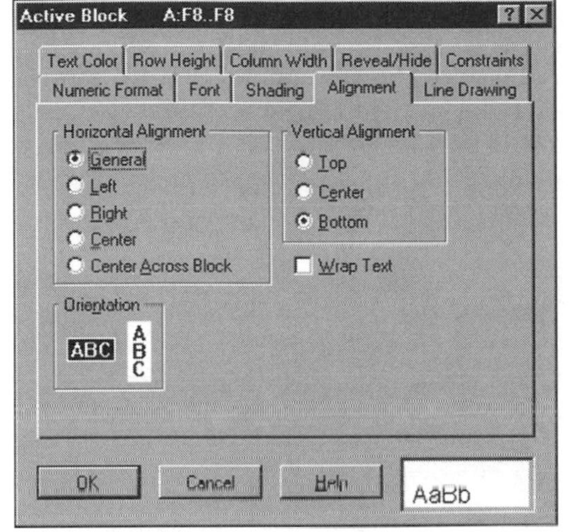

Figure 11-6: Click on the Alignment tab of the Active Block dialog box to see cell alignment options.

- You have three vertical alignment options. Top aligns the data with the top of the cell, Center places the data smack dab in the middle of the cell, and Bottom sinks the data to the bottom of the cell. The default is Bottom.
- When you turn on the Wrap Text option, Quattro Pro expands the cell vertically to accommodate any text that exceeds the width of the cell. It then wraps the overflow text to the next line in the cell. Figure 11-7 shows an example. By default, this setting is turned off.

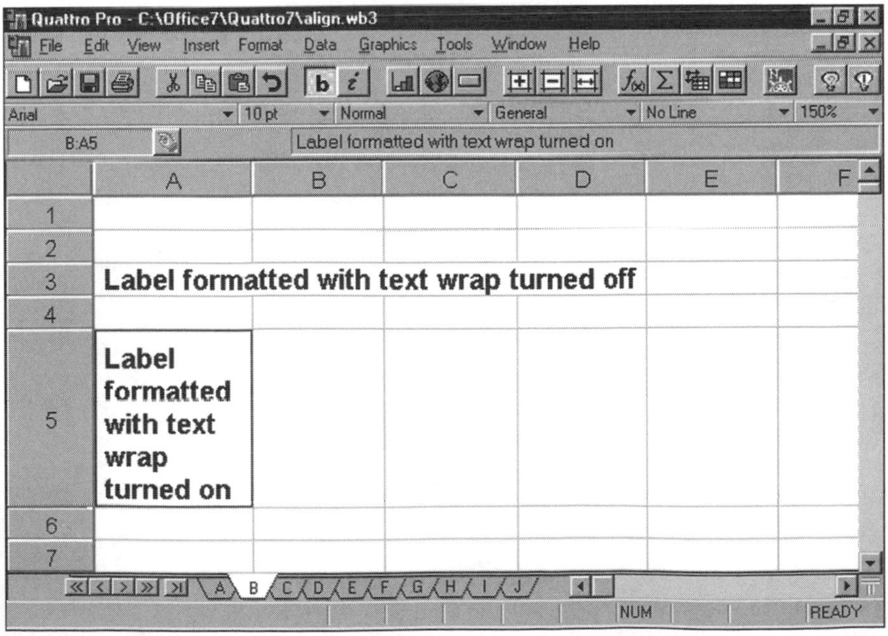

Figure 11-7: When text wrap is turned off, overflow text spills into neighboring cells (top). When text wrap is on, the cell expands and overflow text wraps to the next line (bottom).

- The Orientation options determine whether your text runs horizontally or vertically in the cell. As you can probably tell by looking at the two orientation options in Figure 11-6, the option on the left represents horizontal orientation and the one on the right represents vertical orientation. The default setting is horizontal orientation.

This chapter covers just the basic formatting you can do in Quattro Pro. For information on how to add even more spice to your spreadsheets, see Chapters 14 and 15.

Chapter 12

The Formula for Success

In This Chapter

- Understanding how formulas work
- Structuring your formulas
- Adding, subtracting, multiplying, and dividing
- Using absolute and relative cell addresses
- Using Quattro Pro's built-in formulas
- Naming your cells
- Resolving error messages

Remember back in algebra class, when you had to solve lots of inane problems involving *x* and *y* and two trains headed for the same station at different speeds? Well, if you really got into that sort of thing, you'll love this chapter, which shows you how to use those old algebra skills to write equations (a.k.a. *formulas*) for Quattro Pro to solve.

If, on the other hand, you spent most of your time in algebra class like I did, alternately wailing in frustration or complaining loudly that you didn't know why you needed to *know* this stuff anyway, then you may be turned off by the fact that Quattro Pro requires you to create formulas before it does any work for you. Don't be.

First of all, most formulas you'll use will be simple, involving basic addition, subtraction, multiplication, and division. Secondly, Quattro Pro offers some built-in formulas — called *functions* — that make it easy for you to create more complex equations.

Creating a Basic Formula

Writing a formula is like being back in algebra class — only this time, you're the teacher. You give Quattro Pro a formula to solve, and it does the math for you.

You can enter formulas in two ways: You can type the formula directly into the cell, or you can use the combination type-and-click approach. This section gives you the lowdown on both methods.

Typing formulas for simple calculations

You can use formulas to perform a simple calculation such as 45 + 87. To enter a formula such as this, do the following:

1. **Click on the cell where you want the *answer* to the calculation to appear.**

   As you type a formula, it's displayed in the cell. But after you press Enter in Step 3, Quattro Pro displays the answer to the formula in the cell and hides the formula itself.

2. **Type a plus sign (+) followed by your formula.**

   The plus sign tells Quattro Pro to be on the alert for a formula. If you wanted to enter the formula 45 + 87, for example, you would enter

   ```
   +45+87
   ```

   Formulas can also start with a parentheses, as discussed in the upcoming section "Telling Quattro Pro What to Calculate First," or with the function symbol (@), as covered in the section "Working with Built-in Functions."

3. **Press Enter.**

   You see the answer to the formula in the cell. The formula itself shows up in the Input line.

Typing formulas using cell addresses

Although you can use Quattro Pro to perform simple calculations such as the one discussed in the preceding section, more often than not, you want to perform some calculations on values that are stored in different cells in your spreadsheet. You can have Quattro Pro add the values in one row of cells, multiply that value by the value in another cell, and so on. You can even do calculations involving cells on different pages of your notebook.

Entering this kind of formula is no different than entering the formula described in the preceding steps. This time, however, you use cell addresses instead of actual numbers to identify the values you want to calculate.

Take a look at Figure 12-1. This simple spreadsheet calculates total bookstore sales for each quarter. To find the total for Quarter 1, you can enter the following formula into cell B9, where you want the total to appear:

```
+B4+B5+B6+B7+B8
```

The formula tells Quattro Pro to add the values in cells B4, B5, B6, B7, and B8. The totals in columns C, D, and E use the same formula, except with different cell addresses — C4, C5, and so on for column C, for example.

When you add a long row or column of numbers, you really don't have to type each cell address in the row, as in the preceding formula. Instead, you can use the much quicker @SUM function or QuickSum button, explained in the upcoming section, "Adding Things Up with QuickSum."

Suppose that after finding the quarterly sales totals in Figure 12-1, you want to calculate the total sales for all four quarters and put the result in cell F9. You would click on cell F9 and enter the following formula:

```
+B9+C9+D9+E9
```

If you then wanted to find the average quarterly sales for the year, you would use this formula:

```
+F9/4
```

Input line

Quattro Pro - C:\EXCELFIL\Notebk3.wb3

A:B9 +B4+B5+B6+B7+B8

	A	B	C	D	E
1	**Kristen's Bookstore**				
2					
3		**Qtr. 1**	**Qtr. 2**	**Qtr. 3**	**Qtr. 4**
4	**Adult Fiction**	$45,389	$52,782	$48,989	$65,982
5	**Adult Nonfiction**	$33,213	$32,004	$42,092	$45,192
6	**Children's Books**	$27,902	$32,892	$26,542	$38,943
7	**Periodicals**	$18,342	$16,754	$15,678	$22,800
8	**Other**	$10,892	$9,876	$7,890	$12,349
9	**Totals**	$135,738.00	$144,308.00	$141,191.00	$185,266.00

Figure 12-1: Cell B9 displays the results of the formula in the Input line.

The preceding formula tells Quattro Pro to divide the value in cell F9 (which contains the total sales for all four quarters) by 4. The slash is the symbol for division in Quattro Pro. Table 12-1 lists other mathematical symbols — called *operators* in spreadsheet country.

If you want to perform a calculation on cells contained on different pages of your notebook, you have to include the page name before the cell address in the formula. For example, to add the value of cell B9 on Page A to the value of cell B9 on Page B, you enter the formula:

```
+A:B9+B:B9
```

If you named your page, as explained in Chapter 10, in the section "Naming Your Pages," substitute that name in the cell address. For example, if page A has the name July and page B has the name August, you write the preceding formula like this:

```
+July:B9+August:B9
```

Table 12-1 Smooth Operators

Operator	*Function*
+	Addition
-	Subtraction
/	Division
*	Multiplication
%	Percentage
^	Exponentiation

Entering cell addresses with the mouse

If you're creating a long formula and you're weary of typing in cell addresses — this computing business is *such* hard work, after all — you can use the mouse and your clicker finger to enter the addresses instead. Here's the path to follow:

1. **Click on the cell where you want the answer to the formula to appear.**
2. **Type a plus sign.**
3. **Click on the cell you want to reference in the formula.**

   For example, if you want to enter the formula +B4*52, you click on cell B4, as in Figure 12-2. The far right end of the status line changes to display the word *Point,* and the cell address appears in the Input line and in the cell where you're entering the formula. In Figure 12-2, you enter the formula in cell C4.

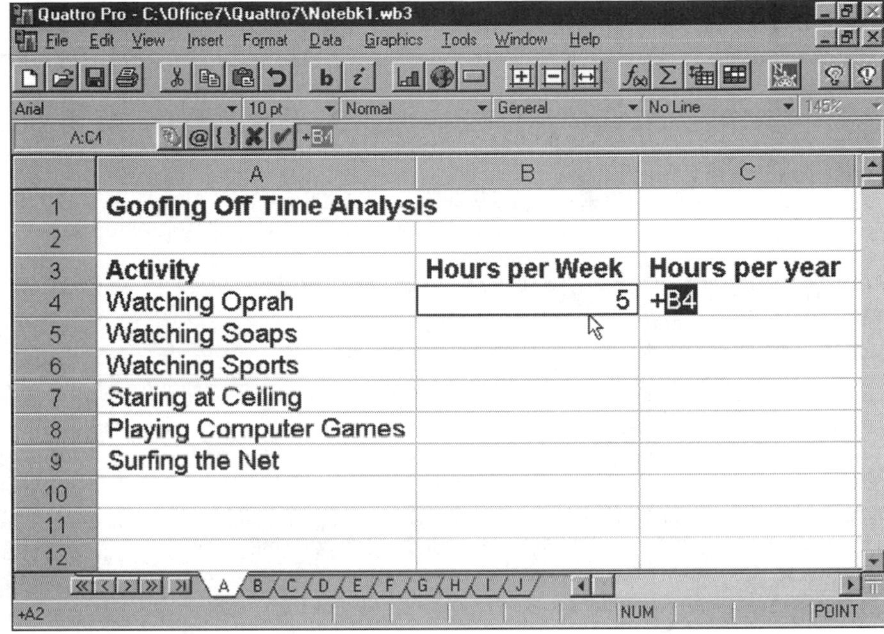

Figure 12-2: To enter a cell's address into a formula, just click on that cell.

4. **Type the next operator in the formula.**

   To continue the formula used in Figure 12-2, you would type the asterisk (the operator for multiplication) after +B4. When you type the operator, the cursor jumps back to the cell where you're entering the formula.

5. **Continue clicking on cells and typing operators or known values until the formula is complete.**

   In the case of the formula in Figure 12-2, all I would need to do to complete the formula is to follow +B4 with 52.

6. **Press Enter.**

Telling Quattro Pro What to Calculate First

When you have a formula that contains more than one type of operator, you need to tell Quattro Pro the order in which you want to calculate the formula.

Take a look at this formula:

```
+B1+B2*B3
```

Would you like that address relative or absolute?

After you create a formula, you can copy it to other cells to save yourself the trouble of entering it again and again. (The how-to's are presented in the next chapter.) When you create formulas that you want to copy to other cells, it's important to consider whether you want to use a *relative* or *absolute* cell address.

If you don't do anything special to your formulas, relative addressing is in force. Here's how a relative address works: Suppose that you have four columns of numbers — let's call them Column A through Column D. Each column contains three rows of numbers, and you want to find the total of each column. To do this, you enter the formula +A1+A2+A3 in cell A4. Then you copy the formula to cells B4, C4, and D4. Quattro Pro is smart enough to realize that you don't want to calculate exactly the same thing as you did in the first column, and so it adjusts the formula to match each column. For example, in cell B4, it changes the formula to +B1+B2+B3. In other words, the formula always calculates the sum of the three cells directly above it.

Now what if for some reason you *don't* want Quattro Pro to tamper with your formulas in this way when you copy them? You need to notify Quattro Pro that you want to use absolute addressing. You do this by putting a dollar sign before the column and the row name, as in +$A$1+$A$2+$A$3. With this formula, Quattro Pro always refers strictly to cells A1, A2, and A3 when it calculates your answer, no matter where you copy the formula.

You can mix absolute and relative cell addresses in the same formula, by the way. You can even make one part of the address absolute and the other part of the address relative, if you're so inclined. For example, you could use the address $A1 to make the column address absolute and the row address relative.

If you enter this formula, you may expect Quattro Pro to work its way from left to right, adding B1 and B2 and then multiplying the sum by B3. But in fact, Quattro Pro first multiplies B2 by B3 and then adds B1 to the result.

If you substitute numbers for the cell addresses, you can see that you get two different answers depending on which order you calculate the formula. Suppose that B1=4, B2=5, and B3=6. If you add 4 and 5 and then multiply the sum by 6, you get 54. If you multiply 5 times 6 and then add 4, you get 34.

So how does Quattro Pro decide which numbers to work on first? By following a set of mathematical rules called *order of precedence.* Translated into non-nerd terms, the rules assign a certain level or importance to each operator. A multiplication sign, for example, is more important than an addition sign, so the multiplying gets done first. If the formula contains several operators that are the same, Quattro Pro calculates the numbers separated by the left-most operator first and then works its way to the right through the rest of the formula.

Table 12-2 shows the order of precedence for the most common operators. But the truth is, you really don't need to remember this stuff — unless you like filling your head with complex technical data, of course. You can tell Quattro Pro how to calculate your formulas using another method you probably learned in algebra class — don't you wish you paid closer attention now? You can use parentheses to indicate which parts of your formula you want Quattro Pro to calculate first, second, third, and so on.

Table 12-2 Operator Order of Precedence

Operator	*Precedence*
^ (exponentiation)	1
* (multiplication)	2
/ (division)	2
+ (addition)	3
- (subtraction)	3

Suppose that you want to add B1 to B2 and then multiply the sum by B3. Enter the formula this way:

```
(B1+B2)*B3
```

When your formula begins with a left parenthesis, as here, you don't need to add the plus sign at the beginning as you do with other formulas. If you do, however, you won't hurt anything.

In long formulas, you may need to create several sets of parenthetical expressions (that's geek talk for equations inside parentheses), one inside of the other. For example, here's how you would enter a formula that finds the sum of B1 and B2, multiplies the sum by B3, subtracts the result from B4, performs the same calculations on cells C1, C2, C3, and C4, adds the two results together, and divides the whole shooting match by 2:

```
((B4-((B1+B2)*B3)) + (C4-((C1+C2)*C3)))/2
```

To dissect this formula, Quattro Pro first calculates whatever parts of the formula are enclosed by the most sets of parentheses. In this case, that's B1+B2 and C1+C2, which are each enclosed by four sets of parentheses. It then works its way outward, evaluating the expressions enclosed by three sets of parentheses, and then two sets, and then one set, before moving on to divide the entire result by 2.

Now that I have your head completely spinning, let me just give you one more little nugget of information. When you type a left parenthesis, Quattro Pro initially displays it in red. When you type the corresponding right parenthesis, it displays both parentheses in neon green. This Christmas-tree color coding — or I guess you could consider it stoplight color coding — is Quattro Pro's way of helping you make sure that you always have a right parenthesis to match every left parenthesis.

If you're missing a right parenthesis, Quattro Pro adds it at the end of your formula — which may or may not be okay, depending on the formula. If you're missing a left parenthesis, Quattro Pro displays a message warning you that you've made a syntax error. Click on OK and put in the missing parenthesis. (Note that you can also get syntax error messages for other types of formula problems.)

Well, now. I think that's just about enough of *that,* don't you?

Working with Built-in Functions

Quattro Pro wants to be your friend, it really does. And because it realizes that creating formulas can be a bit of a drag, your little math buddy thoughtfully provides some prefab formulas to make your life easier. These built-in formulas are formally called *@functions,* pronounced *at functions.* (Just because Quattro Pro wants to be your friend doesn't mean that it's willing to speak to you in plain English, unfortunately.)

To see a list of the available functions, choose Insert⇨Function. Or click on a cell, press F2, and click on the @ symbol that appears on the Input line. Either approach displays the Functions dialog box, shown in Figure 12-3. Click on a category in the Function Category list, and the functions related to that category appear in the Function list box. (If you choose the ALL category, all available functions appear in the list box.) At the bottom of the dialog box, Quattro Pro gives you some information about what the function does.

Quattro Pro 7 provides scores of functions, including everything from formulas that only high-level engineers would need to formulas that handle complex statistical problems. The following sections focus on some of the simpler, more common functions you're likely to use.

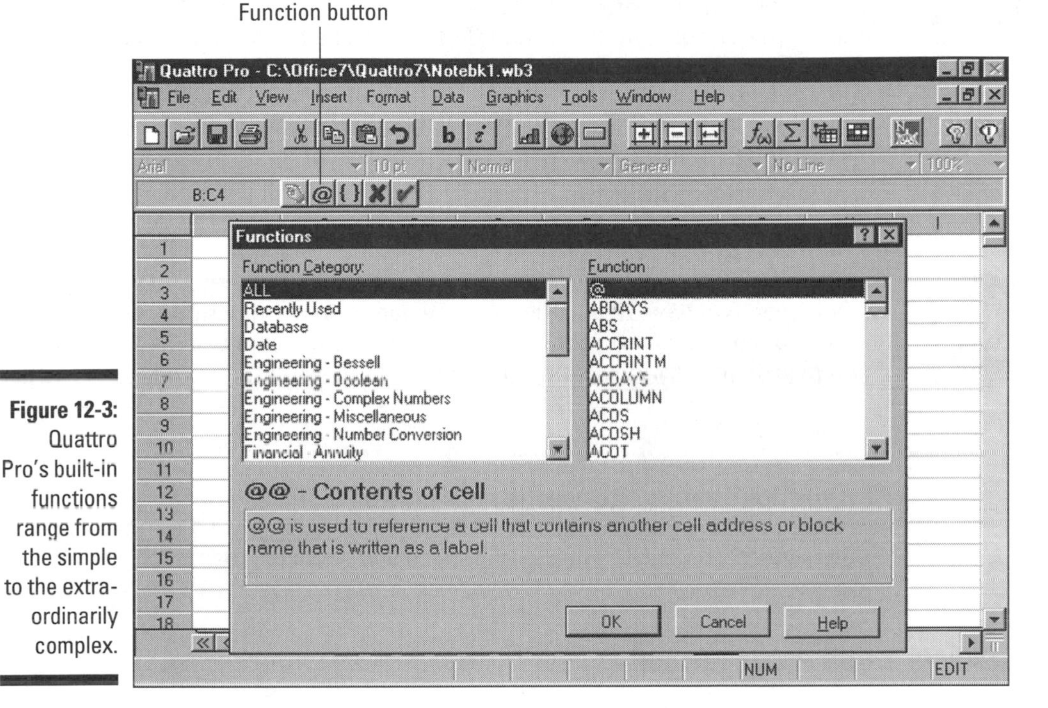

Figure 12-3: Quattro Pro's built-in functions range from the simple to the extra-ordinarily complex.

Writing formulas using functions

One of the functions you're likely to use most often is the @SUM function, which adds up the values in a range of cells. Say that you want to add the values in cells B1 through B20. You could type in +B1+B2+B3+B4 and so on, entering the addresses of all the cells one by one. Or you could get the same results by entering the following formula:

```
@SUM(B1..B20)
```

The @ symbol tells Quattro Pro that you're about to enter a function; SUM is the name of the function. The parentheses contain the *argument* — that is, the data that you want to calculate with the function. The two periods in the formula are Quattro Pro shorthand for *through*. So this formula tells Quattro Pro to find the sum of cell B1 through cell B20.

Functions always begin with the @ symbol. If your formula begins with a function, you don't need to put in the plus sign that you use to begin other formulas; the @ sign is enough. But you won't hurt anything if you forget and put in the plus sign. Also, Quattro Pro always displays function names in all caps. But you don't have to enter the names in all caps; lowercase letters are fine.

If you prefer, you can enter cell addresses using the mouse method discussed earlier in this chapter, in the section "Entering cell addresses with the mouse."

If you want to add values that aren't in a continuous block of cells, you separate the numbers with commas instead of periods. If you want to find the sum of cells B1 though B20, C2, and C6, for example, you enter

```
@SUM(B1..B20,C2,C6)
```

To have a function calculate data that's found on different pages of your spreadsheet, you have to include the page names in the function argument. To find the sum of cells A1 through A3 on page A plus the sum of cells A1 through A3 on page B, for example, enter the page range and then the cell range, like this:

```
@SUM(A..B:A1..A3)
```

Or, if you don't want to include the same cells on both pages — for example, if you want to add the sum of cells A1 through A3 on page A with the sum of cells A4 through A6 on page B, enter both ranges and separate them with a comma, like this:

```
@SUM(A:A1..A3,B:A4..A6)
```

Note that you can use functions as part of a longer formula. If you wanted to add the values in cells B1 though B20 and then divide the result by 4, you would enter

```
@SUM(B1..B20)/4
```

When you're entering functions, you really only need to enter one period to indicate a range of cells — Quattro Pro automatically adds the second one for you after you press Enter. It also adds the closing parentheses if you forget. What a pal!

If you want to add a column or row of continuous cells, you can often do it more quickly by using the QuickSum button than using the @SUM function. See the section "Adding Things Up with QuickSum," later in this chapter, for more information.

Finding the average and median values

Suppose that you run a flower shop and want to find your average daily sales for the month of May. The daily sales totals are stored in cells A1 through A30. To find the average daily sales, use the @AVG function, entering the formula like this:

```
@AVG(A1..A30)
```

Now suppose that you're an eighth-grade teacher (you just do that flower-shop thing on the side) and you've stored all the scores for your final exams in cells A1 through A26. You can use the @MEDIAN function to find the median score. The median score is the score that's smack dab in the middle of all the scores. In other words, half of the scores are better than the median and half of them are worse. Write the formula this way:

```
@MEDIAN(A1..A26)
```

Inserting the current date

If you want a certain cell to always display the current date, enter @TODAY into the cell. Quattro Pro initially displays the date as a serial number — trust me, you don't want to even hear about why this is so. To display the date as a real date, you need to change the numeric format. Choose the Date option from the Style drop-down list on the Power Bar, as explained in Chapter 11 in the section "Changing the numeric format." Or press F12 to open the Block Properties dialog box, which lets you choose from several date formats.

Figuring out some other cool stuff

Table 12-3 shows some of the other available functions and what they do. Some of them are a little complex and require you to enter your formula arguments in specific ways. For complete guidance and examples of how each function is used, consult Quattro Pro's Help system. (And if you need help using the Help system, see Chapter 3.)

Table 12-3 Some Additional Functions to Explore

Function	What It Does
@AMAINT	Calculates interest paid on a loan after x number of payments
@PMT	Calculates monthly or annual loan payments
@FVAL	Calculates the future value of an investment
@MTGACC	Calculates the effects of paying extra monthly principal on a loan
@DOLLARDE	Converts a fractional stock price, such as 1 15/16, into dollars
@DFRAC	Converts a decimal number to a fraction
@MEMAVAIL	Tells you how many bytes of memory are currently available in your computer system (!)

Adding Things Up with QuickSum

If you want to add up a bunch of numbers, you can use the @SUM function as described in the earlier section "Writing formulas using functions." But an even quicker way to add up a column of *continuous* cells is to click on an empty cell at the bottom of the column and then click on the QuickSum button, labeled in Figure 12-4.

If there are any empty cells in the row or column of cells you want to sum, select all the cells you want to sum *plus* an empty cell at the bottom of the column or end of the row to hold the sum. (To select a bunch of cells, you drag over them, as explained in Chapter 13.) Then click on the QuickSum button.

To find the sum for several columns and/or rows at a time, as in Figure 12-4, select the cells *plus* enough empty cells to hold the sums. In Figure 12-4, for example, the first three empty cells in row 11 will hold the monthly sales totals for January, February, and March. The first five empty cells in column E will hold the quarter sales totals for each category of goods. The empty cell at the bottom right corner of the block of cells (cell E11) will hold the total sales for the entire quarter.

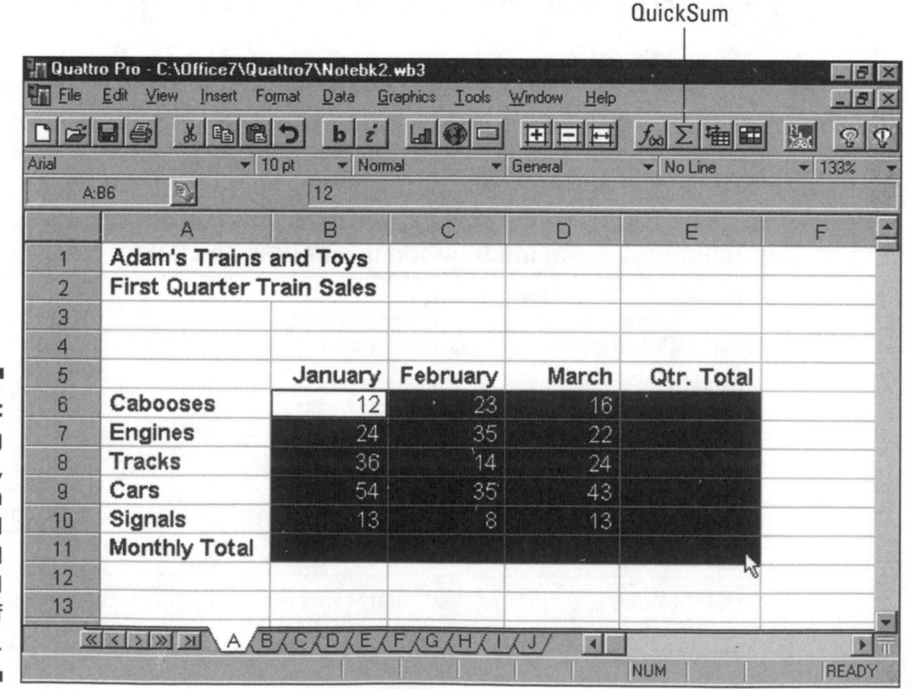

Figure 12-4: Using QuickSum, you can quickly add up several rows and columns of numbers.

Fighting the ERR Message

Sometimes Quattro Pro displays the letters ERR or NA in a cell after you enter a formula and press Enter. This message is Quattro Pro's not-so-subtle way of letting you know that you goofed. Something is wrong with your formula.

If, after checking things out, you can't figure out what went wrong, try clicking on the cell containing the ERR or NA value. Then press F5 or choose Edit⇨Go To and press Enter. Quattro Pro activates the cell that is the source of the problem.

Of course, if the problem is the way you entered the formula rather than in some cell you referenced in the formula, the Go To trick just takes you right back to the cell that contains the formula. That's no help at all. If you're entering a function, call up the Help screen for that function and make sure that you've structured the function argument properly. When all else fails, beg your local Quattro Pro guru for assistance. It helps to offer some sort of little math-related bribe — a slide rule or one of those tiny calculator keychains is always good.

Chapter 13

Editing Your Spreadsheet

In This Chapter

- Undoing mistakes
- Editing and deleting cell contents
- Selecting stuff before you format
- Inserting, deleting, and adjusting columns and rows
- Copying stuff from one cell to another
- Moving data around
- Transposing data

Don't you wish people would react to your mistakes the way they do when those celebrities on TV blooper shows muff their lines? Oh sure, it's funny when somebody *famous* goofs up, but when *you* make a mistake, nobody laughs hysterically and shouts, "That'll be a great one for the blooper reel!"

Well, I'm sorry to say that it'll probably be some time before the stuffy network brass who control our nation's TV viewing realize the appeal of a show like *World's Funniest Quattro Pro Bloopers and Blunders.* So you may as well go ahead and fix those typos, faulty formulas, and other laughers that found their way into your spreadsheet — after enjoying a good chuckle about the mishap, of course.

This chapter shows you how to undo mistakes, edit data, and otherwise wipe all traces of comedy out of your spreadsheets. It also explains how to make other sorts of changes, such as inserting rows and columns and turning your spreadsheet on its ear.

Getting Rid of Bloopers

Type the wrong thing in a cell? You have several choices for putting things right:

- Retype everything correctly, as explained in the following section "Replacing cell contents."

- Edit the data using one of the techniques covered in the upcoming "Editing tricks and techniques."
- Erase the data entirely, as explained in the section "Deleting versus clearing cell contents."

Replacing cell contents

If the data you want to edit is short, the fastest method for fixing mistakes is to simply retype the data. Just click on the cell, type the data again — more carefully this time — and then press Enter. Quattro Pro replaces the existing cell contents with the new data.

Editing tricks and techniques

If you want to make a minor change to a long or complex piece of data (such as a formula), editing the data is probably easier than retyping it. You can make your edits either in the cell or in the Input line. But you first must shift Quattro Pro into edit mode, which you can do in three ways:

- Click on the cell and press F2.
- Double-click on the cell.
- Click on the Input line.

Whichever method you choose, the right end of the status bar displays the word Edit to show that you have indeed entered the editing zone, as shown in Figure 13-1.

Editing data in Quattro Pro is pretty much the same as editing text in WordPerfect 7. Here's a recap of the basics:

- That flashing vertical bar is the *insertion marker.* The insertion marker indicates where the next entry you type will appear.
- When you pass your mouse cursor over the cell you're editing or the Input line, the cursor changes from an arrow to something that looks like a capital letter *I* — hence it's name, the *I-beam.* You click the I-beam to position the insertion marker in your text or data.
- You can also move the insertion marker by using the left- and right-arrow keys.
- Press Delete to erase the character just to the right of the insertion marker; press Backspace to wipe out the character to the left of the insertion marker.

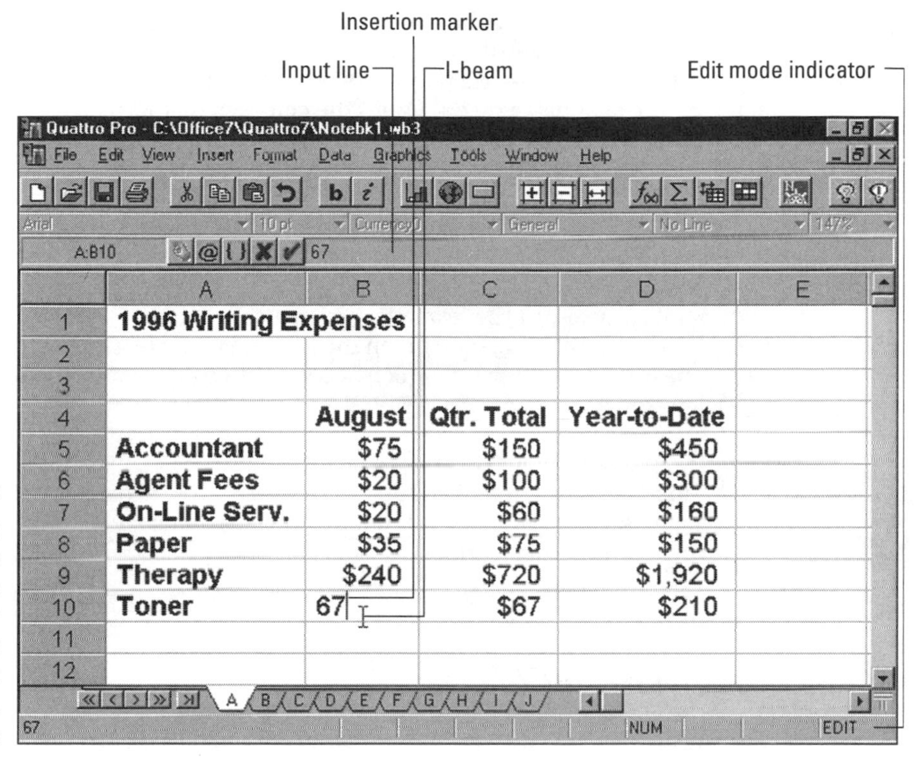

Figure 13-1: The insertion marker shows I'm ready to edit cell B10.

- Normally, Quattro Pro operates in *insert* mode. Any character you insert shoves the characters that follow to the right. If you press the Insert key, you switch to *overwrite* mode, and new characters you type take the place of existing characters. Press Insert again to get back to insert mode. (Quattro Pro also returns you to Insert mode when you press Enter.)

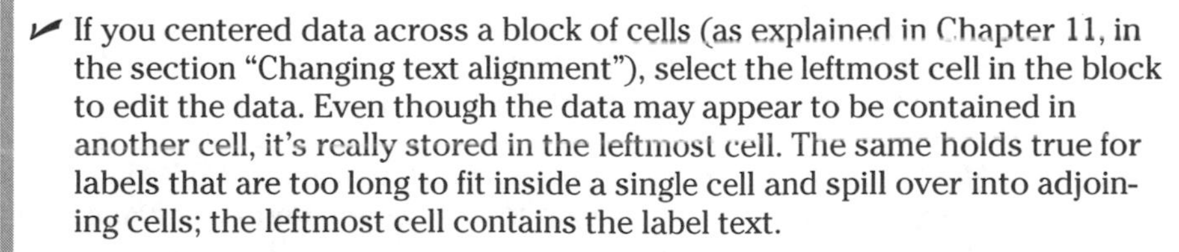

- If you centered data across a block of cells (as explained in Chapter 11, in the section "Changing text alignment"), select the leftmost cell in the block to edit the data. Even though the data may appear to be contained in another cell, it's really stored in the leftmost cell. The same holds true for labels that are too long to fit inside a single cell and spill over into adjoining cells; the leftmost cell contains the label text.

- After you fix up the cell contents, press Enter to make your changes official. Or, if you want to put things back the way they were before you began editing, press Esc instead.

Deleting versus clearing cell contents

If you want to get rid of the contents of a cell completely, click on the cell and press Delete. Simple enough, right?

Ah, but Quattro Pro throws in a little curve when it comes to deleting cell contents. The Delete key does wipe out the *contents* of a cell, but any formatting you applied to the cell — such as numeric style, type size, and so on — remains intact. So the next data you enter into the cell uses that formatting, too.

To wipe out the formatting along with the cell contents, click on the cell and choose Edit⇨Clear. Or right-click on the cell and choose Clear from the resulting QuickMenu. Quattro Pro zaps the data and returns all the formatting to the default settings.

If you want to clear just the formatting from a cell, choose Edit⇨Clear Formats. As for that Clear Values command on the Edit menu, it clears just the values and leaves the formatting intact — which accomplishes the same thing as pressing the Delete key.

To delete or clear a bunch of cells, select them first, as explained in the upcoming section "Selecting Stuff." To delete an entire row or column of cells, follow the steps in the section "Inserting and Deleting Columns and Rows." (Don't you just love these imaginative titles?)

Undoing Bad Moves

Like WordPerfect, Quattro Pro has an Undo command that can take you back in time, to the moment before you made that awful decision that you now regret. You can undo most editing and formatting commands, but not actions such as saving and printing.

Unfortunately, Quattro Pro's Undo command can only reverse your last action — you can't undo several actions at once, as you can using WordPerfect's Undo/Redo History command.

To undo your last action, click on Edit⇨Undo. Or press Ctrl+Z or click on the Undo button on the toolbar (it looks like a curving, left-pointing arrow).

After you choose the Undo command, it changes to the Redo command. If you change your mind about the undo, choose the Redo command to undo your undo, scooby dooby doo.

The names of the Undo and Redo commands change depending on what you last did — for example, if your last action was to enter some data, the command name is Undo Entry. If you're not sure what action you'll be undoing or redoing, look at the command name before you proceed.

If Undo doesn't seem to be working, it may not be *enabled* — that's the chiphead way of saying that the feature may be turned off. You can undo *some* actions with the Undo feature disabled, but not all. Choose Edit⇨Preferences to open the Application dialog box, click on the General tab, and look at the Undo Enabled check box. If the box is checked, Undo is turned on. If the box isn't checked, click on it to activate Undo.

Selecting Stuff

Before you can do much at all to your spreadsheet — whether you want to format it or edit it — you must *select* one or more cells. Selecting tells Quattro Pro exactly where to apply your next command or change.

If you select a single cell, Quattro Pro displays a black border around the cell. If you select only part of the data in a cell or select several cells, the selection appears highlighted on-screen, as in Figure 13-2. Note that the active cell — the first (or sometimes the last) cell in a range of selected cells — does *not* appear highlighted but is still part of the selection.

Here's a list of the most popular selection techniques known to man and Quattro Pro:

- To select a single cell, just click on it. The black border around the cell shows that it's the active (selected) cell.

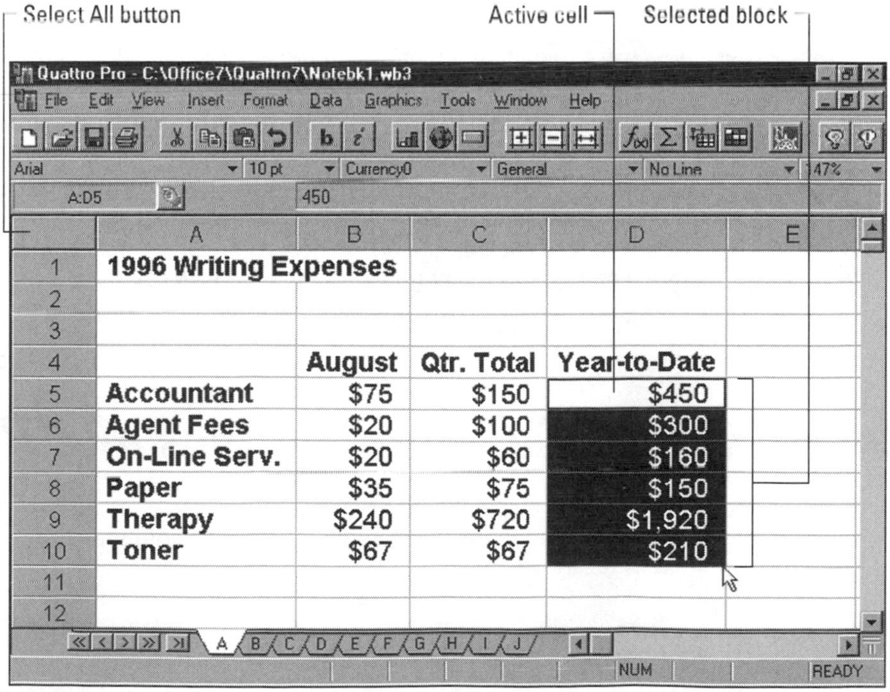

Select All button

Active cell

Selected block

	A	B	C	D
1	1996 Writing Expenses			
2				
3				
4		August	Qtr. Total	Year-to-Date
5	Accountant	$75	$150	$450
6	Agent Fees	$20	$100	$300
7	On-Line Serv.	$20	$60	$160
8	Paper	$35	$75	$150
9	Therapy	$240	$720	$1,920
10	Toner	$67	$67	$210

Figure 13-2: Selected text appears highlighted — except for the first cell in the selection, which looks like an ordinary active cell.

- To select part of the data in a cell, first get into edit mode by double-clicking on the cell, clicking on the cell and pressing F2, or clicking on the Input line. Then drag over the data you want to select.
- To select a block (range) of cells, click on the first cell in the range and drag to highlight the rest of the range.

- If a little hand cursor appears when you try to select cells, Quattro Pro thinks you want to move stuff rather than select it. Click again on the first cell and try selecting the cells again, this time beginning your drag a little quicker after you click.
- If you don't like dragging, click on the first cell you want to select, press Shift, and use the arrow keys to add adjacent cells to the selection.

- Here's an even quicker way to select a large block of cells: Click on the cell in the upper-left corner of the block you want to select. Then hold down the Shift key as you click on the cell in the lower-right corner of the block.
- To select all cells in the notebook, choose Edit⇨Select All. Or click on the Select All button, labeled in Figure 13-2.
- To select an entire row of cells, click on that row in the row border. (Your cursor changes into a fat, right-pointing arrow when you move it onto the border.) To select several rows at once, just drag across them in the row border.
- To select an entire column of cells, click on the column name in the column border. To select several columns, drag across them in the column border.

- If you want to edit data that's centered across a block of cells or that spills over from one cell into adjoining cells, select the leftmost block in the group. That's the one that contains the data, even though it may appear otherwise on-screen.

- To select two or more noncontiguous cells — that is, cells that aren't touching — click on the first cell you want to select. Then hold down the Ctrl key as you click on the other cells you want to select. You can use this same technique to select noncontiguous blocks of cells.
- To "unselect" stuff, just click again.

Inserting and Deleting Columns and Rows

You can add an empty row or column of cells any time, any place, with just a few mouse clicks and drags. You can delete rows or columns from your spreadsheet just as easily.

Inserting an empty row or column

If you insert a row or column, Quattro Pro adjusts formulas in other cells as needed. For example, if you have the formula +A1+A2 in cell A3, and you insert a row before row A1, Quattro Pro changes the formula to +A2+A3 to accommodate the new arrangement of the cells. This automatic adjustment is the result of Quattro Pro's relative addressing feature, explained in the sidebar "Would you like that address relative or absolute?" in Chapter 12.

Here's how to insert a row or column of empty cells:

- To insert a row, click in the row border on the row immediately *below* where you want the new row to appear. Then click on the Insert toolbar button (it looks like a plus sign and is labeled in the upcoming Figure 13-3).
- To insert several rows at once, select however many rows you want to insert in the row border. For example, if you want to insert three rows, select three rows in the row border. Then click on the Insert button. Quattro Pro inserts the new rows immediately above the top row in your selection.
- To insert a column, click in the column border, on the column immediately *left* of where you want the new column to appear and then click on the Insert button. To insert several columns, select the number of columns you want to insert and then click on the Insert button. Your new columns appear just to the left of the leftmost column in your selection.
- You can also insert rows and columns by using the Insert⇨Block command. Click on any cell in the row or column that's immediately before the position where you want the new row or column to appear. Then choose the command, select either the Columns or Rows radio button in the resulting dialog box, and click on OK. But really, it's a heck of a lot easier to simply use the Insert button on the toolbar.

Deleting rows and columns

Make sure that when you delete rows or columns, you aren't deleting cells that are referenced in formulas found elsewhere in your spreadsheet. If you do, you wind up with formulas that Quattro Pro either can't calculate or calculates incorrectly.

To delete a row or column, just click on it in the row or column border, as in Figure 13-3. Then click on the Delete toolbar button, which looks like a minus sign and is sandwiched between the Insert button and the QuickFit button (and is also labeled in Figure 13-3). Alternatively, you can choose the Edit⇨Delete Column(s) or Edit⇨Delete Row(s) command (the command name changes depending on whether you clicked on a column border or row border before choosing the command).

Insert button
Delete button

	A	B	C	D	E
1	1996 Writing Expenses				
2					
3					
4					
5		August	Qtr. Total		Year-to-Date
6	Accountant	$75	$150		$450
7	Agent Fees	$20	$100		$300
8	On-Line Serv.	$20	$60		$160
9	Paper	$35	$75		$150
10	Therapy	$240	$720		$1,920
11	Toner	$67	$67		$210
12					

Figure 13-3: To delete a column, click on it in the column border and click on the Delete button on the toolbar.

Whichever approach you take, Quattro Pro tosses the column or row into the electronic wastebasket and shifts the remaining rows and columns over to fill up the empty space.

To delete several rows or columns at once, select them in the column or row border and then click on the Delete button on the toolbar or choose Edit➪Delete.

The Delete button on the toolbar does *not* do the same thing as the Delete key on your keyboard. The Delete button deletes the entire column or row, while the Delete key just deletes the contents of the cells in the column or row.

Adding a Page

If you need to insert a blank page between two pages of data in your notebook, click on the page tab for the page that falls immediately after the place where you want the new page to appear. Then click on the Insert button on the toolbar or choose Insert➪Block. The Insert Block dialog box, shown in Figure 13-4, appears. Click on the Pages radio button and the Entire radio button and then click on OK.

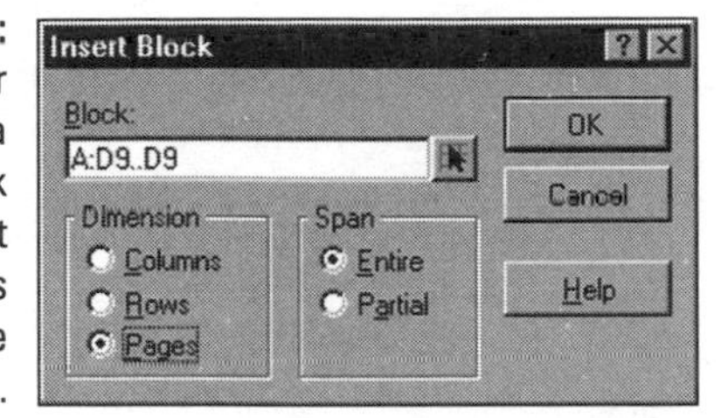

Figure 13-4: To delete or insert a notebook page, select the Pages and Entire options.

To delete a page, click on its page tab and click on the Delete button on the toolbar. After the Delete Block dialog box appears, click on the Pages radio button and the Entire radio button and click on OK. (The Delete Block dialog box looks the same as the Insert Block dialog box except for the name.)

Resizing Columns and Rows

When you first open a spreadsheet, Quattro Pro fills the page with columns that are about nine characters wide, given the default type size and font (10-point Arial). You can shrink or enlarge the columns to fit your data at any time, however. You can also change the height of any row in your spreadsheet.

If you see a row of asterisks in a cell, if Quattro Pro displays some screwy-looking formula instead of the number you typed, or if a label appears to be cut off at the knees, your cell is too small to accommodate all its data. Column A in Figure 13-5 shows examples of all these symptoms of cramped cell disorder. Column C shows the data that I actually typed in the cells in Column A.

To fix things, you need to enlarge the cell by changing the row height or column width. (Alternatively, you can reduce the type size you're using, as explained in Chapter 11, "Changing the font, type size, and type style.")

- The easiest way to change the column width is to place your mouse cursor in the column border, directly over the line that separates the column you want to resize from its neighbor to the right. When you see the cursor change to a two-headed arrow, as shown in Figure 13-5, drag right or left to resize the column.
- You can change row height by dragging up or down on the line that separates the row you want to resize from the row directly beneath it.
- To resize several rows or columns at once, select them in the row or column border and then drag the bottom or left border of any of the selected rows or columns. Remember that you can select nonadjoining columns or rows by selecting the first one and then holding down Ctrl as you click on the other ones you want to select.

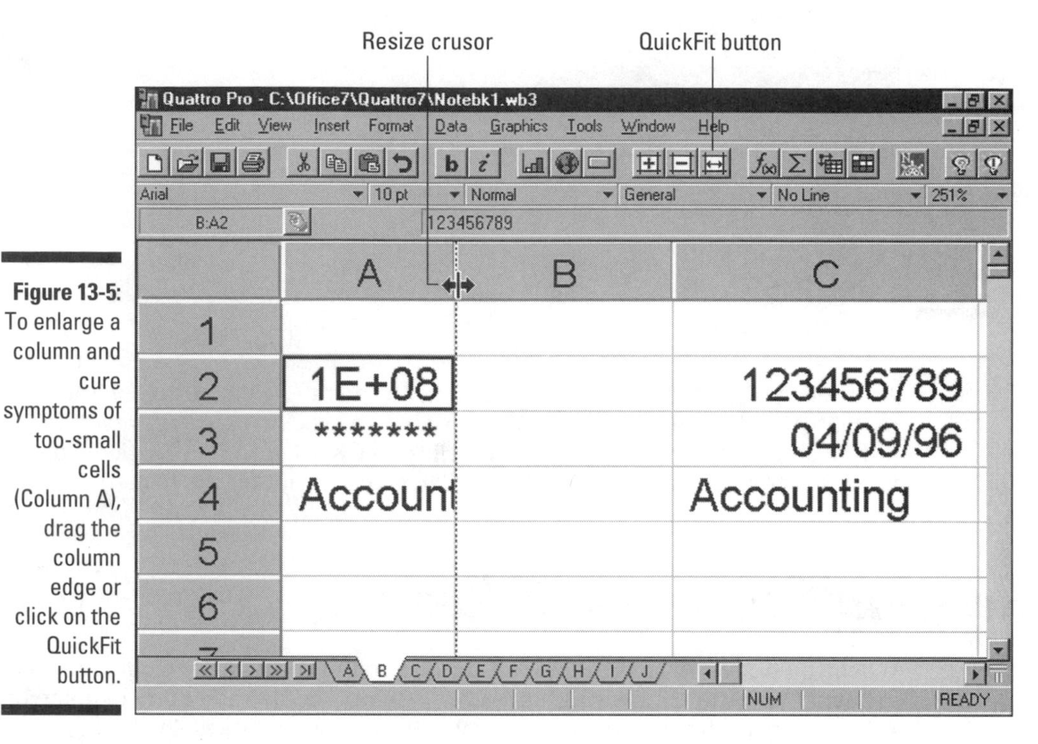

Figure 13-5: To enlarge a column and cure symptoms of too-small cells (Column A), drag the column edge or click on the QuickFit button.

- To have Quattro Pro automatically fit the row or column size to fit the longest entry in the column or row, click on the column or row border and click on the QuickFit button, labeled in Figure 13-5.

If you want more precision over your column and row sizes than the methods just described offer — for example, if you want each column to be exactly 1 1/2 inches wide — you have to open the Active Block dialog box, shown in Figure 13-6. Click on any cell in the column or row you want to adjust and then press F12, choose Format⇨Block, or right-click on the block and choose Block Properties from the QuickMenu.

- To set the column width, click on the Column Width tab. Specify the width value in the Column Width option box and select the Set Width radio button. If you select the Auto Width radio button, Quattro Pro sizes the column to fit the widest entry in the column.

- You can choose from three measurement units for your columns: Characters, Inches, and Centimeters. I recommend that you avoid the Characters option because it's pretty vague. The number of characters you can fit in the cell depends on the type size you use, the font, and the type style (bold or italic). In other words, you may set the column width at 15 characters, but you may be able to fit only 13 characters in the cell if those characters are boldfaced.

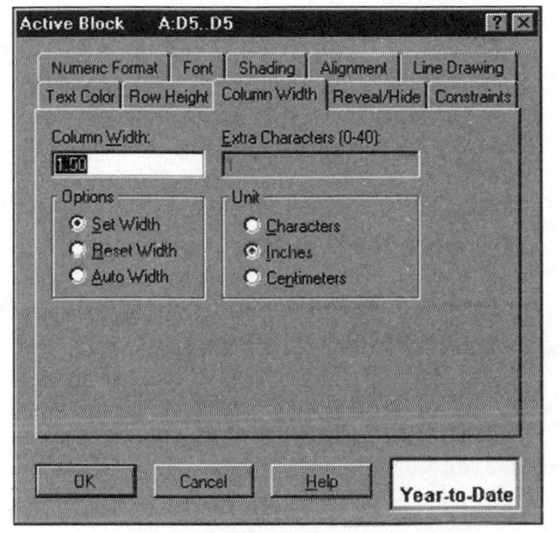

Figure 13-6: To make your columns or rows a precise size, head for this dialog box.

- To set the row height, click on the Row Height tab. Enter your height in the Row Height option box, click on the Set Height button, and click on one of the Unit radio buttons to establish the unit of measurement. You can set your row height in terms of *points* (a point is a publishing unit of measure equal to $^1/_{72}$ inch), inches, or centimeters.
- Click on OK or press Enter to exit the Active Block dialog box and get back to your spreadsheet.
- If you want to change the column or row back to its original default size, select the Reset option on the Column Width or Row Height tab of the Active Block dialog box.

Copying Data from Here to There

If you have a label or formula that you need to use in more than one spot in your spreadsheet, don't keep entering it again and again — instead, save yourself some time and effort and copy it.

Quattro Pro offers several methods for copying data, which are outlined in the following sections. But before you begin your grand copying adventure, you need to be aware of two little pieces of business:

- If you move or copy data to a cell that already contains data, Quattro Pro overwrites the existing data with the stuff you're copying or moving — without giving you any warning at all. The exception is when you use the drag-and-drop method of moving or copying data. In that case, Quattro Pro displays a box warning you that you're about to overwrite the existing data. If that's okay with you, click on Yes. If not, click on No to cancel the copy.

- If you copy a formula, Quattro Pro automatically adjusts the formula relative to its new location, as explained in the sidebar, "Would you like that address relative or absolute?" in Chapter 12. Be sure to read this sidebar before you copy a formula; you may want to do some rewriting of the formula first.

In addition to reading the upcoming sections, be sure to read Chapter 20, which offers some additional copying techniques.

Dragging and dropping a copy

For simple copy jobs, the quickest method is to drag and drop the copy, like so:

1. **Select the data you want to copy.**

   You can copy a single cell or a block of cells. (Selection techniques are outlined earlier in this chapter, in the section "Selecting Stuff.")

2. **With your cursor on the selected cell or block, press and hold down the Ctrl key and then press and hold the left mouse button.**

   Your cursor should change to a little hand with a plus sign next to it, as shown in Figure 13-7. Be sure that you see a little plus sign next to the hand cursor — otherwise, you're simply moving the selected cells rather than copying them.

3. **Drag the cell or block to its new location and release the mouse button.**

Using Copy and Paste to copy data

Although the drag-and-drop method is the quickest way to copy things, using the Copy and Paste commands offers more flexibility. With Copy and Paste, you can copy the same data into many different cells at the same time. Copying data between notebook pages is also easier using Copy and Paste. You *can* drag and drop data between notebook pages, but that method is more cumbersome than using the Copy and Paste method.

To copy data using the Copy and Paste commands:

1. **Select the cell or block of cells you want to copy.**

2. **Choose Edit⇨Copy or click on the Copy button on the toolbar.**

   The Copy button looks like two overlapping pages of paper (it's labeled back in Figure 13-7). Alternatively, you can press Ctrl+C or right-click on the selected cell(s) and choose Copy from the QuickMenu. Quattro Pro sends the data to the Windows Clipboard, where it stays until the next time you use the Copy or Cut command.

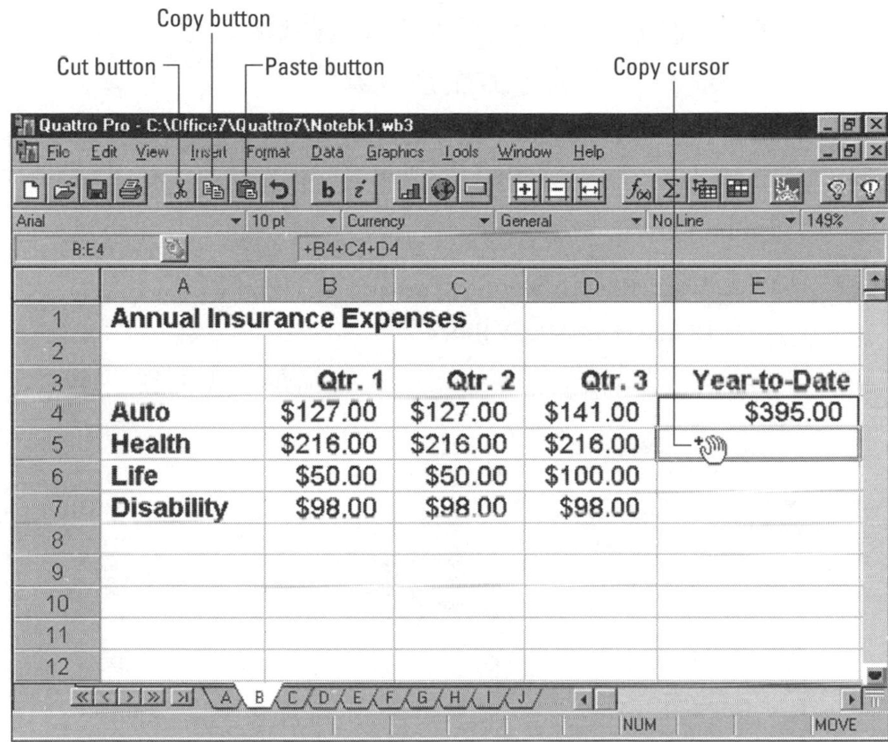

Figure 13-7: To copy a formula or data to another cell, just Ctrl+drag it.

3. **Click on the cell where you want to place the copy.**

   If you're copying a block of cells, click in the upper-left cell of the block where you want to put the copy. You can put the copy on any page in your spreadsheet or even in another spreadsheet, if you like.

   Make sure that you don't copy the data to cells that already contain data. If you do, Quattro Pro replaces the existing data with the data you're copying — and doesn't warn you first.

4. **Choose Edit⇨Paste or click on the Paste toolbar button.**

   The Paste button, labeled in Figure 13-7, is just to the right of the Copy button. You can also just press Ctrl+V or right-click on the cell where you want to place the copy and choose Paste from the QuickMenu. Quattro Pro pops your copy into its new home.

If you want to copy the data to yet another cell, just click on the cell and use any of the methods in Step 4 to paste the data again. You can paste the data as many times as you want.

You can paste the contents of a single cell into a whole block of cells at the same time. To do so, select the block of cells right before you choose the Edit⇨Paste command. Quattro Pro duplicates the data in every cell selected.

Getting more specific with the Copy Block command

If you want to copy some parts of a block, but not all, the Copy Block command in the Edit menu is the ticket. Using this command, you can specify whether Quattro Pro copies formulas, numbers, labels, formatting, objects, and row and column sizes used in the block. Here's how:

1. **Select the cell or block you want to copy.**
2. **Choose Edit⇨Copy Block.**

   The Copy Block dialog box, shown in Figure 13-8, appears.

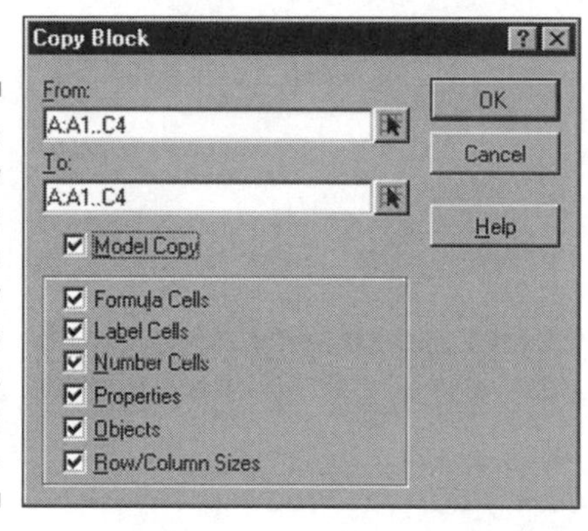

Figure 13-8: The Copy Block dialog box lets you specify which parts of a block you want to copy.

3. **Enter the address of the cell where you want to place the copy in the To option box.**

   If you're copying a block of cells, enter the address of the cell in the upper-left corner of the block where you want to place the copy.

   Quattro Pro doesn't warn you if you're about to copy data to cells that already contain data. It simply overwrites the existing data with the data you're copying. So be careful when specifying a location for the copied data.

4. **Click on the Model Copy box to select it.**
5. **Check the boxes for the elements you want to copy.**

   Formula Cells copies any formulas in the block; Label Cells copies labels in the block; Number Cells copies cells that contain plain old numbers; Properties copies the cell formatting; Objects copies any graphs or other objects in the block; and Row/Column Sizes copies, er, the row and column sizes.

6. **Click on OK or press Enter.**

   Quattro Pro copies just those elements of the block that you specified in the dialog box.

Moving Data Around

Moving the contents of a cell — or a block of cells — from one spot to another is a cinch. You can drag and drop the stuff you want to move or use the Cut and Paste or Move Block commands on the Edit menu.

When you move cells that contain formulas, Quattro Pro *does not* adjust the cell addresses as it does when you copy cells that contain formulas. If you move the formula +A1/A2 from cell A3 to cell B3, the formula doesn't change to +B1/B2, for example, as it does when you copy it. The formula continues to refer to the same cells it did before you moved it.

However, if you move a cell that's referenced in a formula, Quattro Pro adjusts the formula so that it continues to reference that same cell. For example, if you enter the formula +A1+A2, and then move cell A2 to cell A3, Quattro Pro adjusts the formula to read +A1+A3.

If you're moving cells just a short distance, using the drag-and-drop method is usually easiest:

1. **Select the cell or block you want to move.**

   If you're moving a single cell, just click on it. To select a block of cells, use the selection techniques presented earlier in this chapter, in the section "Selecting Stuff."

2. **Put the mouse cursor on the selected cell or block and press the left mouse button until you see the little hand cursor.**

3. **Drag the cell or block to its new home and release the mouse button.**

If you try to use the drag-and-drop method to move data into cells that already contain data, Quattro Pro displays an alert box to warn you. If you want to replace the current contents of the cells with the data you're moving, click on Yes to tell Quattro Pro that you know what you're doing and to leave you alone. Click on No to abort your mission.

If you want to move data to another page of your notebook or to another spreadsheet, you may find using the Cut and Paste or Move Block commands easier than dragging and dropping. The Cut/Paste method also lets you paste the same data repeatedly into as many different cells as you want. Here's the lowdown on the Cut/Paste technique:

1. **Select the cell or block you want to move.**
2. **Choose Edit⇨Cut or press Ctrl+X.**

   Or you can click on the Cut button on the toolbar — bet you'd never guess that the Cut button looks like a pair of scissors. (The button's labeled back in Figure 13-7.) You can also right-click on the selected cell and choose the Cut command from the QuickMenu.
3. **Click on the cell where you want to move the data.**

   If you're moving a block, click on the cell that you want to appear in the upper-left corner of the new block.

   If you use this method of moving data, Quattro Pro *doesn't* warn you that you're about to move data into cells that already contain data. It simply overwrites the existing data with the moved data.
4. **Choose Edit⇨Paste or press Ctrl+V.**

   Or click on the Paste button on the toolbar or right-click and choose Paste from the QuickMenu. Quattro Pro dumps the moved data into its new home. Well, *dumps* sounds a little uncaring, doesn't it? Okay, then, Quattro Pro lovingly slides the data into its new home.

The third and final method for moving data is to use the Edit⇨Move Block command. Select the cells you want to move, choose the command, and enter the address of the cell where you want to place the data in the To box of the Move Block dialog box.

As with the Cut and Paste method, the Move Block command gives you no advance warning if you're about to move data into cells that already contain data. Quattro Pro assumes that you know what you're doing and replaces the existing data with the moved data.

Be sure to check out Chapter 20 for more techniques you can use to move data between documents.

Transposing Cells

You're halfway through creating your spreadsheet, and you realize that you'd be better off if you oriented your data in a different way. You want to change your spreadsheet so that your columns become rows and vice versa — as I did with the data in Figure 13-9.

No problem; Quattro Pro is happy to transpose your data for you. Just select the block you want to flip and then choose Tools⇨Numeric Tools⇨Transpose. The Transpose Cells dialog box, shown in Figure 13-10, appears. The From box shows the cell range for the block you selected. In the To box, enter the address of the upper-left cell of the block where you want to put the transposed data. Or just click on the cell. Then click on OK or press Enter. Quattro Pro obediently turns your data on its ear.

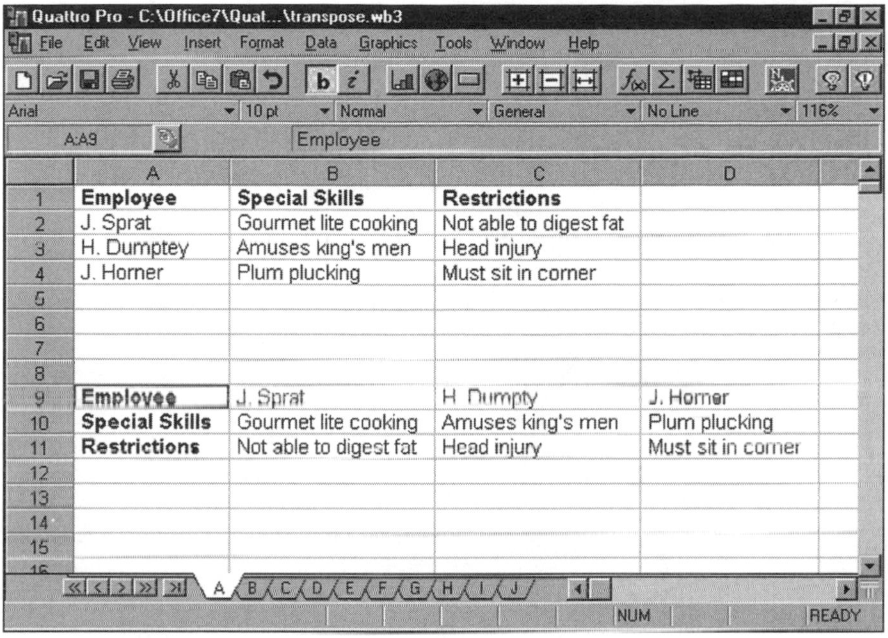

Figure 13-9: With the Transpose command, you can turn your columns into rows and your rows into columns.

Don't try to transpose blocks that contain formulas. Quattro Pro's brain simply isn't up to the task, and your formulas get completely messed up.

If you tell Quattro Pro to put the transposed data into cells that already contain data, it overwrites the existing data — without a word of warning to you. So be very careful when you set the upper-left corner of the block that will hold the transposed data.

Did anyone but me notice that the hotkeys for opening the Transpose Cells dialog box are *TNT?* Just thought I'd ask.

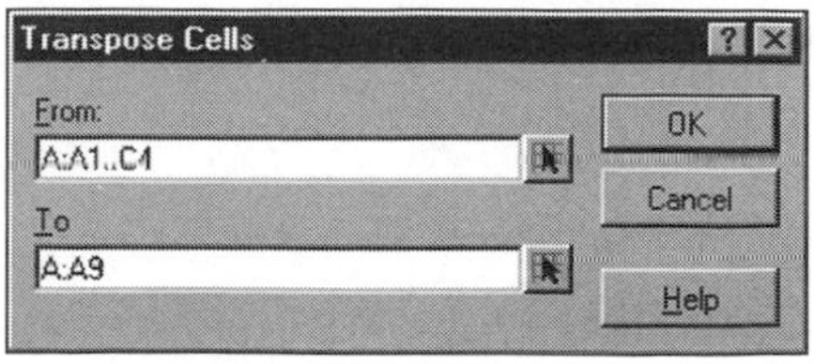

Figure 13-10: Enter the address of the upper-left cell in the block where you want to put the transposed data in the To box.

Chapter 14
Charting Your Course

In This Chapter

- Turning a boring block of numbers into a dazzling chart
- Uncovering the Chart menu
- Choosing a chart type and layout
- Editing chart data and design
- Naming your charts
- Printing charts from the Objects page

With Quattro Pro's graphics capabilities, you can quickly turn a batch of boring numbers into an eye-catching chart that would make Ross Perot's heart pound. Charts not only add some flash to your spreadsheet, they help people make sense of your numbers.

Consider the chart in Figure 14-1, for example. The chart makes it much easier to see which types of shows are more heavily watched than the table of numbers to the left.

This chapter gives you a lightning-fast tour of Quattro Pro charting capabilities so that you, too, can captivate audiences with pie charts, bar charts, and just about any other type of chart you can dream up.

Because this book can hold only so many pages — well, for $19.99, anyway — I can just skim the surface of Quattro Pro's chart-making features in this chapter.

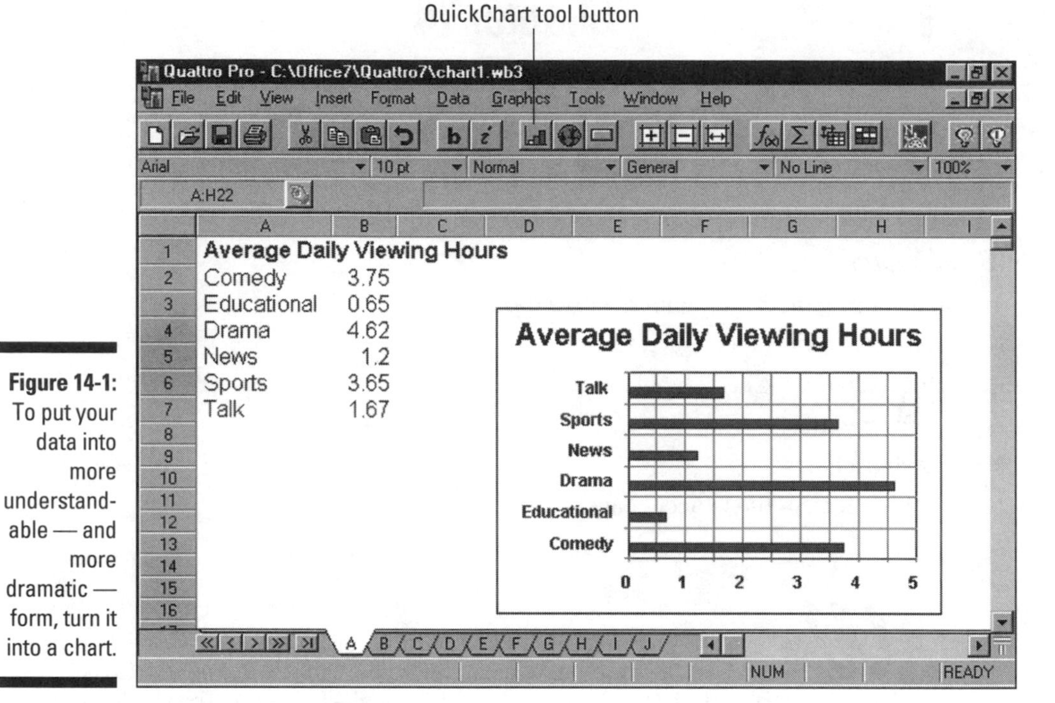

Figure 14-1: To put your data into more understandable — and more dramatic — form, turn it into a chart.

Creating a New Chart

Quattro Pro gives you two quick ways to create a chart:

- Use the Chart Expert. The Expert walks you through the steps of selecting a chart type, adding labels, picking colors, and making other decisions regarding your chart. Using this method, you can put your chart right on a spreadsheet page or in a separate window. You may want to put the chart in a separate window if you want to print it on its own page instead of with your spreadsheet.
- Use the QuickChart tool button, labeled in Figure 14-1. With this tool, Quattro Pro takes a guess at the kind of chart that best fits your data and creates the chart for you right on the spreadsheet page. You can edit the chart if you want to change the chart type, labels, and so on.

In the interest of full disclosure, I should tell you that you can also create a chart in its own window by using the Graphics⇨New Chart command. But that method is much less intuitive and complicated than using the Expert or QuickChart tool, so I don't cover it. After you get familiar with making charts the easy way, you may want to give the New Chart command a whirl, but only if you like making things more difficult than they need to be.

Using the Chart Expert

The Chart Expert is supposed to be self-explanatory, but if you ask me, it's not. So here's how to use the Expert:

1. **Select the data you want to turn into a chart.**

   Select the column and row labels if you want them included in the chart — but *don't* select any titles or subtitles you may have given your spreadsheet. You add those to your chart later.

2. **Choose Tools⇨Experts⇨Chart.**

   The dialog box shown in Figure 14-2 appears. In the example window, Quattro Pro gives you a look at the chart that it thinks best suits your data. But don't worry; you get a chance to change the chart type later. The two check boxes in the dialog box let you rearrange the order of the data in the graph. To see what the options do, check and uncheck them — the preview updates to show you the difference the options make to your chart.

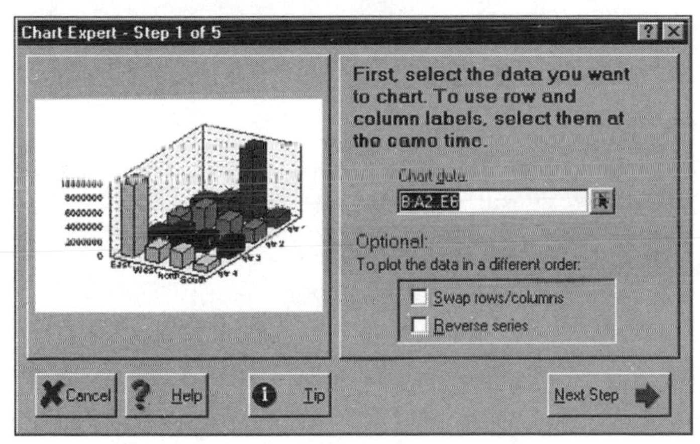

Figure 14-2: You can rearrange the data in your chart by using the two check boxes in the first panel of the dialog box.

3. **Click on the Next Step button to advance through the remaining panels of the Chart Expert.**

   You advance first to a panel that asks you to select a general chart type. Click on Next Step again, and you get to refine your chart type a little more. And with the third click of Next Step, you can select a color scheme for your chart. As you make selections, the sample window updates to show what your chart will look like.

If you're planning to print your chart on a black-and-white printer, use either the Grayscale or Black and White Patterns option in Step 4 of the Expert for best results.

At any point, you can return to the previous panel and change a setting by clicking on the Prev Step button, shown in Figure 14-3.

When you get to the fifth panel of the Expert, shown in Figure 14-3, you can add a title, subtitle, and axis labels to your chart. The preview updates to show you where each label or title will appear.

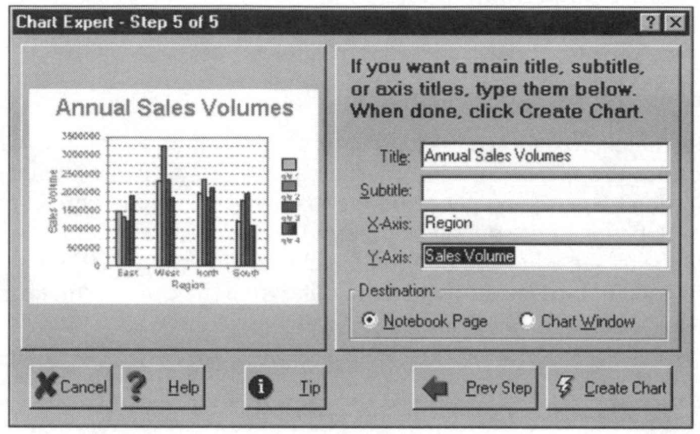

Figure 14-3: You add titles and labels to your chart in the last panel of the Chart Expert.

4. **Select a Destination radio button.**

   If you select the Notebook Page option, your chart appears on the current notebook page. If you select Chart Window, the chart appears in its own window.

5. **Click on Create Chart.**

   If you chose the Chart Window option in Step 4, Quattro Pro creates your chart and displays it in the window. (To return to your spreadsheet, choose its name from the Window menu.)

   If you chose Notebook Page, Quattro Pro returns you to the spreadsheet page, and your cursor looks like a little chart. Place the cursor at the spot where you want to put the upper-left corner of the chart and drag to the opposite corner, as shown in Figure 14-4. After you release the mouse button, Quattro Pro draws your chart.

Creating charts with the QuickChart tool

To use the QuickChart tool, just select the data you want to chart, click on the QuickChart button in the toolbar (labeled back in Figure 14-1), and drag with the chart cursor to set the boundaries for the chart, as in Figure 14-4. After you release the mouse button, Quattro Pro draws the chart that it believes is most appropriate for your data. You can change the chart layout, titles, colors, and other features as explained in the next section.

Chart boundary

Chart cursor

	A	B	C	D	E
1	1996 Sales Figures				
2		qtr 1	qtr 2	qtr 3	qtr 4
3	East	$1,500,687	$1,345,678	$1,235,673	$1,897,654
4	West	$2,302,987	$3,265,382	$2,365,438	$1,876,352
5	North	$1,978,630	$2,348,765	$1,876,392	$2,123,482
6	South	$1,234,897	$1,786,493	$1,984,732	$1,098,362

Figure 14-4: Drag with the chart cursor to set the boundaries for your chart.

Editing a Chart

To change the data in a chart, change the original spreadsheet data you used to create the chart. Any changes to the spreadsheet are automatically reflected in the chart.

To change design-related aspects of your chart — chart type, label font, titles, and so on — you edit the chart itself. Upcoming sections give you the specifics of changing particular elements of your chart, but here's a general overview of how you get to the various editing commands and options:

- To edit a chart on a spreadsheet page, right-click on the chart to display a QuickMenu of editing options related to the overall chart design, as shown in Figure 14-5. Little black boxes, called *selection handles,* appear around the perimeter of the chart to show you that the chart is selected.

  To edit the fine details of the chart, double-click on it. Depending on how you created the chart, one of two things happens. The chart becomes surrounded by a dotted blue border, as shown in Figure 14-6, the Chart menu replaces the Data menu on the menu bar, and the toolbar changes to

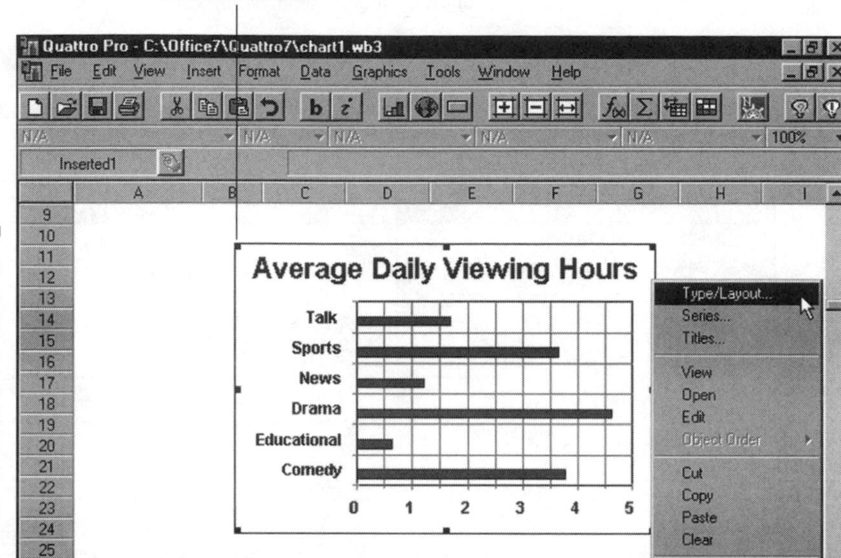

Figure 14-5: To make general changes to the chart, right-click on it and select an editing option from the QuickMenu.

display some handy chart editing and drawing tools. (I added the nifty arrow in Figure 14-6 using the Arrowhead Line tool, by the way.) Or the chart opens in its own chart window, which also offers the special chart editing commands and tools.

Either way, you then right-click on the element you want to edit and choose the Properties command from the QuickMenu to open up a dialog box of editing options. (The name of the Properties command changes depending on what you right-clicked.)

- To edit a chart that you created in its own window, choose the chart name from the Window menu (if you're not already looking at the chart, of course). You can then use the drawing tools, Chart menu commands, and QuickMenu commands to edit your chart.

- You can also edit any chart by clicking on the QuickTab button, labeled in Figure 14-6, to go to the Objects page. The Objects page contains a little icon representing each chart in your spreadsheet, as shown in Figure 14-7. Double-click on the icon for the chart you want to edit. Quattro Pro opens the chart in its own chart window.

Unfortunately, the little icons on the Objects page don't look anything like the charts they represent, and Quattro Pro gives your charts vague names like Chart 1, Chart 2, and so on. You can give a chart a more meaningful name by right-clicking on its icon on the Objects page, choosing the Icon Properties item from the QuickMenu, and entering the name in the resulting Name dialog box, as shown in Figure 14-7.

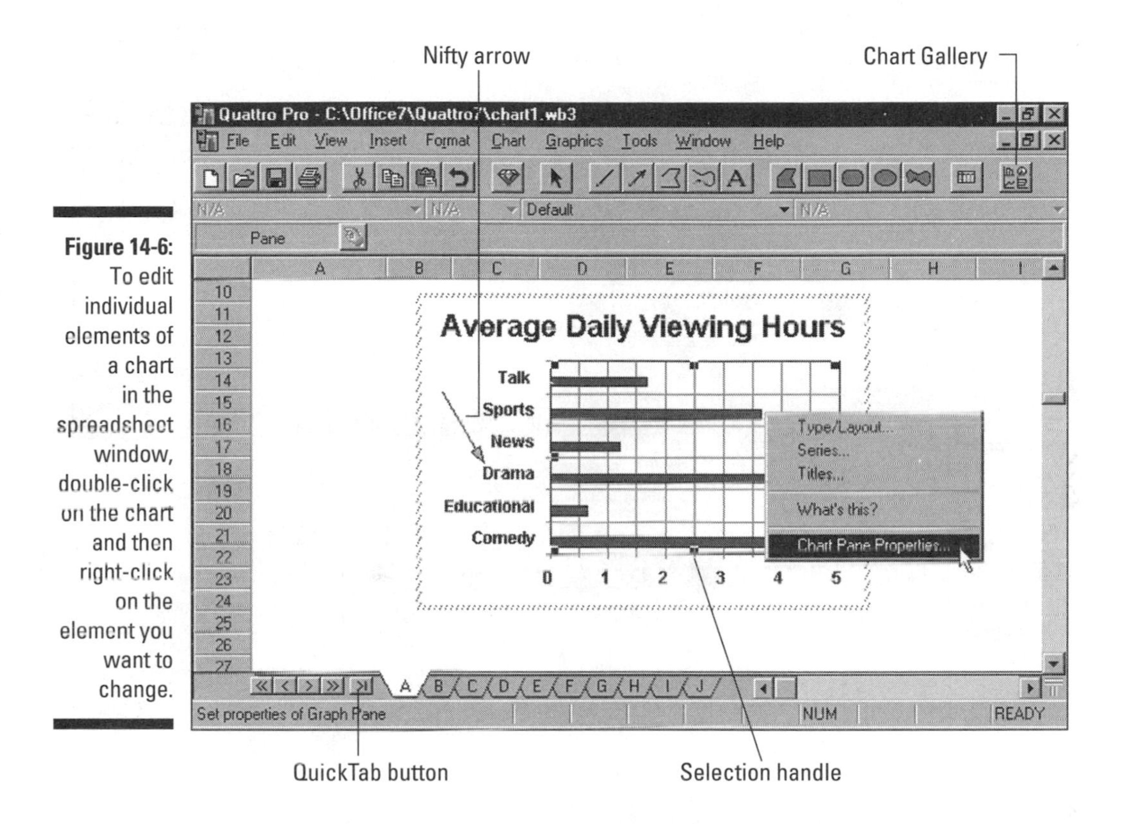

Figure 14-6: To edit individual elements of a chart in the spreadsheet window, double-click on the chart and then right-click on the element you want to change.

To switch from the chart window to your spreadsheet window, choose the spreadsheet window name from the Window menu. Any changes you made to your chart are automatically made in your spreadsheet as well.

Changing the chart type and color scheme

If you want to change the chart type or layout, right-click on the chart and select the Type/Layout option from the QuickMenu. Quattro Pro displays a dialog box that lets you select an overall chart category and specific chart layout.

If you want to change the color scheme of the chart, click on the Chart Gallery button on the toolbar, labeled in Figure 14-6, or choose Chart⇨Gallery to display the Chart Gallery dialog box, shown in Figure 14-8. (If the Chart menu and Chart Gallery toolbar buttons aren't available, double-click on the chart to display them.)

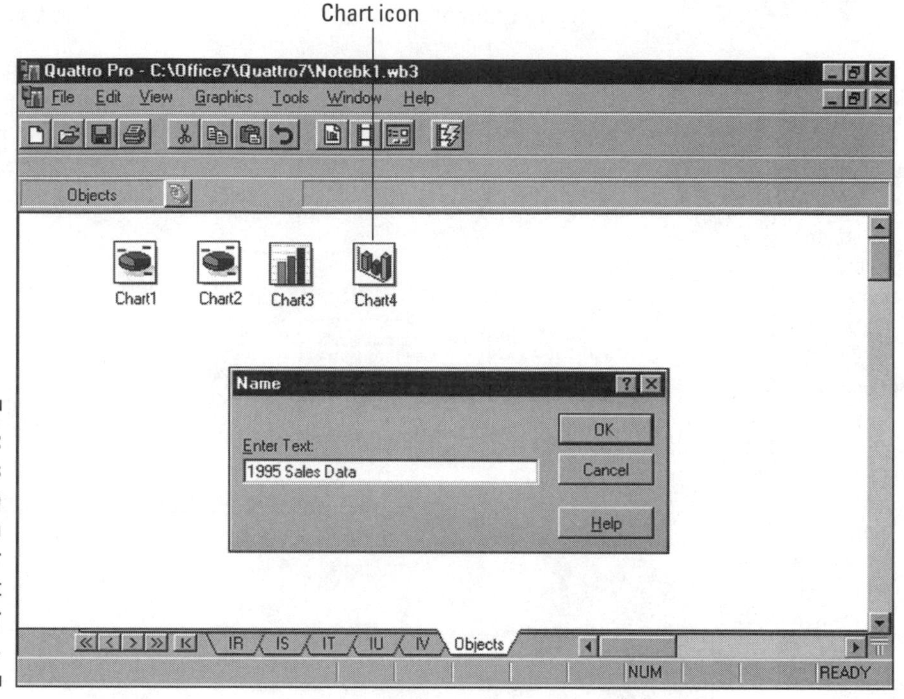

Figure 14-7: The Objects page contains an icon for every chart in your spreadsheet.

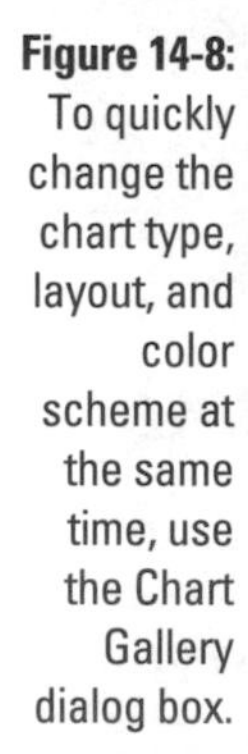

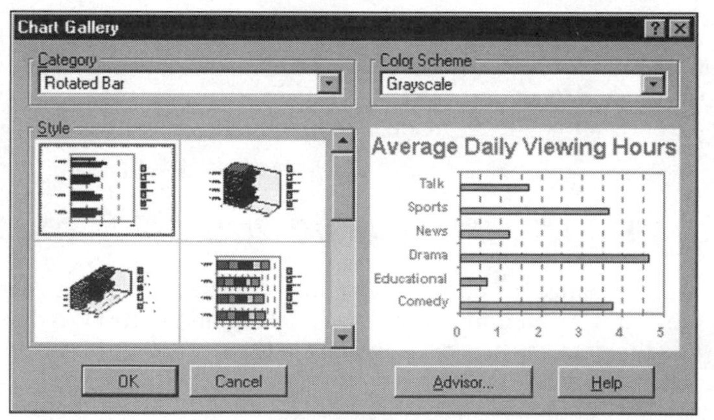

Figure 14-8: To quickly change the chart type, layout, and color scheme at the same time, use the Chart Gallery dialog box.

Select the color arrangement you want to use from the Color Scheme drop-down list. You can also change the chart type and layout in this dialog box. Select a chart category from the Category drop-down list and select a specific chart layout from the Style list box. The preview box shows how your chart looks with the selected changes. Click on OK to apply your changes.

Giving your chart a title and a border

To add a title, subtitle, or axis title to your chart, choose Chart⇨Titles (double-click on your chart to display the Chart menu, if it's not visible) or right-click on the chart and choose Titles from the QuickMenu. Quattro Pro displays a dialog box that lets you enter a main title, a subtitle, and labels for the X and Y axes (for charts that have them). (The X axis is the horizontal one; the Y axis is the vertical one.) Click on OK to apply your titles.

If you want to change the border around your chart, the steps depend on whether you're working in the spreadsheet window or a chart window:

- In the spreadsheet window, right-click on the chart and choose the Chart Properties command. The border options are found on the Box Type and Border Color tabs.
- In a chart window, choose Chart⇨Background or right-click near the edge of the chart and choose the Background Properties item. The border settings are found on the Box Settings tab. Select one of the border style buttons and then select a border color from the Fill Color drop-down list.
- If you don't want a border, select white as your border color — assuming that you're printing on white paper, of course.

Editing individual chart elements

As with adding borders to your chart, you edit the individual elements of a chart — for example, to change the font used for the titles — a little differently depending on whether you're working in the spreadsheet window or in a chart window.

In the chart window, you simply right-click on the element you want to change and choose the Properties item from the bottom of the resulting QuickMenu. The name of the item changes according to what you right-click. If you're working in the spreadsheet window, you must first double-click on the chart.

The type and scope of the elements you can change depend on what type of chart you're using; right-click all over your chart and play around with the different options to discover the possibilities. The selection handles indicate which part of the chart is selected.

To return to the spreadsheet window from a chart window, choose the spreadsheet's name from the Window menu.

Adding lines and callouts

Quattro Pro's drawing tools, listed in Table 14-1, let you add lines, arrowhead lines, and callouts (text) to your chart. (If the tools aren't visible, double-click on your chart to display them.)

To add a line, just click on one of the line tools and drag to create your line. If you're drawing a line with the Polyline tool, double-click to end your line.

To add a box filled with text, click on the Text tool and drag to create the box. Then type the text that you want to appear in the box. To edit text in a text box, double-click on the text box. You get the standard insertion marker you get when editing text in a regular cell.

The shape tools (rectangle, ellipse, and so on) let you add solid shapes to your chart. You probably won't have much call for them, but that doesn't mean that you can't play around with them to amuse yourself on a slow day.

After you create a line, shape, or text box, you can right-click on it to change its properties, as you can with any chart element.

Table 14-1 Quattro Pro's Drawing Tools

Icon	Tool	How You Use It
	Line tool	Drag to create a straight line.
	Arrow tool	Drag to draw a straight line with an arrowhead at one end.
	Polyline tool	Draws lines with more than one segment. Drag to create the first segment, release, drag to create the next segment. Double-click to end the line.
	Freehand Polyline	Drag to draw a freehand line.
A	Text tool	Drag to create a text box, type your text, and click outside the text box.
	Polygon tool	Creates a polygon shape; drag to create the first segment, release the mouse button, and drag to create the remaining segments. Double-click to finish the shape.
	Rectangle tool	Drag to create a rectangle; Shift+drag to create a square.
	Rounded Rectangle tool	Drag to create a rectangle with rounded edges; Shift+drag to create a square with rounded edges.
	Ellipse tool	Drag to create an ellipse; Shift+drag to create a circle.
	Freehand Polygon tool	Drag to create a freehand polygon shape.

Exchanging rows and columns

Take a gander at Figure 14-9. I got this arrangement of data when I first created my chart. Obviously, this arrangement is not the best way to present this particular data; the arrangement shown in Figure 14-10 makes it much easier to see how each gender reacts to the various life irritants.

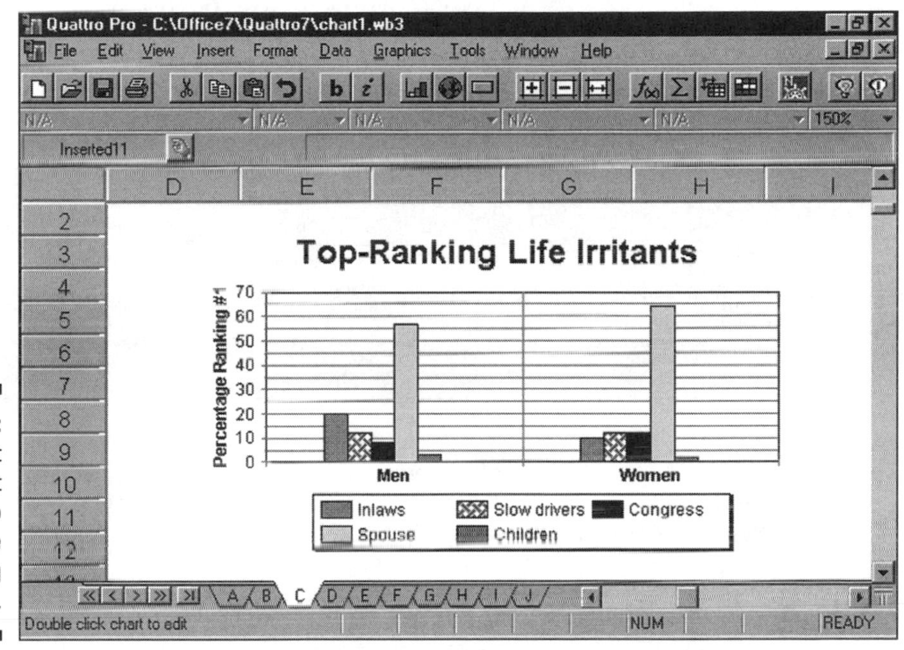

Figure 14-9: This chart makes it difficult to absorb the data being presented.

To change the arrangement of the data in your chart, you could go back and re-enter the data in the spreadsheet, changing your rows into columns and vice versa. Or you could take the easy way out: Right-click on your chart, choose the Series item from the QuickMenu, and select the Row/Column Swap option in the Chart Series dialog box. Click on OK to make the swap official.

Moving, Resizing, and Deleting Charts

Want to move that chart from one place in your spreadsheet to another? Click on it to select it and then press and hold the left mouse button down. When you see the little hand cursor appear, drag your chart to its new home.

You can also move a chart by using the Cut and Paste commands. Select the chart, choose Edit⇨Cut, click at the spot where you want to place the chart,

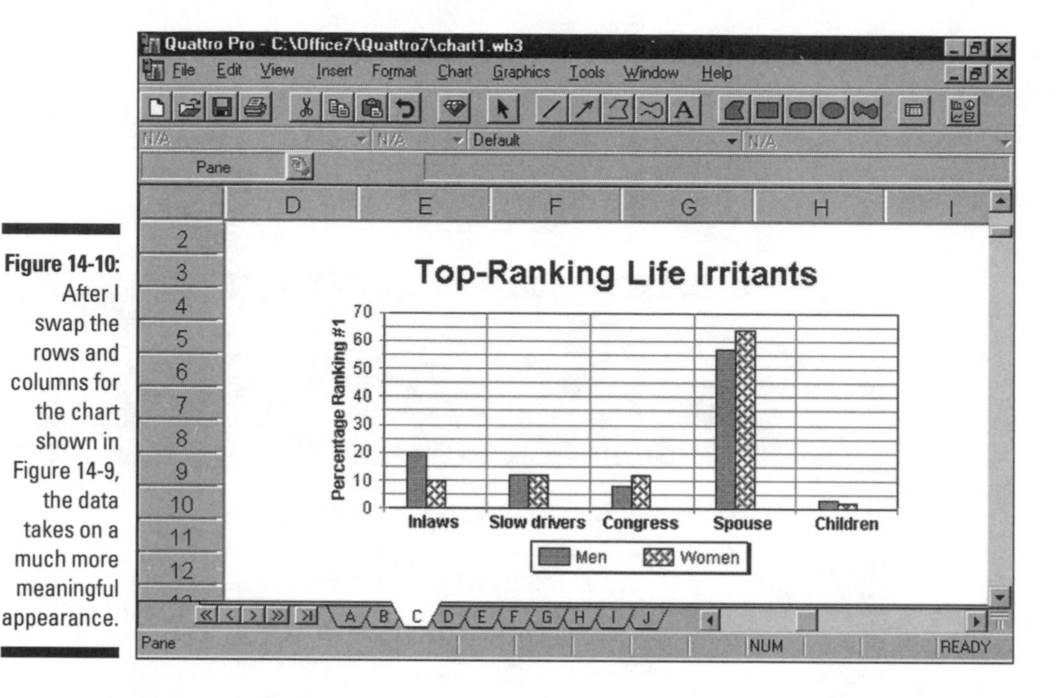

Figure 14-10: After I swap the rows and columns for the chart shown in Figure 14-9, the data takes on a much more meaningful appearance.

and choose Edit⇨Paste. After you choose the Cut command, Quattro Pro tells you that you're about to delete the chart and asks whether you want to delete it from the Objects page also; go ahead and click on Yes.

As you may have already guessed, you can also use the Copy and Paste commands to copy charts. You can use this method to copy a chart created in its own window to a spreadsheet page, for example. Either choose Edit⇨Select All in the chart window and then choose the Copy command, or right-click on the chart icon on the Object page and choose Copy from the resulting QuickMenu.

To resize a chart in the spreadsheet window, click on it to display its selection handles. Drag a top or bottom handle to change the height of the chart only; drag a side handle to change the width only; drag a corner handle to change both the width and height. You can't resize a chart in a chart window, but you can reduce or enlarge it for printing by using the print-scaling options described in the "Changing the page setup" section in Chapter 15.

Finally, to delete a chart from your spreadsheet, select it and press Delete. Quattro Pro asks whether you want to delete the copy of the chart that's stored on the Objects page. If you want to delete the copy, choose Yes; if you want to delete the chart on the current page but not the copy on the Objects page, choose No.

To delete a chart in a chart window, click on its icon on the Objects page and press Delete.

Printing a Chart without Its Spreadsheet

Chapter 15 spells out the steps for printing a spreadsheet. If you created your chart on your spreadsheet page and want to print both the spreadsheet data and chart, follow the instructions given in that chapter.

If you want to print your chart without the spreadsheet data, however, follow these steps instead:

1. **Click on the chart to select it.**

   If you created the chart in its own window, you can skip this step.

2. **Choose File⇨Print or press Ctrl+P.**

   The Chart Print dialog box appears, as shown in Figure 14-11. The Select Printer, Print Preview, and Page Setup options work as outlined in the printing sections of Chapter 15.

3. **Select the number of copies you want to print in the Copies option box.**

4. **Click on Print or press Enter.**

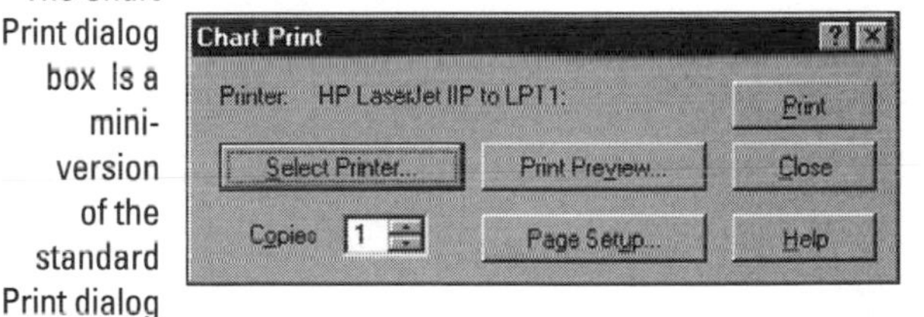

Figure 14-11: The Chart Print dialog box is a mini-version of the standard Print dialog box.

If your notebook contains several charts, you can print them all at the same time by using their icons on the Objects page. Click on the QuickTab button to go to the Objects page (the button's labeled back in Figure 14-6), and Shift+click on the icon for each chart you want to print. Then choose the Print command, set the number of copies you want of each chart, and press Enter.

Chapter 15

The Finishing Touches

In This Chapter

- Formatting in a flash with SpeedFormat
- Adding lines, borders, and colors
- Adding headers and footers
- Hiding columns or rows temporarily
- Inserting a page break
- Printing your spreadsheet

Packaging is everything. Think about it: Would you rather open a present that's encased in shiny, colorful wrapping paper and topped with a matching bow, or one that's stuffed carelessly in a dirty, wrinkled paper bag that smells suspiciously like last night's Chinese carryout? Why, given the right presentation, even a cheap gift can convey the impression that somebody really cares about you.

The same is true with spreadsheets. You make a much better impression on the folks who see your spreadsheet if you fancy up the page with charts, borders, headers, and the like. In fact, a nicely formatted spreadsheet can help divert everyone's attention from the actual information you're presenting, which can be really helpful on occasion.

Of course, you won't always want to dress up your spreadsheets in their Sunday best. For everyday number-crunching, you just want to enter your formulas, run your calculations, and then print out the results. For those times, skip to the end of this chapter, which tells you how to print your spreadsheet.

But if you want your spreadsheets to really wow your audience — whatever your motives — play around with the advanced formatting options discussed in the rest of this chapter. (Chart-making techniques are covered in Chapter 14.) With a little effort on your part, you can make even the most horrible spreadsheet data look as delightful as a gift-wrapped box from Tiffanys.

Using SpeedFormat

Don't want to spend much time formatting your spreadsheet? Afraid of making some awful formatting faux pas? Let Quattro Pro's SpeedFormat command take care of everything for you. The SpeedFormat command lets you apply a predesigned set of formatting attributes to your data — font, shading, alignment, and more — with a wave of your hand (or rather, with a few clicks of the old mouse).

To use this handy feature, select the cells you want to format, as explained back in Chapter 13, in the section "Selecting Stuff." Then click on the SpeedFormat toolbar button (it's near the right end of the toolbar and looks like a miniature spreadsheet), choose Format⇨SpeedFormat, or right-click on the block and choose the SpeedFormat command from the QuickMenu. The dialog box shown in Figure 15-1 appears.

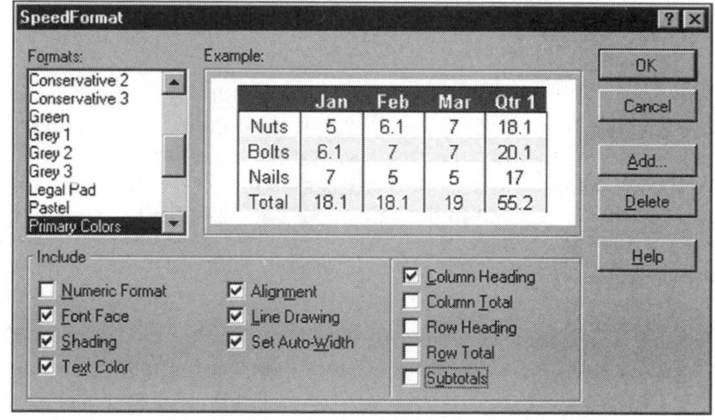

Figure 15-1: To quickly turn your spreadsheet from dull to dazzling, use one of the formatting templates available through the SpeedFormat command.

You can select from a variety of different spreadsheet designs, which are listed in the Formats list box. Click on a design name to display an example of that format in the Example box.

At the bottom of the dialog box are check boxes that enable you to select which parts of the design you want to incorporate into your spreadsheet. For example, if you don't want to use the font that the template applies, uncheck the Font Face option box.

When you're satisfied with your selections, click on OK or press Enter to apply the formatting. If you don't like what you see, choose Edit⇨Undo or press Ctrl+Z. Or select the Normal option from the Style drop-down list on the Power Bar to return to Quattro Pro's default formatting.

You can add your own template to the SpeedFormat dialog box. Just format a block, open the SpeedFormat dialog box, click on the Add button, and give your template a name. Any time you want to use that same format again, you can apply it from the SpeedFormat dialog box.

Adding Lines, Borders, and Colors

Quattro Pro lets you draw lines around cells, surround blocks with borders, and even paint your spreadsheet with color. To whet your artistic appetite a little, the spreadsheet in Figure 15-2 shows an example that incorporates all these formatting options.

Notice anything different about the spreadsheet in Figure 15-2? The cell gridlines that normally appear on-screen are missing. When you're adding lines, borders, and color to your spreadsheet, turn the gridlines off so that you can get a better idea of how your printed spreadsheet will look. (Gridlines normally don't print, as explained in the printing section later in this chapter.)

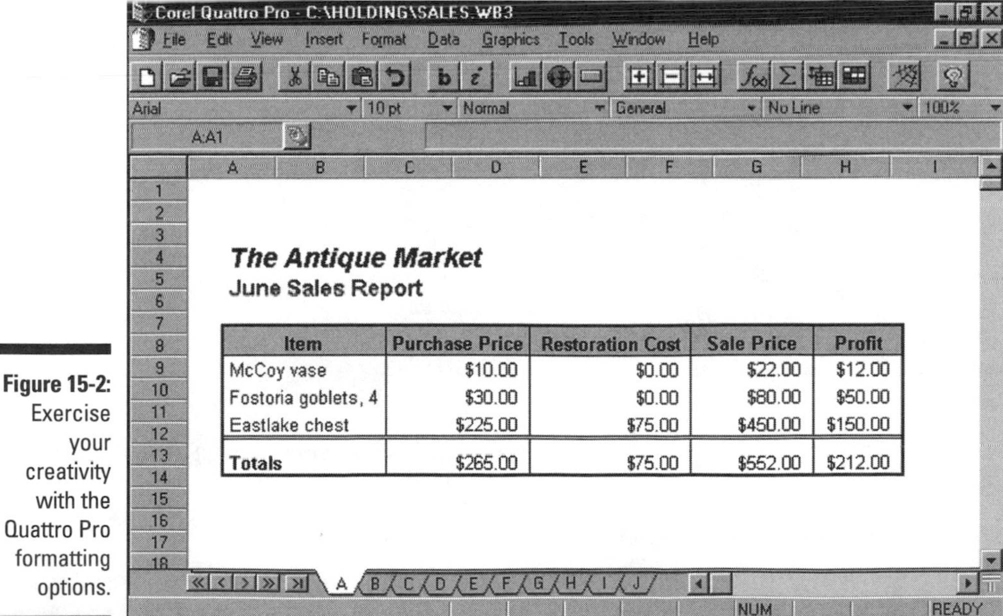

Figure 15-2: Exercise your creativity with the Quattro Pro formatting options.

To turn off the gridlines, right-click on the page tab or choose Format⇨Page to display the Active Page dialog box. Then uncheck the gridlines check boxes on the Display tab and press Enter.

Drawing lines and borders around cells

Putting a line under a cell is easy. Just select the cell (or cells) you want to format and select one of the line options from the Line drop-down list on the Power Bar. (The drop-down list button is labeled No Line when no line is applied to the current cell.) You get four choices: Thin Line, Double Line, Thick Line, and No Line. To remove a line under a cell, just select the cell and select the No Line option.

Adding lines elsewhere — around a block of cells, between cells, at the top of cells, and so forth — is a little more complicated. Select the cells you want to format and then press F12, choose Format⇨Block, or right-click on the block and choose the Block Properties item from the QuickMenu. When the Active Block dialog box appears, click on the Line Drawing tab to display the line options, as shown in Figure 15-3.

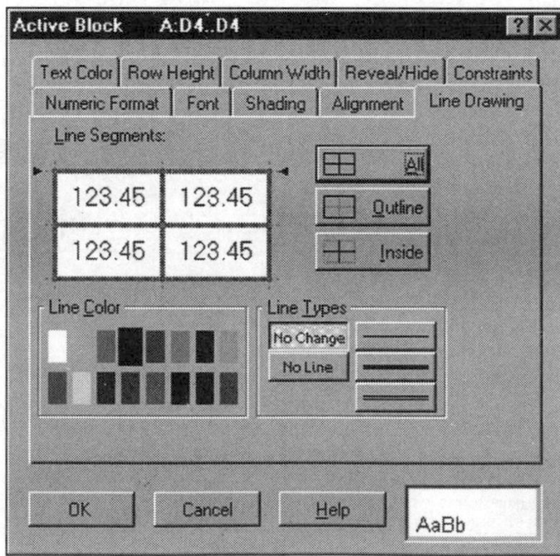

Figure 15-3: Drawing borders around blocks or lines between cells isn't really as complicated as this dialog box makes it appear.

This particular dialog box has to be one of the most confusing in all of Quattro Pro-land. I'll try to make it as simple as I can:

1. **Specify where you want lines to appear.**

   You make your choices in the Line Segments portion of the dialog box. If you click on the All button, you get lines around each and every selected cell. If you click on the Outline button, Quattro Pro draws a line around the selected block only. And if you click on the Inside button, you get lines between the cells but not around the perimeter of the block.

You aren't limited to the All, Outline, or Inside options, however. You can select whatever lines you want by clicking in the example grid. If you click at the intersection of two lines — on a corner, for example — both of the intersecting lines become selected. To select a line by itself, click anywhere on the line except at the point where it intersects with another line.

The little black arrows in the example grid indicate which lines are selected and will be added to your spreadsheet. In Figure 15-3, the arrows indicate that a line will be added to the top of the block.

You can add a line to the selection by Shift+clicking on it. To delete a line from the selection, Shift+click on it again.

2. **Select one of the Line Types buttons.**

   You can select a thin, thick, or double line. If you want to remove a previously drawn line, select the No Line option. If you want to cancel your changes to the line, select the No Change option.

3. **Select a Line Color swatch.**

   The default line color is black. If you want to select another color, just click on its swatch.

   Remember, though, that your colors won't print in color if you don't have a color printer — and some colors translate to a yucky, muddy shade of gray when printed on a black-and-white printer.

4. **Click on OK or press Enter.**

   When you finish applying your lines, press Enter or click on OK to see the results. If you don't like what you see, go back to the Line Drawing panel to make some changes or just press Ctrl+Z to get rid of all the lines you just applied.

You can specify as many different types of lines in the dialog box as you want. For example, you can add a thick line to the top and bottom borders and put a thin line on the right and left sides of the block. For each line type, just select the lines you want to format in the Line Segments grid and then select a line type and color.

If you're curious, here's how I created the lines in Figure 15-2: I first applied a thick line around the perimeter of the block by clicking on the Outline button and selecting the thick line type. Then I added a thin line between cells by selecting the center vertical line in the Line Segments grid and choosing the thin line type. Next, I closed the dialog box, selected the cells in the top row of the block, and selected the Thin Line option from the Power Bar. Finally, I selected the fourth row in the block and selected the Double Line option from the Power Bar.

Applying color to text and backgrounds

If you have a color printer or if you're creating an on-screen presentation, you may want to add some color to your spreadsheet. Even if you plan to print your spreadsheet on a black-and-white printer, you can get some nice effects by coloring the background of some cells with shades of grey or by reversing your text (putting white text on a dark background).

To change the color of spreadsheet text, select the cells you want to format and then press F12 to open the Active Block dialog box. (Or, if you insist on using the menus, choose Format⇨Block or right-click and choose the Block Properties command.) Then click on the Text Color tab and click on one of the color swatches on the tab. The preview box in the bottom-right corner of the dialog box shows what your colored text will look like on its current background.

To change the background color of a cell, click on the Shading tab of the Active Block dialog box. The Shading tab appears in all its glory in Figure 15-4. To fill the cell with a solid color background, click on a swatch in the Color 1 palette and then click on the leftmost swatch in the Blend palette.

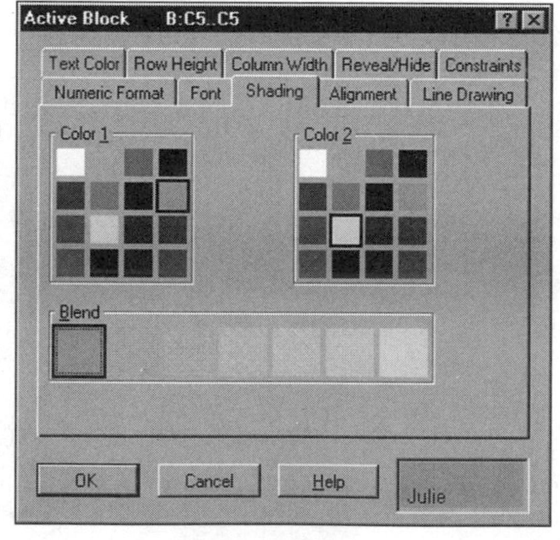

Figure 15-4: Nothing brightens up a spreadsheet like a little splash of color, known in Quattro Pro as shading.

To fill the cell with a *blend* — that is, a mixture of two colors — click on a color in the Color 1 palette and another color in the Color 2 palette. Quattro Pro fills the Blend palette with swatches that start with the Color 1 color and gradually blend into the Color 2 color. Click on the mixture that you want to use.

After you're done playing around with text and background colors, and you're ready to do some real work again, click on OK or press Enter.

Inserting Page Breaks

When you enter spreadsheet data, Quattro Pro automatically inserts a page break at the bottom of the page. To find out the size of your paper (so that it knows where to put the page break), Quattro Pro checks the Paper Type setting in the Spreadsheet Page Setup dialog box (discussed in the section "Changing the page setup," later in this chapter).

If you want to insert a page break at some other spot, select the leftmost cell in the row where you want the break to occur. For example, if you want the break to be at row 30, click on cell A30. Then choose Insert⇨Page Break. If the cell where you want to enter the page break is empty, you can enter the characters |:: into the cell instead of using the menu commands, if doing so would add some spice to your life. That's a vertical bar — which you get by pressing Shift and the backslash key (\) — followed by two colons.

The page breaks that Quattro Pro inserts are called *soft page breaks*. The page breaks that you insert are called *hard page breaks*.

Hiding a Row or Column

Suppose that you created a bang-up spreadsheet that lists each of your employees' names, titles, phone numbers, years at the company, and salary. Someone asks you for an employee information list, and the spreadsheet immediately pops into your head. It would be a quick way to deliver the information, but the person who needs the information isn't supposed to know how much money everybody makes.

Here's the solution: You can temporarily hide the salary information for printing or on-screen viewing. Just select the border of the row or column you want to hide and press F12, choose Format⇨Block, or right-click and choose Block Properties to open the Active Block dialog box. Then click on the Column or Row radio button (depending on what you want to hide), select the Hide radio button, and click on OK or press Enter.

When you hide a row or column, the following rows or columns shift over to fill the empty space. But the row numbers and column letters don't change — which gives you one easy way to see that you hid some data.

To redisplay a hidden row or column, select the rows or columns on both sides of the hidden row or column. Then follow the same procedure outlined for hiding data, but this time select the Reveal radio button.

You can also hide and reveal rows and columns using the mouse, but doing so is a little tricky:

- To hide a column, drag its right border to the left until you reach the right border of the preceding column. In other words, to hide Column B, drag its right edge all the way to the right edge of Column A.
- To reveal a hidden column, put your cursor *slightly to the right* of the border separating the two neighboring columns. To reveal hidden column B, for example, put your cursor just to the right of the border between columns A and C; then drag right.
- To hide a row, drag up on the bottom row border until you reach the bottom border of the preceding row.
- To reveal a hidden row, put the cursor *slightly below* the border between the two neighboring rows. Then drag down to uncover the hidden row.

Going from Screen to Printer

Ready to make the leap from digital spreadsheet to printed page? The following steps give you the basic how-to.

Printing a chart is slightly different than printing a regular spreadsheet. For more information, see the last section in Chapter 14.

1. **Choose File⇨Print or press Ctrl+P.**

   Or, if you're the toolbar type, click on the button that looks like a little printer with a sheet of paper coming out of the top. The Spreadsheet Print dialog box, shown in Figure 15-5, appears from out of nowhere.

   If the print commands are dimmed, you're in edit mode. Click outside the active cell to get out of edit mode and access the print commands.

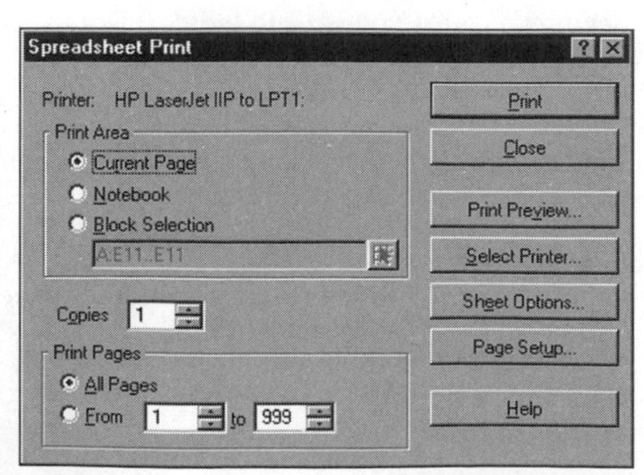

Figure 15-5: The Spreadsheet Print dialog box is Grand Central Station for all printing options.

2. **Select the print area.**

   Select Current Page to print just the current notebook page. Select Notebook to print more than one page in the notebook (you set the specific pages to print in Step 4). You can also print just selected cells by selecting them before you choose the Print command and then selecting the Block Selection radio button.

3. **Enter the number of copies you want to print in the Copies option box.**

4. **Select which pages to print.**

   If you selected the Notebook radio button as the print area in Step 2, you need to specify which pages print. Select the All Pages radio button to print all pages in your notebook. To print a range of pages, enter the starting page number in the first From option box and enter the last page number in the second option box. (You don't have to bother clicking on the From radio button; it automatically becomes selected when you enter values into the option boxes.)

5. **Click on Print or press Enter.**

   Assuming that your printer is properly set up and configured to work with your computer, your spreadsheet should come sliding out of your printer any minute now.

If you're hooked into a network and have access to several printers, you can select a printer by clicking on the Select Printer button.

Previewing before you print

Before you print, you may want to take a look at what the printed piece will look like. You may decide that you want to shrink or enlarge the margins, adjust the type size or font, or make other formatting changes before you actually transfer your spreadsheet to paper.

To preview your spreadsheet, choose File➪Print Preview to open the Preview window, shown in Figure 15-6. Or click on the Print Preview button in the Spreadsheet Print dialog box. The figure shows the preview of a budget spreadsheet I created to track everyday expenses. You'll notice that I've zoomed way out on the page so that no one can see how much I spend per week on sugar-free Fudgesicles and *Soap Opera Digest.*

The Preview window offers a number of helpful tools and options:

- When you first open the preview window, it shows you a full-page view of the first page in your notebook. Click to zoom in; right-click to zoom out. Keep clicking or right-clicking until you reach the magnification you want to use.

- Alternatively, you can zoom in and out by clicking on the Zoom buttons at the top of the window. The one with the plus sign in the center zooms in; the one with the minus sign zooms out.
- To see a different page of your notebook, enter the page number in the Page option box or click on the Next Page or Previous Page button.
- The two buttons that have crayons on them switch you between black-and-white view and full-color view. If you applied colors to fonts or used color in charts or graphs, you may want to preview the colors; otherwise, there's not much point in using the full-color display.
- To display or hide margin guidelines (labeled in Figure 15-6), click on the Margins button. You can drag the guidelines to change the page margins, as explained later in this chapter, in the section "Changing the page setup."
- Click on the Page Setup button to open the Spreadsheet Page Setup dialog box. In this dialog box, you can select a paper size and orientation and reduce or enlarge your spreadsheet for printing. These options are covered in the section "Changing the page setup."

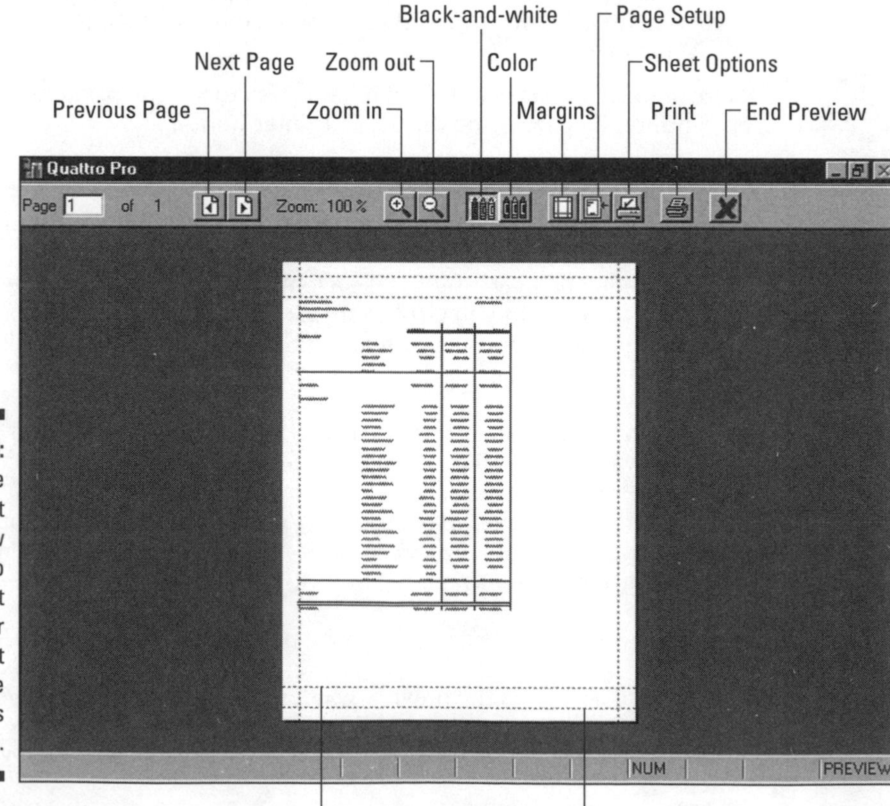

Figure 15-6: Use the Print Preview command to see what your spreadsheet will look like when it's printed.

- Click on the Sheet Options button to open the Spreadsheet Print Options dialog box, where you can make still more adjustments to the way your spreadsheet prints. For more information, see the upcoming section "Choosing print options."
- To go ahead and print your spreadsheet, click on the Print button. To close the Preview window, click on the End Preview button or press Esc.

Changing the page setup

If you want to print your spreadsheet on a special size paper, change the page orientation (the direction it prints), or enlarge or reduce your spreadsheet to fit on the printed page, you need to head for the Spreadsheet Page Setup dialog box, shown in Figure 15-7.

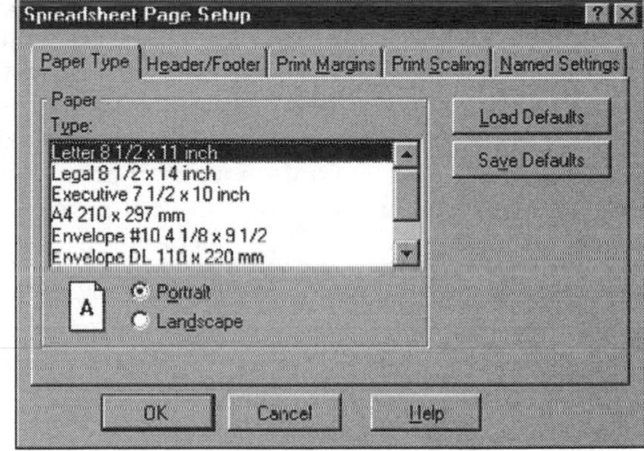

Figure 15-7: Choose the paper size, orientation, and other print options in the Spreadsheet Page Setup dialog box.

You can open this dialog box either by clicking on the Page Setup button in the Print Preview window (labeled in Figure 15-6) or by clicking on the Page Setup button in the Spreadsheet Print dialog box, shown back in Figure 15-5.

This dialog box contains five different panels of options. To switch between panels, click on the tabs at the top of the dialog box.

- Select your paper size from the Type list box on the Paper Type tab of the dialog box.
- Select the paper orientation by clicking on either the Portrait or Landscape radio button. In Portrait orientation, the rows of your spreadsheet run parallel to the short edge of the paper. In Landscape orientation, things print out sideways, so that the rows print parallel to the long edge of the paper.

- The Print Scaling tab offers two options: Print to Fit, which enlarges or reduces your spreadsheet to fit the paper; and Scaling, which enables you to enter a specific enlargement or reduction percentage. A value of exactly 100 percent prints the spreadsheet at its actual size; a value lower than 100 percent reduces the spreadsheet; and a value higher than 100 percent enlarges the spreadsheet.
- The Named Settings tab enables you to save all your page setup settings under a specific name so that you can easily reuse those same settings when you print another spreadsheet. To save your settings, enter a name in the New Set option box and click on the Add button. To reuse a setting, select it from the settings list box and click on the Use button. (You can't save print settings for a chart, however.)
- Set your page margins and header/footer margins on the Print Margins tab. Alternatively, you can drag the margin guides in the Print Preview window, as explained in the section "Previewing before you print."
- When you create a spreadsheet, Quattro Pro inserts automatic page breaks at the bottom of each page, checking the Paper Type tab settings to determine the size of your pages. The Break Pages check box on the Print Margins tab controls whether your pages print with or without these page breaks. If the option is selected, the page breaks are active; if the check box is turned off, the spreadsheet prints without the page breaks. You may want to turn the option off to print on continuous-feed printer paper, for example. (For more information on inserting your own page breaks, see the section "Inserting Page Breaks," earlier in this chapter.)
- The Header/Footer tab lets you add a header (text that appears at the top of every page) and a footer (text that appears at the bottom of every page). For example, you may want your name to appear on the bottom of every printed page. By default, the headers and footers are left-aligned and separated from the notebook data by the amount of space indicated by the header/footer margins.

  You can change the font of a header or footer by clicking on the corresponding font button on the Header/Footer tab. If you want to change the alignment of a header or footer, you have to type in some special Quattro Pro codes with your header/footer text. To see a list of the available codes, choose the Headers and Footers item in the Help index. You can also use the codes to insert dates, times, and multiple lines of text. Be forewarned, though, that using the codes is a bit complicated and messy.
- After you choose your page setup settings, click on OK or press Enter to return to the Spreadsheet Print dialog box or the Print Preview window.

Any settings you make in the dialog box are stored with your spreadsheet and remain in effect until you change them again.

If you want to return all the settings to their default values, click on the Load Defaults button. To save your current page setup values as the new default values, click on the Save Defaults button.

Choosing print options

The Spreadsheet Print Options dialog box, shown in Figure 15-8, offers still more ways to fine-tune your printout. To get to this dialog box, click on the Sheet Options button in the Print Preview window (labeled in Figure 15-6) or click on the Sheet Options button in the Spreadsheet Print dialog box.

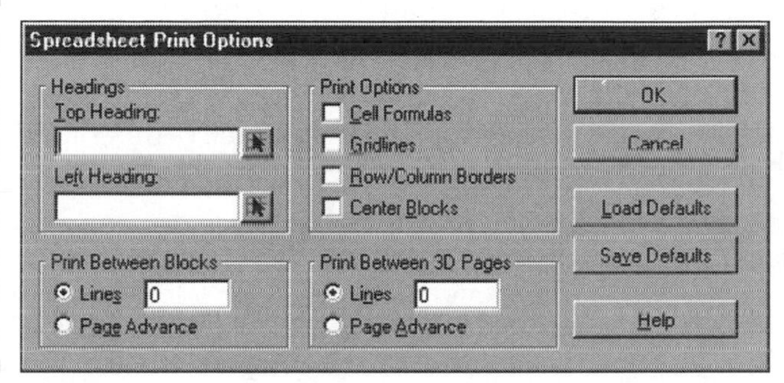

Figure 15-8: Options in this dialog box enable you to change the appearance of your printout.

The various options in the dialog box work as follows:

- If you have a long spreadsheet that won't print entirely on a single page, you may want to print the top row and/or left column of the spreadsheet on every page. Why? Because the top row and left column usually contain the titles of the rows and columns of data in your spreadsheet, and without those titles, it's easy to forget what type of information each row and column holds. Enter the name of the row (or rows) you want to print on each page in the Top Heading option box; enter the name of the column (or columns) you want to print on each page in the Left Heading option box.

  When you use these options, you need to print your document in a special way. Select everything *except* the top row or left column that you specified as the Top Heading or Left Heading. Then print using the Block Selection option in the Spreadsheet Print dialog box. Otherwise, the top row and left column print twice on the first page of your printout.

- Normally, Quattro Pro prints the answers to formulas and not the formulas itself. But if you want to print the formulas rather than the answers for some reason, check the Cell Formulas check box. One reason you may want to do this is if you're having trouble making your spreadsheet work and you want to have a Quattro Pro guru review the formulas you're using. Note that some print features, such as Gridlines and Center Blocks (explained next), are disabled when you use this option.

- Normally, the gridlines marking the boundaries of each cell on-screen don't print. If you want these gridlines to print, check the Gridlines option box. But be forewarned that including the gridlines increases the amount of printer memory you need to print your spreadsheet.

- If your printer memory isn't sufficient to print gridlines, you may be able to create "fake" gridlines by drawing them with the Line Drawing options discussed in "Drawing lines and borders around cells" in this chapter. Select the part of your spreadsheet that needs gridlines; then choose the All line segments button and the thin Line Types option on the Line Drawing panel of the Active Block dialog box.
- If you want to print row and column borders, check the Row/Column Borders option box. You may want to do this if you want to know the exact cell address of each cell in the printed spreadsheet so that you can go back and edit specific cells easily. But unless your spreadsheet's really big, printing the borders is probably overkill.
- To center the spreadsheet on the page, check the Center Blocks check box. Otherwise, the spreadsheet is aligned to the left margin.
- If you chose the Block Selection printing option and are printing more than one block of your spreadsheet, select the Page Advance radio button in the Print Between Blocks section of the dialog box to print each block on a separate page. If you select the Lines option, the different blocks are printed on the same sheet of paper but are separated by the number of lines you enter in the Lines option box. (To find out how to select multiple blocks to print, see the section "Selecting Stuff" in Chapter 13.)
- If you want each page of your notebook to start on a new sheet of paper, select the Page Advance radio button in the Print Between 3D Pages section of the dialog box. If you just want to separate the different pages with a few lines of space, select the Lines radio button and enter the number of line spaces you want in the option box.
- To reset the print options to Quattro Pro's defaults, click on Load Defaults. To make your settings the new default settings, click on Save Defaults.
- After you select all your print options, click on OK or press Enter to return to the Spreadsheet Print dialog box or the Print Preview window.

You now know more than you ever wanted to know about printing spreadsheets in Quattro Pro. That headache you have is a sure sign that your brain is growing by leaps and bounds.

Part IV
Those Other Programs

AFTER SPENDING 9 DAYS WITH 12 DIFFERENT VENDORS AND READING 26 BROCHURES, DAVE HAD AN ACUTE ATTACK OF TOXIC OPTION SYNDROME.

In this part . . .

This part of the book is a heaping smorgasbord of information about the programs not covered in Parts I, II, and III. It dishes up tasty servings of techniques and tips for using Presentations, Envoy, Netscape Navigator, Sidekick, Dashboard, CorelFLOW, and Corel Address Book. And for dessert, it offers valuable insights on how to use all the programs in the suite together to save yourself some time and effort.

Dig in, and bring a hearty appetite. As they say, there's something here to satisfy every taste. And at this buffet, you can fill your plate as many times as you want without winding up with that uncomfortable, bloated feeling or any extra pounds.

Chapter 16

Let's All Get Together and Put on a Show!

In This Chapter

- Creating multimedia slide shows
- Adding text and graphics to slides
- Adding sounds, animation, and other special effects
- Creating simple drawings
- Playing your presentation on someone else's computer

Hoo, boy. You really stepped in it this time, didn't you? When they asked if you'd give a presentation to the big brass at the annual company meeting, you didn't even *hesitate* before saying yes. Okay, maybe you hesitated just a little, but you didn't want to look uncooperative, so you acted as if the idea was a good one. Or maybe you out and out refused, but they said that if you didn't agree to their evil plan, you'd be looking for another employer.

Well, however you got yourself into this predicament, Presentations can help get you out of it. With Presentations, you can create a multimedia slide show that you can play back on any computer — even one that doesn't have Presentations installed. You can also create regular 35mm slides, transparencies, and printed drawings.

This chapter shows you how to use Presentations to create a show that not only entertains and informs your audience, but also draws attention away from the fact that you spilled salad dressing on your shirt during lunch.

Starting and Stopping

To start Presentations, click on the Presentations DAD icon or click on the Start button on the Windows 95 taskbar, choose the Corel WordPerfect Suite 7 item from the Start menu, and then choose Corel Presentations 7 from the submenu.

After your computer gurgles and churns for a bit, Presentations pops to life and immediately presents you with the dialog box shown in Figure 16-1. You see this same dialog box every time you start the program or close all your open documents — Presentations doesn't feel comfortable with the windows closed, evidently.

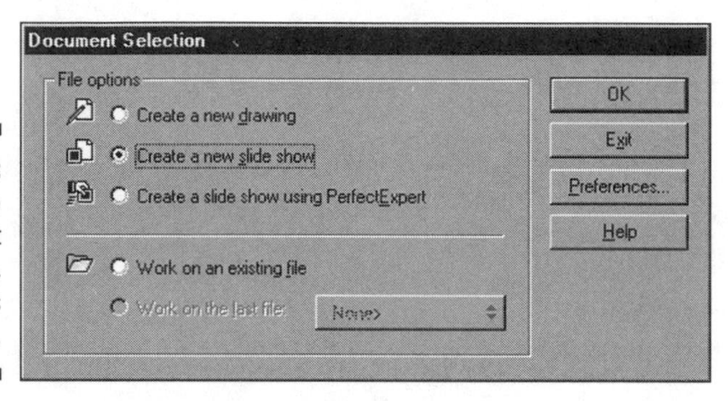

Figure 16-1: Each time you start Presentations, you see this dialog box.

- You can choose to create a new drawing, create a new slide show on your own (with this book's help, of course), create a new slide show using the PerfectExpert, or edit an existing slide show.
- If you click on the Work on an Existing File radio button, the Open dialog box appears so that you can select the file you want to edit. (If you're not familiar with using the Open dialog box, see the section "Figuring out the Open dialog box" in Chapter 5.)
- The Work on the Last File button gives you quick access to the files you worked on most recently. Click on the button next to the option to display a list of files and select the one you want.

After you make your choice in the Document Selection dialog box, click on OK or press Enter. If you're creating a new slide show, Presentations takes you next to the New Slide Show dialog box, explained in the upcoming section "Building a Really Big Shew." If you're creating a new drawing, a shiny new drawing page appears, where you can use the tools described in the section "Adding Pretty Pictures" to create simple drawings. And if you're editing an existing show or drawing, the show or drawing appears on-screen.

The Presentations window contains many of the same elements as WordPerfect, Quattro Pro, and other programs in the WordPerfect Suite, including a toolbar, Property Bar, and menu bar. For more information on using the different window elements, see the section "Basic Stuff You Need to Know" in Chapter 2. The Presentations window also has a second toolbar that runs down the left side of the program window. This toolbar — which, for the sake of convenience, I refer to as the drawing toolbar — contains drawing tools plus buttons that enable you to switch between viewing modes when you're creating a slide show.

If you're not sure what a toolbar button or Power Bar button does, pause the mouse cursor over the button for a second. Presentations displays a box explaining the purpose of the button.

If you want to create a second Presentations document while the first one is still open, choose File⇨New, press Ctrl+N, or click on the New button on the toolbar. To open a second existing file, choose File⇨Open, press Ctrl+O, or click on the Open button on the toolbar. The New button is the first button on the toolbar (the one that looks like a blank sheet of paper), and the Open button lives right next door.

To close a drawing or presentation, choose File⇨Close, press Ctrl+F4, or click on the document window Close button. To shut down Presentations, choose File⇨Exit, press Alt+F4, or click on the program window Close button.

Building a Really Big Shew

To understand how Presentations works, you need to understand that each slide has three layers:

- The Background layer contains a picture or design that appears behind the text and graphics on your slides.
- The Layout layer is a template that contains preformatted areas to hold your slide text. You select a template for each type of slide you create — such as title slide, bullet chart, and so on.
- The Slide layer holds the actual text and graphics that you put on the slide.

The following sections show you how to combine these three layers to create your slides. Later sections explain how to edit your slides and save, print, and play your show.

Step 1: Choosing a Master

After you tell Presentations that you want to create a slide show, it presents you with the New Slide Show dialog box, shown in Figure 16-2. As you can see from the dialog box, your first decision involves choosing a *Master.*

The Master determines the overall look of your show. The Master includes the background for your slides and templates with preformatted areas to hold different types of slide text. Although the purpose of the Master is to give your show a consistent design, you can override the background and layout template for any slide.

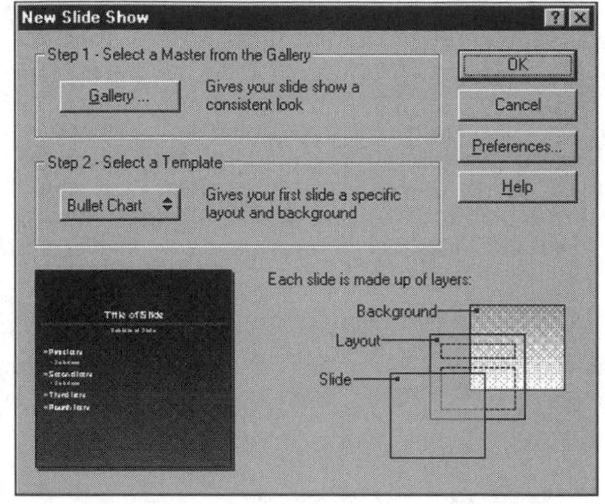

Figure 16-2: The first step in creating a slide show is to select a Master.

To select a Master, click on the Gallery button in the New Slide Show dialog box. The Master Gallery dialog box, shown in Figure 16-3, appears.

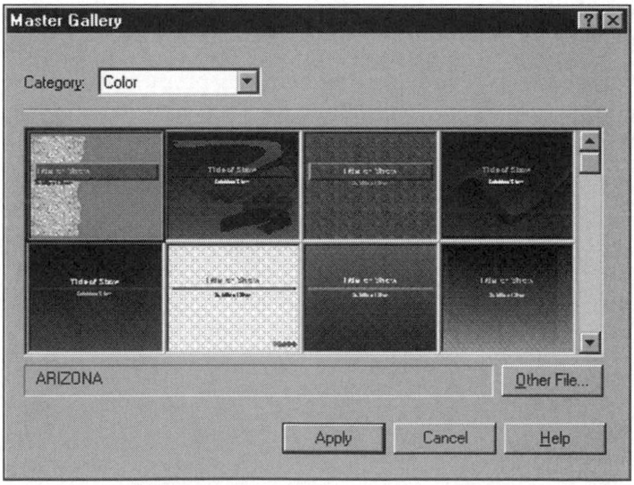

Figure 16-3: Select the Master you want to use and click on Apply.

The Category drop-down list offers three options:

- Select the Color option if you'll be showing your presentation on a color monitor.
- Select the 35mm slide option if you plan on converting your presentation to 35mm slides for use in a slide projector.

- Select the Printout option if you're going to print your show as black-and-white transparencies or print black-and-white copies of your slides to use as handouts. (You can also convert a color slide show to black-and-white handouts during printing, as explained later in this chapter, in the section "Printing Your Masterpieces.")

Use the scroll bar on the right side of the dialog box to view the different Masters. Click on the one you want to use and click on Apply or press Enter to make your choice official. You return to the New Slide Show dialog box to select a template.

Step 2: Choosing a slide template

After you select a Master, the next step is to select the template for your first slide. You select a template from the drop-down list in the Select a Template area of the New Slide Show dialog box, shown back in Figure 16-2. Your choices are:

- None: a plain white background and no preformatted text boxes
- Background: the background image from the Master Gallery but no preformatted text boxes
- Title (on Background): the background from the Master Gallery plus text boxes formatted to hold a title and subtitle
- Bullet Chart (on Background): the background and formatted text boxes to hold a title, subtitle, and bulleted list of information
- Text (on Background): the background plus areas formatted for a title and paragraph text
- Org Chart (on Background): the background and areas formatted to hold a title and an organizational chart
- Data Chart (on Background): the background plus areas formatted for a title and a data chart (such as a bar chart or pie chart)
- Combination (on Background): the background and formatted areas for a bulleted list and a data chart

In most cases, you want the first slide to contain the title of your show, so you select the Title template in the New Slide Show dialog box. Click on OK, and the main Presentations window appears with your first slide on-screen, as shown in the upcoming Figure 16-4.

Step 3: Adding titles and regular text

To add text to a slide, double-click on a text box (labeled in Figure 16-4). The text box border changes and selection handles appear to show that the box is selected, as in the top text box in Figure 16-4. You also see the standard blinking insertion marker and I-beam cursor used for entering text in WordPerfect, Quattro Pro, and almost every other Windows program.

- The insertion marker indicates where the next character you type will appear. To reposition the insertion marker, click at the spot where you want it to appear. Or use the arrow keys to move the insertion marker.
- When the characters you type fill up the text box, the box enlarges and text wraps to the next line. You can also press Enter to start a new line of text. After entering your text, click outside the text box to deselect it or press Esc to deselect the text but leave the text box selected.
- Text boxes in which you don't enter text don't show up on your finished slide.

- To create an additional text area, press and hold the mouse button down on the Text Objects button on the drawing toolbar (labeled in Figure 16-5). A flyout menu offering three tools appears: the Text Area tool, which creates a regular text box; the Text Line tool, which creates a text box for a single line of text; and a Bullet Chart tool, which creates a text box formatted to hold a bulleted list. Drag across the flyout menu to select the tool you want to use. Drag with the Text Area or Bullet Chart tool to create a text box, as shown in Figure 16-5. Just click with the Text Line tool to create a one-time text box.

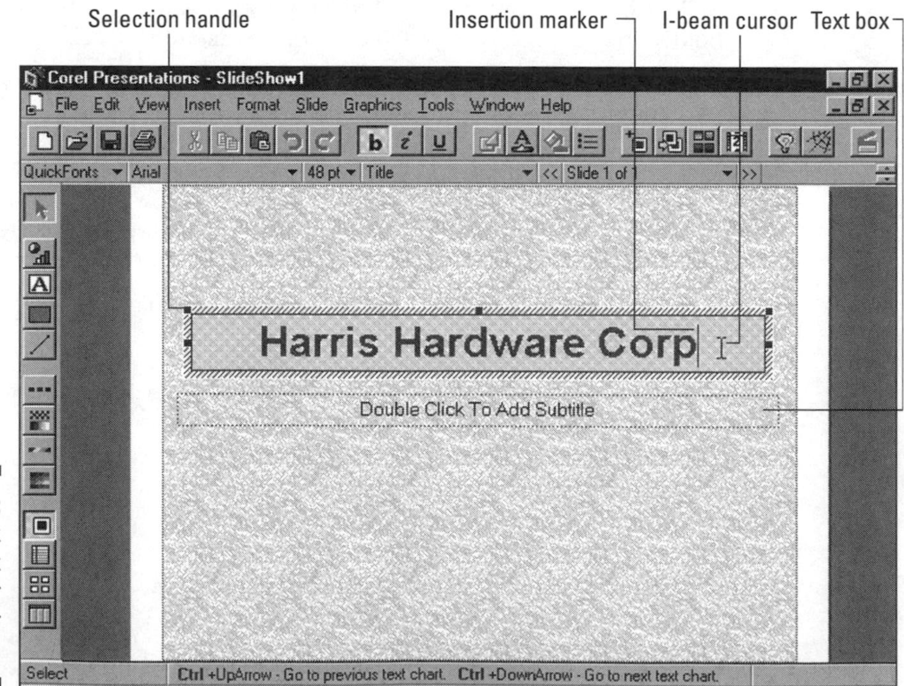

Figure 16-4: Double-click on a text box to enter or edit your text.

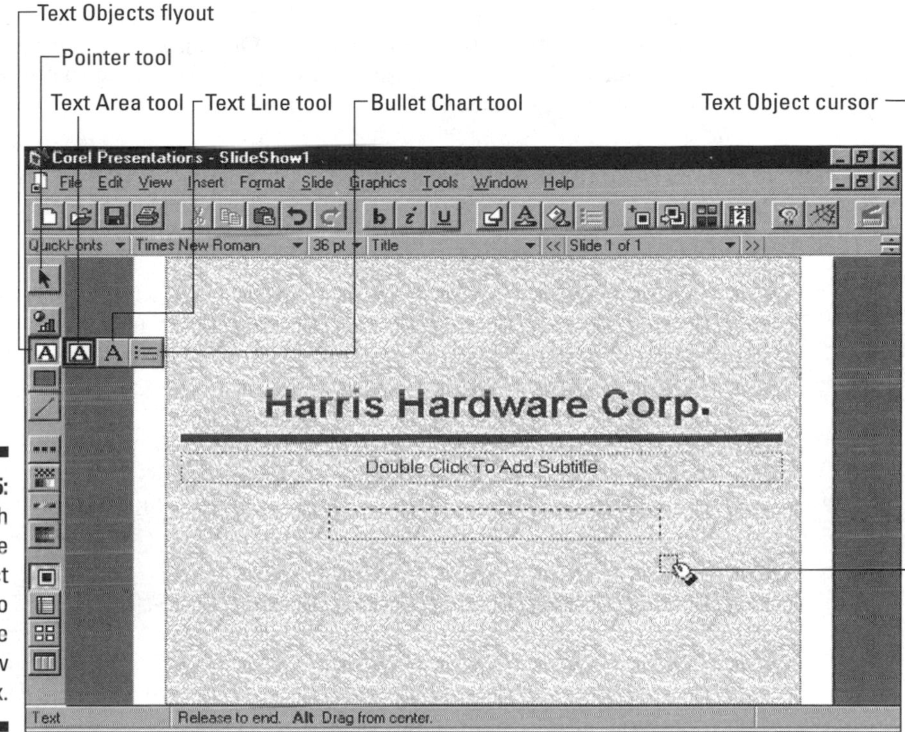

Figure 16-5: Drag with one of the Text Object tools to create a new text box.

After you drag or click to create a text box, the text box becomes selected and ready for you to enter your text. Click outside the text box after you're done. If you change your mind about creating a text box, click on the Pointer tool to return to the regular arrow cursor.

- When you double-click on a text box for a data chart, Presentations displays the Data Chart Gallery dialog box, where you select a chart type and layout. Presentations then creates a sample chart and displays a data sheet that's prefilled with sample data. You replace the sample data with your data. (If you don't want Presentations to display sample data, deselect the Use Sample Data check box in the Data Chart Gallery dialog box.) As you fill in the data sheet, Presentations draws your chart on the slide. Close the data sheet window after you're finished entering data. Click outside the data chart to deselect it.

You can add a chart you created in Quattro Pro to your Presentations slide. For information about bringing items created in one program into another program, see Chapter 20.

- To enter text for an organization chart, double-click on the text box. Then double-click on a box in the chart to enter a person's name and title into the box. Click outside the box to deselect it. Click outside the organization chart area to deselect the entire chart.

- If you don't like the chart style created by the Org Chart template, choose Insert➪Organization Chart or click on the Organization Chart tool (on the Chart and Graphics flyout, as shown in Figure 16-8). Drag to create a text box. You can then choose a new chart style.
- To enter text into a bullet chart text box, double-click on the box. A bullet appears for the first item in your list. Type the item and then press Enter to create a bullet for the second item in the list. If you want to put a second-level item underneath a bulleted item, press Tab. To change an item from a second-level item to a first-level item, click at the beginning of the line and press Shift+Tab; press Tab to change a first-level item to a second-level item. You can create as many levels of bulleted text as you want by pressing Tab to move to a lower level and Shift+Tab to move up a level.

You can change the font, size, alignment, color, and other aspects of your text after you create it. For the lowdown, see the section "Editing and formatting text" later in this chapter. You can also add charts, clip art images, and other graphics to your slide, as explained in the section "Adding Pretty Pictures."

Step 4: Creating additional slides

To add the next slide to your show, choose Slide➪Add Slides or click on the Add Slide button on the toolbar, labeled in Figure 16-6. The Add Slides dialog

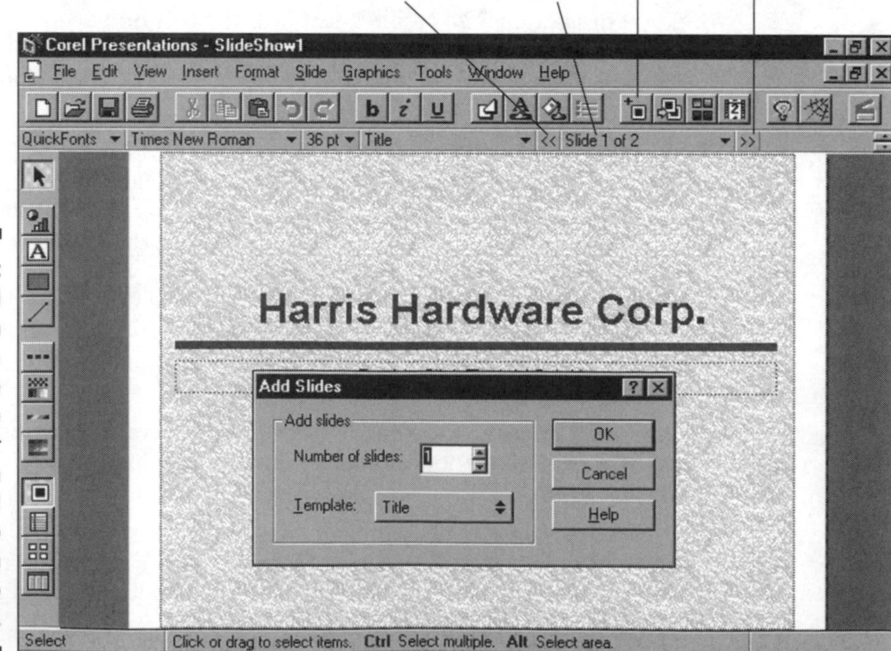

Figure 16-6: Use the Add Slide button to add a slide; use the Slide Selector drop-down list and buttons to move from one slide to another.

box appears, as shown in the figure. Enter the number of slides you want to add and select a template for the slides. You can either add all your slides at one time, changing the template later as needed (as explained in the section "Editing Your Slides"), or add them one by one, choosing the template for each slide in the Add Slides dialog box.

Click on OK to create your new slide(s) and enter the text for each one. To move from one slide to the next, use the Slide Selector drop-down list on the Power Bar, or click on the Next Slide or Previous Slide buttons, which are all labeled in Figure 16-6.

Adding Pretty Pictures

Nothing's as dull as a presentation that includes screen after screen of plain text. To liven up your show — and help keep audience snoring to a minimum — you can add clip art, photographic images, and even your own homemade drawings to your slides.

Using the QuickArt browser to add graphics

To add one of the clip art images that comes with WordPerfect Suite 7 to your slide:

1. **Choose Insert⇨QuickArt.**

   Or select the QuickArt icon from the Chart and Graphics flyout menu on the drawing toolbar, labeled in the upcoming Figure 16-8. (The QuickArt icon looks like a green diamond.) Your cursor turns into a little hand holding a box.

2. **Drag to create a graphics box.**

   Drag to create a frame to hold the graphic. (You can resize and move the frame later if needed.) The new QuickArt Browser appears. Double-click on the Standard.qad icon to display folders of graphics that are installed with the WordPerfect Suite, as shown in Figure 16-7.

3. **Double-click on a folder to view the images in the folder.**

   The dialog box changes to display subfolders within the folder. Double-click on one of these subfolders, and Presentations displays a preview of the images stored in the folder. If you don't see one you like, click on the Folder icon at the right end of the Look In option box to return to the category folders and select another category.

4. **Double-click on the image you want to use.**

   Or click once and press Enter or click on Insert. Presentations politely places the image on your slide. The image is selected and ready to resize, move, or otherwise edit, as shown in Figure 16-8.

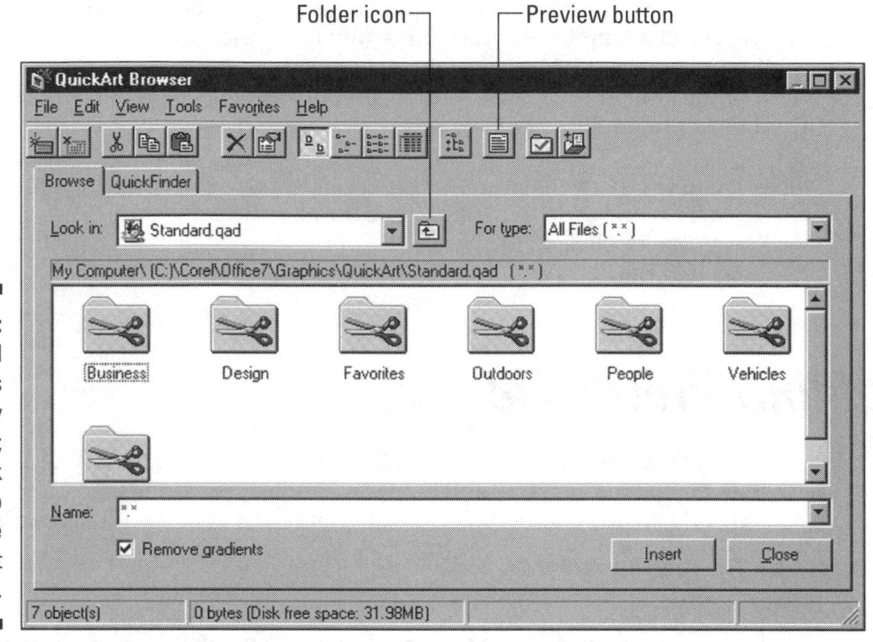

Figure 16-7: The Corel clip art is stored by category; double-click a folder to see the images it contains.

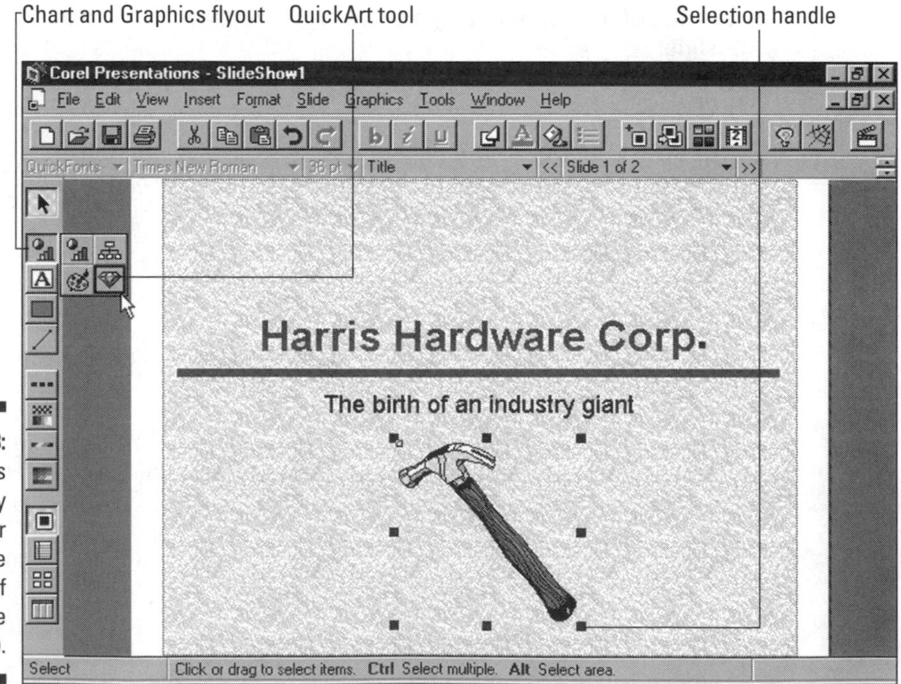

Figure 16-8: Graphics can really hammer home the message of your slide (yuk, yuk).

You're not limited to using the graphics in the QuickArt folder. You can find additional graphics in the Graphics folder of the Office 7 folder, for example, and in the Photos folder on the Suite CD. To use one of these graphics or a graphic created in some other program, locate the graphic file you want to use in the QuickArt browser and click on it. To see a preview of the image, click on the Preview button, labeled in Figure 16-7. Double-click on the file to add the graphic to your slide.

Creating simple graphics

Presentations offers some tools that you can use to create basic drawings such as the one in Figure 16-9. I'm not sure what that big white circular thing is, but I think it's a giant tennis ball descending on a spoiled tennis star who's shouting at a line judge.

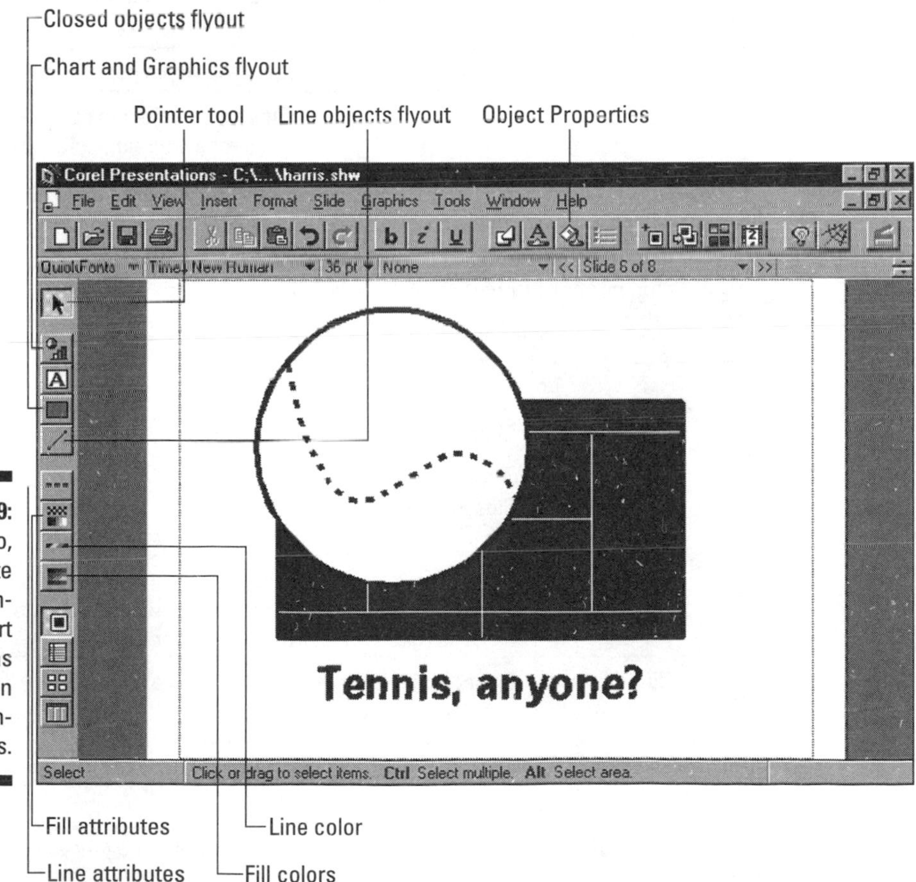

Figure 16-9: You, too, can create museum-quality art such as this in Presentations.

To create a drawing on a slide, just select the drawing tool you want to use and sketch away. To create a new drawing in its own window (that is, not on a slide), choose File➪New and select the Create a New Drawing radio button in the New Document dialog box. Your ever-willing slave, Presentations immediately displays a big blank drawing page. The toolbars change slightly; the main toolbar offers a few additional drawing tools, and the slide view icons disappear from the drawing toolbar.

The various drawing tools and flyout menus are labeled in Figure 16-9. Table 16-1 gives you more information on what each tool does and how you use it. For the most part, you click on a tool and then drag to draw a line or shape. In some cases, you use the Pointer tool to select the portion of the graphic you want to edit and then click with a drawing tool to apply a color or pattern to the selected shape.

To select several objects at once, drag with the Pointer tool to create a big selection box around them.

Table 16-1 Presentations Drawing Tools

Icon	*Tool*	*Flyout Menu*	*How You Use It*
	Pointer		Click on an object to select it; Shift+click to select a second object; drag around several objects to select them all.
	Chart	Chart and Graphics	Drag to create a data chart.
	Organization	Chart and Graphics	Drag to create an organization chart.
	Bitmap	Chart and Graphics	Drag to create a bitmap image.
	QuickArt	Chart and Graphics	Drag to add an imported graphic to a drawing or slide.
	Rectangle	Closed Objects	Drag to create a rectangle. Shift+drag to create a square.
	Rounded Rectangle	Closed Objects	Drag to draw a rectangle with rounded corners; Shift+drag to create a square with round corners.
	Circle	Closed Objects	Drag to draw a circle.
	Ellipse	Closed Objects	Drag to draw an ellipse; Shift+drag to draw a circle.
	Polygon	Closed Objects	Drag to create the first segment in a polygon; drag to create additional segments; double-click to end the shape.

Icon	*Tool*	*Flyout Menu*	*How You Use It*
	Closed Curve	Closed Objects	Drag to create the first segment of the curved shape; click and drag again to start another segment; double-click to end the shape.
	Arrows	Closed Objects	Click to position the head of the arrow and then click to set the end of the arrow. To create a curved arrow, drag to start the arrow, release the mouse button, move the mouse to shape the arrow, and click to end the shape.
	Regular Polygon	Closed Objects	Draws a polygon with sides that are all the same length. Click on the tool, set the number of sides in the Regular Polygon dialog box that appears, and drag to create the shape.
	Line	Line Objects	Drag to create a straight line. Shift+drag to draw a perfectly vertical, horizontal, or diagonal line.
	Curved Line	Line Objects	Drag to create the first segment in a curved line, click to set the curve, and drag to create the next segment. Double-click to end the line.
	Elliptical Arc	Line Objects	Drag to create an elliptical arc (section of an ellipse); Shift+drag to create a circular arc.
	Freehand	Line Objects	Drag to create a freehand line.
	Polygon Line	Line Objects	Drag to create a line that has several angles. Drag to create the first segment, click to start the second segment, and double-click to end the line.
	Bezier Curve	Line Objects	Drag to create a line using Bezier curve theory (if you don't know what that means, stay away from this tool).
	Circular Arc	Line Objects	Drag to set the size of the arc, release the mouse button, move the cursor to shape the arc, and click.
	Line Attributes		Click to change the width and style of a selected line.
	Fill Attributes		Click to change the fill pattern of the selected object.
	Line Color		Click to apply a color to a selected line.
	Fill Colors		Click to select a new pattern color and a new background color for the selected object.

You can also access the fill and color options, as well as some additional options for lines, by selecting the object and clicking on the Object Properties button on the toolbar, labeled in Figure 16-9. Or right-click on the object and choose Object Properties from the QuickMenu.

Working with bitmap images

The main Presentations drawing tools create *vector drawings,* which are graphics that the computer creates by using mathematical formulas to generate lines, arcs, and other shapes. Presentations also offers some tools that enable you to create *bitmap images,* which are composed of tiny squares called *pixels,* which are sort of like the tiles in a mosaic. Scanned photographs or graphics created in a painting program such as CorelPHOTO-PAINT! are bitmap images.

Creating and editing bitmap images requires some expertise and experience, however. And if you have that kind of knowledge, you probably also have full-fledged image editing software — in which case, you're better off doing your bitmap work in that program.

If you want to play around with the bitmap tools, choose Insert⇨Bitmap and drag the cursor to create a frame for the graphic. Presentations takes you to the bitmap editing window, which contains tools specifically for working with bitmap images. (See the section "Play with Special Effects in Presentations" in Chapter 21 for a look at one of these tools in action.) After you're done fooling around, choose File⇨Close Bitmap Editor to put your bitmap image on your slide or drawing page. Or choose File⇨Cancel Bitmap to close the bitmap editor without adding your image to the slide or drawing.

Editing graphics

Before you edit a graphic, first determine whether it's a bitmap image or a vector drawing. To find out, right-click on the graphic. If the top item in the QuickMenu is Edit Bitmap, you're dealing with a bitmap image. Otherwise, the graphic is a vector drawing. The distinction is important because the two types of graphics have different editing rules.

- To change a vector drawing's color, border, pattern, and other characteristics, click on it to select it and then use the fill, line color, and other graphics tools. Or right-click on the graphic and choose the Properties item from the QuickMenu to display a dialog box of object options related to the graphic.
- To edit an individual element in a vector drawing, double-click on the graphic to select it. Then click on the element you want to edit. Any drawing commands or tools you use then affect the selected element only. You can also right-click on the element and choose an editing command from the QuickMenu. (You can also zoom in for a closer look by choosing one of the Zoom commands from the View menu.)

- To edit a bitmap image, double-click on it. The image appears in the bitmap editing window, which you can read more about in the preceding section.

Moving, resizing, and deleting graphics is discussed later in this chapter, in the section "Moving, deleting, resizing, and copying stuff."

Editing Your Slides

After you create your slides, you'll no doubt want to make some changes. This section explains how to wreak all sorts of havoc on your text, layouts, and backgrounds. Tips for editing graphics are found in the preceding section as well as in the upcoming section "Moving, deleting, resizing, and copying stuff."

Changing the background

You can change the slide background in several ways. To change the background behind all slides, choose Slide⇨Master Gallery and pick a new master just as you did when first creating your slide show.

Going this route changes both the background and the layout of your text according to the template that the Master uses.

If you want to modify the background only, choose Slide⇨Background Layer. Everything but the background disappears from sight. You can now add graphics and text to the background. You may want to use this approach to put your company logo on every slide, for example. Choose Backgrounds⇨Slide Layer to return to the normal slide view.

What if you want to change the background behind some slides, but not all? You need to create a new, second background. Follow these steps:

1. **Choose Slide⇨Background Layer.**

   When you do, the Slide menu changes to the Backgrounds menu and offers commands related to backgrounds.

2. **Choose Backgrounds⇨Add Background or press Ctrl+Enter.**

   A dialog box appears and asks you to enter a name for your background. Enter the name and click on OK or press Enter.

3. **Create your background.**

   A blank slide appears that you can fill up with graphics and text.

   You can also select from some predefined backgrounds by choosing the Backgrounds⇨Background Gallery command.

To create a plain, colored slide, drag with the Rectangle tool to create a rectangle that fills up the entire slide. To change the color or pattern of the rectangle, use the Fill Colors and Fill Attributes buttons on the drawing toolbar.

4. **Choose Backgrounds⇨Slide Layer to display your slide again.**
5. **Choose Slide⇨Apply Template.**

   The Apply Template dialog box appears, as shown in Figure 16-10. Check the Override Assigned Background check box and select your new background from the neighboring drop-down list. In the Apply To area of the dialog box, select a radio button to tell Presentations which slides get the new background. You can change the current slide by using the black arrows at the top of the dialog box.
6. **Click on OK or press Enter.**

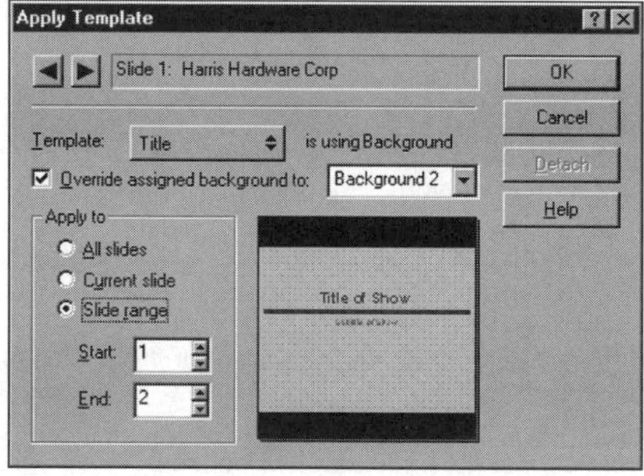

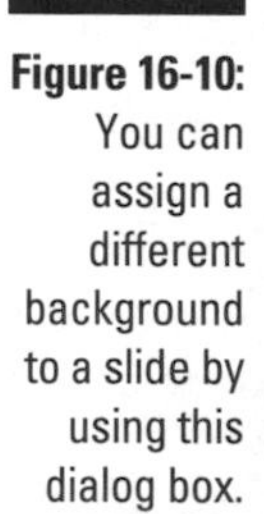
Figure 16-10: You can assign a different background to a slide by using this dialog box.

Editing the template

To change the template used on your slides, choose Slide⇨Apply Template to display the Apply Template dialog box shown in Figure 16-10. Select a new template from the Template drop-down list and select an Apply To option to tell Presentations which slides get the new template. Use the black arrows at the top of the dialog box to change the current slide.

If you want to change the template for just one slide, you don't need to bother with the dialog box. Just select a new template from the drop-down list on the Power Bar (see Figure 16-11).

You can edit the template itself to make changes to all slides using that template. For example, if you want to delete the subtitle text box from all the slides that use the title template, go to a slide that uses the template. Choose Slide⇨Layout Layer. Click on the subtitle text box to select it and press Delete. Then choose Layout⇨Slide Layer to return to your normal slide view.

Editing and formatting text

If you need to make some changes to text in a regular text box, first select the text block by double-clicking on it. You can then use most of the standard text-editing techniques you use to edit text in WordPerfect (these techniques are described in Chapter 6).

To edit the data in a data chart, double-click on the chart to select it. Then right-click and choose Display Datasheet from the QuickMenu and edit the values in the chart. Close the Data Chart window after you're done. The QuickMenu also offers commands that let you change other aspects of the chart, such as whether labels are displayed.

To edit the data in an organization chart, double-click on the chart to select it. Then double-click on the chart box you want to edit.

You can also use various formatting commands to add artistic touches to your text, as shown in Figure 16-11. Before you can format text, you have to select the text block (by double-clicking on it) *and* select the characters you want to format (by dragging over them).

Here are just some of the different ways to make your text look cool:

- To change the font, type size, type style, or font color, choose Format⇨Font or click on the Font Properties button on the toolbar (labeled in Figure 16-11) to display the Font Properties dialog box. Make your selections on the Font tab of the dialog box and click on OK or press Enter.
- You can also use the Font and Type Size drop-down lists on the Power Bar to change the font and size of your text. The B, I, and U buttons on the toolbar make text bold, italic, and underlined, just as they do in WordPerfect.
- As in WordPerfect, the QuickFonts drop-down list gives you quick access to the font combinations you used recently.

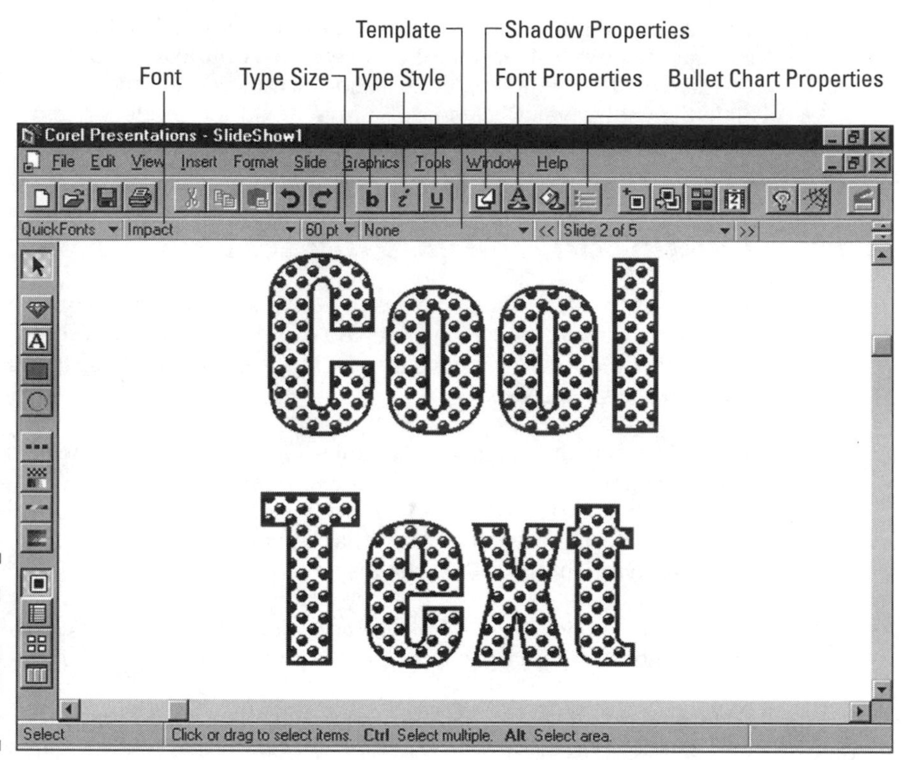

Figure 16-11: You can create all kinds of cool text effects.

- To outline your text, click on the Outline tab of the Font Properties dialog box and deselect the No Line check box. You can then pick an outline type, size, and color.
- If it looks like nothing is happening when you make changes to your text, zoom in for a closer look. (Choose one of the Zoom commands from the View menu.) Some effects aren't visible if you're zoomed out.
- To fill your text with a pattern, click on the Fill Attributes tab of the Font Properties dialog box, shown in Figure 16-12. Deselect the No Fill option and select a pattern and a color for the pattern and the background. If you want to fill your text with a blend of two colors, select the Gradient option from the Fill Style drop-down list.
- To add a shadow behind your text, select the text box *only.* (If the individual characters are selected, you can't access the shadow attributes.) Choose Format⇨Shadow Properties or click on the Shadow Properties button, labeled back in Figure 16-11. Deselect the No Shadow option and then play around the shadow options until you see an effect you like.

- In case you're dying to know, the text in Figure 16-11 is 60-point Impact type with a thin black outline and a pattern fill that uses white as the background color and black as the pattern color.

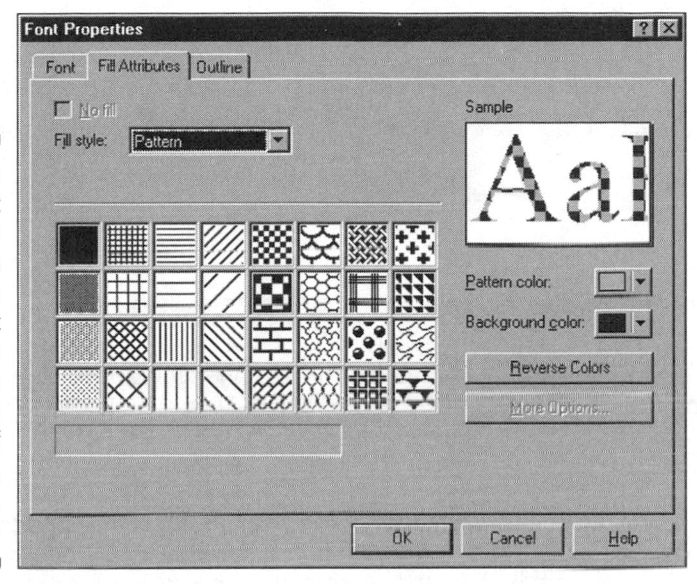

Figure 16-12: The Font Properties dialog box contains options that let you dress up your text in all kinds of colors, patterns, and fonts.

You can also adjust the alignment, line spacing, indents, and other formatting of your selected text by using the Line, Paragraph, and Justification commands on the Format menu. If you want to change the formatting of a bulleted list, choose the Bullet Chart Properties command from the Format menu or click on the Bullet Chart Properties button on the toolbar (labeled in Figure 16-11).

In addition to choosing commands from the menu bar and toolbar, you can right-click on a text box or object to display a QuickMenu of commands related to whatever you're doing at the moment.

Moving, deleting, resizing, and copying stuff

Still not happy with how things look? Here are some other editing maneuvers you can make:

- To move a text box or graphic, just click on it to select it and then drag it to a new position.
- To resize a graphic or text box, select it and then drag one of its selection handles.

- Be careful when resizing a bitmap image. Enlarging a bitmap can make it look all blurry and yucky.
- To delete a text block or graphic, select it and press Delete. To delete the text inside a text block but leave the text block intact, select the individual characters inside the block and press Delete.
- To undo your last action, press Ctrl+Z or choose Edit⇨Undo.

- To delete an entire slide, display the slide (by choosing it from the Slide Selector) and choose Slide⇨Delete. Presentations asks whether you're really sure you want to delete the slide; click on Yes to confirm your decision.
- You can copy a graphic or text block by selecting it and choosing Edit⇨Copy or pressing Ctrl+C. Click at the spot where you want to put the copy and choose Edit⇨Paste or press Ctrl+V.

Getting Another View of Your Show

The figures you've seen up to this point in the chapter all show the primary Presentations view mode, which is called Slide Editor view. Presentations offers some other modes that can be helpful if you're creating a long or complicated slide show:

- Outliner view presents your slide text in outline form on a background that looks like a piece of notebook paper. You can edit text, add slides, and delete slides in this view, just as you can in Slide Editor view.
- Slide Sorter view displays thumbnails (miniature views) of your slides so that you can see several of them on-screen at one time. You can rearrange slides by dragging them.
- Slide List view shows you the number and title of each slide, along with information about the transition and advance options that you selected. As in Slide Sorter view, you can drag the slides to rearrange their order.

To switch between modes, choose the mode you want from the View menu or use the mode icons, which are the last four buttons on the drawing toolbar. From top to bottom, they are: Slide Editor view, Outliner view, Slide Sorter view, and Slide List view.

Adding Transitions and Other Special Effects

Back in the days before interactive multimedia, people didn't expect a whole lot from a presentation. But if you want to captivate an audience today, you have to add a little sizzle to your show. This section explains how to add transitions, sound clips, and other effects that create the kind of pizzazz that makes a presentation memorable.

Be careful not to overload your show with too many effects — you want to enhance the messages on your slides, not detract from them.

Choosing a transition

A *transition* determines what the viewer sees when you switch from one slide to the next. You can have the two slides dissolve seamlessly into each other, so that the viewer hardly notices the transition, or you can use a more dramatic effect. Presentations offers more than 50 different transition effects, including one that fills the screen with little happy faces — a choice I don't recommend, by the way.

To set up your transitions, choose Slide⇨Slide Transition to open the dialog box shown in Figure 16-13. (Or click on the Slide Transition button on the toolbar; it's the one that has two little slides and a yellow arrow on it.) Use the arrows at the top of the dialog box to select the slide that gets the transition. (For example, if you want to create a transition between Slide 1 and Slide 2, select Slide 1 in the dialog box.) If you want to use the same transition between all your slides, check the Apply to All Slides option box.

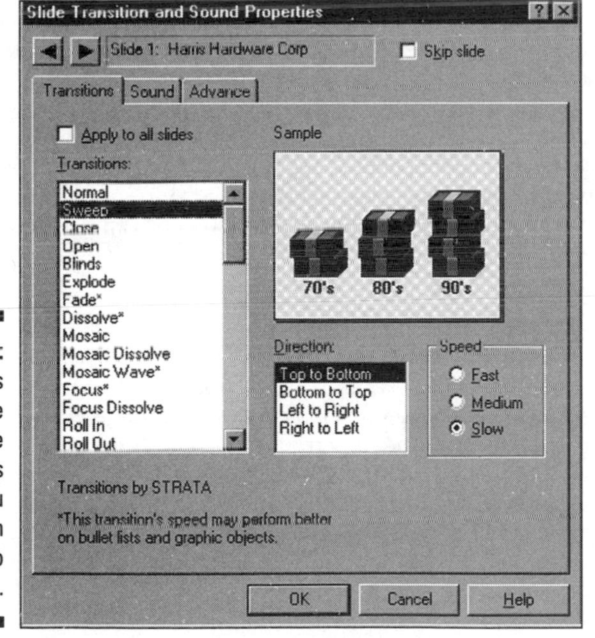

Figure 16-13: Transitions determine what the viewer sees when you move from one slide to the next.

As you click on the different options in the Transitions list box, you see a preview of the effect in the Sample box. You can adjust the speed of the transition by selecting one of the Speed radio buttons. For some transitions, you can set the direction of the transition. After you set the transitions for all your slides, click on OK or press Enter.

The Skip Slide option, contrary to what you may expect, doesn't really have anything to do with transitions. This option tells Presentations to skip the slide altogether when you play your show.

To apply the same transition to several slides at the same time, select the slides in Slide Sorter view before choosing the Slide Transition command. Click on the first slide you want to select and Ctrl+click on the others.

Choosing an advance mode

You can also choose whether each slide advances on its own after a specified period of time or advances only when you click the mouse button or press the spacebar.

To get to the advance options, choose Slide⇨Slide Transition or click on the Slide Transition button on the toolbar. Then click on the Advance tab of the Slide Transition and Sound Properties dialog box (shown back in Figure 16-13). To set the advance for a specific slide, select the slide by clicking on the right- or left pointing arrow at the top of the dialog box. To use the same advance option throughout your show, check the Apply to All Slides option box.

If you want to advance the slides via a mouse click or pressing the spacebar, select the Manually option. (This is the default setting.) If you want the slides to advance automatically, select Time Delay and set the amount of time you want each slide to be displayed in the Number of Seconds Per Build option box.

Adding sounds

Remember the days of filmstrips? (Come on, I'm not *that* much older than you!) Anyway, a little bell inside the projector dinged to signal the teacher that it was time to advance the filmstrip to the next frame. Presentations lets you add a similar sound effect between your slides — only these sounds are much cooler than your average filmstrip-projector ding. You can even have a music clip play through your entire show. (All this depends, of course, on whether or not the computer you're using to play the show has a sound card installed that can play the sound files you use.)

To add a sound to a slide, choose Slide⇨Sound. The now-famous Slide Transition and Sound Properties dialog box opens with the Sound tab selected, as shown in Figure 16-14. To select which slide gets the sound effect, click on the right- and left-pointing arrows at the top of the dialog box. The sound will play when the selected slide appears on-screen during playback.

You can add three types of sounds to your slides: .WAV files, MIDI files, and tracks from regular music CDs. For your amusement, WordPerfect Suite 7 provides some .WAV and MIDI sound files; select the Wave or MIDI option and then click on the little white file folder at the end of the neighboring option box to locate the files. (I'm personally quite taken with KISS_UP.WAV, which makes a smooching sound similar to the ones that corporate managers often make when discussing important issues with their vice presidents.)

If you check the CD check box, a little CD icon appears at the end of the option box. Click on the icon to open a dialog box that lets you select which CD track you want to use and how much of the track you want to play.

You can also set the volume for your sounds in the dialog box. Keep in mind that you won't be able to access volume controls from the Windows 95 taskbar as you normally can (by right-clicking on the little speaker icon) because the taskbar disappears when you play your show.

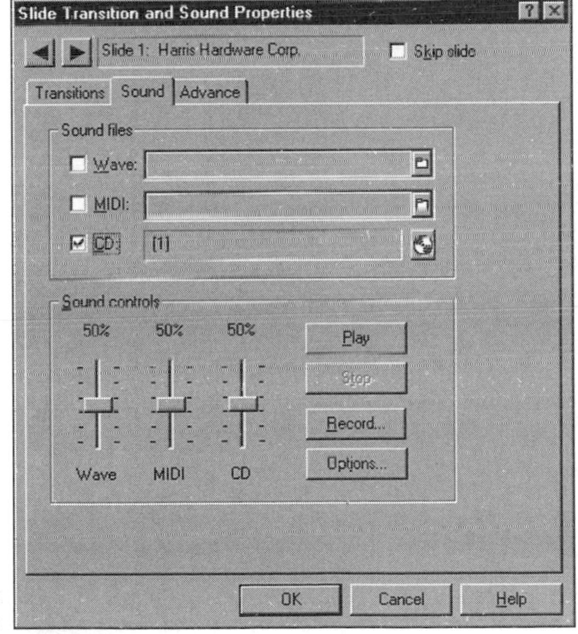

Figure 16-14: All kinds of sound effects are available from the Sound tab of the Slide Transition and Sound Properties dialog box.

If you want to have one sound file or CD track play for several slides, attach it to the first slide in the sequence. Click on the Options button in the Sound dialog box and select the Loop Sound option for the type of sound you're adding. The sound file or track plays until the show reaches the next slide that has a sound file attached.

Animating an object

Okay, here's a cool effect you have to try, if only to enjoy a laugh on a rainy day. You can bring a graphic or text box to life by applying an animation effect. Try it out: Click on a graphic or text box to select it. Then choose Slide⇨Object Animation to display the dialog box shown in Figure 16-15. Deselect the No Effect check box, select the Animation option from the Effects drop-down list, and click on an effect in the Effects list box. You see a preview of the effect in the Sample box. You can adjust the direction and speed of the animation if you want.

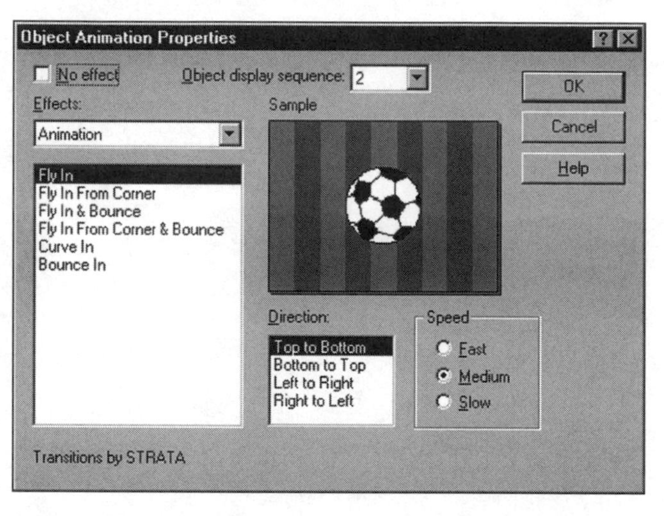

Figure 16-15: You can make graphic objects move across the screen by applying an animation effect.

If you assign animation effects to more than one object on a slide, you can specify which one moves first by using the Object Display Sequence option box. Assign number 1 to the object you want to move first, number 2 to the second object, and so on. Click on OK or press Enter after you're done.

Jazzing up bulleted lists

One more fun effect before we get back to serious business: You can add special effects to bulleted lists on your slides. Click on the text box that holds your bulleted list and choose Slide⇨Object Animation to display the Bullet Chart Animation Properties dialog box, shown in Figure 16-16. Deselect the No Effect check box. If you select the Transition option from the Effects drop-down list, you can apply transitions between bullet points similar to the transitions you apply between slides. If you select the Animation option from the Effects drop-down list, you can animate your bulleted list as if it were a graphic object. Play around with the different options until you find a combination that strikes your fancy; the Sample box shows you a preview of the effect as you select different options.

Playing Your Show

When you're ready to view the results of your creative genius, choose Slide➪Play Slide Show or click on the Play Show button on the toolbar — the button looks like a filmstrip frame with the number 2 in it. The Play Slide Show dialog box, shown in Figure 16-17, appears.

Use the Starting Slide scroll bar or option box to indicate where you want the show to begin — at the first slide, second slide, or some other slide. If you want the show to repeat continuously, check the Repeat Slide Show box.

The Highlighter enables you to draw on-screen with the mouse as the show plays — sort of like how TV sports commentators draw little Xs and Os over slow-motion replays. You set the color and width of the highlighter pen in the Play Slide Show dialog box.

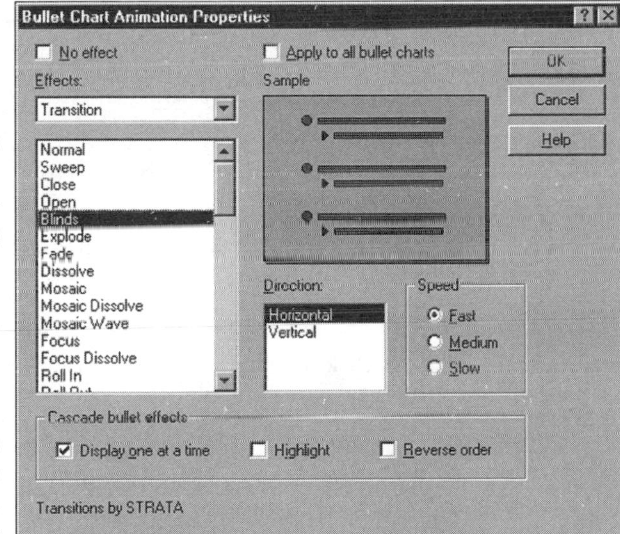

Figure 16-16: If you really want to get fancy, you can add transitions to bulleted lists and even send your lists flying across the screen.

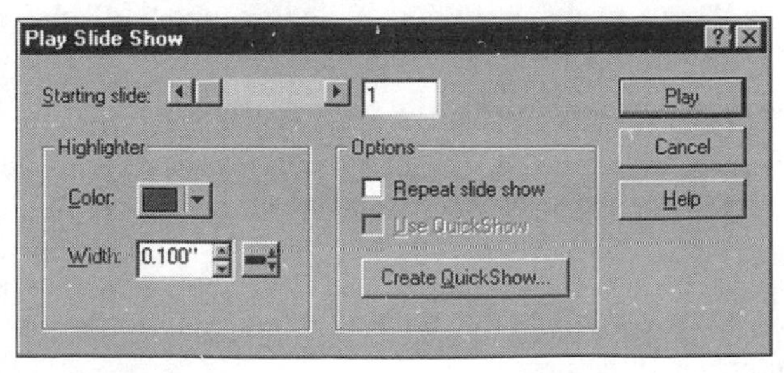

Figure 16-17: You can specify the starting slide in your show and choose to repeat your show.

The Create QuickShow option creates a version of your show that advances the slides faster than usual — which you may want to do when checking out how a certain editing choice works, for example. However, QuickShow files are very large and take up much more of your computer's resources than a regular file. To play the QuickShow version, select the Use QuickShow option.

When you click on Play or press Enter, your computer screen turns black for a few seconds and then your show begins. If you're using the manual advance option (as explained back in the section "Choosing an advance mode," click the left mouse button or press the spacebar to advance to the next slide or animation effect. Right-click or press PgUp to go back one slide.

Drag with the mouse to use the highlighter. Using the highlighter temporarily halts the show; click or press the spacebar to advance the show.

To stop the show at any point, press Esc. You return to the Presentations window when you stop the show or it finishes playing.

Playing Your Show on Someone Else's Computer

Playing your slide show on your own computer is all fine and dandy, but chances are you won't want to lug your system with you when you need to show a presentation. That's why Presentations offers an option that makes your show portable.

You can save your show to a floppy disk or other portable storage device (such as a Zip drive or SyQuest cartridge) as a Runtime file. A Runtime file contains the show files plus the Presentations program files needed to play the show. You can then play the show on any computer that uses Windows — without having to install Presentations. (You need to make sure that the computer can accept your type of floppy disk or storage device, of course.)

To create a Runtime file:

1. **Open your show and choose Slide⇨Make Runtime to display the dialog box shown in Figure 16-18.**
2. **Enter the name of your show in the Name option box.**
3. **Enter the name of the disk or directory where you want to store the Runtime file in the Copy Runtime File To box.**

   For example, if you want to save the show to your floppy disk drive, and that drive is Drive A, enter A:\ in the box. Or click on the white button at the end of the box to access the Select Location dialog box, and select a drive, folder, and directory.

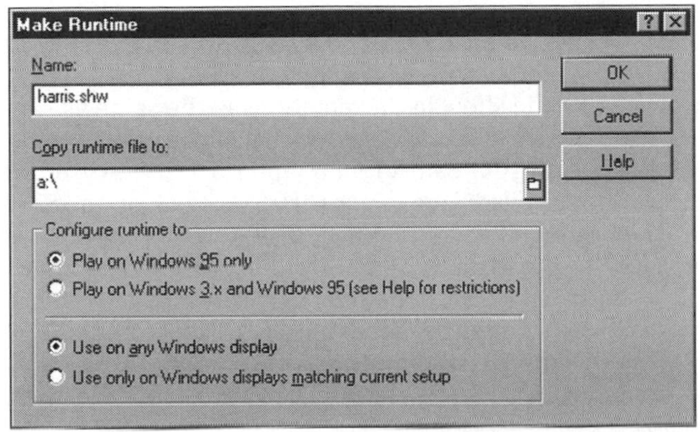

Figure 16-18: To play your show on a computer that doesn't have Presentations installed, create a Runtime file.

4. **Select your configuration options.**

   You can select one radio button in each pair of radio buttons. If the computer you'll be viewing the show on uses Windows 95, select the Play on Windows 95 Only option. You can also configure the show to play on computers that use Windows 3.x, but special transitions or animation effects in your show won't work.

   If you select the Use on Any Windows Display button, the show will play on any computer capable of displaying 256 colors at a 480 × 640 resolution (which includes most computers running Windows today). If you select the other display option, the Runtime show uses the display settings that are in force on your monitor only; this restriction can cause display problems if the computer that you play the show on doesn't use the same monitor settings.

5. **Click on OK or press Enter.**

To play your slide show in Windows 95, click on the Start button and select Run from the Start menu. For example, if the show is on a floppy disk that's in Drive A, type A:\Show70.exe. Type the name of the drive and Show70.exe. Then type the name of the show file you want to view (show files have the extension .PQF). Press Enter or click on OK.

After you save a Runtime file, *don't* rename it. If you do, the Runtime program files won't work properly. Also, be aware that video and sound drivers (the files that run the computer's sound card and video card) aren't copied with the Runtime file. The computer you use to play the show must have a sound card that's capable of playing the type of sound files used in your show, and the video display depends on the computer's video capabilities.

In other words, always test out your show in advance to make sure that everything works properly. That way, you give yourself time to make adjustments or find another display computer if needed.

Saving Slide Shows and Drawings

Saving a drawing or slide show in Presentations is the same as saving a file in WordPerfect or Quattro Pro. For detailed saving information, see the section "Saving Your Work (and Your Sanity)" in Chapter 5. But here's a brief reminder of the process: Choose File⇨Save, press Ctrl+S, or click on the Save button on the toolbar (the button looks like a floppy disk) to open the Save dialog box. Enter a name for your work in the Name option box, and specify where you want the file to be saved (drive and folder). Click on OK or press Enter to save the file. Presentations assigns the file extension .SHW to slide shows and .WPG to drawings (WPG is the WordPerfect graphics format). After you save a file for the first time, just press Ctrl+S or choose File⇨Save to resave it without opening the Save dialog box.

To save the file under a different name or in a different location, choose File⇨Save As or press F3.

Printing Your Masterpieces

If you want to create a printed copy of the slides in your show, choose File⇨Print, press Ctrl+P, or click on the Print button on the toolbar. The Print dialog box, shown in Figure 16-19, appears. In the Print drop-down list, you can choose to print black-and-white handouts that have a specified number of slides printed on each page, print each slide on its own page, or select from a variety of other printing options. The Print Options tab of the dialog box offers more printing choices, including one that lets you print the slide number on each page.

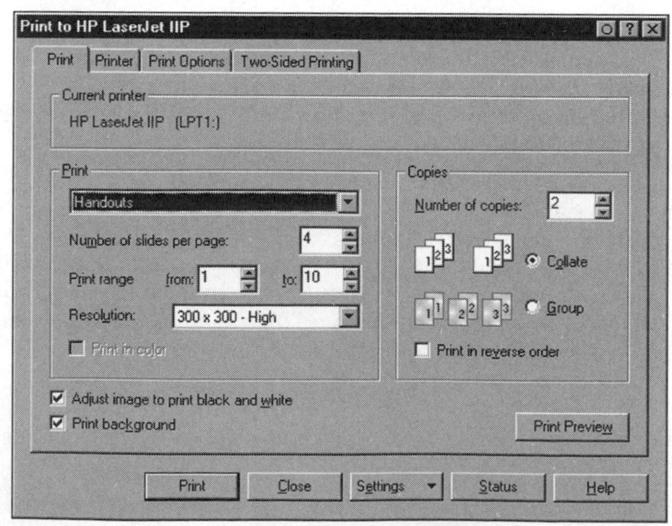

Figure 16-19: The Print dialog box lets you print your slide shows and drawings in a number of ways.

Unless you have a color printer, check the Adjust Image to Print Black and White option. Presentations automatically adjusts the colors in your slides to appropriate shades of gray. You can select this option only if Print Background is also selected. If you deselect the Print Background option, the text and graphics on your slide print but the background doesn't.

If you have a film recorder hooked up to your computer, you can print your show as 35mm slides. If not, you can save your show to disk and take it to a service bureau for conversion to 35mm slides. Be sure to ask the service bureau what format you should use when saving the show to disk.

The WordPerfect Suite includes a little program called Graphicsland, which you can find by clicking on the Windows 95 Start button and then choosing Corel WordPerfect Suite 7⇨Accessories. The program enables you to use a modem to send your Presentations slides to Graphicsland, a slide imaging company, for processing as 35mm slides or overhead transparencies. If you don't have a modem, you can send your Presentation files to Graphicsland on floppy disk. You can find out pricing information and other details by reading the instructions that appear when you start the Graphicsland program.

Printing a drawing is simple; just press Ctrl+P or choose File⇨Print. Select the Full Document option from the Print drop-down list, specify the number of copies you want to print, and select the Print in Color option if you have a color printer and want a color printout. Then click on Print or press Enter.

Chapter 17

Envoy: A Tree's Best Friend

In This Chapter

- Preserving paper by using Envoy
- Saving a document as an Envoy file
- Reading documents in the Envoy window
- Adding notes and highlights to Envoy pages
- Sending the Envoy Viewer to other computer users

One of the great promises made by the grand poohbahs of computerdom is that computers will one day enable us to create the paperless office. Instead of churning out reams of paper from our computer printers and copy machines each day, we'll create, store, and share all our documents electronically.

I'm not quite sure that this vision of the future will ever come to pass — at least, not until someone creates a computer that's guaranteed not to crash, taking your 350-page manuscript with it. But it's true that more and more people are sharing ideas and documents via their computers these days instead of on the printed page, which is good news for the world's tree population.

You, too, can join the wave of the future — and save a forest or two along the way — by using Envoy. An electronic publishing program, Envoy enables your coworkers and colleagues to view and annotate (add notes to) your documents on their computers even if they don't have the software you used to create the documents.

Turning a Document into an Envoy File

To turn a document into an Envoy document, you save it in the Envoy file format. But you don't use the Save File dialog box, as you do when saving files in other programs. Instead, you use the Print dialog box — which is why the process of saving files as Envoy documents is called "printing to Envoy" or "publishing to Envoy."

The following steps show you how to print a WordPerfect or Presentations document to Envoy.

1. **Open the document in the program you used to create it.**
2. **Choose File⇨Publish to Envoy.**

   Your computer hems and haws for a few seconds and then the document appears in the Envoy program window. Note the name of your document; the name appears in the Envoy title bar. When you close the document, Envoy prompts you to save the file. If you want to save the file under a different name choose File⇨Save As.

In Quattro Pro, the Print dialog box appears when you choose the Publish to Envoy command. Click on the Print button to open your document in an Envoy window.

If you're printing to Envoy from a program that doesn't have a Publish to Envoy command or if you want to take advantage of some other special options, follow these steps instead. (The steps here give instructions for WordPerfect; the names of the Print dialog box buttons may be a little different depending on the program you're using.)

1. **Open the document in the program you used to create it.**
2. **Choose File⇨Print to open the Print dialog box.**
3. **Select the Envoy 7 printer driver.**

   The way you select a printer driver differs depending on the program; in WordPerfect, click on the Printer tab and select the Envoy 7 Driver option from the Name drop-down list.

   Don't forget to change the printer driver back to your regular printer driver after you finish creating your Envoy files.

4. **Click on the Properties button to open the Envoy 7 Driver Properties dialog box.**

   Again, the name of the button may vary depending upon the program.

5. **Click on the Destination tab and choose a destination and format.**

   When you click on the Destination tab, the dialog box shown in Figure 17-1 appears.

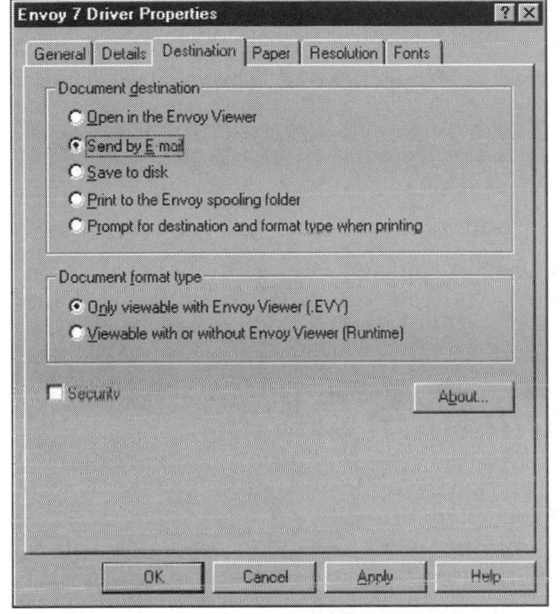

Figure 17-1: You can create an Envoy file in several different ways by making selections in this dialog box.

You can choose from several options:

- Open in the Envoy Viewer launches Envoy and opens your document in the Envoy window.
- Send by E-mail starts your e-mail program and sends the file as an attachment to an e-mail message.
- Save to Disk saves the file to a floppy disk or hard drive. (You select the disk or hard drive later.)
- Print to the Envoy Spooling Folder lets you create several Envoy files at the same time. The files are stored in a special folder until you give the final go-ahead to print.
- Prompt for Destination and Format Type When Printing lets you set different options when you're creating more than one file at a time.
- Only Viewable with Envoy Viewer (.EVY) creates a file that can be opened on a Macintosh or a PC running Windows 95 that has the Envoy 7 Viewer installed. (The Envoy Viewer is free, and you can share it with other users, as explained in "Sending Someone Else an Envoy File.")
- Viewable With or Without Envoy Viewer (Runtime) creates a file that can be opened on a Windows 95 system that does not have the Envoy Viewer installed. These files won't work on a Macintosh, however. Also, files saved with this option have the file extension .EXE (regular

Envoy documents use the .EVY extension). Note that this option isn't available if you select the first or last Document Destination options.

6. **Click on OK to exit the Properties dialog box and return to the Print dialog box.**

   You may need to click on OK a couple times to get back to the dialog box, depending on the program you're using.

7. **Click on the Print button.**

   If the Save As dialog box appears, enter the name of the file and the drive and/or folder where you want to store the file and then click on Save.

Viewing a Document in Envoy

To launch Envoy and view an Envoy document, click on the Windows 95 Start button, choose the Corel WordPerfect Suite 7 item from the Start menu, and then choose Envoy 7 from the submenu. The Envoy window appears, with almost every command and toolbar button dimmed except the Open button. Click on the button, or choose File⇨Open, or press Ctrl+O to display the Open dialog box and select the file you want to view. (If you need help navigating the dialog box, see "Figuring out the Open dialog box" in Chapter 5. The dialog box is slightly different in Envoy, but works pretty much the same way as the WordPerfect dialog box discussed in Chapter 5.)

Envoy files have the extension .EVY.

Figure 17-2 shows a page from the Envoy documentation, which is included as an Envoy file in the Reference Center (see Chapter 3 for Reference Center information). Like other programs in the WordPerfect Suite, the Envoy window has a menu bar, toolbar, status bar, scroll bar, and other elements common to Windows 95 screens. For information on these elements, read Chapter 2, "Basic Stuff You Need to Know."

You can view document pages in several different ways:

- Choose View⇨Thumbnails⇨Top to display miniature versions of the document pages across the top of the screen, as in Figure 17-2. Viewing the thumbnails can be helpful if you're trying to get an overall look at a document such as a newsletter or brochure.
- If you want the thumbnails displayed on the left side of the window, choose View⇨Thumbnails⇨Left. To hide the thumbnails altogether (the default setting), choose View⇨Thumbnails⇨Hidden.
- You can also click on the Thumbnails button on the toolbar (labeled in Figure 17-2) to toggle back and forth between the different thumbnail options.

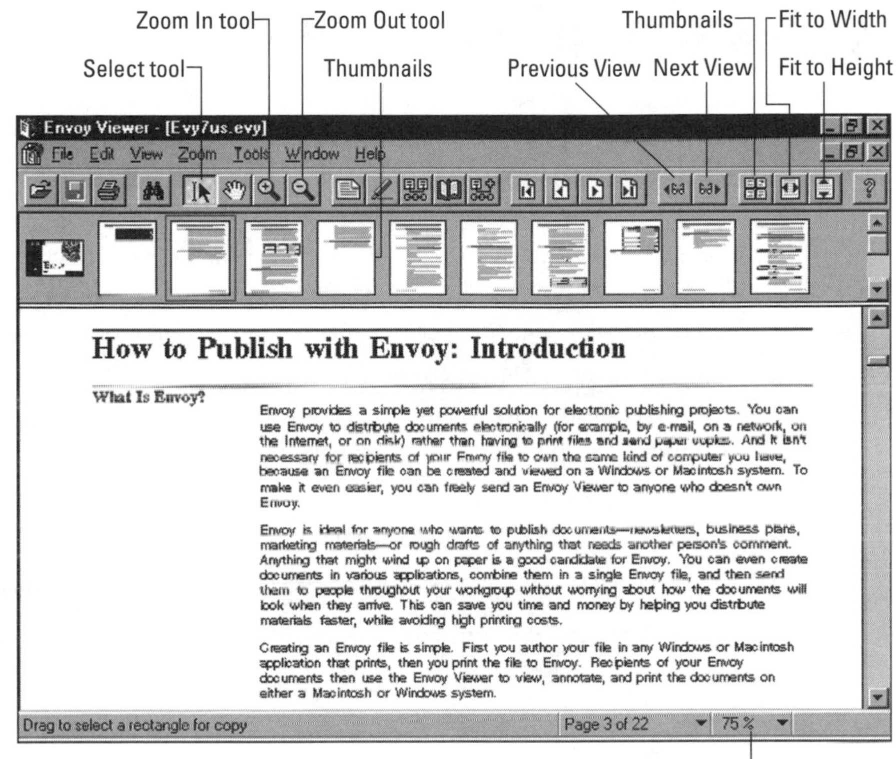

Figure 17-2: Envoy gives you lots of different tools for changing the on-screen display.

- To see page numbers displayed with the thumbnails, choose View⇨Thumbnails⇨Show Page Numbers. To turn the page numbers off, choose View⇨Thumbnails⇨Hide Page Numbers.
- To zoom in or out on a page, click on one of the Zoom buttons on the toolbar and then click on the page. Keep clicking to keep zooming. Click on the Select tool in the toolbar to deselect the Zoom tool and return to the regular cursor. You can also zoom by using the commands on the Zoom menu.
- The Fit Page to Height button enlarges or reduces the page so that you can see the entire length of the page in the window. The Fit Page to Width button magnifies the page so that its entire width appears on-screen. These commands are found on the Zoom menu, too.
- Just in case one of the preceding zoom options doesn't grab you, you can click on the Zoom button on the status bar and select a zoom magnification from the pop-up menu.
- The Previous View and Next View toolbar buttons switch you back and forth between the last view you were using and the current view.

Flipping through Your Pages

Here are some of the bazillion ways you can move from page to page and move about within a page:

- Click on the page navigation buttons on the toolbar (labeled in Figure 17-3).
- Double-click on a thumbnail with the Select tool to go to that page.
- Click on the Page button on the status bar to display the Go To Page dialog box. Enter the page number you want and press Enter or click on OK.
- Click on the scroll arrows or drag the scroll box.
- Click on the Hand tool, labeled in Figure 17-3, to get the hand cursor. Then drag with the cursor to move the page around on-screen.

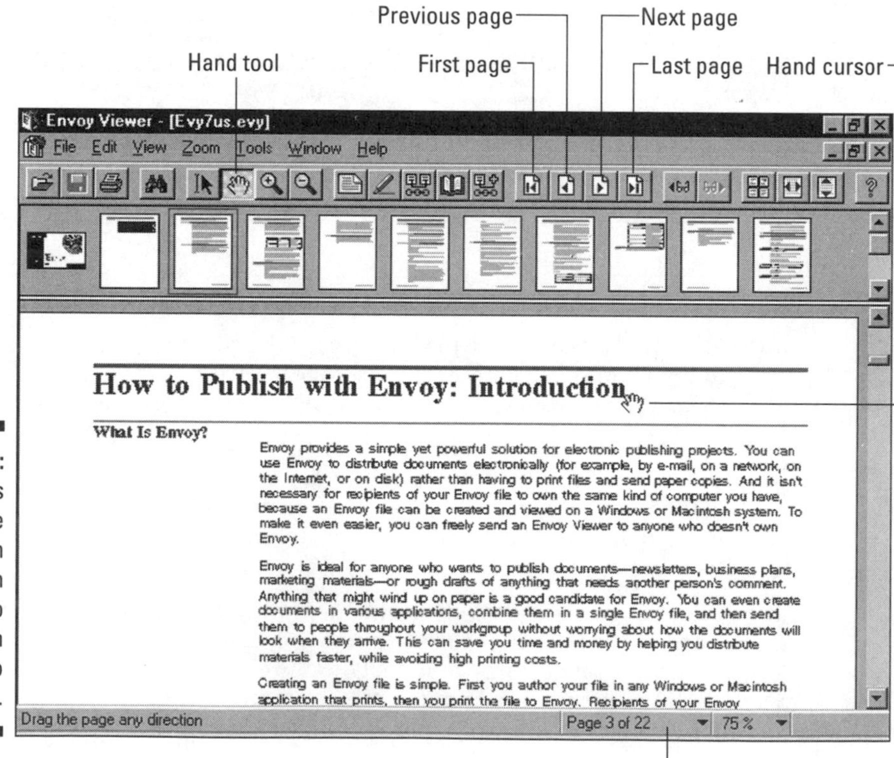

Figure 17-3: Envoy gives you more than enough ways to move from page to page.

Adding Notes and Highlights

Although you can't make many editing changes to an Envoy document, you can mark sections with the equivalent of a highlighter pen and add comments or questions on little electronic notes called QuickNotes. These tools provide a great way to route a document through a committee for approval or input.

Highlighting important stuff

To highlight something, click on the Highlight tool, labeled in Figure 17-4. The cursor changes into a little highlighter pen. Drag across the text or graphic you want to highlight. To change the highlight color, right-click on a highlighted area and choose Highlight Properties. Envoy displays a dialog box that lets you change the color and even assign a different color to different authors (people who open and view the document). If you prefer, you can change the highlighter so that highlighted text appears as strikeout text. (If you want strikeout highlights, be sure to start dragging *inside* the text. You should see the I-beam cursor instead of a plus sign next to the highlighter cursor.)

To remove highlighting, right-click on the highlighted area and choose Clear from the QuickMenu. To jump to the next highlighted text in the document, right-click and choose Find Next Highlight from the QuickMenu.

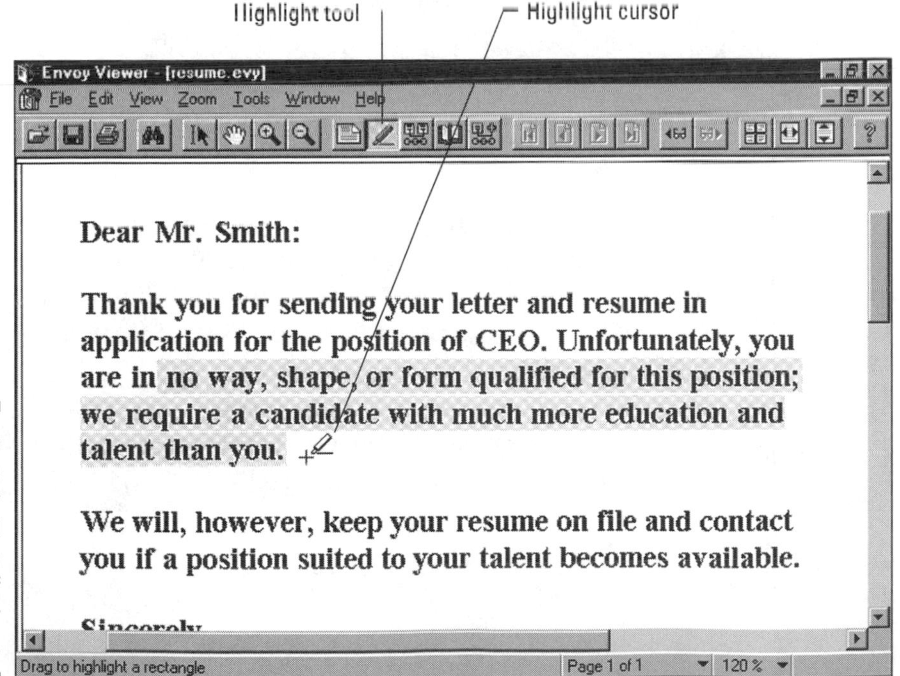

Figure 17-4: Use the Highlighter tool to call attention to portions of your document.

Adding a QuickNote

To attach a note to a page, click on the QuickNote tool button, labeled in Figure 17-5. Then click at the spot where you want the note to appear. Envoy creates a box for your note. Type your note and click outside the box after you're finished. To edit the note, double-click on the note box with the Select tool.

To move or resize the note, click on it with the Select tool. Black selection handles appear around the note, as in Figure 17-5. Drag anywhere inside the note to move it; drag a selection handle to resize the note. To delete a note, right-click and choose Clear from the QuickMenu, or just click on the box and press Delete.

Having a bunch of note boxes scattered throughout your document can make it pretty darned hard to read the document itself. That's why Envoy has a system that lets you shrink notes to an icon. People reading your document click on the icon to read the note and then shrink the quick note back to an icon. You can see a QuickNote icon in the upper-right corner of Figure 17-5.

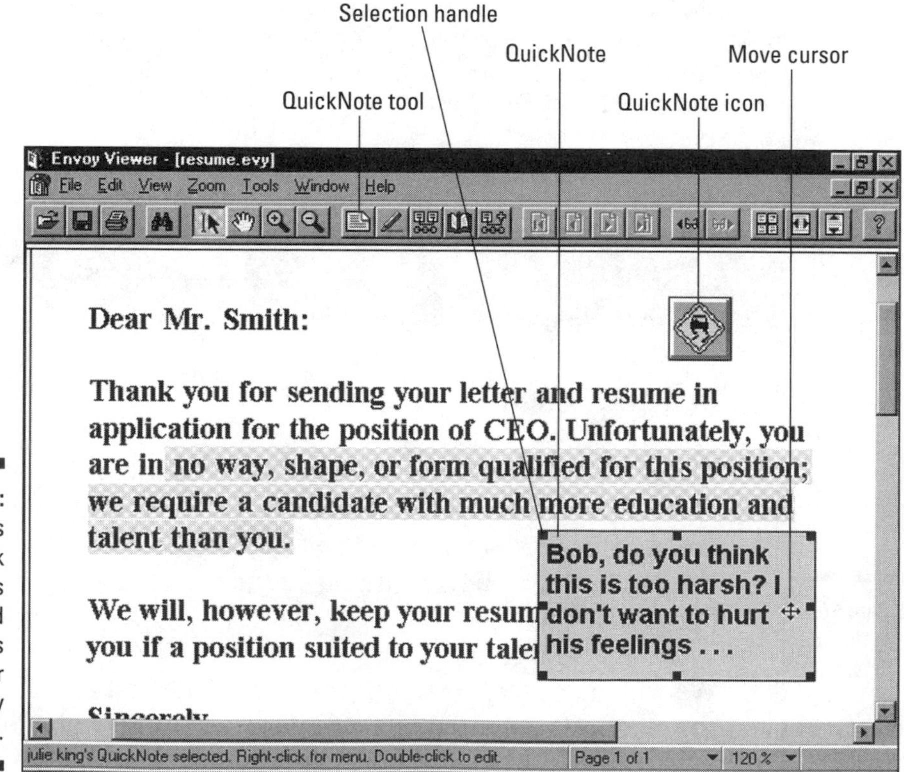

Figure 17-5: QuickNotes let you stick questions and comments into your Envoy documents.

To shrink a note to an icon, click on it to select it and then press F2. Or right-click on the note and choose Close QuickNote from the resulting QuickMenu. To redisplay the note, press F2 again or right-click and choose Open QuickNote from the QuickMenu.

If you right-click on a note box or icon and choose QuickNote Properties, you can select a different icon for your notes. You can also select a different text color, font, note box color, and text alignment. You can even assign a distinct set of note properties to different people who will be viewing your document. This feature is handy if a coworker always writes stupid notes that you don't want to waste your time reading.

Adding, Deleting, and Rearranging Pages

You can't edit an Envoy document as you can a regular WordPerfect document — you can't change text, for example — but you can perform a few editing maneuvers:

Be careful when making these editing changes, because Envoy doesn't have an Undo function:

- To copy a text or graphic from one Envoy document and insert it in another Envoy document, choose the Select tool and then drag to select the text or drag around a graphic to enclose it in a selection box. Then choose Edit⇨Copy or press Ctrl+C. Choose Edit⇨Paste or press Ctrl+V and then click at the spot where you want to put the copy. Copied text is inserted as a QuickNote.
- To move a page from one Envoy document to another, first open both documents. Then choose Window⇨Tile Top to Bottom so that you can see both documents on-screen. Turn on thumbnail views for each document. Then, with the Select tool, click on the thumbnail of the page you want to move and drag it onto an empty spot in the thumbnail area of the other document. To make one of the documents take up the entire window again, click on its Maximize button.

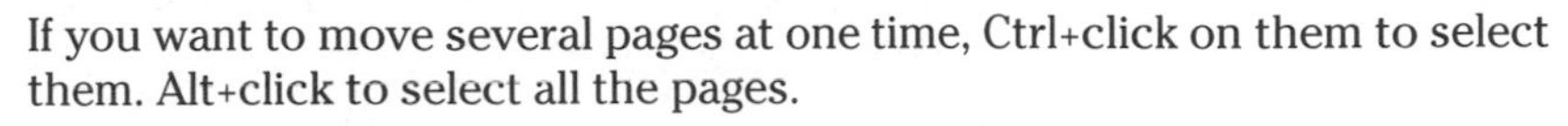

If you want to move several pages at one time, Ctrl+click on them to select them. Alt+click to select all the pages.

- To delete a page, click on its thumbnail with the Select tool and press Delete.
- To rearrange pages, choose the Select tool, click on the thumbnail of the page you want to move, and drag it to its new position.

Marking Your Place with a Bookmark

If you're viewing a long document — or sending a long document to others — you may want to use bookmarks to make finding important sections of the document easier. After you create a bookmark, a Bookmarks list appears on the status bar, as in Figure 17-6. To move quickly to the spot where you placed a bookmark, you just choose the bookmark name from the list.

To create a bookmark, click on the Bookmark tool button on the toolbar. Your cursor changes to a little book, as shown in Figure 17-6. Drag over the text you want to mark with the bookmark cursor.

When you release the mouse button, the Bookmark Properties dialog box, shown in Figure 17-7, appears. Enter the name that you want to appear on the Bookmarks list in the Bookmark Name option box. If you check the Select Bookmark Content After Jump option box, Envoy selects the bookmarked text each time you select the bookmark from the Bookmark list. (You may want to do this to make it easy for people to copy or print the text, for example.)

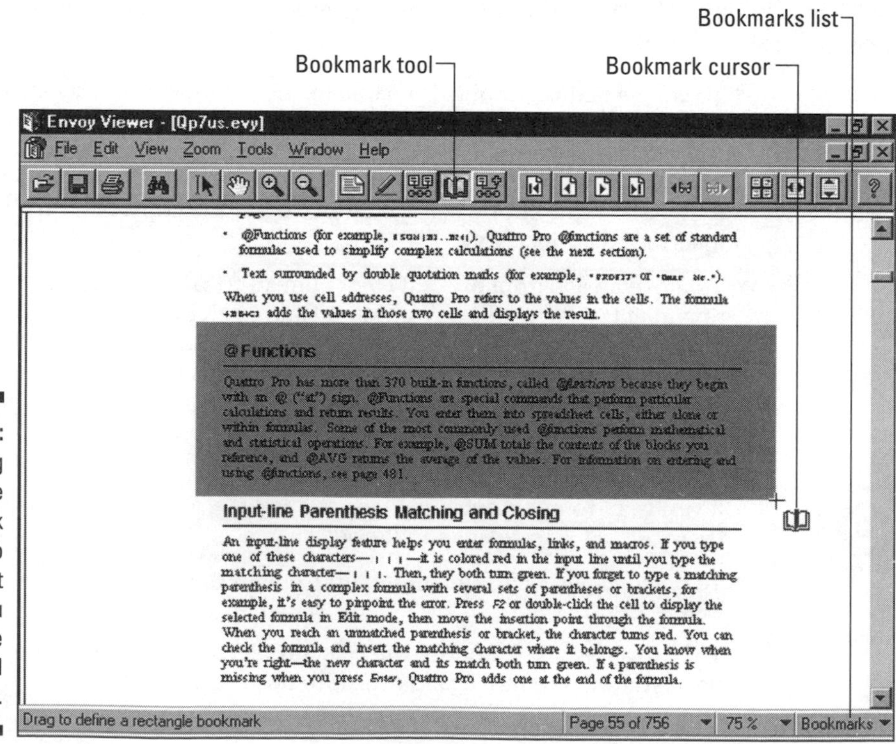

Figure 17-6: Drag with the bookmark cursor to mark text that you want to be able to find later.

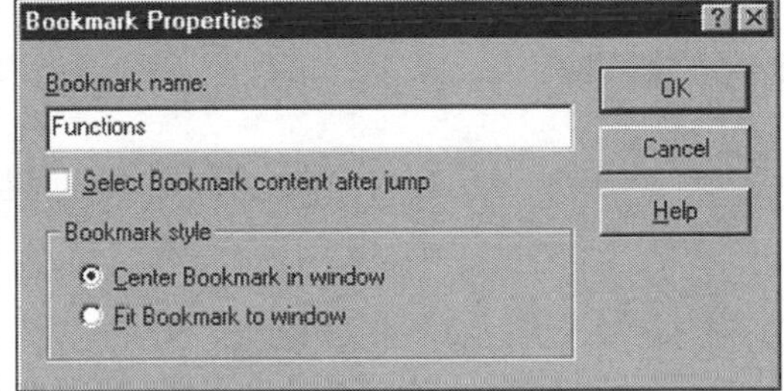

Figure 17-7: Tell Envoy how you want bookmarked text to appear.

If you select the Center Bookmark in Window radio button, the bookmarked text appears in the center of the Envoy window when you jump to it. If you select the Fit Bookmark to Window option, Envoy enlarges or reduces the bookmarked text so that it all appears on-screen when you jump to it.

To change the settings in the Bookmark Properties dialog box after you create a bookmark, just right-click on the bookmarked text with the Bookmark cursor and choose the Bookmark Properties command from the QuickMenu. To delete a bookmark, right-click and choose Clear from the QuickMenu. And to quickly jump to the next bookmark in the document, choose Find Next Bookmark from the QuickMenu.

Creating and Using Hypertext

If you surf the Internet or use any interactive media, you're probably familiar with the concept of hypertext. When you click on a graphic or piece of text that's formatted as a hypertext link, your cursor jumps to another page that contains related information.

You can create a hypertext link to another page in the same document or in another Envoy document. Here's how:

1. **Choose Tools⇨Hypertext or click on the Hypertext tool.**

   The Hypertext tool is labeled in Figure 17-8. When you click on the tool or choose the Hypertext command, the cursor changes into a . . . well, I guess it sort of looks like two little pages linked by a chain and topped by a plus sign.

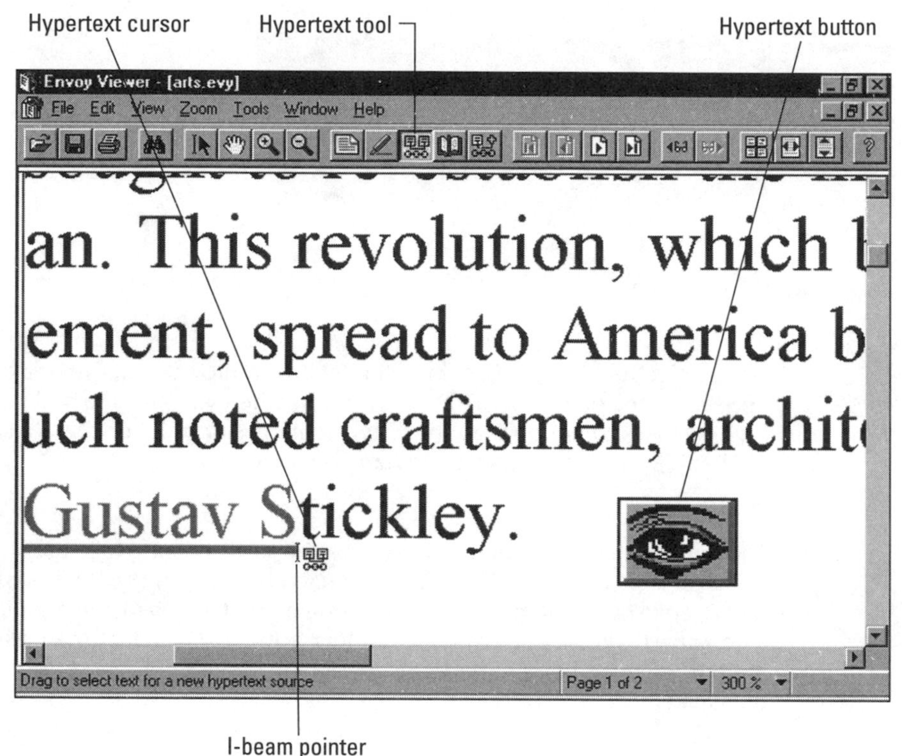

Figure 17-8: Clicking on a hypertext link jumps your cursor to a page containing related information.

2. **Drag to highlight the word or phrase that you want to format as hypertext.**

   When you put the hypertext cursor inside a block of text, the plus sign on the cursor changes to the I-beam pointer, as shown in Figure 17-8. In the figure, I'm in the process of highlighting the name Gustav Stickley with the cursor.

   You can also create a hypertext button that viewers can click on to jump to related information. To create a button, place the cursor where you want the button to appear (it must be a spot where there is no text) and drag to create the button. Figure 17-8 shows a hypertext button that I created. By default, the button looks like a rectangle; I changed the button face to this "eye-catching" design by editing the hypertext properties, as explained a little later in this section.

   After you complete your drag, that little plus sign above the hypertext cursor becomes enclosed in a circle.

3. **Select the linked text.**

   In other words, find the text that you want people to jump to when they click on the hypertext or hypertext button you created in Step 2. You can link to text in the same document or in another open document.

Drag to enclose the text in a box. When you release the mouse button, the text is surrounded by a black rectangle with selection handles. You can move the box by dragging it or resize the box by dragging one of the selection handles.

4. **Click on the Hypertext tool again to deselect it.**

   Or, set up more hypertext links, if you like, and click on the tool after you're finished.

After you create a link, check to make sure that it works. With the Select tool, pass your cursor over the hypertext link or button. The cursor should change into a little hand with a pointing finger. Click on the link to make sure that you jump to the right spot.

One of the formatting options for a hypertext button causes the button box to be invisible (people sometimes use this option if they want to print a document that uses hypertext buttons). If you can't find a hypertext button after you create it, chances are this option is turned on. To find the button, click on the Hypertext tool. The button's outline should appear. If you switch back to the Select tool, the outline disappears. But if you pass the cursor over the now invisible button, you get the little hand with a pointing finger and can click to jump to the linked text. The button's invisible, but it still works. (Don't you wish the same could be said for some of the people in your office?)

If you want to change the button's appearance, right-click on the button with the Hypertext tool and choose Properties from the QuickMenu. The dialog box shown in Figure 17-9 appears. You can choose how you want the button to appear — as a framed rectangle, as an invisible rectangle, or as a button icon like the one shown in Figure 17-8. Use the scroll arrows to see the available icon choices for your button.

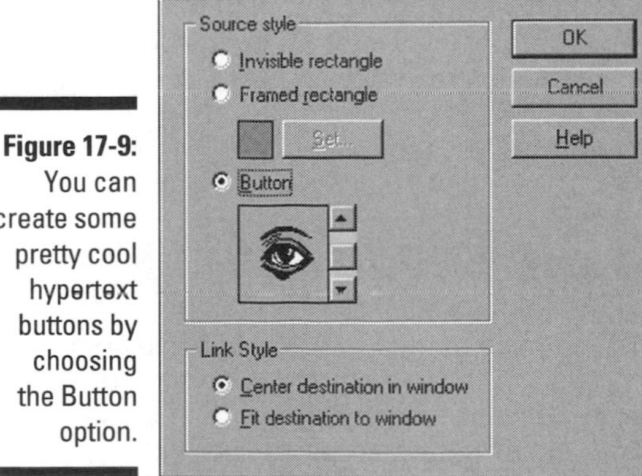

Figure 17-9: You can create some pretty cool hypertext buttons by choosing the Button option.

You can edit a hypertext text link by choosing the Hypertext tool and placing your cursor over the link until you see an arrow appear. Then right-click to display a QuickMenu. Choose Properties to display the dialog box shown in Figure 17-10, where you can specify what formatting you want to use to indicate hypertext (colored text, underlined text, or both). You can also specify whether you want Envoy to center the linked text in the window when a user jumps to it or whether you want the text enlarged or reduced so that it fits entirely within the window.

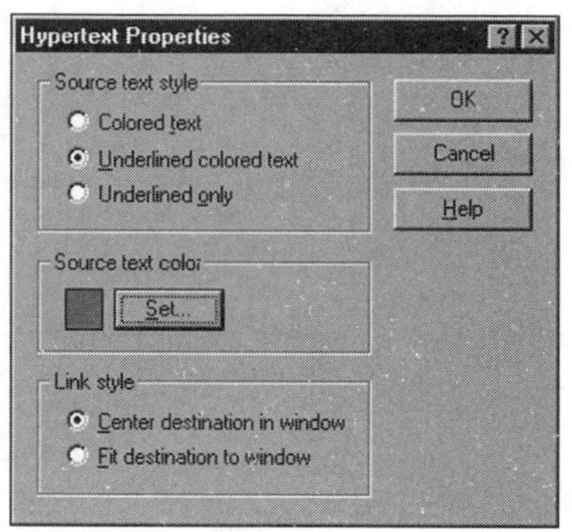

Figure 17-10: You can make a hypertext link appear as colored text, underlined text, or colored and underlined text.

Choose Edit Link from the QuickMenu to change the linked text associated with a hypertext link or button; choose Edit Source to change the button or text that viewers click to jump to the linked text. To remove a hypertext link, right-click on the link text or button with the Hypertext tool and choose Clear from the QuickMenu.

The WebLink tool, which is two buttons to the right of the Hypertext tool, enables you to create links to pages on the Internet or to non-Envoy documents. If you want to try it out, you can find the how-to's by choosing the Web Links item from Index tab of the Envoy Help dialog box. (For information on using the Help system, see Chapter 3.)

Sending Someone Else an Envoy File

You say you created an incredible Envoy file that you want to send to your Grandmother in Omaha, but she doesn't have Envoy installed on her computer? No sweat. You can either send her a copy of the Envoy Viewer or you can create a Runtime file that she can view without installing the Envoy Viewer.

Grandma needs to be using Windows 95; Envoy files and Runtime files created in Windows 95 won't open in Windows 3.1. If Grandma uses a Macintosh, she needs a copy of the Envoy 7 Viewer for Macintosh to view your Envoy files. You can get a copy via the Internet by visiting the site `http://www.tumbleweed.com`.

To copy the Envoy Viewer, choose Run from the Windows 95 Start menu and type the following into the Open box: **C:\Corel\Office7\Envoy7 \DVSETUP.EXE.** (This command assumes that Envoy is stored on your hard drive and that C is the name of that hard drive.) Then click on OK or press Enter.

A dialog box appears, asking you to agree to certain software licensing terms. Respond in the affirmative. In the Output Path box, enter the name of the drive, directory, and folder where you want to save the Viewer. Click on OK to make the copy.

A regular floppy disk is too small to hold the entire Viewer. So if you want to copy the Viewer to a disk, first copy it to a folder on your hard drive. It's a good idea to create a new folder to hold the copy so that you don't get confused about which files are the Viewer files. After you copy the viewer files to your hard drive, you can use a program such as WinZip to compress the files so that they fit on one floppy disk. You can then delete the files from the folder you created on your hard disk. If all this sounds like Greek to you, grab a computer guru to help you out.

To create a Runtime version of your file, choose File⇨Save As, enter a name for your file in the File Name option box, specify the drive, directory, and folder where you want to save the file, and select Envoy Runtime Files in the Save As Type drop-down list. Click on Save or press Enter to save the file. Runtime files have the file extension .EXE. All Grandma has to do to view that file is choose Run from the Windows 95 start menu and enter your filename in the Open option box.

Saving, Printing, and Shutting Down

To save an Envoy file, use the same steps you use to save any file in the WordPerfect Suite. To save a file for the first time, choose File⇨Save or press Ctrl+S to display the Save dialog box, give the file a name, specify the drive, directory, and folder where you want to store the file, and select a file type. (Regular Envoy files get the extension .EVY; if you want to create a Runtime version of the file, see the preceding section for the lowdown.) Click on Save or press Enter to finish the tortuous saving process. To resave the file, just press Ctrl+S again.

To save the file under a different name, to a different location, or as a different file type, choose File⇨Save As or press Ctrl+F3. (If you need more details about how to save a file, see "Saving Your Work (and Your Sanity)," in Chapter 5. Saving a file in Envoy is similar to the save process described there.)

To print a document from Envoy, choose File⇨Print or press Ctrl+P. You get the standard Print dialog box, where you can select the number of copies and pages you want to print. Click on OK or press Enter to send your file off to the printer.

If you changed the printer driver to the Envoy 7 driver to create your Envoy file, don't forget to change it back to your regular printer driver before printing on paper.

To close an Envoy document, choose File⇨Close, press Ctrl+F4, or click on the document window's Close button. And finally, to send Envoy into the deep, dark, digital night, choose File⇨Exit, press Alt+F4, or click on the program window Close button.

Chapter 18

Internet Adventures

In This Chapter

- Getting acquainted with Netscape Navigator
- Exploring the World Wide Web
- Marking your favorite Web pages so that you can find them again
- Sending e-mail over the Internet
- Participating in newsgroups
- Printing and saving pages and messages

Not too long ago, Netscape Communications sent Wall Street into a tizzy with the initial public offering of its stock, which soared to unbelievable (and some say ridiculous) heights minutes after its debut. The stock offering brought even more attention to the company that became famous for its Navigator software, a product that made finding your way around the Internet's World Wide Web a heck of a lot easier than it had been before.

If you were lucky enough to grab some Netscape shares at a decent price, I'd like to congratulate you (and get the name of your broker, please). If not, well, at least you can take some satisfaction in owning Netscape Navigator, which is included in the WordPerfect Suite. Okay, I know that's sort of a lame substitute for making a killing on Wall Street. But the software will undoubtedly entertain and inform you long after the market bulls move on to some other hot new stock.

This chapter shows you how to explore the Internet and the World Wide Web using Netscape Navigator — which, by the way, folks refer to as *Netscape* and not *Navigator.* You find out how to move between pages, send e-mail, post messages to newsgroups, and do all those other things you hear everyone talking about these days.

If you want to know more about the Internet and Netscape — and there's much more to explore than I can cover in this book, check out *Netscape and the World Wide Web For Dummies,* 2nd Edition, by Paul Hoffman, or *The Internet For Dummies,* 3rd Edition by John Levine, Carol Baroudi, and Margaret Levine Young. Both of these books (published by IDG Books Worldwide, Inc.) offer the low-down on surfing the Internet.

A Crash Course in Internet Lingo

Like most things related to computers, the Internet has its own vocabulary. Here are just a few basic terms to make your exploration of the Internet easier (and help you avoid sounding like a rube at parties):

- The *Internet* — also called the *Net* — is nothing more than a big group of computers located all over the world and tied together via modems and other communication devices. The Internet is not unlike the computer network you may have in your office, only it's much bigger and offers you access to much cooler stuff. On the Internet, you can find information about every topic under the sun, buy products from local and international vendors, carry on conversations with other computer users, and send and receive electronic mail.
- Individuals and corporations who want to distribute information, products, and services create and maintain Internet *sites.* Computer users around the world can "visit" those sites by *logging in* (connecting via a modem) to the Internet.
- The *World Wide Web* is one part — the flashiest part — of the Internet. When you visit many sites on the Internet, all you see are pages (screens) full of plain-looking text. Web sites, on the other hand, usually incorporate stylish text formatting, full-color graphics, and sometimes even sound and video clips.
- Web pages also contain *hypertext* links. A hypertext link is a graphic, button, or piece of text that you can click on to move from one Web page to another page offering related information.
- A Web *browser* is a software program designed for finding and accessing information on the World Wide Web. Netscape is the leading Web browser today. Netscape not only enables you to find and view Web pages, but also provides access to other Internet services, such as e-mail and newsgroups.
- A *newsgroup* is a group of people who carry on conversations with each other by sending messages back and forth through an Internet service called *Usenet.* Different newsgroups focus on different topics. When people send messages to a newsgroup, they say that they're *posting an article* or *posting news.*
- *URL* stands for *Uniform Resource Locator.* A URL is, in essence, an address on the Web.

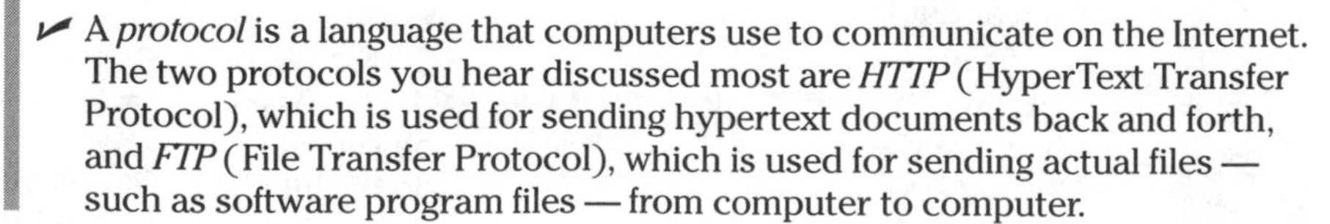

- A *protocol* is a language that computers use to communicate on the Internet. The two protocols you hear discussed most are *HTTP* (HyperText Transfer Protocol), which is used for sending hypertext documents back and forth, and *FTP* (File Transfer Protocol), which is used for sending actual files — such as software program files — from computer to computer.

- *HTML* is short for *HyperText Markup Language*. This language is the most popular language for creating Web pages.

  By the way, WordPerfect 7 offers a QuickTask that walks you through the process of creating an HTML document; choose File➪Internet Publisher to check it out. Or choose the Create Web Page option from the QuickTask dialog box (QuickTasks are discussed in Chapter 3.)

Leaping onto the Net

Before you can access the Internet with Netscape — or with any other software — you must sign up with an Internet service provider (and have a modem, of course). You also need to establish some settings in Netscape so that your modem can communicate with the service provider's computers. Your service provider should help you do this setup work.

The Corel WordPerfect Suite includes AT&T WorldNet Service software, which enables you to sign up with AT&T as your Internet service provider. The software also provides you with a special, AT&T version of the Netscape Navigator browser. You can use the browser with other service providers, but you may want to investigate AT&T's services if you're just beginning with the Net. At press time, AT&T was offering five free hours of online time per month for one year to AT&T long-distance customers. To link up with AT&T as your Internet provider, click on the Windows 95 Start button and then choose Programs➪AT&T WorldNet Service. Then double-click on the Set Up Account icon in the window that opens.

After you get set up with an Internet service provider, you can start Netscape by double-clicking on the AT&T WorldNet Service shortcut icon on your desktop. Or choose Start➪Programs➪AT&T WorldNet Service and double-click on the AT&T WorldNet Service icon in the window that appears. You can also click on the Internet toolbar button in WordPerfect, Presentations, and Quattro Pro. And, as if those weren't enough options, you can connect to a specific Internet site by clicking on the DAD QuickConnect icon.

If you're not using AT&T as your service provider, you may need to connect to the Internet through your service provider's software before you start the AT&T Netscape browser.

After you connect to the Internet, you see a window looking something like the one in Figure 18-1. If you double-clicked the AT&T WorldNet Service icon to start your Internet session, the browser automatically loads the Netscape Web site's home page (a *home page* is the first page you see when you visit a Web site). If you start the Netscape browser by clicking on the Internet button in WordPerfect, Quattro Pro, or Presentations, you start at the home page for Corel's Web site.

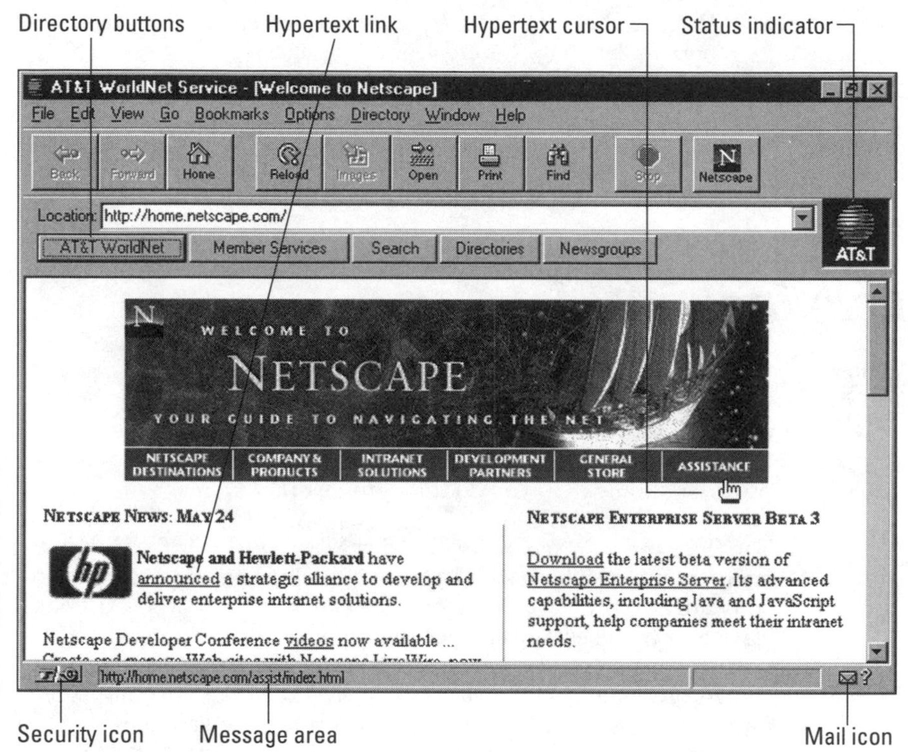

Figure 18-1: The Netscape program window and home page.

The following list gives you the blow-by-blow of the different components of the browser window:

- That big AT&T icon is the *status indicator.* When Netscape is transferring information to your computer, the icon becomes animated.
- The little envelope in the bottom-right corner of the screen is the Mail icon. You can click on this icon to get to Netscape's e-mail features, as explained later in this chapter, in the section "Sending Electronic Mail on the Internet."
- When you pass your cursor over a hypertext link — which could come in the form of a button, graphic, or colored, underlined text — the cursor changes into a little hand with its button-pushing finger extended. Click to jump to the linked information.
- The message area gives you information about the status of data being transferred to your computer. This area also displays the address of the page you will jump to if you click on a particular hypertext link.

- The security icon tells you whether you're looking at a *secure* document. Many vendors who sell stuff on the Internet build security precautions into their pages to make sure that cyberthiefs can't get their hands on your credit card number or other confidential information. A broken door key on a gray background, like the one in the figure, indicates a non-secure page. A complete key on a blue background tells you that the page is secure. (But keep in mind that even secure pages are sometimes broken into, just like homes with the best security systems.)
- The Location box at the top of the window shows you the address of the current page. If you know the address of a site you want to visit, you can enter the address in the box and press Enter to move to that site.
- The row of buttons beneath the Location box are the Directory buttons. Each button takes you to another Web page or spot on the Internet.
- Like other program windows, the Netscape window offers a menu bar, toolbar, Close button, Minimize and Maximize/Restore buttons, and scroll bar. For more information about these window features, see Chapter 2, "Basic Stuff You Need to Know."

You can turn some window elements on and off by clicking on them in the Options menu. You may want to turn off the toolbar and Directory buttons at times, for example, so that you can display more of a Web page on the screen at one time.

The various Preferences commands on the Options menu enable you to control many other aspects of Netscape. You can change the default home page that appears when you start the program, for example, and change the font used to display your e-mail messages.

Becoming a Page Jumper

To view the contents of a Web page, you simply use the scroll bar on the right side of the Netscape window to scroll the page. Most pages contain one or more hypertext links that you click on to jump to pages that contain related information. Hypertext links can be indicated by colored, underlined text, buttons, icons, or other special formatting. You know that you've found a link when your cursor changes into the little pointing finger, as explained in the preceding section.

- As you jump from link to link, Netscape remembers the addresses of the last several pages you viewed. So if you want to return to the previous page, you can just click on the Back button or choose Go⇨Back. To go forward a page, click on the Forward icon or choose Go⇨Forward.

- To go backward or forward several pages, choose the page location from the bottom of the Go menu.
- Clicking on the Home button or choosing Go➪Home takes you to the Netscape home page.
- Some pages, such as the one in Figure 18-2, have *frames,* which are like pages within pages. Clicking on a link within a frame may jump you to an entirely new page or simply display a new page inside the frame. You can resize any frame by dragging its border.

Of course, you won't always want to follow a trail of links to travel from one page to another. If you know the URL (address) of the site you want to visit, just type it into the Location option box and press Enter to go to that site. Click on the down-pointing arrow at the end of the Location box to display a drop-down list of pages you've viewed recently. Click on a page to jump to it.

The information on some Web pages gets updated frequently (on pages offering current stock market quotes, for example). Some pages don't update automatically after you download them, however. To reload the page so that you can view the most current version of the page, choose View➪Reload or click on the Reload button on the toolbar.

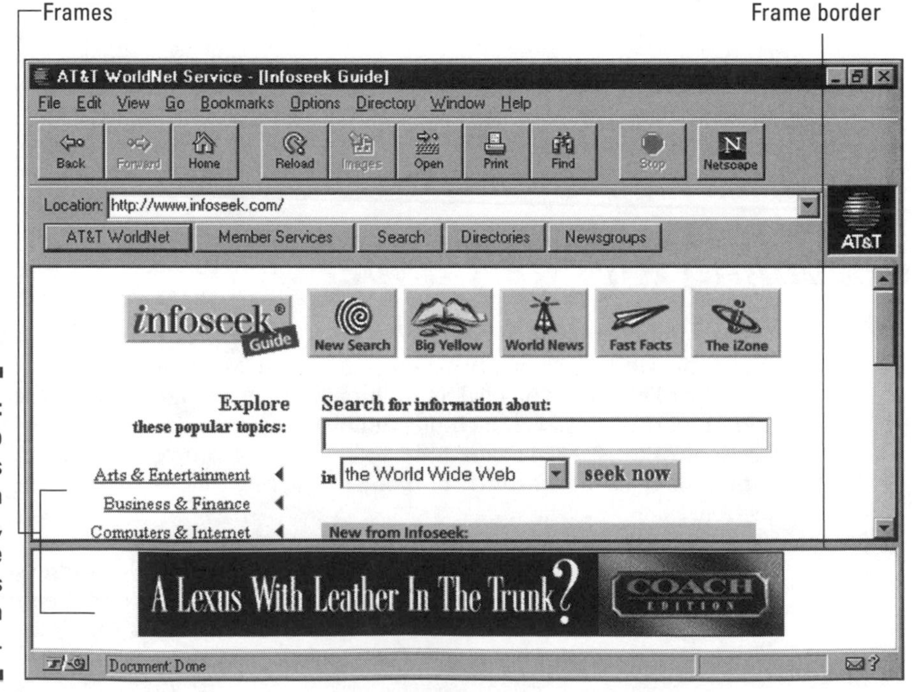

Figure 18-2: Some Web pages contain frames, which are like pages within pages.

Finding Sites that Interest You

The Web is jam-packed with information to read, products to buy, files to download, and services to use. So many Web sites exist, in fact, that finding the ones that interest you is perhaps the biggest challenge of life on the Internet. On top of that, much of the stuff on the Web is junk — either low-grade content or slimy advertising that tricks you into visiting a site by promising something more than what's really there.

Netscape offers several tools to help you find the good Web sites and bypass the not-so-good:

- The Search and Directories buttons take you to pages offering links to search tools and directories — tools for finding Web sites that deal with a particular topic. You can also click on the Net Search hypertext link on the Netscape home page to go to the page shown in Figure 18-3, which offers access to search tools and directories.
- Different search tools search different areas of the Internet; some search for only text pages, some search only the Web, and so on. Although each search tool works a little differently, you usually type the topic you want to find in an option box and then click on a Search button. You next see a display of links to sites matching your search request. Often, the sites are described briefly and rated in terms of the type and quality of content they offer. To go to the site, just click on the link.

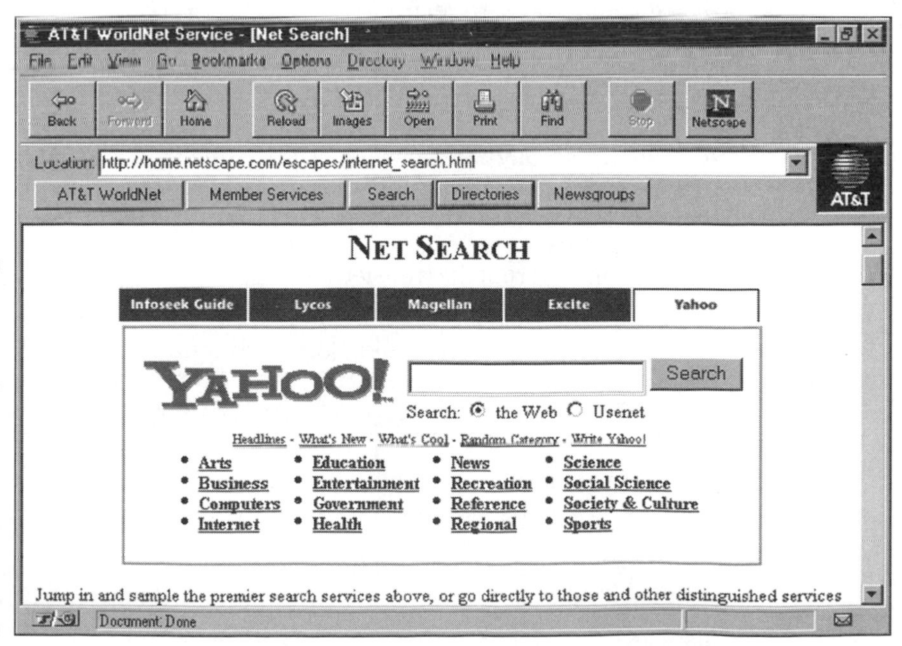

Figure 18-3: Begin a search for a particular topic using one of the services offered on this Netscape page.

- Directories display links and site information by category. For example, you can click on the Arts hypertext link shown in Figure 18-3 to display a list of arts-related sites in the Yahoo! directory.
- Click on the Bookmarks menu to display a list of bookmarks for popular Web sites. Click on a bookmark to jump to that site. Bookmarks are explained further in the section "Saving Online Time (and Money)."
- On the Netscape home page, click on the What's Cool and What's New hypertext links to jump to lists of pages recommended by the folks at Netscape.

You can also find many books and Internet directories that provide descriptions and addresses of good Web sites. I recommend *The Web After Work For Dummies*, IDG Books Worldwide, Inc.

One Web site you should definitely check out is the Corel Corporation Web Site, which you can visit at the address `http://www.corel.com`. (The site is included in the list of bookmarks under the Bookmarks menu.) The Corel site offers news about Corel's products, as well as technical support information. Also check out Chris Dickman's CORELNET at `http://www.corelnet.com`, which offers discussion areas through which Corel users can share information.

Saving Online Time (and Money)

One of the first things you notice about cruising the Web is that it can take a long time for information to get from the Web to your computer screen. Because most Internet providers base their fees on the number of hours you spend online, it pays to become a more efficient Webber. Here are a few tips to help you make the most of your online time:

- If a Web site is really popular — which means that many people are trying to download the same stuff at the same time — accessing the site can take a long time. If you get tired of waiting or if you get a page downloaded halfway and realize that it's not what you expected, click on the Stop button or press Esc to interrupt the transfer.
- You can access Web pages much faster if you choose Options and uncheck the Auto Load Images command. Netscape then downloads just the text parts of a page and displays the graphics as little icons. If you want to see the graphics on a particular page, choose View⇨Load Images or click on the Images toolbar button.
- If you find a page you like and think you may want to visit again, choose Bookmarks⇨Add Bookmark or press Ctrl+D. Netscape adds the site or page name to a list of bookmarks that you can access from the Bookmarks menu or by choosing Window⇨Bookmarks to open the Bookmarks window. Double-click on an item in the window to jump to that page.
- Instead of taking the time to read a long document on-screen, save it to disk or print it and read it after you log off the Internet. You can find the how-to's in the section "Printing and Saving Pages and Messages."

- Also, don't compose long e-mail or newsgroup messages while you're online. Instead, compose your messages in Netscape before you log onto the Net, as discussed in the sections "Sending e-mail" and "Posting a message to a newsgroup."

Sending Electronic Mail on the Internet

In addition to browsing Web pages, you can send and receive e-mail (electronic mail) over the Internet using Netscape. To open the Mail window, click on the envelope icon in the bottom-right corner of the Netscape window or choose Window➪AT&T WorldNet Mail. A window looking like the one in Figure 18-4 appears.

Before Netscape lets you receive or send any mail, it asks you to enter your e-mail password (assigned by your Internet provider). You can avoid having to do this each time you open the Mail window by choosing Options➪Mail and News Preferences, clicking on the Organization panel in the resulting dialog box, and checking the Remember Mail Password option box.

Receiving and reading your mail

The Mail window has three different panes, labeled in Figure 18-4, which you can resize by dragging the pane borders. After you click on a folder in the Mailbox pane, the Message Header pane displays a list of messages in the folder. Click on a message in the Message Header pane to display the entire message in the Message pane.

- The Message Header pane displays some identifying information about the message, such as the name of the person sending the message and the subject matter of the message.
- The little icons to the right of the sender's name can be used to flag a message that you want to be able to find again later or mark as important. Just click on the icon to turn the flag on or off. The other icon marks your messages as read or unread; a green diamond indicates an unread message. Again, you can just click on the icon to toggle it back and forth between on or off.
- You can drag the borders between the different column titles to display more or less of the information in that column. For example, you may want to shrink the size of the Sender column so that you can see more text in the Subject column.
- By default, Netscape puts all your messages into a mail folder called Inbox. You can create other folders so that you can store messages by category if you want; choose File➪New Folder to create a folder. To move a message into the folder, just drag it to the folder.

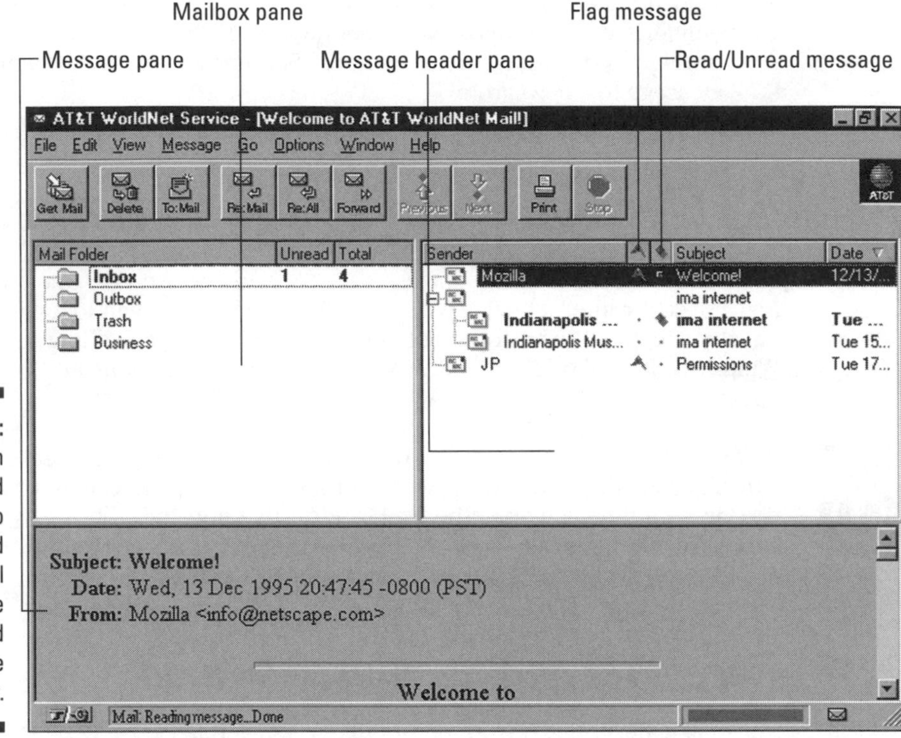

Figure 18-4: You can send messages to friends and family all over the world through the Internet.

- To delete a message, click on it in the Message Header pane and click on the Delete button on the toolbar.

When you first open the Mail window, Netscape checks to see whether any new messages arrived for you. When this happens, the question mark next to the envelope icon at the bottom of the program window disappears. If you want Netscape to check for messages while you're online, choose Options⇨Mail and News Preferences, click on the Servers tab of the resulting dialog box, and change the Check for New Mail option from Never to Every. In the Every option box, specify how often you want the program to check for new mail. When new mail arrives, a little exclamation point appears next to the envelope icon. Click on the Get Mail button to retreive the mail.

Sending e-mail

To send a new mail message to someone, choose File⇨New Mail Message or click on the To: Mail button on the toolbar. The Message Composition window shown in Figure 18-5 appears. In the Mail To box, type the e-mail address of the recipient. If you want to send a copy of the message to other people, enter their addresses in the CC box. Type a brief subject heading in the Subject box and then type your message in the message area. Click on the Send button to launch your message into cyberspace.

To reply to a message, click on it and then click on the RE: Mail button. The recipient's name and address are entered for you in the Message Composition window. The text of the original message is included in your response.

You can compose your messages in Netscape before you log onto the Internet to reduce the amount of time you spend online. Start Netscape but don't connect to the Internet. Create your mail message as usual, but choose Options⇨Deferred Delivery before you click on the Send button. Netscape stores the message in a folder called Outbox in your Mailbox pane. When you log onto the Internet, choose File⇨Send Mail in Outbox or press Ctrl+H to send all the messages in the Outbox folder.

Using the address book

To avoid avoid having to enter someone's e-mail address every time you send a message to that person, add the address to Netscape's address book. Choose Window⇨Address Book to open the address book, choose Item⇨Add User, and enter the person's name and address. Or, to add the address of someone from whom you've received a message, click on that person's message in the Message Header window and choose the Message⇨Add to Address Book command.

When you want to send that person a message, choose Window⇨ Address Book and double-click on the person's name. Netscape opens up a Message Composition window and fills in the person's name and address for you. You can also access the address book inside the Message Composition window by clicking on the Address button. Click on the person's name and then click on the To: or CC: button to indicate whether you want to insert the name into the Mail To option box or the CC option box.

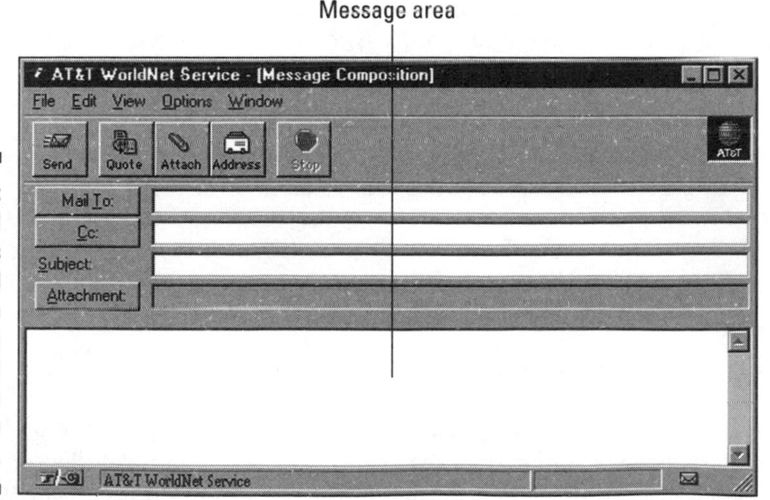

Figure 18-5: Create and address your mail messages in this dialog box and then click on Send to "mail" them.

Chatting in Newsgroups

Newsgroup is the Internet term for a group of people who exchange messages about a particular area of interest. You can find newsgroups for almost every topic, from using computers to creating craft items.

To see what newsgroups are all about, click on the Newsgroups button or choose Window⇨AT&T WorldNet Newsgroups. Netscape opens a window that looks similar to the one in Figure 18-6. Like the Mail window, the News window has three panes: a Newsgroup pane, Message Header pane, and Message pane. Drag the border of any pane to resize it. Drag the column header borders to resize the columns in the panes.

Newsgroups are organized into folders in the newsgroup pane. Each folder contains newsgroups related to a specific subject. After you double-click on a folder in the newsgroup pane, you see a list of all the newsgroups in the folder. The number in the Unread column indicates how many of the newsgroup messages you haven't read yet, and the number in the Total column tells you the total number of newsgroup messages. A checkmark next to a newsgroup name means that Netscape is set up to automatically display the newsgroup in the newsgroup pane and to keep track of which messages you've read and haven't read.

Catching up on the latest "news"

After you click on a newsgroup name, a list of messages for the newsgroup appears in the Message Header pane. Click on a message in the list to display the entire message in the Message pane.

The icons after the sender name indicate the same thing they do in the e-mail window. The first icon flags messages that you want to be able to locate easily later; click on the icon to turn the flag on or off. The second icon marks a message as read or unread. After you read a message, the icon shrinks and turns grey. Click on the icon to turn it from "read" to "unread" and vice versa.

Replies to a newsgroup message are positioned next to the original message. The original message and all replies are said to be *threaded,* as in strung together. If you click on any message in the thread and then click on the Thread button, you can mark all the messages in a thread as read (and make a clever rhyme at the same time).

Subscribing to a newsgroup

By default, Netscape displays a couple of newsgroups in the Newsgroup pane. To see a list of other newsgroups, choose Options⇨Show All Newsgroups. Then go get a cup of coffee while Netscape downloads the list, which can take several minutes.

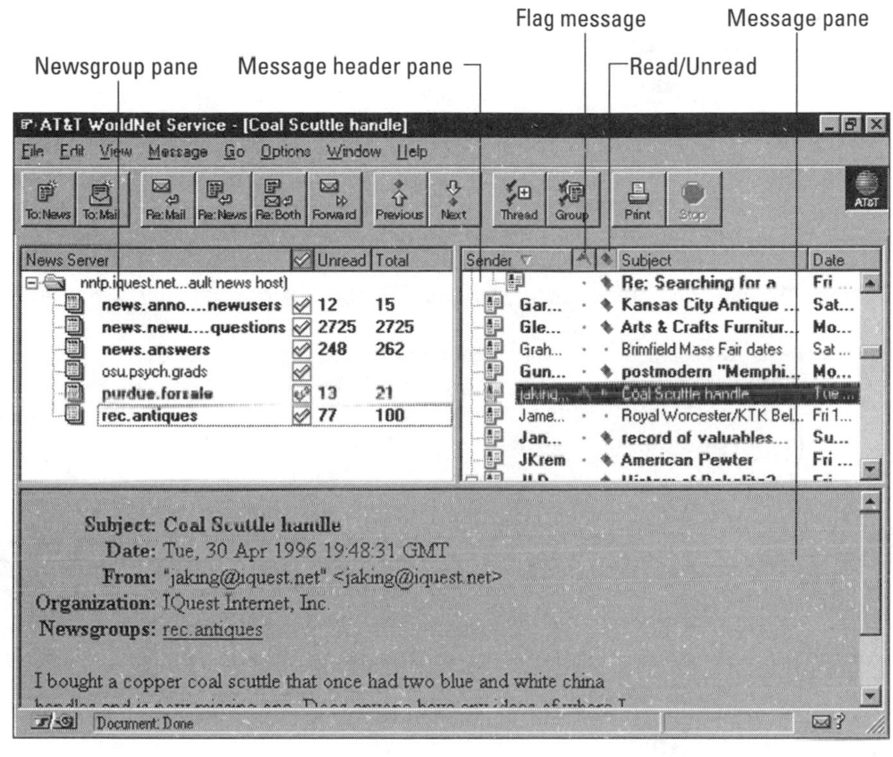

Figure 18-6: The Netscape News window lets you converse with computer users around the world.

You'll quickly discover, as you scroll through the newsgroup list, that a newsgroup's name often doesn't reveal its subject matter. But you can get a vague idea by looking at the beginning of the newsgroup name. For example, *comp.* indicates newsgroups dealing with computers; *sci.* indicates scientific newsgroups; *rec.* indicates a focus on recreational activities such as hobbies or sports; and *soc.* indicates groups interested in social interests or socializing.

To see whether you want to join a newsgroup, read a few of the messages. If you like what you see, you can *subscribe* to the newsgroup. All you have to do to subscribe is check the box next to the newsgroup name in the Newsgroup pane. Subscribing to a newsgroup simply tells Netscape to display that newsgroup every time you open the Newsgroup window — provided, of course, that you turn off the Options➪Show All Newsgroups command and turn on the Options➪Show Subscribed Newsgroups command.

The Options menu contains many other settings that you can use to control how and when newsgroup messages are displayed. For example, you can tell Netscape to show all messages or show only unread messages. If you want the settings you select in the Options menu to remain in effect after you end your current online session, choose Options➪Save Options.

The View⇨Sort command lets you specify the order in which newsgroup messages are displayed — by date, sender, subject, and so on.

Posting a message to a newsgroup

Ready to be bold and put in your two cents worth about the newsgroup topic at hand? To post a new message, choose File⇨New News Message or click on the To: News button. To reply to the message that's currently displayed in the Message pane, choose Message⇨Post Reply or click on the Re: News button.

If you want to send a private e-mail message to the author of the message you're replying to, choose Message⇨Mail Reply or click on the Re: Mail button. To post a reply to the newsgroup and send an e-mail to the author, click on Re: Both or choose Message⇨Post and Mail Reply.

Printing and Saving Pages and Messages

To print the current Web page, e-mail message, or newsgroup message, just click on the Print button on the toolbar or choose File⇨Print. If you're looking at a page that uses frames, the command changes to File⇨Print Frame and prints the contents of the currently selected frame only. If you're printing a mail or newsgroup message, the Print command changes to Print Message(s).

To save a Web page to disk, choose File⇨Save As or press Ctrl+S to display the Save As dialog box. If you select the Source option in the Save as Type option box, the pages is saved as an HTML file, which you can view in Netscape after you log off the Internet by choosing the File⇨Open command, just as you would open a document in any other program.

If you select the Plain Text option in the Save as Type option box, only the text on the page is saved, and most of the text formatting is lost. However, you can open the page in most programs.

You can save newsgroup and mail messages to disk by choosing File⇨Save As and giving the message a filename with the .TXT file extension. (You must type in the extension for mail messages; for newsgroup messages, you can select the extension from the Save File as Type option box.)

If you right-click on a hypertext link, you can save the linked page without going to that page. Just choose Save This Link As from the QuickMenu that appears when you right-click.

Chapter 19

And the Rest . . .

In This Chapter

- Looking at the other programs in the WordPerfect Suite
- Using Corel Address Book
- Keeping track of your life with Sidekick
- Directing operations from Dashboard
- Charting and diagramming with CorelFLOW

Have you ever bought something from one of those mail-order companies that sends you a grab bag full of surprise goodies when you order a certain amount of merchandise? You usually wind up with one or two things you use a lot, some that you use once in a blue moon, and some that you know you'll never, ever need and can safely give as Christmas presents to people you don't like very much.

When you buy Corel WordPerfect Suite 7, you receive a similar bundle of goodies. Along with the main components in the suite — WordPerfect, Quattro Pro, and Presentations — Corel threw in a bunch of other programs. Some of them, such as Netscape and Sidekick, you may use on an almost daily basis. Others, such as CorelFLOW, can come in handy on occasion. And others, you'll probably open once to see what they're all about and then never look at again.

This chapter concentrates on the programs that you're most likely to find helpful: Sidekick, Dashboard, Corel Address Book, and CorelFLOW. You can explore the others by reading about them in the Reference Center (as discussed in Chapter 3) or by starting them up and then getting information from the Help menu (also discussed in Chapter 3).

By the way, if you're considering giving any of the programs you don't use as Christmas presents, you should know that you'll break software licensing laws if you do. Not to mention breaking the heart of your third cousin, who was really counting on getting that automatic coffee-filter dispenser from you this year.

Using Corel Address Book

Corel Address Book gives you a convenient way to store and access the names, addresses, and phone numbers of all your friends, business contacts, and so-called friends. After entering names and addresses into Corel Address Book, you can print mailing labels and envelopes, add a contact name and address to a letter or other WordPerfect document, and even get your computer to dial the contact's phone number, e-mail address, or Internet address for you.

Sidekick, another program included with the WordPerfect Suite, offers similar address-book features plus appointment calendars, contact management tools, and a whole lot more. Think of Address Book as one of those little pocket-sized address books you buy in a dime store; think of Sidekick as one of those expensive personal organizers you buy from a specialty store or catalog.

You can start Corel Address Book by clicking on the Windows 95 Start button, choosing the Corel WordPerfect Suite 7 item, and then the Accessories item, and then the Corel Address Book item. Or, if you're working in WordPerfect, you can choose Tools⇨Address Book or click on the Address Book button on the toolbar to temporarily access the Address Book. (The icon is at the far right end of the toolbar, next to the Spell Checker button.) Whichever route you take, the Address Book window appears, as shown in Figure 19-1.

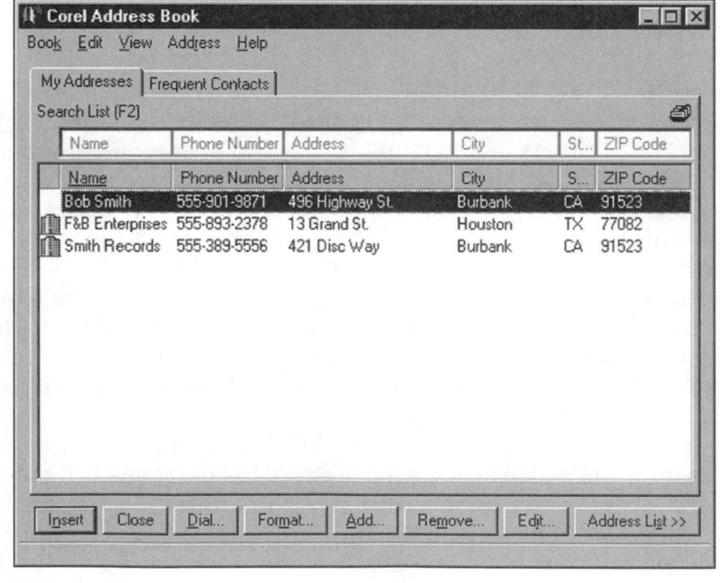

Figure 19-1: The Address Book gives you a simple way to store addresses, phone numbers, and other contact information.

Each of the tabs in the dialog box represents a different address book. You can use just one of the books for all your contacts if you like, or you can separate your addresses into categories to make them easier to find. You can store the same contact on more than one tab, if you want, and you can create as many additional address books as you like by choosing Book⇨New. To open or close an address book, choose Book⇨Open and Book⇨Close, respectively.

Adding and deleting contacts

To add a name to an address book, choose Edit⇨Add Name or click on the Add button at the bottom of the window. A dialog box appears, asking you to specify whether you want to add an address for an organization or a person. Select the category you want and then click on OK.

If you select the Person category, the Properties dialog box shown in Figure 19-2 appears; a slightly different dialog box opens if you choose the Organization category. Fill in the blanks and click on OK to add the contact to the address book.

- Organization entries appear with a little skyscraper icon in the address book, as shown in Figure 19-1.
- If you fill in the Organization blank when adding a person to an address book, a separate entry automatically appears for the organization.
- To make changes to an entry, click on it and then click on the Edit button to redisplay its Properties dialog box. When you edit an entry in one address book, it's updated in all address books in which it's stored.

- When editing an individual's address information, you can edit the information for that person's organization by clicking on the Edit button next to the Organization box to edit the organization information.

- You can copy entries from one address book to another by clicking on the entry to select it and then choosing Edit⇨Copy Names. A dialog box appears and asks you to choose the address book where you want to paste the names. You can also drag the names to the tab of the address book where you want to add them.
- To delete an entry, click on it and press Delete or click on the Remove button.

- To select more than one address to copy or delete, Ctrl+click on each address you want to select.

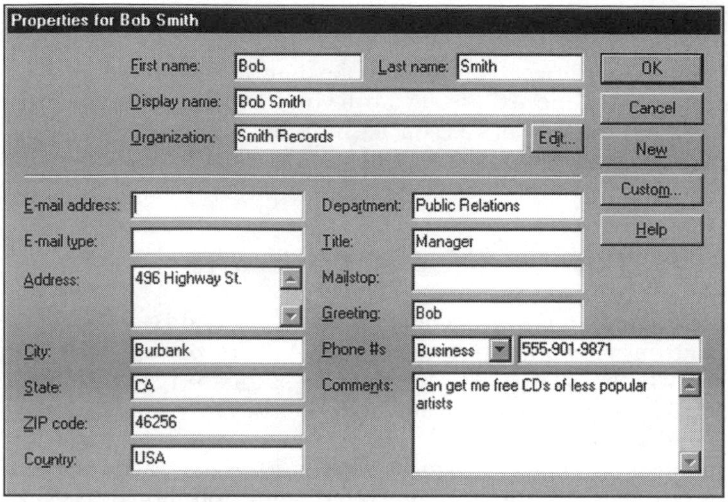

Figure 19-2: Enter contact information for an individual in this dialog box.

Searching for a long-lost loved one

After you get many addresses entered into the Address Book, it can be time-consuming to hunt down the one you want. To track down an address quickly, use the Search List option boxes at the top of each address book tab. If you want to search by name, for example, click inside the Name box and begin typing the name of the contact you want to locate. If you want to search for a particular phone number, type it into the Phone Number box. Almost before you're finished typing, the Address Book finds the listing and highlights it for you in the Address Book window. Click outside the Search List box to end your search. If the search doesn't turn up the contact, the status bar displays a message saying that the search failed.

The Address Book can search for names in the current address book only.

Changing the display of information

By default, the Address Book window displays the name, phone number, address, city, state, and zip code for a contact. If you want to display other items, choose Edit⇨Columns to display a submenu of available items. If you see a checkmark next to an item, that item will display in the window. Click on an item to turn the checkmark on or off.

Drag the borders between the column headings in the Address Book window to change the width of the columns.

Printing and inserting addresses in WordPerfect

If you're working in WordPerfect, you can insert contact addresses into the document by choosing Tools⇨Address Book. A new button, Insert, appears at the bottom of the Address Book. Click on the address you want to insert and then click on Insert. You can also insert addresses onto envelopes that you create using WordPerfect's Format⇨Envelope command. The Envelopes dialog box that appears contains icons that let you select both the return address and mailing address from the Address Book.

If you want to print mailing labels, you can create them using WordPerfect's Format⇨Labels command. But using the Address Book Mailing Labels QuickTask is even easier. Click on the QuickTasks icon on the DAD bar or the Windows 95 Start button, the Corel WordPerfect Suite7 item, the Accessories item, and then the Corel Office QuickTasks item. The mailing labels QuickTask is the second one on the All tab of the QuickTasks dialog box. (You can find out more about QuickTasks in Chapter 3.)

Dialing for dollars

Are you hooked into the Internet or otherwise connected by modem to the outside world? You can use the Address Book to dial an e-mail, Internet, or regular phone number. Click on the name of the person or organization you want to contact and then click on the Dial button. In order for the Dial options to work, the contact's Address Book listing must contain a phone number.

Keeping Tabs on Your Life with Sidekick 95

Sidekick 95 is the Address Book on steroids. The digital equivalent of a personal organizer, Sidekick has tools that help you keep track of appointments and phone calls, log business expenses, store contact information, create To Do lists, and more.

When you first start Sidekick (by choosing it from the Corel WordPerfect Suite 7 menu on the Windows 95 Start menu), the screen appears in Calendar view, which is one of six different views available in Sidekick 95. To switch to a different view, you click on one of the first six icons on the right side of the screen or choose the view from the View menu. Each view offers different tools and features, which are described in the upcoming sections.

If you have an earlier version of Sidekick installed on your system, Sidekick 95 doesn't overwrite that version when you install the program (assuming that you use the default installation directory). If you want to use your existing Sidekick files in Sidekick 95, you must first open them in Sidekick 95. Then save them as Sidekick 95 files by using the File➪Save As command.

Using the calendar and appointment scheduler

In Calendar view, your screen resembles a page from an appointment book, as shown in Figure 19-3. To switch to Calendar view, just click on the Calendar icon, press F6, or choose View➪Calendar.

You can record appointments and keep track of your many chores with the calendar. You can also set alarms to remind you that it's time for lunch and print your calendar so that you can show your boss why you're simply too busy to take on another project.

By default, the Calendar appears in daily view, which displays the current day's activities. You can get a longer-term look at your life by clicking on the Weekly, Monthly, or Yearly view tabs at the bottom of the window. To flip to another day's calendar page, choose the month, year, and date in the mini-calendar at the top of the window.

When you close Sidekick, don't forget to save your calendar (the Program prompts you to do this). Otherwise, all your appointments and other information are erased.

Recording appointments

Click on one of the time slots in the Appointments window to record an appointment. Double-click on the entry to set a precise appointment time (such as 9:50, for example), to add more detailed information, or to tell Sidekick to sound an alarm when the appointment time draws near. (Remember that the alarm only sounds if Sidekick is running.)

To see a list of all your appointments for the day, click on the Appointment List icon, labeled in Figure 19-3. Click on the Appointment Times icon to return to the other appointment view.

When you enter an appointment, a little stopwatch icon appears next to it, as shown in Figure 19-3. To change the time of an appointment, just drag the icon to another time slot. To move the appointment to another day, right-click on it and choose Reschedule Activity. You can then choose a new date and time for the appointment. To delete an appointment, drag its icon to the Delete wastebasket in the bottom-right corner of the Sidekick window.

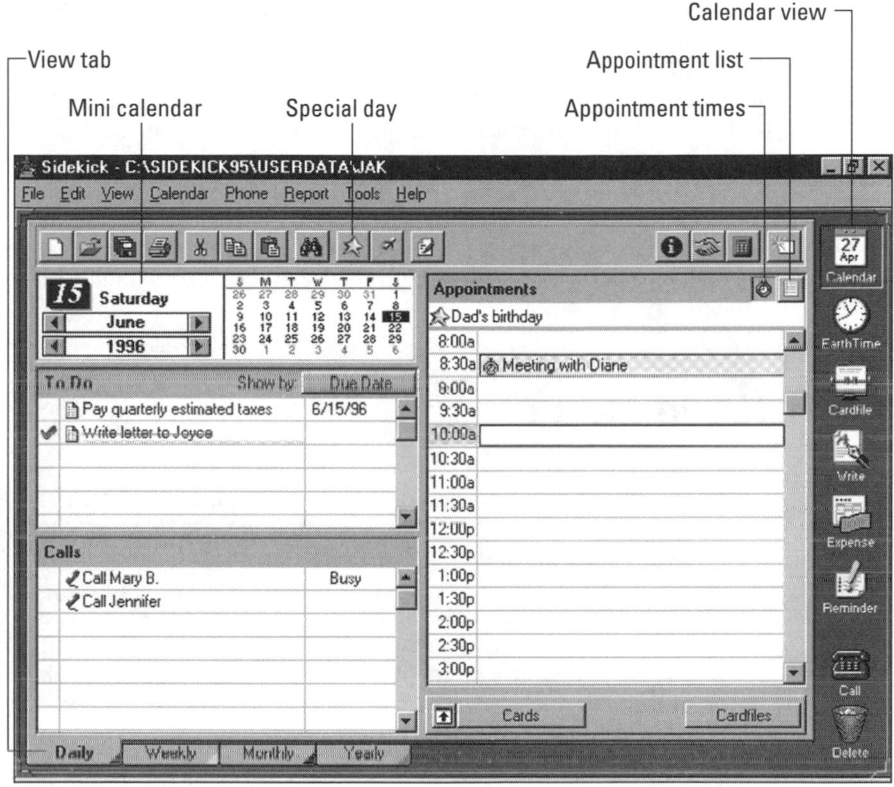

Figure 19-3: The Calendar helps you keep track of your overburdened schedule.

Click on the Special Day icon on the toolbar to record the date of special days you want to remember, such as birthdays and anniversaries. A reminder appears at the top of the day's Appointments window, as in Figure 19-3.

Creating a To Do list and call list

To add items to your To Do list, just click on a blank line in the To Do window and begin typing. Double-click in the right column to assign a category (such as business or personal) to the task, assign a priority (high, medium, or low), and change other attributes of the task. Select which attribute appears in the right column by clicking on the button above the column.

After you complete a task, click in the left column to mark it as done. Any tasks that aren't checked off as completed are forwarded to the next day's page at the end of the day. To reschedule a task, right-click on it, choose Reschedule Activity from the QuickMenu, and then select the new date. To delete a task, drag its icon to the Delete wastebasket in the bottom-right corner of the Sidekick window.

You can list the calls you need to make separately from your other tasks if you want. You enter calls into the Calls window the same way you enter tasks into the To Do window. When you double-click in the right-hand column of the window, you get a dialog box in which you can record topics you want to discuss during the call and the level of urgency of the call.

If you have to do a certain task or make a particular call on a regular basis, you don't need to keep entering it over and over again. Just right-click on the task or call and choose Recurring from the QuickMenu. You can then set up the task or call so that it appears in the Calendar automatically on the dates you specify.

Using the Cardfile

In Cardfile view, you find all sorts of contact-management tools. You can store addresses, phone numbers and other information, and even place calls via your computer modem, if you have one. To switch to Cardfile view, click on the Cardfile view icon, labeled in Figure 19-4.

The Cardfile is set up to work similar to a regular desktop cardfile — you know, one of those boxes or spinning-wheel thingies that holds little index cards on which you store people's phone numbers and addresses. In Sidekick, your cards are organized into *cardfiles,* which are simply folders in which you store groups of related addresses.

Sidekick gives you a blank cardfile to get you started; you can create as many additional cardfiles as you want.

To open a cardfile, choose File⇨Open Cardfile; to close it, choose File⇨Close Cardfile. To switch to another open cardfile, click on its cardfile tab, labeled in Figure 19-4. To create a new cardfile, choose File⇨New Cardfile and follow the steps in "Setting up a new cardfile." To save a cardfile, choose File⇨Save.

On the left side of the Cardfile window is the Card List, which displays brief identifying information for each card. The right half of the window shows detailed information for the selected card. To select a card, just click on it in the Card List. To move quickly to a section of the cardfile, click on the Alphabet tab to the right of the card list. For example, click on the B on the alphabet tab to display cards beginning with the letter B. You can also drag the slider on the alphabet tab or use the scroll arrows and scroll box on the left side of the list to move through your cards.

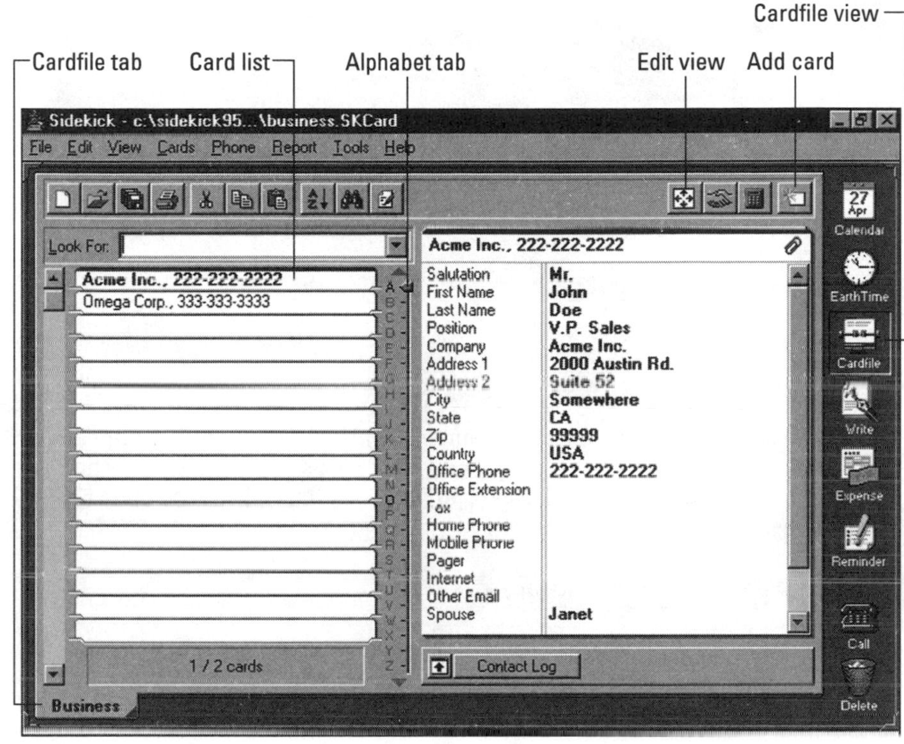

Figure 19-4: The Cardfile is a beefed-up address book and information manager.

Setting up a new cardfile

Before you can add cards to a cardfile, you first have to set up the cardfile, as follows:

1. **Choose Cards⇨Define Cardfile Fields.**

   The mysterious Select Cardfile Template dialog box, shown in Figure 19-5, appears. (The dialog box appears automatically if you choose File⇨New Cardfile to create a new cardfile.) In this dialog box, you select the *template* that will be used for all the cards in your cardfile. The template determines what fields (categories) of information you can add to each card.

2. **Select a template from the Cardfile Template drop-down list.**

   The drop-down list contains several prefab templates that Sidekick provides. After you select one of the templates, the fields that it offers appear in the Field Names list box so you can see whether the template meets your needs. (Keep in mind that you can add and delete fields if needed later.) If you don't see a template that will work for your cardfile, select the (None) item from the drop-down list.

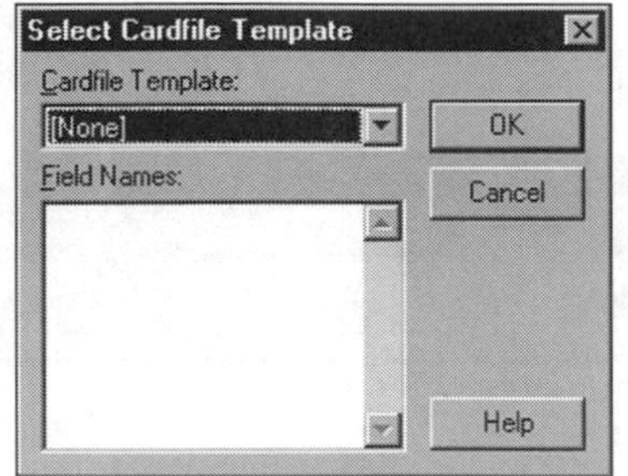

Figure 19-5: The first step in creating a cardfile is to select a template in this dialog box.

3. **Click on OK or press Enter.**

   If you use one of the built-in templates, the cardfile appears in the Cardfile window. You can now add your cards, as described in the next section. Otherwise, the Define Cardfile Fields dialog box, shown in Figure 19-6, appears.

Figure 19-6: You choose which categories of information can appear on the cards in a cardfile by creating fields in this dialog box.

4. **Enter the fields you want to appear on each card.**

   Enter the first field in the Field Name box and click on the Add button. Continue adding fields to the Field Name box and clicking on the Add button until you've entered all the fields.

   The fields appear on your cards in the order they appear in the Field Name list box. To insert a field before an existing field, type it into the Field Name box and then click on Add Before. To change or delete a field, click on it in the list box and then click on the Change or Delete button.

5. **Click on OK.**

   Your cardfile appears in the Sidekick window.

Adding and deleting cards

To add a card to a cardfile, click on the Add Card button on the toolbar, labeled back in Figure 19-4. Or press Ctrl+A or choose Cards⇨Add Cards. Sidekick presents you with a dialog box in which you can enter the card information. Use the scroll bar on the right side of the dialog box to move through all the option boxes, if necessary. Click on Add to store the information as a card and then enter the information for another new card; click on Close to close the dialog box.

The type of information you can add to a card is determined by the *fields* (categories of information) established for the cardfile. For information on editing the fields, see "Editing cards and cardfile fields."

To delete a card, just drag it from the Card List to the Delete wastebasket in the bottom-right corner of the Sidekick window.

After you add cards to the cardfile, choose File⇨Save Cardfile to save the cardfile and give it a name. Otherwise, your cardfile information isn't saved.

Selecting and marking cards

To select a single card in the cardfile, just click on it in the Card List. To select several cards, Ctrl+click on each card. To select all cards in the cardfile, click on the first card and then Shift+click on the last card.

If you right-click on some elements in the Sidekick window, you display a QuickMenu of commands. But if you right-click on a card in the Card List, you *mark* it. Marking is another way of selecting cards for some functions, such as printing and moving cards. Marked cards remain marked until you right-click on them again, which can be handy at times. If you find yourself printing the same cards over and over, for example, you may want to mark them instead of selecting them. A little triangle appears to the left of a marked card.

Editing cards and cardfile fields

To update the information on a card, click on the card in the Card List. Then just edit the information in the card information window on the right. If you want to get a wider view of the card information, click on the Edit View button (labeled back in Figure 19-4). Click on the button again to return to the normal view.

Want to change the categories of information that appear on the cards in your cardfile? Choose Cards⇨Define Cardfile Fields. You then get the Define Cardfile Fields dialog box, explained in the preceding section and shown back in Figure 19-6. You can add, delete, and change the cardfile fields in the dialog box.

If you simply want to rearrange the order of the fields in the cardfile, however, choose Cards⇨Reorder Cardfile Fields to display a dialog box showing all the fields. Double-click on each field in the Current Order list in the order that you want the fields to appear in the cardfile. For example, if you want the Name field to appear first, double-click on it first. After you double-click on a field, it appears in the neighboring New Order list.

Searching for cards

For a quick way to locate a particular card, use the Cardfile's Look For box to search for the card. Type the information that's stored in any field displayed in the Card List into the Look For box above the Card List. For example, if the cards in the Card List display the contact name, city, and phone number, you can search by contact name, city, or phone number. Press Enter to begin the search. (You can choose different Card List fields by changing the cardfile sort order, as explained in the section "Changing the Card List display.")

You can search through the cards in one cardfile at a time only. To switch to a different cardfile, click on its cardfile tab at the bottom of the window. After the search is complete, the first card to match the search criteria becomes selected. Others appear in the Look For drop-down list.

Changing the Card List display

You can change the information that appears in the Card List by choosing Cards⇨Sort Cardfile to display the dialog box shown in Figure 19-7. You can display up to three fields in the Card List. Click on the fields you want to display in the Field Name list box and then click on the Add Field button (labeled in Figure 19-7) to place them in the Sort By list box. To remove a field from the Sort By list box, click on it and click on the Remove Field button.

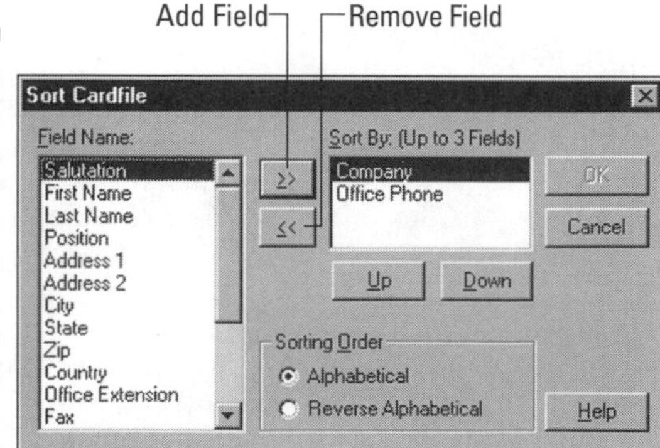

Figure 19-7: To change the fields that appear on your cards in the Card List, head for the Sort Cardfile dialog box.

The order that the fields appear in the Sort By list box is the order they appear on the cards in the Card List; use the Up and Down buttons to rearrange the order of the fields in the Sort By list box.

By default, the cards are displayed in the Card List in alphabetical order by the first field on the card, and then the second, and then the third. If you want to display them in reverse alphabetical order instead, select the Reverse Alphabetical radio button. Click on OK to make your changes official and return to the cardfile.

Ringing up a contact

If you have a modem connected to your computer, you can place a call to a contact by choosing Phone⇨Call or pressing F9. The Phone Dialer dialog box, shown in Figure 19-8, appears. You can select which of the contact's numbers to dial (e-mail, fax, phone, and so on), log notes about the call, and even record the length of the call. (Click on the watch icon to start the clock on your call.) Click on Dial to make the call.

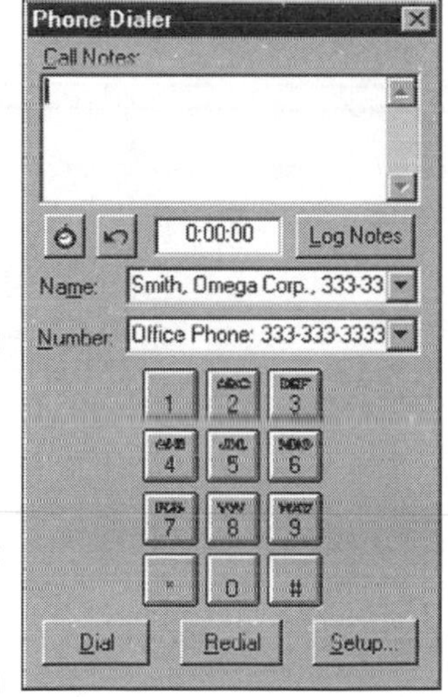

Figure 19-8: The Phone Dialer dialog box lets you reach out and dial someone.

For an even speedier way to dial, drag the contact's card from the Card List to the Call icon in the bottom-right corner of the Sidekick dialog box. Your call is automatically dialed according to the default settings in the Phone Dialer dialog box. To choose the default phone number that Sidekick dials, choose Phone⇨Speed Dial Field. To change other default settings, choose Phone⇨Setup.

Checking out the Write view

If you click on the Write icon, labeled in Figure 19-9, you switch to Write view. In this view mode, Sidekick offers you tools for creating letters, keeping a journal, or otherwise recording text information that you don't want to store in your cardfile or calendar.

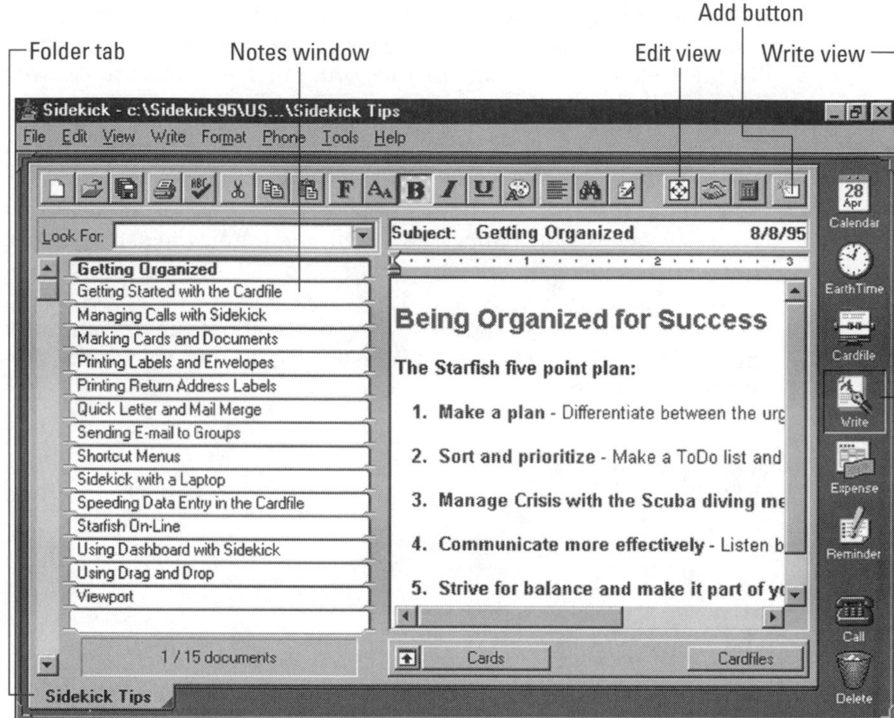

Figure 19-9: The Write window offers some simple document creation tools.

Stuff in the Write window is organized into documents and folders, just as in WordPerfect, Quattro Pro, and other programs. The documents in a folder appear in the Notes window on the left; the contents of the selected document appear in the right half of the dialog box. To select a document, click on it in the Notes window. To display the entire contents of a document, click on the Edit View button.

To create a document, click on the Add button. Enter a subject name, press Enter, and type your document text. To create a new folder, choose Write⇨Folder⇨New Folder. To save your work, choose File⇨Save Write File.

I'm guessing that you probably won't use the Write window all that much because you have WordPerfect, a much more powerful word processor, at your disposal. But Sidekick does offer some prefab letters you may want to check out by choosing Tools⇨QuickLetter. You can find templates for baby announcements, complaint letters, and all sorts of other types of correspondence. You can edit the letter just as you would in WordPerfect; the toolbar offers you some formatting tools such as font, type size, and type style.

Using the Viewport

When you're working in Cardfile, Calendar, or Write view, you can use the Sidekick Viewport. (Don't you just love that name? Sounds so *Star Trek*-y!) Similar to the picture-in-picture feature found on high end television sets, the Viewport lets you see information from a different part of Sidekick. For example, if you're working in Cardfile view, you can see your daily appointments in the Viewport, as shown in Figure 19-10.

To open the Viewport window, click on the up-pointing arrow next to the Viewport button. The arrow then changes to a down-pointing arrow, which you click to shut the window. When the window is open, click on the Viewport button to select what you want to display in the window.

Printing cards, calendars, and other information

Having all your contact and appointment information stored in your computer is fine, but you may also want to have a printed copy of that data at times. Here are some of the printing options you have:

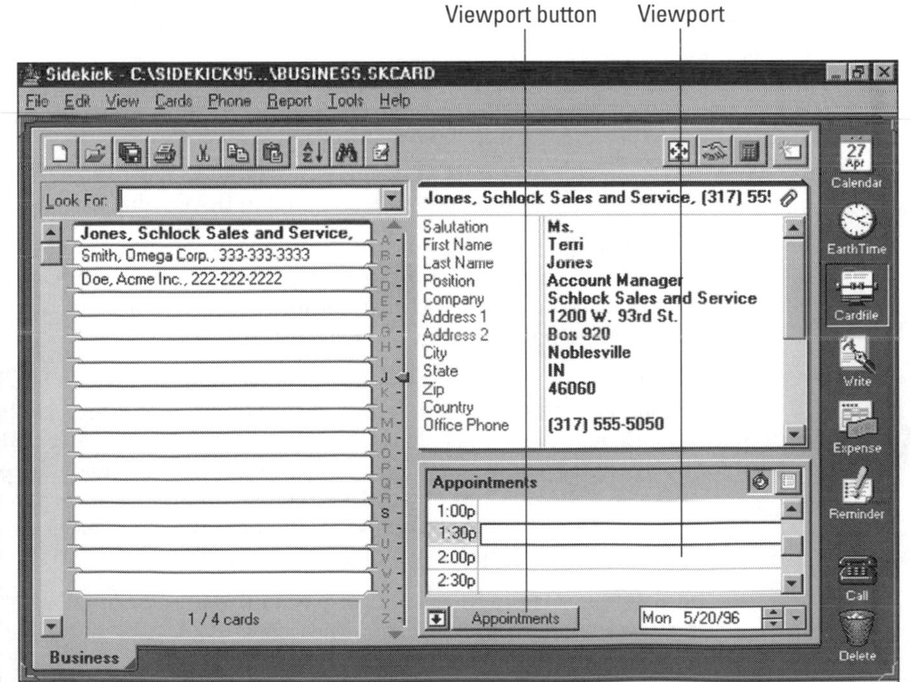

Figure 19-10: The Viewport lets you see information from two areas of Sidekick at the same time.

- To print cards in your cardfile, choose File⇨Print⇨Print Cards. The Print dialog box then gives you several different printing options. You can choose to print specific cards or the entire card list, print or hide field names, and choose how many cards print per page, among other things.
- When you're working in Cardfile view, the File⇨Print submenu also offers options that enable you to print address labels, envelopes, and even an address book containing information from selected cards or all the cards in your cardfile.
- To print a page from your calendar, switch to Calendar view and choose File⇨Print. A submenu appears that lets you print your pages in several different formats, including formats designed to fit some popular brands of personal organizers, such as Filofax. You can print a page for a single day, week, month, or year; just click on the calendar tab for the view you want to print.
- To print a document from Write view, just choose File⇨Print.

Exploring other tools

The preceding sections give you a broad overview of Sidekick's abilities, but the program offers lots more that I don't have room to detail here. The following list explains some of the additional features that you'll want to investigate. You can find out more about these features in the Sidekick documentation in the Reference Center (see Chapter 3 for information about using the Reference Center).

- In the top-right corner of the toolbar is an icon that looks like two hands clasped in a handshake. Click on this icon to open the Contact Manager, where you can get a look at all activity related to the person or organization listed on the card currently selected in the Cardfile.
- The Contact Log, which you can open by using the Viewport button (labeled back in Figure 19-10), provides an area where you can record and view notes about phone calls and other contacts related to the currently selected card in the Cardfile.

  You can add information about calls that you make through Sidekick's dial commands to the Contact Log by clicking on the Log Notes button in the Phone Dialer dialog box. The date and time of the call, along with any notes that you add in the Phone Dialog dialog box, are transferred to the Contact Log. If you want appointment dates and times added to the log, double-click on the appointment in Calendar view and select the Enter in Contact Log option in the Appointment dialog box.
- The Calculator icon at the far-right end of the toolbar opens up a calculator, surprisingly enough. Click on the calculator buttons just as you would press the buttons on a regular calculator to do all calculations you can't do in your head or on your fingers.

- The Expense icon on the right border of the Sidekick window opens up a window that's full of tools and options for tracking and reporting business and travel expenses.
- Click on the Reminder icon to see an agenda for the current day. You can get a list of activities for the next day, the next week, next month, and other times by clicking on the Look For drop-down list.
- Last, but not least, is the Earth Time icon. I'm willing to bet that this was the very first thing you clicked after you started Sidekick for the first time — it certainly was for me. I was hoping that clicking on the icon would enable me to switch to Mars time or Jupiter time, but what this feature really does is display the current time at selected cities around the world. If you right-click on a city and choose Facts About City from the QuickMenu, you display snippets of data about the location, such as population and area code.

Peering Over the Dashboard

You say you don't like the way that you start programs, open files, and switch between programs in Windows 95? Dashboard 95 gives you an alternative way to do all those things.

If you want to take Dashboard for a spin (sorry, just couldn't resist the driving analogy), click on the Windows 95 Start button and choose the Corel Word Perfect Suite 7 item on the Start menu. Then click on the Accessories item and, finally, the Dashboard 95 item. You see a screen that looks similar to the one in Figure 19-11. (I maximized the Dashboard window to give you a better look at all its bells and whistles; you can resize the window as you would any program window.)

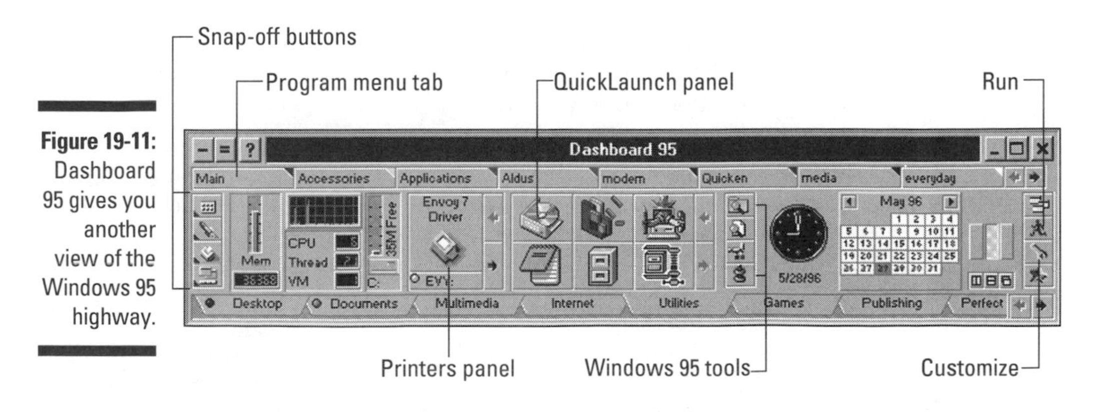

Figure 19-11: Dashboard 95 gives you another view of the Windows 95 highway.

The Dashboard window is chock-full of icons, tabs, and buttons. Here's a look at some of the ones you're likely to use the most:

- The Program menu tabs represent program groups found on the Windows 95 Programs menu. Click on a tab to display a list of programs in the group; click on the program to start it up.
- The QuickLaunch panel contains QuickLaunch buttons you can click to start programs and open documents. Click on the tabs at the bottom of the Dashboard window to display different groups of QuickLaunch buttons.

  Click on the Documents tab to display QuickLaunch buttons for files you worked on recently — the same files you'd find if you chose the Documents item from the Windows 95 Start menu. As with the Documents item, you need to periodically purge the documents on the panel to make room for new documents. To do this, right-click on the Windows 95 taskbar, choose the Properties item, click on the Start Menu Programs tab, and select the Clear button.

  To add a QuickLaunch button for a program, drag the program from its Program menu tab to the QuickLaunch panel. You can't add a button to the QuickLaunch panel when the Documents or Desktop tab is selected.
- Use the scroll arrows to display hidden tabs and panel buttons.
- Click on a printer button in the Printers panel to select that printer. You can print a document by dragging its QuickLaunch icon to the printer button.
- The tech-y looking display at the left end of the Dashboard window gives you feedback about your computer's resources — available memory, hard drive space, and so on. The Clock and Calendar display at the right end of the Dashboard helps you keep track of your fleeting youth.
- You can separate the QuickLaunch panel, Printers panel, and Program menu tabs from the Dashboard so that they appear by their lonesome on your screen. Click on the appropriate Snap Off button to send the element on its way. To bring a snapped-off panel back into the Dashboard fold, click on the Snap Off button again. The bottom Snap On/Off button controls the taskbar, a variation of the Windows 95 taskbar.
- To the right of the QuickLaunch panel are icons that access Windows 95 tools: Explorer, the Control Panel, Find, and Task Manager. You can change the tools that appear on the Dashboard by right-clicking one of the tool icons and choosing the Customize command from the QuickMenu.
- The Run button opens a dialog box that lets you enter a DOS command, just like the Run item on the Windows 95 Start menu does.
- The Customize button opens up the dialog box shown in Figure 19-12. (You can also display the dialog box by right-clicking on certain elements of the Dashboard.) In the dialog box, you can control how the various elements of the Dashboard appear. When you click on an item in the list box on the

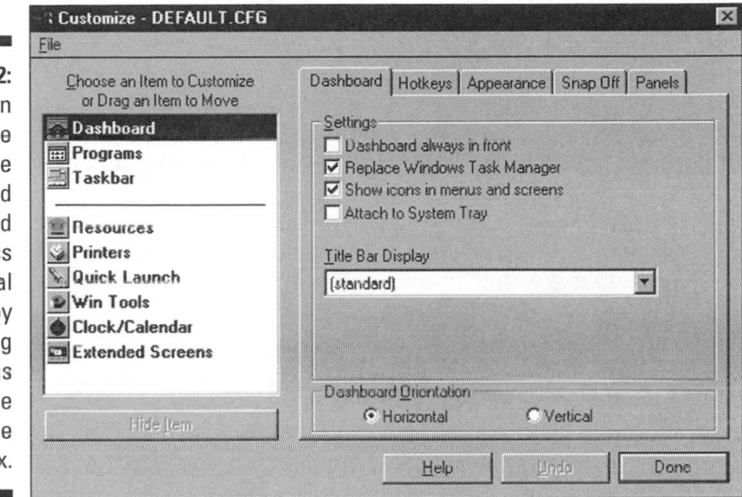

Figure 19-12: You can customize the Dashboard display and access additional tools by changing settings in the Customize dialog box.

left side of the dialog box, the panels on the right change to display options related to that item.

- If you're not sure what a particular item on the Dashboard does, pause your mouse cursor over it for a second to display a label that identifies the item. Or click on the Help button and then click on the item. The Dashboard Help system springs to life with information about the element.

You can do lots of other stuff with Dashboard, including setting alarms to wake you from your afternoon nap. Spend some time cruising around the Customize dialog box to see what other options and tools are available to you. You can also find out more about the program by skimming through the Sidekick documentation in the Reference Center, as explained in Chapter 3.

You may or may not find the Dashboard more convenient than the Windows 95 desktop for managing your programs and files. It depends on your fondness for cool gadgets — and the Dashboard certainly looks cooler than the Windows 95 desktop — and your willingness to spend some time learning how to work all the controls.

Drawing Diagrams with CorelFLOW

If you love drawing diagrams, you'll love CorelFLOW. This program gives you tools to create just about any sort of diagram, from a family tree to a project flow chart.

The version of CorelFLOW included with the WordPerfect Suite 7 is a limited version of CorelFLOW 3. Unfortunately, the suite version doesn't include many of the templates, and libraries of diagramming and charting objects you get if you buy the program separately. These features make the program much easier to use, so if you find yourself using CorelFLOW frequently, you may want to buy the full version of the product.

If you just want to create a simple organization chart or bullet chart, you may find the charting tools in Presentations easier to use than those in CorelFLOW. And if you need to create a data chart, such as a chart depicting your annual sales figures, you're better off using the chart tools in Quattro Pro. CorelFLOW is best reserved for creating more complex charts and diagrams.

Getting the lay of the land

When you first start CorelFLOW (which you do via the Windows 95 Start menu or DAD icon on the taskbar), the program gives you several options. You can start a new diagram, create a diagram built on a template, or work on an existing document. After you make your selection, the CorelFLOW program window opens, looking something like the one in Figure 19-13. In the figure, a diagram-in-process appears on the drawing page; if you're starting a new diagram, the page is blank.

To change the page size, orientation, or margins, choose File⇨Page and Diagram Setup.

Here's a lightning-fast introduction to the elements in the program window:

- The toolbox, on the left side of the window, contains tools you can use to draw lines and objects, create text, zoom in on your work, and add colors and shadows to lines and objects. The different tools are explained in the upcoming section "Drawing your own objects."
- The little triangle in the bottom-right corner of a toolbox button indicates that you're looking at a *flyout menu.* Press and hold the mouse button on the toolbox button to display the flyout menu, which contains several related tools. Click on the tool you want to use.

- If you display a flyout menu and then double-click on an empty area of the menu (that is, not on a button), the menu transforms itself into a separate palette of tools that remains displayed on-screen, making it easier to access the flyout menu's tools. To close the palette, click on the Close button in the palette's upper-right corner.
- Use the tools on the Zoom flyout to zoom in and out on your page. Drag with the Panning tool to move the page around in the document window. Or use the scroll arrows and scroll bar on the right and bottom side of the window to scroll the view of your page.
- A Smart Library is a collection of predrawn objects that you can place on your page, as explained in "Using Smart Libraries."

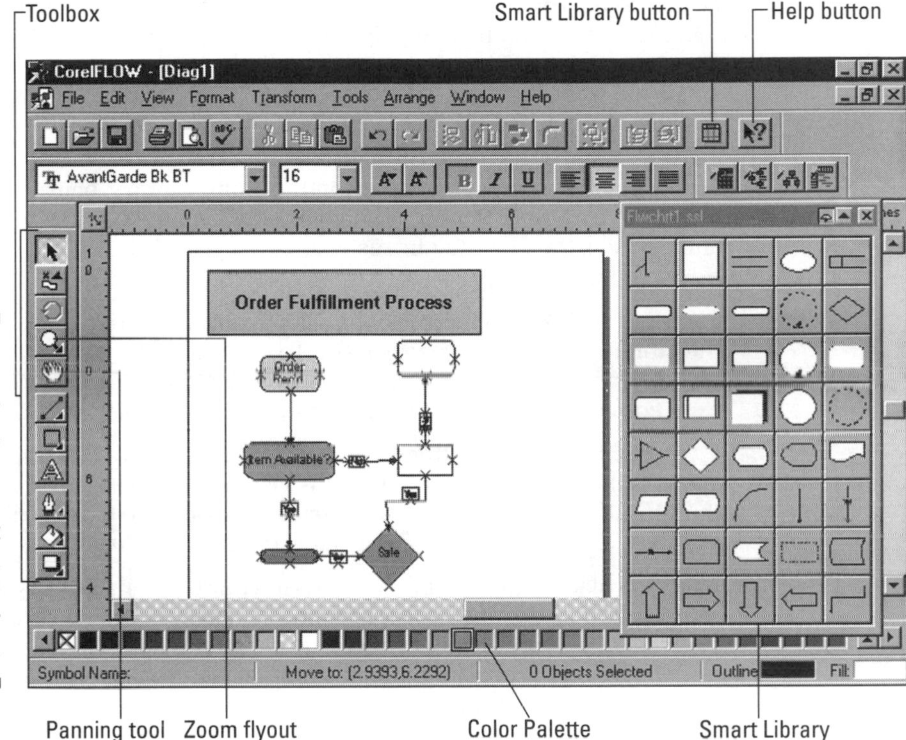

Figure 19-13: The CorelFLOW window gives you an overwhelming assortment of tools, buttons, and other gadgets.

- You can use the color palette at the bottom of the window to quickly apply a background (fill) color and outline to a select object. Click on a color block to apply that color as the fill; right-click to apply an outline in that color. If you click or right-click when no object is selected, you establish new default fill and outline colors. Click on the arrows at the end of the palette to see additional colors.
- If you're stumped about the purpose of an on-screen element, click on the Help button and then click on that element. The CorelFLOW Help window opens, displaying information about the element that's troubling you.

Using Smart Libraries

Depending on what kind of diagram you're creating, CorelFLOW displays one or more Smart Libraries filled with objects that you can use in your diagram. Using the Smart Library objects saves you the time and hassle of drawing diagram objects yourself.

To display other Smart Libraries, click on the Smart Library button (labeled in Figure 19-13). Then choose a Smart Library from the Open dialog box. Smart Libraries have the file extension .SSL and are stored in the SmartLib folder, which is inside the Flow folder, which is inside the Flow3 folder.

To place an object from a Smart Library into your diagram, just click on the object in the Library and then drag it onto your diagram page. Or click on the object and then click on the diagram page with the rubber stamp cursor that appears. If you want to put additional copies of the object on your page, just keep clicking with the rubber stamp cursor.

- To get a close-up look at an object in the Smart Library, pause your cursor over it for a second. CorelFLOW shows you an enlarged view of the object and displays the object's dimensions.
- If a Smart Library gets in your way, click on the arrow in the right-hand corner to shrink the Library so that all you see is the title bar. To redisplay the Library, click on the arrow again. To move a Library, drag its title bar. To put the Library away for good, click on the Close button in the upper-right corner of the Library window (the button's marked with an X).
- That little thumbtack button in the upper-right corner of the Smart Library anchors the Library so that it remains visible on-screen. If you click on the thumbtack button (so that it appears to raise up), the Library disappears after you place an object from the Library into your diagram.
- After you place a Smart Library object in your diagram, little black boxes called *selection handles* appear around the object to indicate that the object is selected. You can then resize and manipulate the object, as explained in "Playing with objects," later in this chapter. To deselect the object, click on the Pick tool (labeled in 19-15) and then click outside the object. Or, if the Pick tool is already selected, just click outside the object.
- The little Xs and hollow circle or square on the object represent connection points and connector pins, as explained in the next section.

Understanding points and pins

By default, each CorelFLOW object has one or more *connector pins* — which look like either hollow circles or squares, as shown in Figure 19-14. Most Smart Library objects also come with *connection points,* which appear as little Xs. Connection points are always displayed; connector pins appear only when the object is selected, as in the figure. (The black squares around the object are the selection handles, which appear to show that an object is selected.)

Connector pins and points join two objects together. When a connector pin comes into contact with a connection point, the two objects snap together and are joined. A red dot indicates that the point and pin are snapped together.

Using points and pins enables you to manipulate joined objects in special ways. When you move one object, for example, all objects connected to it also move. If you move two objects that are joined by a line, the line stretches and shifts to accommodate the move. You can also use the Autorouted Line tool to automatically create a line between two objects, as explained in the section "Drawing your own objects."

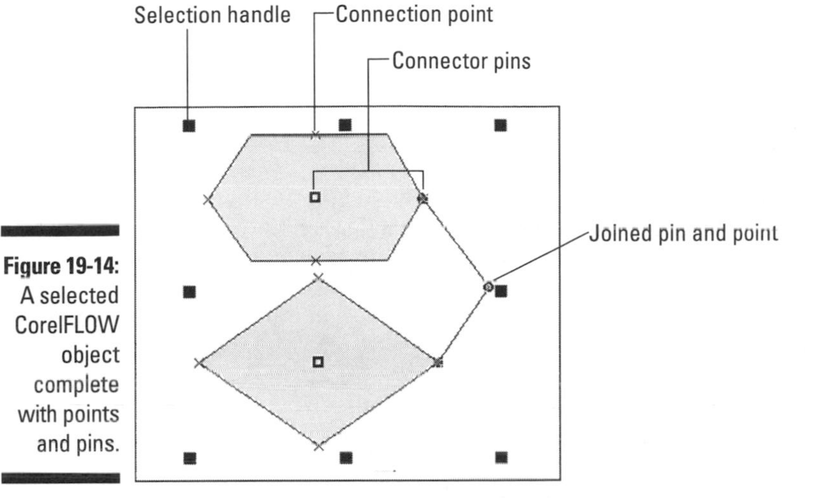

Figure 19-14: A selected CorelFLOW object complete with points and pins.

Here are the basics of using points and pins:

- To add a connection point to an object, click with the Connector tool. The Connector tool (labeled in Figure 19-15) is the second tool from the top in the toolbox.
- To join two objects, drag one of them (using the Pick tool labeled in Figure 19-15) until the connector pin on one object comes into contact with the connection point of the other object. When the pin turns red, the objects are joined.
- To break two joined objects apart, drag the one that has the joined connector pin away from the other object.
- To reposition an object's connector pin, first select the object by clicking on it with the Pick tool. Then select the Connector tool and drag the pin with that tool.
- To move a connection point, drag it with the Connector tool. To delete a connection point, click on it with the Connector tool. Then press Delete. (You can't delete a point that's joined to a pin.)
- To disable an object's connection points, select the object (with the Pick tool) and choose Format⇨Symbol to display the Shape Properties dialog box. Click on the Misc tab and uncheck the Connectors Enabled check box. To disable the connector pin, click on the None radio button. To disable points and pins for all new objects you draw, check the Set as Default check box. (Unfortunately, you can't turn off points and pins for all new Smart Library objects you use; you have to select each object after you place it in your diagram and then disable the points and pins.)

This section gives you only the tip of the connector pin/point iceberg. You can adjust the point and pin settings in the Shape Properties dialog box so that connected objects behave in different ways, for example. If you want to learn more about using connector points and pins, the CorelFLOW Help system can tell you everything you need to know.

Drawing your own objects

If you can't find a Smart Library object that suits your needs, you can draw your own objects using the drawing tools, labeled in Figure 19-15. (The toolbox is shown horizontally in the figure to make it easier for you to see the tool names. If you prefer this horizontal arrangement of the toolbox, just drag the toolbox off the left edge of the drawing window. You can then move the toolbox around by dragging its title bar.)

If you're not sure what a particular tool does, pause your cursor over it for a moment. A QuickTip appears to indicate the tool's purpose.

- Tools on the Line tool flyout draw various types of lines. To draw a straight line, choose the Line tool. Click at the point where you want the line to begin and double-click at the spot where you want the line to end. To draw a multi-segmented line, click to begin the line, click to set the end of the first segment, and then continue clicking to create additional segments. Double-click to end the line.

Figure 19-15: A look at the CorelFLOW toolbox.

- The Autorouted Line tool determines the best path between two objects and draws a line along that path to join the objects. With the tool selected, click on a connection point on the first object and double-click on a connection point on the second object. CorelFLOW draws a line between the two points, snaking the line around or between other objects when necessary. (Connection points are described in the preceding section; points must be turned on for this feature to work.)
- The Curved Line tool draws lines using Bézier curve theory. If you're familiar with Bézier drawing tools, you may enjoy this tool; otherwise, it will confound you. An easier way to draw curved lines is to use the Freehand Line tool, which makes the process more intuitive. Just drag to create your line, letting up on the mouse button to end the line.
- The Shape tool flyout contains tools for drawing rectangles, ellipses, and polygons. Click on the tool you want to use and then drag to create the shape.

- To draw a perfect square, press Ctrl+drag with the Rectangle tool; to draw a circle, Ctrl+drag with the Ellipse tool. To change the number of sides in polygons you draw with the Polygon tool, choose Format➪Polygon, as you click on the Polygon tab of the resulting Shape Properties dialog box and change the Number of Value.

- Objects take on the default fill and outline shown on the right end of the status bar. (To change the default fill or outline, click or right-click on a color square when no object is selected.)
- To add text to your diagram, you can simply click with the Text tool at the spot where you want to place the text and begin typing. Or you can drag with the Text tool to create a frame for your text and then begin typing. The advantage of using frames is that you can use more advanced text formatting features — indents, automatic text wrap, and so on.

- If you click with the Text tool inside an object, the object's border serves as the text frame. You can then access all the formatting features you can with a regular text frame.
- The Outline, Fill, and Shadow flyouts enable you to add a border, color, and shadow to selected objects, as explained in the next section. The Rotate tool lets you spin an object on its axis, also explained in the next section.

Playing with objects

After you create an object, you can move it, resize it, color it, and do all sorts of other things to it. But before you can make any changes to an object, you first have to select it:

- To select a single object, click on it with the Pick tool. To select several objects, shift+click on them or drag around them with the Pick tool to enclose them in a selection marquee (outline). Black squares (selection handles) appear around selected objects.
- If you select the Pick tool and click on text, you select the text's background — which is invisible unless you apply a color or shadow, as explained in the following list. To select the text itself, drag over the text with the Text tool.
- After you select multiple objects, you may want to group them. When objects are grouped, you can select them all by clicking on one object in the group. You can also move and format the objects en masse. To group selected objects, choose Arrange➪Group. To ungroup objects, select the group and then choose Arrange➪Ungroup.
- To deselect an object, just click outside it with the Pick tool.

Here are just some of the things you can do to a selected object or selected text:

- To move a selected object, just drag it with the Pick tool.

- To change the size, color, spacing, alignment, and other formatting attributes of selected text, choose Format⇨Text to display the Shape Properties dialog box. Make your selections in the dialog box and click on OK to close the dialog box.

- The horizontal toolbar at the top of the CorelFLOW window contains some buttons and drop-down lists that let you change some text formatting attributes, such as type size and font, without going to the Shape Properties dialog box. Pause your cursor over the different toolbar buttons and drop-down lists to see what's what.
- To resize a selected object, drag one of its selection handles with the Pick tool.
- To fill a selected object with a solid color, click on one of the color squares in the color palette. To apply a pattern or gradient (blended) fill, choose one of the other options from the Fill flyout.
- To apply a colored outline to an object, right-click on a color swatch in the color palette. To change the width of the outline, select another width from the Outline flyout.
- Choose an option from the Shadow flyout to create a shadow beneath the selected object.
- To rotate a selected object, click on the Rotate tool and drag one of the object's corner selection handles.
- Another way to change the formatting of a selected object or piece of text is to right-click on it and choose the Properties command from the QuickMenu. CorelFLOW displays the Shape Properties dialog box, which offers different formatting options depending upon the type of object or text that's selected. The dialog box offers some formatting options (such as pattern fills) not available from flyout menus.
- To delete selected text or objects, just press Delete.

Previewing, printing, and saving

To get a preview of what your diagram will look like when printed, choose File⇨Print Preview or click on the Print Preview button (it looks like a magnifying glass). To close the preview window, click on the Close button.

To print your diagram, choose File⇨Print or press Ctrl+P and choose your printing options from the Print dialog box. To save your diagram, choose File⇨Save or File⇨Save As and specify the document name, storage folder, and file type as you normally do when saving documents in Windows 95. (For more help on printing and saving documents, see Chapter 5; the CorelFLOW Save dialog box works similarly to the dialog box discussed in that chapter.)

Chapter 20

Using Everything Together

In This Chapter

- Getting your programs to pass the ball
- Using different programs to create one document
- Making copies that update automatically when the original data changes
- Editing copied data when you don't have access to the original file
- Making friends with OLE
- Dragging and dropping stuff from one program to another
- Copying and moving data between programs with the Cut, Copy, and Paste commands

Imagine coaching a team of basketball players who all refused to play if they weren't the one with the ball. The minute one player got the ball, all the other players stomped off the court and sat on the bench.

Well, in the old days of computing, programs worked just like that. If one program was active, all the others rushed to the sidelines. But today, programs know how to play together as a team. And unlike some NBA superstars who shall remain nameless, the players in the WordPerfect Suite don't charge into the stands to beat up fans, cover themselves with tattoos, or otherwise behave like unruly children.

This team computing philosophy means that you can call on the collective strengths of all the programs in the WordPerfect Suite to create a single document. Suppose that you want to create a report that contains text and a data chart. You open a WordPerfect document and create your text. You then tell WordPerfect that you want to create a chart, and it passes the digital basketball to Quattro Pro, which is, after all, the team member best equipped for creating charts. After you build your chart, Quattro Pro passes the ball — and your chart — back to WordPerfect.

Although you can get good results by working with each member of the WordPerfect team individually, you can accomplish a whole lot more in less time if you learn the art of tag-team document creation. At the risk of carrying the sports analogy one step too far, this chapter gives you the game plan for doing just that.

You're about to encounter some scary technical lingo such as *Object Linking and Embedding* and *OLE server.* If these words make your eyes glaze over — as they rightly should — just skip over them and follow the steps for accomplishing the various tasks. If you want to understand more about how and why a feature works — which can be helpful in figuring out the best way to get something done — take a deep, relaxing breath and dig in to the text marked with the tech stuff icons. The information isn't really that difficult to grasp, just a little dry. Okay, a lot dry. But it's useful information just the same.

Saving Time and Effort with OLE

The key to getting your programs to work together is *Object Linking and Embedding,* which is called OLE (pronounced *olé*) for short. OLE isn't a command or a tool; it's a background technology built into many Windows programs, including those in the WordPerfect Suite.

OLE enables you to do several things:

- Create data in one document, put a copy of that data into another document, and have the copy automatically updated any time you make changes to the original. For example, you can create a chart in Quattro Pro and then copy it into a WordPerfect document. When you update the chart in Quattro Pro, it's automatically updated in the WordPerfect document as well. (You can turn off this automatic updating if you want to keep the two charts separate.) The upcoming sections "Making Linked Copies that Update Automatically" and "Linking Copies without Automatic Updating" tell all.
- After copying data from one program into another program, you can just double-click on the data to edit it in the original program. Say that you create a drawing in Presentations and copy it into a WordPerfect document. If you want to edit the drawing while you're working in WordPerfect, you just double-click on it. Windows opens the drawing in a Presentations window for you. When you're finished making changes, the Presentations window closes, and your edited drawing appears in WordPerfect. This magical editing process is discussed in the section "Editing without Leaving Home," later in this chapter.
- You can use different programs to create the different elements of your document without leaving the confines of your primary program. Suppose that you're working in WordPerfect and decide that you want to create a simple drawing to illustrate your point. You can launch Presentations, create your drawing, and place it into WordPerfect — all without ever venturing outside WordPerfect. For the inside scoop, see the section "Embedding Objects on the Fly," later in this chapter.

Because of OLE, you can use the program that's best suited to handle each component of your document and then easily combine the different components into one master document. And you don't have to waste time updating all the copies of a particular piece of text or graphic every time you make a change to it — you just let OLE's automatic updating capabilities handle everything for you.

Not all programs support OLE or all the OLE features discussed in this chapter. If a particular feature or command doesn't seem to be working — or even available in the program you're using — chances are that the program doesn't offer OLE support. You should still be able to copy data between documents using the Cut, Copy, and Paste commands, however, as discussed near the end of this chapter, in the section "Sharing Data without OLE."

Deciding Whether to Link, Embed, or Copy and Paste

You can create two kinds of objects with OLE: *linked* or *embedded*. When you create a linked object, Windows establishes a link between the *source* program (the program you use to create the object) and the *destination* program (the program where you place the object).

By the way, you'll hear chipheads referring to the source and destination programs as the *OLE server* and *OLE client*, respectively.

With linking, the object is automatically updated in the destination document any time you make changes to it in the source document. Linking can be a great way to make sure that all your documents contain the same version of some text or graphic that changes frequently. If you ever decide that you don't want the object to be updated automatically, you can change the link settings so that you can update the object manually or sever the link altogether.

What's all this talk about OLE objects?

The term *OLE object* refers to any data — whether it's text or graphics — that you copy or create in one program and place into another using OLE. The computer people found it tiring to keep using the phrase "text or graphics that you copy or create in one program and place into another using OLE," so they came up with a new term. Either that, or they just wanted to make you feel bad because they knew a word that you didn't.

The drawback to linking is that if you want to share your document with other people, you need to give them a copy of the source documents for any linked objects along with the destination document.

With embedding, all the information you need to display *and* edit the object is placed — embedded — in the destination document. If you embed a Quattro Pro chart in a WordPerfect document, for example, you can edit the Quattro Pro chart from within WordPerfect even if you no longer have access to the original Quattro Pro file. It's way cool, but embedding also eats up a great deal of space on your computer's hard disk or floppy disk. And when you edit the original object in the source program, the changes aren't automatically made to the object in the destination program as they are with linking.

If all you want to do is copy or move some data from one document to another and you don't want or need to take advantage of the OLE features just described, you can simply use the Cut, Copy, and Paste commands, as described near the end of this chapter, in the section "Sharing Data without OLE." Cutting, copying, and pasting between documents using these commands is the same as cutting, copying, and pasting within the same document.

Making Linked Copies that Update Automatically

You create a chart in Quattro Pro to illustrate your company's annual sales figures. You copy the chart into a WordPerfect document, where you're writing an executive summary to justify the dismal sales performance to the company's board of directors. You also copy the chart into a separate WordPerfect document in which you're creating the company's annual report and another document you're creating to try to convince stockholders that things really aren't as bad as they appear.

Just when you get the chart copied into all three documents, your boss comes around and says that management wants to make a few minor changes to the sales figures. You could leap up, grab the boss by the collar, and snarl, "Not in this lifetime, pal!" Or you could smile enthusiastically and say, "Sure, no problem at all," secure in the knowledge that you can easily update all the copies at the same time through the wonder of OLE linking.

Of course, if you want to find yourself in this happy, enthusiastic place, you have to create your copies using OLE linking in the first place. The following steps show you how to use OLE linking to copy a Quattro Pro chart into a

WordPerfect document and have that chart update automatically when you make changes to the data in Quattro Pro. The process is the same no matter what programs you're using (as long as those programs support OLE — some programs don't).

You can't link a Presentations slide show file or an object in a slide show file to another program (slide show files have the .SHW file extension). You can link a Presentations drawing file, however.

The source document contains the data you want to copy. The destination document is the one that receives the copy.

1. **Make sure that the source document has been saved to disk.**

   You can't link data from a document that hasn't been saved to disk.

2. **Select the data you want to copy and choose Edit⇨Copy.**

   In most programs, you drag over the data with the cursor to select it or drag a selection box around the data. If you don't know how to select stuff, look in this book's index for information related to the specific program that contains the data you're copying.

3. **Switch to the document where you want to place the copy.**

4. **Click on the spot where you want to put the copy.**

5. **Choose Edit⇨Paste Special.**

   The dialog box shown in Figure 20-1 appears.

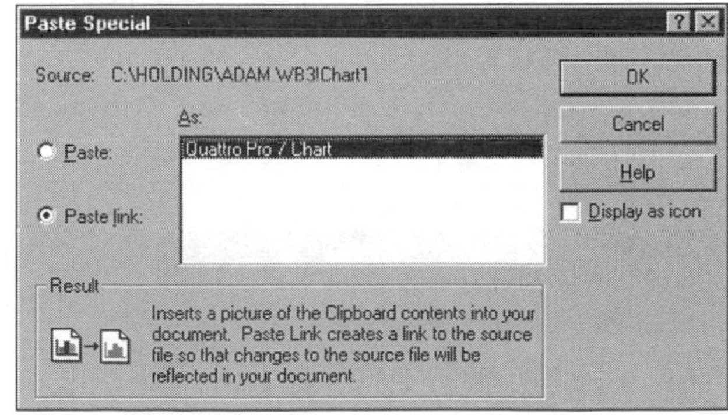

Figure 20-1: If you want the copy to be updated every time you make changes to the original, select the Paste Link option.

Sometimes, you get several file format choices in the As list box. The computer automatically selects the best format for you, so you don't need to fool with this option unless you experience problems.

6. **Click on the Paste Link button to select it.**

   If the button is dimmed, either the source or destination program doesn't support linking. (Or you may have forgotten to save the source document as I begged you to do in Step 1.) You can click on the Paste button to create an embedded object, as explained in "Creating an Embedded Copy," or perform a simple copy and paste, as explained in "Sharing Data without OLE."

7. **Click on OK.**

   The copy appears in your destination document.

Congratulations — you just created a linked OLE object. Any changes you make to the data in the source document are automatically made in the destination document as well.

Linking Copies without Automatic Updating

If you decide that you don't want your linked copies to be updated automatically when you change the original, you can change the link so that you can update the copy manually when needed. Here's how to do it in WordPerfect:

1. **Open the document that contains the copy.**

   Make sure that no text or graphics are selected in the document, or the Edit⇨Links command you use in the next step will be unavailable.

2. **Choose Edit⇨Links.**

   The Links dialog box shown in Figure 20-2 appears. Each linked object in the document is listed in the dialog box.

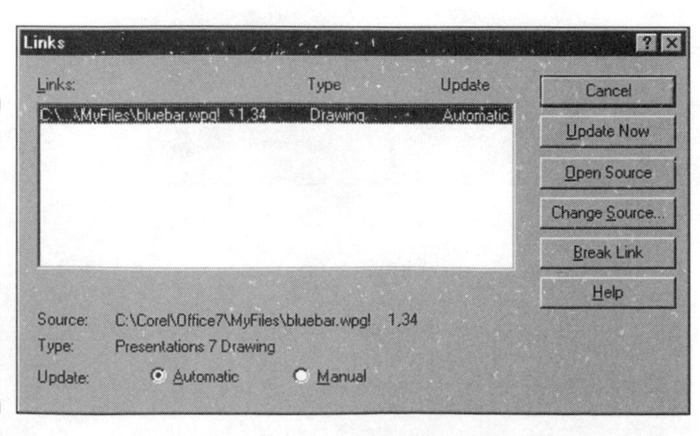

Figure 20-2: The Links dialog box lets you automatically or manually update linked copies.

3. **Click on the linked object whose link you want to change.**
4. **Click on the Manual radio button.**
5. **Click on Close or press Enter.**

If you later change the original and decide that you want to update the copy to reflect the changes, just open the Links dialog box and click on the Update Now button. (If the copy doesn't update, try closing and then reopening the document that contains the copy. Then try updating the link.)

The Links dialog box also offers some other options you may find useful:

- The Open Source button lets you open the source document. You may want to do this to check out the source data to see whether any changes were made since you last updated the linked copy.
- Change Source lets you link the copy to a different source document.
- Break Link severs any and all ties between the copy and the source document.

To edit links in Presentations, you follow these exact same steps. In Quattro Pro, link editing commands appear on a submenu when you choose Edit⇨Links rather than in a separate dialog box. (The commands have slightly different names in Quattro Pro.)

Creating an Embedded Copy

When you *embed* an object through OLE, you copy all the data the computer needs to display *and* edit the object into the destination document. Say that you create a chart in Quattro Pro and embed it into a WordPerfect document on your desktop computer. You then save the document to a floppy disk so that you can work on it on your laptop computer during your business trip to Tasmania. (Hey, as long as you're traveling, you may as well travel somewhere exotic.)

Anyway, assume that you don't have a copy of the original Quattro Pro file on your laptop computer (but you do have Quattro Pro installed). You can still edit that chart on the road. You double-click on the graphic, and all the Quattro Pro commands and tools appear inside the WordPerfect window.

To embed an object, just follow steps 2 through 7 in the section "Making Linked Copies that Update Automatically" but select the Paste radio button rather than Paste Link in step 6.

With embedding, the copy doesn't get updated if you change the original. Also, files that contain lots of embedded objects can take up lots of disk space.

Embedding Objects on the Fly

The preceding section explains how to embed an existing object into your document. But you can also create embedded objects as you work on a document. You can open up a second program, create the object, and embed it without leaving the comfy confines of your first document window. The following steps show you how to create an embedded Presentations object when you're working in WordPerfect. The steps are similar for other programs.

1. **Make sure that nothing is selected in your document.**

   If something is selected, the Insert⇨Object command you use in the next step is unavailable.

2. **Choose Insert⇨Object.**

   The dialog box shown in Figure 20-3 appears.

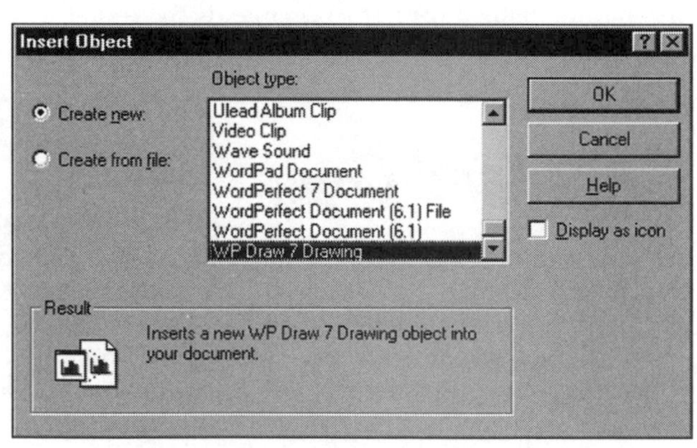

Figure 20-3: You can create a new embedded object without leaving the destination document.

3. **Select the Create New button.**

4. **Select the type of object you want to create from the Object Type list box.**

5. **Click on OK or press Enter.**

   After some grinding noises from your computer, the WordPerfect menu and tools are transformed into the Presentations menu and tools, and a drawing window appears right on your WordPerfect page, as in Figure 20-4.

6. **Create your object.**

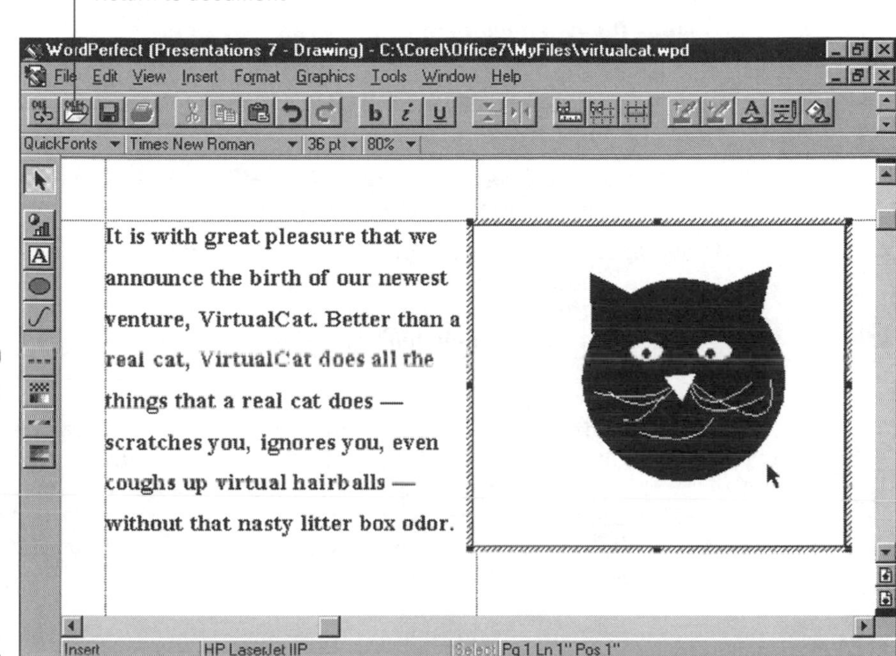

Figure 20-4: You can access all the Presentations drawing tools while working in WordPerfect.

7. **Click outside the object boundaries.**

   Or, in some programs, you can click on a Return to Document button on the toolbar, labeled in Figure 20-4. Your drawing is embedded in WordPerfect and appears selected in the WordPerfect window.

WordPerfect offers some special commands that give you another way to create an embedded Presentations drawing or Quattro Pro chart. To create a drawing in Presentations, choose Graphics⇨Draw. If you want to create an embedded Quattro Pro chart, choose Graphics⇨Chart in WordPerfect. Choosing these commands lets you bypass the Insert Object dialog box. Everything else works the same as in the preceding steps.

Dragging and Dropping between Programs

Many programs — those in the WordPerfect Suite included — allow you to drag and drop data from one program to another. You can use drag and drop to create a linked copy, to create an embedded copy, or to move data from one document and embed it in another. Here's the 1-2-3:

1. **Open both the source document and the destination document.**
2. **Display the two document windows side-by-side.**

   You can do this by right-clicking on the Windows 95 taskbar and choosing Tile Horizontally or Tile Vertically. (You can't have either window maximized or minimized for these commands to work.)
3. **Select and then drag, Ctrl+drag, or Shift+Ctrl+drag the data from the source document to the destination document.**

   Dragging deletes the data from the source document and embeds it in the destination document. Press Ctrl as you drag to copy the data and embed it in the destination document. And press both Shift and Ctrl as you drag to create a copy that's linked to the source document rather than embedded.

Another way to drag and drop data in Windows 95 is to drag the object you want to copy or move from the source program to the destination program's button on the Windows 95 taskbar. When you drag the object to the taskbar, don't release the mouse button — just pause for a second until the destination program window appears. Then drag the object from the taskbar into the destination program window.

You can't create a linked copy unless you've saved the file that contains the data you're copying.

Embedding or Linking an Entire Document

If you want to embed or link an entire file into your document, first make sure that nothing is selected in the document. Then choose Insert⇨Object to display the Insert Object dialog box and select the Create from File option, as shown in Figure 20-5. Enter the name of the file you want to copy or click on the Browse button to locate your file. (In some programs, including WordPerfect, that little white box at the end of the filename option box serves as the Browse button; in other programs, you see a button labeled Browse.) If you want to copy the file as a linked object, click on the Link button. If you want to copy the file as an embedded object, deselect the Link button. Click on OK to make the copy.

Editing without Leaving Home

One of the advantages of OLE linking and embedding is that you can edit an OLE object by simply double-clicking on it. The process varies depending on whether you double-click on an embedded or linked object:

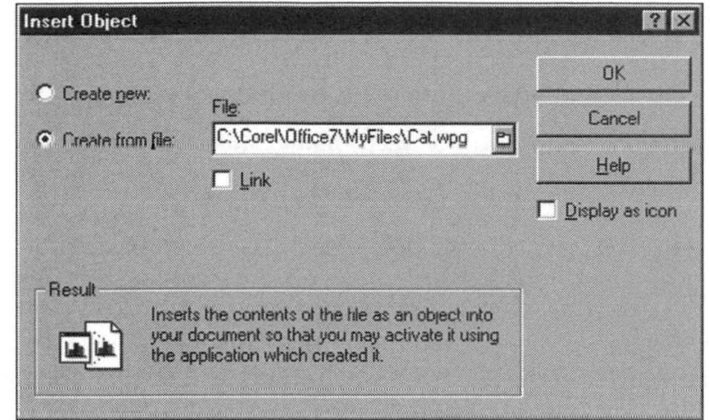

Figure 20-5: The Create from File option lets you link or embed an entire file.

- If you double-click on a linked object, the source document launches and your object appears in its own window, ready for editing. Make your changes and then save them in the source program. Then choose File⇨Exit to close the source program and return to the destination document or just click outside the source document window to return to the destination document and keep the source program open.
- If you double-click on an embedded object, the menus and tools of the source program become available in the current window. Make your changes and then click outside the object boundaries.

Sharing Data without OLE

You don't *have* to use OLE to share data between programs. You can also copy and move data using the Cut, Copy, and Paste commands. If you go this route, you lose some of the advantages of OLE: The copy doesn't get updated when the original changes, and you can't double-click the copy to edit it in the source program. Then again, you don't have to tax your brain with all that OLE linking and embedding rigmarole, either.

The following steps show you how to copy a Quattro Pro chart into a WordPerfect document. You can use the same steps to copy data between any two programs or documents.

1. **Open the document that contains the data you want to copy.**
2. **Select the data you want to copy.**
3. **Press Ctrl+C or click on the Copy button on the toolbar.**

   The Copy button looks like two pages of paper stacked on top of each other. If you're a menu-lover, choose Edit⇨Copy instead.

Either way, the data scurries away to the Windows Clipboard, where it hangs out until the next time you choose the Copy or Cut command.

4. **Open the document where you want to place the copy.**
5. **Click at the spot where you want to insert the copy.**
6. **Press Ctrl+V or click on the Paste toolbar button.**

   The Paste button looks like a Clipboard with a piece of paper attached. If you like choosing things from menus, you can choose Edit⇨Paste instead.

You can paste the same copy repeatedly if you want. Just keep clicking on the spot where you want to put the copy and choosing the Paste command. The copy is available to be pasted until the next time you choose the Copy or Cut command, at which time the Clipboard chucks its current contents to make room for the incoming material.

You can use these same steps to move data between programs. Just choose Edit⇨Cut, press Ctrl+X, or click on the Cut button on the toolbar (it looks like a pair of scissors) in Step 3 instead of using the Copy command.

Part V
The Part of Tens

In this part . . .

Welcome to the short-attention-span part of the book. The next three chapters contain little tidbits of information that you can digest in minutes — seconds, really, in some cases. You discover ten cool tricks to amaze and astound your friends, ten shortcuts you can use to get things done with less effort, and ten tips to trim some time off your workday. If you need a quick fix of information or inspiration, look here first.

Chapter 21

Ten Cool Tricks to Try on a Slow Day

In This Chapter

- Creating drop caps
- Shaping your words with TextArt
- Putting a watermark on your pages
- Displaying the Corel clip art as a screen saver
- Figuring out the pros and cons of refinancing a loan
- Calculating the number of days until your next day off
- Applying special effects to bitmap images
- Turning drawings into three-dimensional, warped copies of their former selves
- Adding sounds to your documents
- Playing with QuickTasks

It's 4:00 on a Friday afternoon, the boss is gone, and you're sitting around trying to kill time until you can shut the door on another long work week. You could fire up one of those games that comes with Windows 95, but frankly, you're a little tired of losing to a machine.

That's the time to check out the ten features described in this chapter. Tucked inside the menu bars of various programs in the WordPerfect Suite are some pretty nifty tools that I haven't covered elsewhere because they're not the sort of features most people need on a regular basis. They are, however, lots of fun to play with — tricks that may even prove useful now and again.

Start Off with a Drop Cap

Many magazines, newsletters, and other publications begin articles with a *drop cap*. A drop cap is a letter that's enlarged and dropped down into surrounding lines of text, as shown in Figure 21-1.

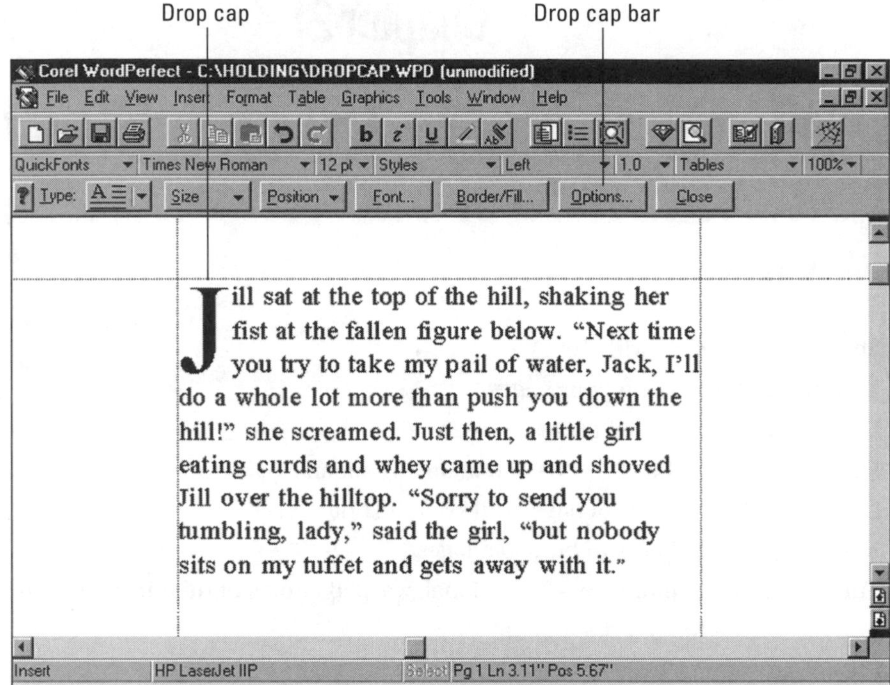

Figure 21-1: A drop cap is a great device to call attention to the start of an article.

WordPerfect makes creating a drop cap easy. Just select the letter that you want to format as a drop cap and choose Format⇨Drop Cap or press Ctrl+Shift+C. WordPerfect turns the letter into a drop cap and displays the Drop Cap bar, which contains several buttons that display drop cap options. Click on the Close button to hide the Drop Cap bar when you're done.

To redisplay the Drop Cap bar, double-click on the drop cap. To remove the drop cap formatting, select the drop cap and choose the No Cap option from the Type drop-down list at the left end of the Drop Cap bar.

Twist and Stretch Your Words

The WordPerfect TextArt feature lets you turn ordinary words into graphic masterpieces, as shown in Figure 21-2. Try it out:

1. **Click at the spot where you want to add a TextArt image.**

   Or select the word in your document that you want to turn into TextArt.

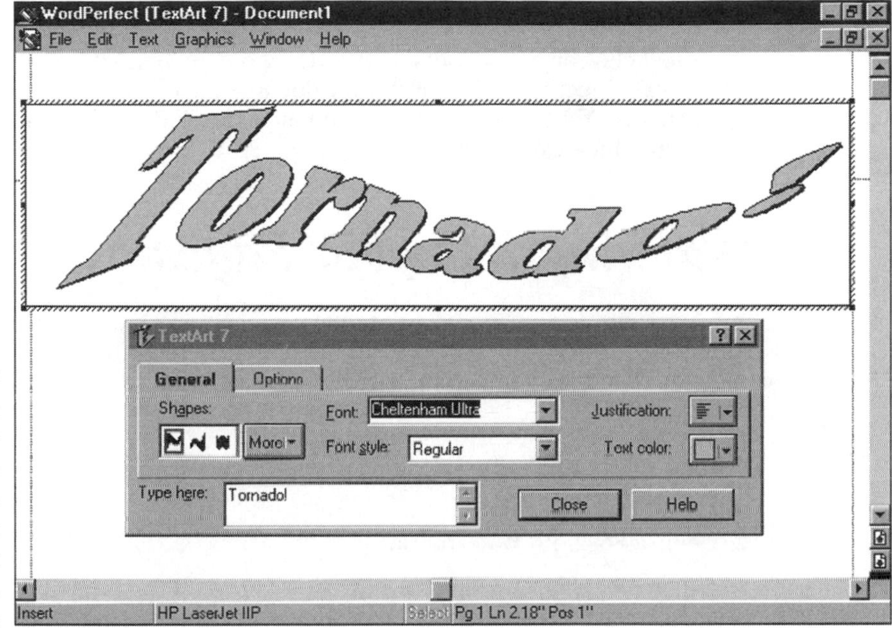

Figure 21-2: Show your artistic flare with the WordPerfect TextArt feature.

2. Choose Graphics⇨TextArt.

A TextArt window appears, as shown in Figure 21-2. The word you selected appears in a TextArt box, or, if you didn't select a word, the word *Text* appears in the box. The TextArt dialog box also opens.

3. Play with your text.

The two panels in the TextArt dialog box are full of options that let you stretch, shape, color, outline, and add other cool effects to your text. Most of the effects are self-explanatory, but a few require some instruction:

- If you want to edit your text, do so in the Type Here option box.
- To change the shape of your text, click on one of the icons in the Shapes option box. Click on the More button to display more shapes.
- Click on the Rotation button on the Options panel to display four little handles around your text. Drag a handle to rotate the text. Or double-click on the Rotation button and enter a specific angle of rotation in the resulting dialog box.
- Unless you're trying to create text with jagged edges, leave the Smoothness setting on Very High. But keep in mind that the higher the Smoothness setting, the longer your computer takes to redraw the text when you make a change.

4. **Click on the Close button in the TextArt dialog box.**

   Or just click anywhere outside the dialog box or TextArt image. Your TextArt object is inserted into your document. To edit it, double-click on the image. You can move, copy, and resize the TextArt object as you can any graphic in WordPerfect.

Add a Watermark to Your Pages

Companies with tons of money pay to have watermarks imprinted on their stationery. (A *watermark* is an image that appears behind the printed text on your page.) You can create a simulated watermark in WordPerfect by following these steps:

1. **Click at the beginning of the page where you want the watermark to first appear.**
2. **Choose Format➪Watermark.**

   A dialog box appears and asks whether you want to create Watermark A or B. You can create two different watermarks per page (A and B). Pick the one you want to create and click on Create. WordPerfect displays a blank page and the Watermark bar, as shown in Figure 21-3.

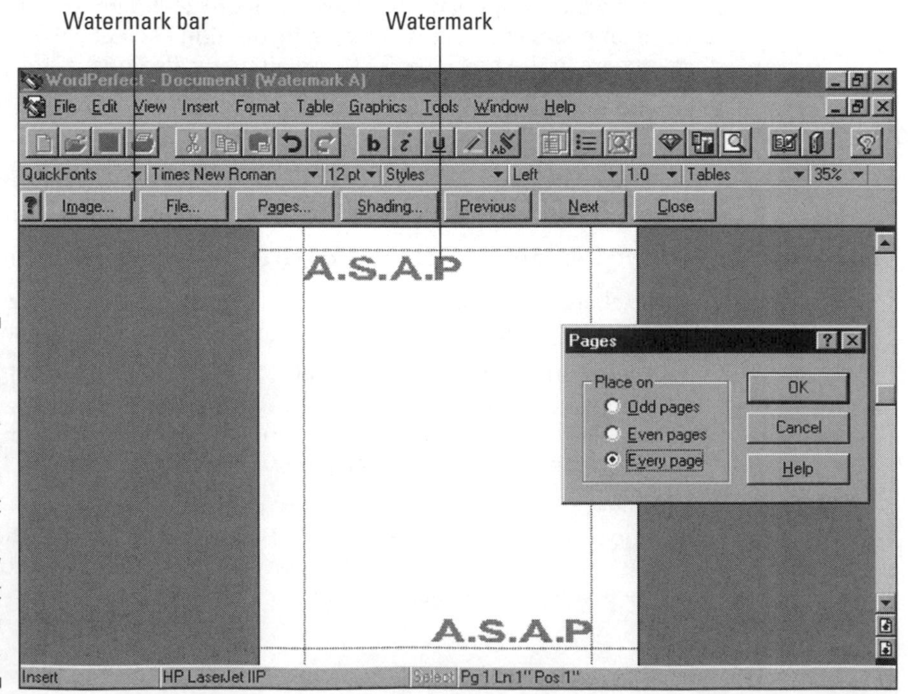

Figure 21-3: You can add a watermark to your page to make sure that everyone knows how important the document is.

3. **Add the text and graphics for the watermark.**

   WordPerfect supplies some images and textual graphics that are ideal for use as watermarks. To insert one of them, click on the Image button on the Watermark bar. You can also add your own text and graphics. Most, but not all, of the normal WordPerfect commands are available when you're creating a watermark.

4. **Adjust the shading.**

   You can make the watermark darker or lighter by clicking on the Shading button on the Watermark bar. Don't make the watermark too dark, though, or it will just look like regular text or graphics when printed.

5. **Click on the Pages button to choose which pages in the document get the watermark.**

   The Pages dialog box, shown in Figure 21-3, appears. You can put the watermark on odd pages, even pages, or every page. Click on OK after you select one of the radio buttons (you can change the settings later, if necessary).

6. **Click on the Close button on the Watermark bar.**

If you want to edit a watermark, click on a page that uses the watermark and choose Format➪Watermark. Choose the watermark that you want to edit (A or B) and click on Edit. The watermark window and Watermark bar appear. To edit a different watermark of the same type (A or B), you can click on the Previous or Next buttons on the Watermark bar.

To discontinue a watermark, click on the page where you want to turn the watermark off, choose Format➪Watermark, select the watermark you want to turn off, and click on Discontinue.

Display Corel Clip Art as Your Screen Saver

People used to use screen savers to prevent images from "burning in" on their computer monitors. Today's monitor technology makes screen savers unnecessary (you really won't do any damage to your screen if you don't use a screen saver), but they still add some flair to your office.

The WordPerfect Suite includes Corel Screen Saver, which displays photo images from the WordPerfect Suite 7 CD-ROM any time the computer is idle for a specified period of time. Aside from providing a visual change of pace, the screen saver gives you a good way to get acquainted with the clip art images included on the CD.

To use the screen saver, choose Settings➪Control Panel from the Windows 95 Start menu. Then double-click on the Display icon in the Control Panel to open the Display Properties dialog box. Click on the Screen Saver tab and select Corel

Screen Saver from the Screen Saver drop-down list. Then click on the Settings button to display a dialog box that lets you change several aspects of the screen saver display.

- If you check the Show File Name option, the name of the image file appears along with the image. I recommend turning this option on so that you can jot down the filenames of images you like. That way, you can quickly find the image files if you want to add the images to a document or slide show.
- The Default Disk shows the name of the drive or directory where the screen saver looks for images to display (that's if you don't have the WordPerfect Suite CD-ROM in the CD drive).
- Click on the WordPerfect Options button to display a list of image categories. You can select which categories you want the screen saver to display.

After choosing your settings, click on OK to return to the Display Properties dialog box. Click on the Preview button to get a quick sample of how your screen saver will appear. Set the time that the computer must be idle before the screen saver starts in the Wait option box. Click on Apply and then click on OK to close the dialog box.

Save by Refinancing a Loan

Trying to decide whether or not you should refinance that mortgage? Don't tax your brain; tax Quattro Pro's brain instead. Choose Tools⇨Experts⇨Analysis to open the Analysis Experts dialog box. Choose the Mortgage Refinancing item from the Analysis Tool list box and click on Next Step. In the Output Block option box, enter the cell address of the top-left corner of the block where you want the results to appear in your spreadsheet. Enter your current remaining mortgage term, balance, and rate. Then enter the proposed new rate and any financing fees and click on the Calculate button. Quattro Pro creates a spreadsheet that spells out your potential savings or loss if you refinance the loan.

Figure Out How Many Days Until . . .

Counting the days till your next day off? Instead of using your calendar — which could look a little obvious to anyone walking by — use Quattro Pro to make the calculation for you. To figure out the number of days between the current date and another day, enter this formula into a cell in a Quattro Pro spreadsheet:

```
@CDAYS(@TODAY,@DATE(year,month,day),1)
```

When you enter the formula, replace *year, month,* and *day* with the date that you're looking forward to. For example, to find out how many shopping days until Christmas 1996, enter **96,12,25**.

The 1 at the end of the formula, in case you care, tells Quattro Pro to count days using the actual number of days in a year rather than using some other arbitrary calendar in its databank.

Play with Special Effects in Presentations

If you import a bitmap image into Presentations, you can apply some special effects to the image. Try it out by inserting one of the images from the Photos folder of the WordPerfect Suite 7 CD into a Presentations drawing. (The folders appear by default when you choose the CD from the Look In drop-down list in the QuickArt Browser dialog box, which is covered in Chapter 16.)

Double-click on the image to open the Bitmap Editor and then choose Tools⇨Special Effects or click on the Effects button on the toolbar (the button looks like a woman's face, for some reason). The Special Effects dialog box, shown in Figure 21-4, appears. The preview in the top-right corner of the dialog box shows the entire image. The previews at the bottom of the dialog box give you before and after views of the portion of the image surrounded by the selection box in the full image preview. Drag the box to move the preview

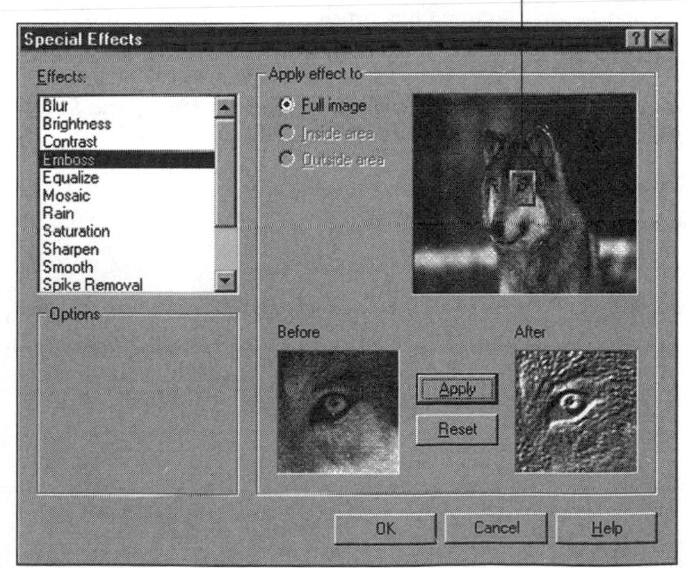

Figure 21-4: You can apply some interesting special effects to bitmap images.

To see what an effect looks like, click on it in the Effects list box. Then click on the Apply button. If you like what you see, click on OK to apply the effect to the image and return to the Bitmap Editor window. Or choose another effect and click on Apply to see what that effect does. After you return to the Bitmap Window, choose File⇨Close Bitmap Editor to save your edits and return to your drawing.

Send an Object into the Third Dimension

The Presentations Quick3-D command adds instant three-dimensional depth to a drawing or text object. Select any object in Presentations and then choose Graphics⇨Quick3-D. The Quick3-D dialog box appears, in which you can add depth to an object, change the perspective, and rotate the object around the X, Y, and Z axes. Figure 21-5 shows a rectangle before (top) and after (bottom left) you apply 3-D effects. You create the bottom-right image by applying the Graphics⇨QuickWarp command to the top rectangle. Like the Quick3-D command, the QuickWarp command gives you some interesting ways to distort and reshape an object.

Make Your Documents Sing

If you have a sound card installed in your computer and have a microphone attached to it, you can record your voice as a sound clip and insert the clip into your WordPerfect documents. Anyone viewing the document on a computer that has a sound card can just click on the clip to hear it. Here's how to record your favorite song and insert it into a WordPerfect document:

1. **In your document, choose Insert⇨Sound to display the Sound Clips dialog box.**
2. **Click on Record.**

   The Windows Sound Recorder launches.
3. **Record your song.**

   The Sound Recorder controls work pretty much like those on a regular tape recorder; click on the Red record button to start your recording and click on the black Stop button to stop recording. Use the Rewind and Play buttons to preview your clip.
4. **Choose File⇨Save in the Sound Recorder and save the clip to disk.**

   Then close the Sound Recorder window.

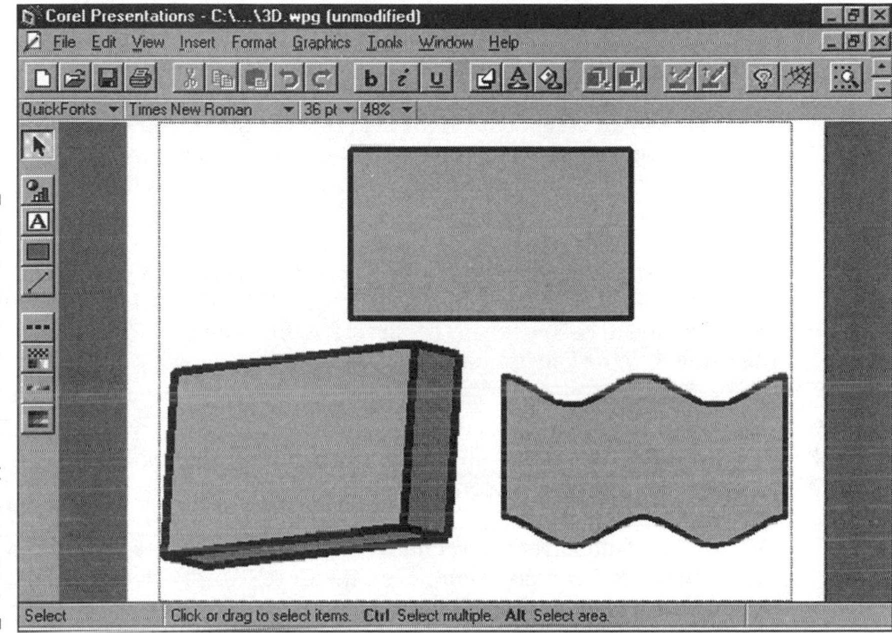

Figure 21-5: A rectangle drawn with the Rectangle tool (top), transformed into a 3-D object (bottom left), and warped (bottom right).

5. **Click on the Insert button in the Sound Clips dialog box.**

   The dialog box shown in Figure 21-6 appears. Enter the name of the sound clip file in the File option box. Select the Store in Document radio button if you're going to send the document to someone else — otherwise, the clip will only play on your computer.

6. **Click on OK.**

   The dialog box closes and your sound is inserted into your document.

Insert Sound Clip into Document
Name
Clip #1
File
Happy.wav
Link to file on disk
Store in document
OK
Cancel
Help

Figure 21-6: Liven up your documents by inserting sound clips through this dialog box.

To play the sound clip, just click on the speaker icon in the left margin of the document. Or choose Insert⇨Sound and click on the Play button in the Sound Clips dialog box.

If you insert two sound clips right next to each other, you see a little balloon with quotation marks in the margin instead of a speaker icon. Click on the balloon to display the speaker icons for each sound clip and then click on the one you want to play.

In addition to sending your friends and coworkers a clip of yourself singing *Don't Cry for Me, Argentina,* you can also insert digital (.WAV) and MIDI sound files into your document. Follow the preceding steps, but skip steps 2 through 4. Enter the file name into the File option box in step 5.

Play with QuickTasks

For still more fun adventures, choose the Corel QuickTasks item from the DAD bar or from the Accessories menu on the Corel WordPerfect Suite 7 menu. A dialog box appears, listing all the available QuickTasks in the Suite. Some of my favorites are:

- Create Certificate: This one helps you create an official-looking certificate, perfect for proclaiming yourself Employee of the Month.
- Create Graph Paper: Ideal for those times when you want to sketch out the floor plan of your dream home, this QuickTask prints a piece of graph paper.
- Create Card: When you don't care enough to send the very best, use the Create Card QuickTask to create and print a homemade thank-you card or greeting card.

Chapter 22

Ten Shortcuts You Can Use All the Time

In This Chapter

- Opening existing documents and creating new documents
- Closing documents
- Moving around in documents and dialog boxes
- Cutting, copying, and pasting data
- Printing documents
- Saving your work
- Undoing mistakes
- Making text bold, underlined, or italic
- Getting help
- Quitting a program

When I was a kid, I was fascinated by the notion that Samantha Stevens, the magical mom of TV's *Bewitched,* could do her household chores simply by twitching her nose. I thought that if I concentrated hard enough, I, too, could make my bed, clean my room, and do other tedious tasks by wrinkling my nose. Alas, I never acquired the touch, or should I say, the twitch.

Imagine my delight, then, when I discovered that computers have built-in shortcuts that enable you to perform certain jobs in one quick step instead of working your way through menu after menu to dig out the commands you want. This chapter shares some of the keyboard shortcuts and toolbar icons that you can use in many Windows 95 programs to get your work done faster and with less effort. It's not magic, mind you, but then again, you don't have to worry about the side effects that so often plagued the Stevens household, where people were forever getting turned into donkeys and other farmyard animals because of a glitch in a twitch.

Not all programs offer all the toolbar buttons shown in this chapter. But you can always create your own toolbar button for a command or feature that you use frequently, as explained in Chapter 23. Also, be sure to check the menus in your programs for additional keyboard shortcuts. Keyboard shortcuts are usually listed next to command names on menus — but not always. Some of the shortcuts in this chapter, for example, aren't on the menus in WordPerfect or Quattro Pro but work fine just the same.

Creating and Opening Documents

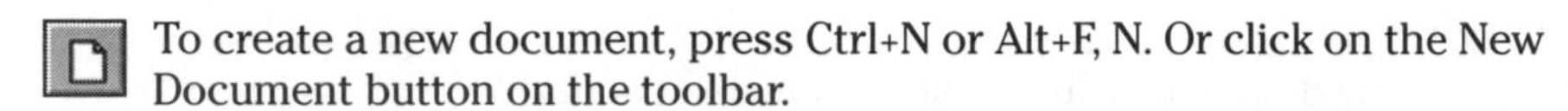

To create a new document, press Ctrl+N or Alt+F, N. Or click on the New Document button on the toolbar.

To open an existing document, press Ctrl+O or Alt+F, O. Or, if you prefer clicking to pressing keys, click on the Open Document button on the toolbar.

Closing the Current Document

To close the current document, press Ctrl+F4 or Alt+F, C. (In Quattro Pro, you can press Ctrl+W to close a document as well.) You can also click on the Close button for the document window. If you haven't already saved the document to disk, you're prompted to do so.

Moving around Your Documents and Dialog Boxes

To jump quickly to the end of your WordPerfect document, press Ctrl+End. To jump to the beginning of the document, press Ctrl+Home. Press Home to move to the beginning of the current line and End to move to the end of the current line. These shortcuts also work in most other word processing programs.

In Quattro Pro, pressing Ctrl+Home moves you to the first cell on the first page in the notebook; pressing Home moves you to the first cell on the current page.

To move from one option to the next inside a dialog box, press Tab or press Alt plus the underlined letter in the option name. To move to the previous option in the dialog box, press Shift+Tab.

Cutting, Copying, and Pasting Data

To make a copy of some text or a graphic, select it and then press Ctrl+C or click on the Copy button. The copy trots off to the Windows Clipboard, where it stays until the next time you choose the Copy or Cut command.

To cut data from one spot and move it to the Windows Clipboard, press Ctrl+X or click on the Cut button. The data remains on the Clipboard until you choose Cut or Copy again.

To paste the contents of the Clipboard into your document, click at the spot where you want to put the data and press Ctrl+V or click on the Paste button. (If you want to paste the contents as an OLE object, as explained in Chapter 20, choose the Paste Special command from the Edit menu instead.)

You can paste the Clipboard contents in multiple places if you want; just keep clicking at the location where you want to paste the data and pressing Ctrl+V.

Printing Documents

To print the current document, press Ctrl+P or Alt+F, P. Or click on the Print button on the toolbar.

Saving Your Work

To save the current document to disk, press Ctrl+S or Alt+F, S or click on the Save button. The first time you save, a Save dialog box appears, and you're asked to give the document a name, specify a file type, and choose where you want to store the document. The next time you press Ctrl+S or click on the Save button, the document is saved using the same Save settings; the dialog box doesn't appear. If you want to save the document using different settings, choose File⇨Save As or press Alt+F, A.

Undoing Mistakes

Screw up bigtime? You can erase all evidence of your mistake by pressing Ctrl+Z, pressing Alt+E, U, or clicking on the Undo button. Undo can reverse most, but not all, actions; you can't undo saving a file, for example. Envoy, unfortunately, has no Undo feature.

If you change your mind about that Undo, press Ctrl+Shift+R or Alt+E, R to reverse your decision. Or click on the Redo button.

Making Text Bold, Underlined, or Italic

If your data's looking dull, give it some flair by applying some character formatting. First, select the text you want to format. Then press Ctrl+B to make it bold, Ctrl+U to underline it, or Ctrl+I to italicize it. Or press on the B, I, or U toolbar buttons. Press the shortcut or click the button again to turn the formatting off.

Getting Help

If you're stumped as to how a particular feature works, click on the feature and then press F1. A Help window appears, displaying information about the feature.

In WordPerfect, Quattro Pro, and Presentations, you can also choose Help➪Ask the PerfectExpert type in a question in the PerfectExpert dialog box.

Some dialog boxes include a question mark button. Click on the button and then click on a dialog box option to find out more about that option.

Quitting a Program

When you've had all you can take of this computing business, press Alt+F4 or Alt+F, X to shut down the current program. Or simply click on the program's Close button. If you have any open documents, you're prompted to save them before you exit the program.

Chapter 23
Ten Ways to Save Time

In This Chapter

- Using the mouse to reach commands faster
- Creating buttons for commands you use all the time
- Taking advantage of Quick commands
- Using styles to speed up formatting
- Protecting yourself from losing data if the power goes out
- Creating data once and reusing it in other documents
- Dragging and dropping stuff from here to there
- Sharing ideas and information on the World Wide Web
- Getting assistance from technical experts
- Swallowing your pride and reading the book

Tick tick tick tick . . . Recognize that sound? It's not a bomb — at least, I don't think so, unless you offended a mobster or something lately. No, that sound is the clock on the wall, reminding you that there are only so many minutes in a day and you haven't even begun to accomplish all the tasks slated for this day's minutes.

With so much to do and so little time, what you need is a way to make your computer work faster. (Certainly *you're* already going as fast as you can go.) With that thought in mind, this chapter continues Chapter 22's time-saving theme by bringing you ten more ways to speed things up. Put these tips into practice, and you may even make up for all that time you spend tooling around the Internet when no one's looking.

Click Once Instead of Twice

Whenever possible, avoid hunting through menus to access commands. Instead, choose a command by clicking on its toolbar button, selecting it from a Power Bar drop-down list, or pressing its keyboard shortcut. (Chapter 22 provides a rundown of buttons and shortcuts for the most frequently used commands.)

You can also save yourself some time by right-clicking to access QuickMenus, which contain commands related to the text, graphic, or other element you right-clicked.

Create Your Own Toolbar and Power Bar Buttons

If a program doesn't have a toolbar or Power Bar button for a command you use often, you can make your own button. The following steps show you how to create a button in WordPerfect 7. The command names for creating and editing buttons may vary slightly in other programs; you should find specifics in the Help menu for the program you're using.

1. **Right-click on the toolbar or Power Bar and choose Edit from the QuickMenu.**

   The Toolbar Editor dialog box, shown in Figure 23-1, appears.

2. **In the Features list box, click on the command you want to turn into a button.**

   Commands are organized by menus; you can switch to a different menu by selecting it from the Feature Categories drop-down list.

3. **Drag the highlighted command to the toolbar or Power Bar.**

   You can also click on Add Button to add the button to the end of the toolbar.

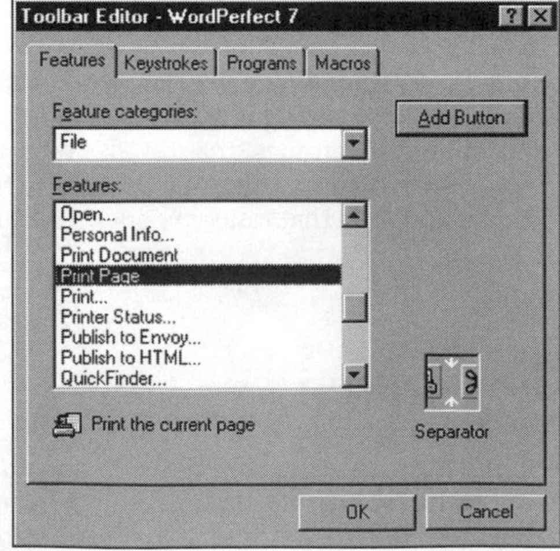

Figure 23-1: You can create your own toolbar and Power Bar buttons for commands you use often.

You can remove a button from the toolbar or Power Bar by pressing Alt as you drag the button off the bar. You can also rearrange buttons and move buttons by Alt+dragging them.

If you don't like the button face that WordPerfect assigns to a command, you can change it. With the Toolbar Editor dialog box open, double-click on the button you want to change. You see a dialog box in which you can change the name of the button and specify what QuickTip text you want to see when you pause the mouse cursor over the button. Click on the Edit button to display a dialog box that lets you edit the colors and design of the button. (Click on the button face display in the zoomed area of the dialog box to change the colors of the pixels that make up the image.)

Use Quick Thinking

The WordPerfect Suite offers several different speed-it-up features that begin with the word Quick: QuickCorrect, QuickTasks, and so on.

Using QuickCorrect, for example, you can correct typing errors on the fly and also set up the equivalent of a keyboard shortcut, as explained in Chapter 6, in the section "Letting WordPerfect Correct Mistakes for You." (QuickCorrect works similarly in other programs in the suite.)

QuickTasks help you blaze your way through various routine tasks such as creating fax cover sheets. You can access QuickTasks by clicking on the Show Me tab of the Help dialog box inside WordPerfect and Presentations; by working your way from the Windows 95 Start menu to the QuickTasks item on the Corel WordPerfect Suite 7 Accessories menu; or by clicking on the QuickTasks DAD icon.

Different programs offer different Quick commands — work your way through the menus looking for commands related to the project you're doing. Be sure to also right-click your way around the screen to display different QuickMenus, which are mini-menus containing commands related to whatever you right-click.

Work in Style

Especially in WordPerfect, it pays to use *styles.* Styles enable you to automatically apply many different formatting attributes at once instead of choosing them one by one from various menus. Styles also ensure that the different components of your document — headlines, body text, and so on — have a consistent look.

For more information about using styles in WordPerfect 7, see "Using Styles to Speed Up Formatting Chores" in Chapter 9. For information about using styles in other programs, check out the Help index in each program.

Keep Automatic Backup Turned On

Most programs offer a feature that automatically saves your document every so often to protect you from losing all your work should the power to your computer go out unexpectedly. But in many cases, you have to turn this automatic backup feature on before it can do its job.

Where you activate automatic backup depends on the program; usually, you can find the option by choosing the Preferences command. In WordPerfect, choose Edit⇨Preferences⇨Files and make sure that the Timed Document backup check box is selected; in Presentations, choose Edit⇨Preferences⇨Backup to access the option. In Quattro Pro, choose Edit⇨Preferences and click on the File Options tab. To locate the option in another program, consult the program's Help system.

Teach Your Programs How to Share Data

Don't keep recreating the same data over and over again; create it once and then use OLE commands or the normal Cut, Copy, and Paste commands to copy and move it into other documents. If you want, you can use OLE to create copies that automatically get updated when you update the original data. You can find out more about these options in Chapter 20 and also in the editing sections of chapters discussing individual programs in the WordPerfect Suite.

Practice the Art of Drag and Drop

If you want to copy or move data, you can select the data, choose the Cut or Copy command, click on the spot where you want to place the data, and then choose the Paste command. Or, you can make life easy and simply select the data and drag it to its new home using your mouse.

You can drag and drop data within the same document, between two open documents in the same program, and, in some cases, between two open documents in different programs.

In most programs, you drag to move data between documents and press Ctrl while dragging to copy data. For more information, see the section "Dragging and dropping" in Chapter 6 and "Dragging and dropping a copy" in Chapter 13. You can use the techniques presented there to drag and drop stuff in most programs.

When dragging between programs, Ctrl+dragging embeds the data as an OLE object and Shift+Ctrl+dragging links the data, as explained in Chapter 20, in the section "Dragging and Dropping between Programs."

Seek Out Online Help

As mentioned back in Chapter 18, Corel Corporation maintains a site on the World Wide Web at `http://www.corel.com`. This site is a great place to find out about the latest Corel products and programs and access technical support. Another Corel related site, Chris Dickman's CORELNET, offers additional Corel product information and a chat area where users can ask for assistance with a particular problem and exchange ideas and information. Check out the site at `http:\\www.corelnet.com`.

Don't Be Shy about Calling for Help

I can't tell you how many hours I lost trying to research and solve my own computer headaches before I finally wised up to the benefits of calling tech support. In some cases, I would have *never* been able to find a solution myself, because the problem was related to some software or hardware bug known only to the folks at tech support.

So if you encounter a problem that you just can't seem to solve, don't waste endless hours trying to track down a solution on your own. Instead, pick up the phone and call the technical support department for the software or hardware component that's causing you fits.

In some cases, you may pay a small surcharge for technical support — and you may have to wait on hold for some time before you get to speak to a real, live person. But if you weigh those drawbacks against all the time you lose if you try to fix things yourself, you almost always come out ahead. (***Note:*** As I write this, Corel is offering free technical support for the WordPerfect Suite. Yea, Corel!)

When All Else Fails . . .

Many people seem to feel that they should be able to install and use a new piece of software just like that, with no instruction and no information about how the program works. They refuse to read the manual that came with the program or any other references, such as this book. As a result, they never learn to use the program to even a bazillionth of its capacity — which means they plunk down a lot of money for a meager return. They also spend much more time than necessary getting things done, because they don't know how to put the program's power to work for them.

Of course, I know that *you* don't fall into this category, because *you* bought this book. But just in case the book was a gift (or was anonymously put on your desk by someone who was tired of hearing you yell at your computer), understand that it is no reflection on your intelligence that you can't learn how computer programs work by osmosis. Heck, you didn't learn how to tie your shoes by osmosis, did you? (Oh . . . is that why you're still wearing sneakers with Velcro closures instead of laces?) So swallow your pride and let this book show you how to use the WordPerfect Suite. If you spend just five minutes a week reading, you can pick up techniques and tricks that will save you hours in the future.

Appendix

Installing WordPerfect Suite 7

Installing the programs in the WordPerfect Suite is relatively painless — the suite's setup program walks you through the entire process. The biggest problem you're likely to face is not having enough space on your computer's hard drive to hold all the programs. Installing all the components in the suite requires more than 200MB of hard drive space.

Before you install the suite, read the first two sections in Chapter 1 to determine whether you want to install all the programs. If you don't think you'll have any use for a particular program, don't install it — save your hard drive space for something else. Remember that you can always go back later and add components that you didn't install the first time.

The WordPerfect Suite runs on Windows 95 only. If you're using Windows 3.11 or earlier, Corel makes a version of the suite designed for you (although it includes older versions of the programs in the suite). To run the WordPerfect Suite, you also need a computer with at least a 486/25 processor and 8MB of RAM; you'll do much better with a faster processor and 16MB or more of RAM, however.

Installing over Older Versions of Suite Programs

The setup program for the WordPerfect Suite doesn't automatically overwrite or remove pre-Windows 95 versions of WordPerfect or other programs in the suite. If your hard drive space is limited, you may need to delete the old programs to make room for the new versions. You can remove the old programs by clicking on the Windows 95 Start button and then choosing Settings⇨Control Panel. Double-click on the Add/Remove Programs icon to access the Windows 95 uninstaller and select the programs you want to remove. You can also delete the program files using the File Manager or by using the Uninstall utility that came with the original program, if one was provided.

If you have Envoy 1.0 or 1.0a installed, you need to remove it before you install Envoy 7.

If you want to be able to use any of the files you created in earlier versions of the suite programs, copy the files to a floppy disk or a folder on your hard drive before you remove the old programs. If you're uncertain of how to do this, ask a Windows 95 guru for help.

Doing a Standard CD-ROM Installation

To install the core programs of the WordPerfect Suite — WordPerfect, Quattro Pro, Presentations, DAD, and Envoy — from the Suite CD-ROM, just follow these steps:

1. **Insert the WordPerfect Suite 7 CD-ROM into your CD-ROM drive.**

   After a few seconds, the Corel WordPerfect Suite 7 screen appears automatically. Click on the WordPerfect Suite Setup button.

2. **Click on the Release Notes button.**

   Clicking on this button displays a window detailing any last-minute installation information from Corel. Software companies use release notes to advise users about any reported problems with certain types of computers and other potential problem areas. Chances are, you won't find anything worth worrying about, but it's always good practice to check. When the Release Notes window opens, click on the notes you want to see and click on View. After you scan the notes, click on the little X button in the upper-right corner of the notes window to close it. Then click on the Close button.

3. **Click on Next.**

   A dialog box appears, asking you whether you agree to the terms of the software licensing agreement.

4. **Click on Yes to signal that you're A-Okay with the terms of the agreement.**

5. **Enter your name, company name (optional), and program serial number and then click on Next.**

   You can find the serial number on the software proof of purchase form. Be sure to keep this number stored somewhere safe; you'll need it if you ever contact Corel's technical support staff.

6. **Choose an installation type and click on Next.**

   You have four installation options:

   - Typical performs a standard installation and requires about 125MB of empty hard drive space.

   - Compact installs the minimum number of components required to run the program. It only takes about 54MB of free hard drive space, but you won't be able to take advantage of many program features if you choose this option.

- Custom lets you pick and choose which components you want to install. The amount of disk space required depends on how many components you install. Information about custom installation is provided in the next section of this chapter.
- Run from CD-ROM lets you install just a few program files on your hard disk and then actually run your programs off the CD-ROM. This option requires only about 10MB of hard drive space, but you'll find that your programs run really, really slowly. Also, you must always have the WordPerfect Suite CD-ROM in the CD-ROM drive to run programs.

7. **Specify the drive and directory where you want to install the suite.**

   Typically, the default options that the setup program picks are fine. But you can change the installation drive and directory if you want.

8. **Click on Next.**

   A dialog box appears, listing all the components that are installed by default. If you don't want to install a particular program, click on its check box to deselect it. (A checkmark indicates that the program is selected for installation.)

9. **Click on Next and then on Install.**

   The installation process takes a few minutes.

When the installation is finished, the setup program displays a dialog box announcing that you're ready to roll. Click on OK to signal your everlasting gratitude. Then click on the Close button (that X button in the upper-right corner of the screen) to close the setup program. Or, if you want to install the other programs on the CD, click on the Bonus Applications button. To install AT&T WorldNet Service software and Netscape Navigator, click on the Internet Service Setup button. The installation steps are the same as for installing the core Suite programs. After you finish installing programs, you should find the WordPerfect Suite 7 program menu at the top of the Windows 95 Start menu.

Performing a Custom Installation

If you want to install just some components of the suite — or install high-end components not installed via the Typical installation option — follow the preceding Steps 1 through 8, and choose the Custom option in Step 6.

The setup program displays a dialog box listing all the major components you can install. If you see a checkmark in the box next to a component, that component will be installed. Click on the box to turn the check on and off.

At the bottom of the setup dialog boxes, the setup program indicates how much disk space you need to install the currently selected components. Each time you select or deselect a component, the disk space information is updated.

For each component, you can click on the Components button to display a second dialog box of options related to that particular component. Click on the options that you want to install. Some components have several layers of options; keep clicking on Components to find all the possible options that you can turn on and off. Click on OK to work your way back to the first layer of components.

When a box is shaded, only part of the component is installed by default. Click on the item and then click on Components to access the other parts of the component and turn them on or off.

When you're done selecting all the components you want to install, click on Next and then click on Install.

Installing from Floppy Disks

If you bought the floppy disk version of the WordPerfect Suite, you can install WordPerfect 7 by putting the first disk in your floppy disk drive. Click on the Windows 95 Start button, click on Run, type **a:\setup.exe** into the Open option box, and click on OK. Follow the on-screen prompts to complete the installation.

All the other programs in the suite are on the CD-ROM, so you need a CD-ROM drive to install them. Or, you can find a friend with a CD-ROM drive, copy the files to floppy disks, and then copy the floppies onto your computer. Get a Windows 95 guru to help you — it will be a long and messy process.

Adding and Removing Installed Components

After you do the initial suite installation, you can go back at any time and install additional components. Just follow the instructions for performing a custom installation, as described in the preceding section.

To remove a program, click on the Windows 95 Start button, click on Settings, and then click on Control Panel. In the Control Panel window, double-click on the Add/Remove Programs icon. When the Add/Remove Programs dialog box appears, select the program you want to remove and then click on the Add/Remove button. The Corel Remove for Windows 95 window appears. Click on Next and select the programs you want to remove. Click on Next and then click on Remove.

Index

• Symbols and Numbers •

* (asterisks)
  operator, 162, 165
  in spreadsheet cells, 151
@ (at symbol) for functions, 167
\ (backslash) in spreadsheet cells, 152
^ (caret) operator, 162, 165
- (minus sign) operator, 162, 165
() (parentheses)
  for function arguments, 167
  order of preference for calculations, 165–166
% (percent sign) operator, 162
+ (plus sign)
  formula indicator, 160
  operator, 162, 165
/ (slash) operator, 162, 165
3-D objects in Presentations, 328
3-D spreadsheets, 140
35mm slides, 224

• A •

abbreviations, replacing as you type, 70
absolute cell addresses, 164
absolute tabs, 82
Action menu, 126
Active Block dialog box
  Alignment, 156–158
  Column Width, 182–183
  Font, 155
  Line Drawing, 208–209
  Numeric Format, 154–155
  Shading, 210
active cell, 136, 139
Active Page dialog box, 138–139, 208
Add Slides dialog box, 228–229
adding programs, 344
addition operator, 162, 165
Address Book, 282–285
  adding entries, 282–283
  customizing display, 284
  deleting entries, 283
  overview, 12, 282
  when to use, 13
address book in Netscape Navigator, 277
advance modes for slides, 242
Advanced Multiple Pages option, 59
alignment. *See* justifying text
all justification, 89–90
animation, 244–245
Appearance attributes of fonts, 77
applying styles, 118
appointments (Sidekick 95), 286–287
arrow keys
  in Quattro Pro, 141
  selecting text, 63
  in WordPerfect, 46, 47
artwork. *See* graphics
Ask the PerfectExpert dialog box, 30–31
asterisks (*)
  operator, 162, 165
  in spreadsheet cells, 151
AT&T WorldNet Service, 12, 269
at symbol (@) for functions, 167
automatic error correction, 69–71
automatic saving
  overview, 338
  Quattro Pro, 145
  WordPerfect, 57
automatic updating of linked copies, 310–312
@AVG function, 168

• B •

Back button on Help windows, 34
back tab indent, 88
back tabbing, 81
Background layer, 223, 235–236
Backgrounds menu, 236
backslash (\) in spreadsheet cells, 152
Backspace key, 44
Balanced Newspaper columns option, 108
bitmap images, 234–235, 239, 327–328
Bksp key, 44
blend, 210
Block command
  Format menu, 154–155, 182, 208, 210
  Insert menu, 179–180

boldface
  text in this book, 6
  type style, 77, 334
bomb symbol, 5
Bookmark Properties dialog box, 260–261
bookmarks
  Envoy, 260–261
  Netscape Navigator, 273–274
Border/Fill command, 113
borders
  around charts, 199
  around graphics, 112
  around spreadsheets, 207–209
  around text, 112–113
  printing for spreadsheets, 218
  See also lines (graphic)
budgets, 134
Bullet Chart Animation Properties dialog box, 244–245
bulleted lists, 96–97
  special effects, 244–245
Bullets & Numbers dialog box, 96–99
bullseye symbol, 5
buttons
  in Dashboard, 298–299
  on dialog boxes, 25–26
  hypertext buttons, 262–263
  in Netscape Navigator, 271
  same button in different programs, 14
  See also Power Bars; toolbars

• C •

Calculator (Sidekick 95), 296
Calendar view (Sidekick 95), 286–288
call lists (Sidekick 95), 287–288
callouts on charts, 200
cancelling bitmaps, 234
Cardfile (Sidekick 95), 288–293
  adding cards, 291
  changing Card List display, 292–293
  deleting cards, 291
  dialing a contact, 293
  editing cards and cardfile fields, 291–292
  new cardfile setup, 289–291
  opening, 288
  overview, 288
  printing cards, 295–296
  searching for cards, 292
  selecting and marking cards, 291
  Viewport, 295
caret (^) operator, 162, 165
CD-ROMs
  installing from, 342–344
  sounds from, 243
cell addresses
  defined, 136
  entering using mouse, 162–163
  in function arguments, 168
  relative versus absolute, 164
  using in formulas, 160–163
cells
  borders, 208–209
  deleting columns or rows, 179–180
  deleting contents, 175–176
  deleting formatting, 176
  editing contents, 173–175
  entering data, 149–153
  formatting data, 154–158
  inserting columns or rows, 179
  line drawing, 208–209
  making active, 139
  moving to, 140
  overview, 136
  QuickFill, 152–153
  selecting cells and data, 154, 177–178
  text alignment, 155–158
  transposing, 188–189
  See also cell addresses; spreadsheets
centering
  spreadsheets on pages, 218
  text on lines (justifying), 89–90
  text on pages, 93
  text on tab stops, 84
character styles. *See* styles
characters
  copying formatting, 122–123
  inserting special characters, 102–104, 152
Chart Expert, 192, 193–194
Chart Gallery dialog box, 197–198
Chart menu (Quattro Pro), 197, 199
Chart Print dialog box, 203
charts, 191–203
  borders, 199
  callouts, 200
  changing type, 197–198
  color scheme, 197–198
  creating using Chart Expert, 192, 193–194
  creating using QuickChart, 192, 194–195
  deleting, 202
  editing, 195–201
  exchanging rows and columns, 201

lines and shapes, 200
moving, 201–202
printing without spreadsheets, 203
Quattro Pro uses, 134
resizing, 202
selecting in Presentations, 227
titles, 199
check boxes, 25
choosing. *See* selecting
clearing
cell formatting, 176
tabs, 83
See also deleting
clicking, 19
clip art screen saver, 325–326
Close button, 22, 54
closing
bitmap editor, 234
dialog boxes, 26
documents, 54, 332
drawings or presentations, 223
Envoy documents, 266
spreadsheets, 143
using Close button, 22, 54
See also shutting down; turning off
codes
Date Code, 101–102
hidden, 66, 75, 120–121
Collate option, 58
colors
for charts in Quattro Pro, 197–198
in CorelFLOW, 306
of parentheses in formulas, 166
in Presentations, 224, 237
for spreadsheets, 210
for text in WordPerfect, 78
Columns dialog box, 108
columns in charts, exchanging with rows, 201
columns in spreadsheets
deleting, 179–180
hiding, 211–212
inserting, 179
overview, 136
QuickSum, 170
resizing, 181–183
selecting, 178
transposing to rows, 188–189
columns of text, 107–110
borders and fills, 113
entering and editing text, 110
setting up, 107–109
commands
conventions in this book, 6, 19–20
grayed out on menus, 20
same command in different programs, 14
underlined letters, 6, 19
See also specific menus
connection points (CorelFLOW), 302–304
connector pins (CorelFLOW), 302–304
Contact Log (Sidekick 95), 296
Contact Manager (Sidekick 95), 296
Contents tab of Help topics, 34
context-sensitive menus. *See* QuickMenus
Control key combinations. *See* keyboard shortcuts
conventions in this book, 6, 19–20
Copy Block dialog box, 186–187
copying
Address Book entries, 283
between Envoy documents, 259
formats in WordPerfect, 122–123
keyboard shortcuts for, 65, 333
linking and embedding versus, 309–310
opening a document copy, 53
Presentations graphics or text blocks, 240
spreadsheet data, 183–187
text in WordPerfect, 63–67
See also Object Linking and Embedding (OLE)
copyright symbol, 104
Corel Corp. Web Site, 274, 339
Corel Screen Saver, 325–326
Corel WordPerfect Suite 7
adding programs, 344
cooperation among programs, 14–15
deleting programs, 344
dragging and dropping between programs, 67
earlier versions, 2, 341–342
installing, 341–344
overview, 10–12
programs covered by this book, 2
shutting down programs, 18
starting programs, 18
switching between programs, 26
uses for each program, 13
using programs together, 307–318
See also programs
CorelFLOW, 300–306
changing objects, 305–306
connector pins and connection points, 302–304

(continued)

CorelFLOW *(continued)*
drawing objects, 304–305
overview, 12, 300–301
previewing diagrams, 306
printing diagrams, 306
saving diagrams, 306
Smart Libraries, 301–302
when to use, 13
CORELNET, 274, 339
CorelOffice Professional 7, 2
counting days, 326–327
Ctrl key combinations. *See* keyboard shortcuts
curly quotes, 103
cursors
mouse cursor, 18
shadow cursor in WordPerfect, 40
custom installation, 343–344
customizing
Address Book, 284
number of undos, 69
Power Bars, 336–337
Quattro Pro, 137–139
screen elements, 23–24
toolbars, 23, 336–337
WordPerfect, 41–44
Cut command
in Quattro Pro, 188
in WordPerfect, 65

• D •

DAD (Desktop Application Director), 22, 24
Dashboard, 12, 297–299
Data Chart Gallery dialog box, 227
Date Code command, 101–102
Date Text command, 101–102
dates
counting days, 326–327
current date function, 169
of files, 53
inserting the current date, 101–102
QuickFilling spreadsheet cells, 152–153
Decimal tab stop type, 84
defaults
font, 74, 76
spreadsheet page setup, 216
spreadsheet print options, 218
tab stops in WordPerfect, 81, 83
Define Cardfile Fields dialog box, 290
Delete key, 44
deleting
Address Book entries, 283
appointments in Sidekick 95, 287
borders around text, 113
bullets, 97
cancelling bitmaps, 234
cards from Cardfile, 291
cell contents, 175–176
cell formatting, 176
charts, 202
connection points in CorelFLOW, 303
e-mail messages, 276
Envoy pages, 259
graphics in WordPerfect, 112
header/footer, 107
highlighting in Envoy, 257
numbered items from lists, 99
page numbers, 101
Presentations text blocks or graphics, 239
programs, 344
slides, 240
spreadsheet columns or rows, 179–180
styles, 120–121
tab stops, 83
text in WordPerfect, 44, 63
text using Find and Replace, 125
To Do list tasks in Sidekick 95, 287
undeleting, 63, 67–68
Desktop Application Director (DAD), 22, 24
Destination dialog box, 253–254
dialing phone numbers
using Address Book, 285
using Cardfile, 293
dialog boxes
navigating, 330
overview, 24–26
question mark buttons, 26, 34
dimmed commands on menus, 20
dimmed options on dialog boxes, 26
directories. *See* folders
Display dialog box, 137–138
Display Preferences dialog box, 41–43
displaying
card list in Cardfile, 292–293
Envoy documents, 254–255
graphics as icons in Netscape Navigator, 274
Header/Footer bar, 106
hidden codes in WordPerfect, 66, 75
hidden symbols in WordPerfect, 85

more toolbar rows, 23, 43–44
newsgroup messages, 278–280
Presentations viewing modes, 240
reading e-mail, 275–276
Web pages, 271–272
See also customizing; hiding; previewing
division operator, 162, 165
Do It for Me option, 33
Document on Disk dialog box, 60
Document Selection dialog box, 222
document styles, 116–117
Document tab of WordPerfect Display Preferences, 42
documents
automatic saving, 57
closing, 54, 332
dragging and dropping text between, 67
embedding or linking, 316
naming rules, 56
opening a copy, 53
opening existing documents, 52–53, 332
opening new documents, 50–52, 332
pathnames, 60
printing, 57–60
saving, 54–57
saving under different name, 56
See also files; spreadsheets
dot leaders
for justified text, 91
for tabs, 85
double indent, 86, 88
double spacing text, 92
double-clicking, 19
dragging, 19
dragging and dropping
between programs, 315–316
copying and moving text, 65, 67
copying spreadsheet data, 184
defined, 19
moving spreadsheet data, 187
saving time using, 338–339
drawing tools
CorelFLOW, 304–305
Presentations, 232–233
Quattro Pro, 200
drop caps, 321–322
drop-down lists, 25

• E •

Earth Time icon (Sidekick 95), 297
Edit menu (Quattro Pro)
Copy Block command, 186–187
Copy command, 184–185
Cut command, 188
Delete Column(s) command, 179
Delete Row(s) command, 179
Move Block command, 188
Paste command, 185, 188
Preferences command, 145
Redo command, 176–177
Undo command, 176–177
Edit menu (WordPerfect)
Copy command, 64–65
Cut command, 65
Find command, 124
Paste command, 65
Preferences command, 23–24
Redo command, 68–69
Select command, 62
Undelete command, 63, 67–68
Undo command, 68–69
editing Cardfile cards and fields, 291–292
editing charts, 195–201
borders, 199
changing chart type, 197–198
changing color scheme, 197–198
editing individual elements, 199
exchanging rows and columns, 201
inserting callouts, 200
lines, 200
overview, 195–197
title, 199
editing graphics
in Presentations, 234–235
in WordPerfect, 111–112
editing hypertext links, 264
editing OLE objects, 316–317
editing slides, 235–240
backgrounds, 235–236
copying graphics or text blocks, 240
deleting graphics or text blocks, 239
deleting slides, 240
layers of slides, 223
moving graphics or text blocks, 239
resizing graphics or text blocks, 239

(continued)

editing slides *(continued)*
special effects, 240–244
templates, 236–237
text, 237–239
undoing actions, 239
editing spreadsheets, 173–189
borders, 207–209
changing cell contents, 173–175
colors, 210
copying data, 183–187
deleting cell contents, 175–176
deleting cell formatting, 175
deleting columns or rows, 179–180
hiding columns or rows, 211–212
inserting columns or rows, 179
inserting pages, 180–181
line drawing, 207–209
moving data, 187–188
page breaks, 211, 216
resizing columns or rows, 181–183
selecting cells and data, 154, 177–178
transposing columns and rows, 188–189
undoing actions, 176–177
See also formatting spreadsheet data
editing styles, 119–120
editing text, 60–71
Address Book entries, 283
automatically with QuickCorrect, 69–71
in chart text boxes, 200
in columns, 110
copying and moving text, 63–67
in CorelFLOW, 306
deleting text, 63
finding and replacing text, 123–126
formatting after copying or moving, 66
headers and footers, 106
selecting text, 62–63
in slides, 237–239
undeleting text, 63, 67–68
undoing edits, 68–69
when finding and replacing, 125
See also formatting text; page layout
electronic publishing. *See* Envoy
em dashes, 103–104
e-mail
address book, 277
composing offline, 275, 277
deleting messages, 276
icons after sender's name, 275
printing messages, 280
receiving, 275–276
sending, 276–277
embedding. *See* Object Linking and Embedding (OLE)
en dashes, 104
End key, 47
Enter key, 81
entering spreadsheet data
basics, 149–152
building spreadsheets, 148–149
copying data, 183–187
entering text
Address Book entries, 282–283
automatic error correction, 69–71
in chart text boxes, 200
in columns, 110
composing e-mail offline, 275, 277
in Presentations bullet charts, 228
in Presentations slides, 225–228
in Sidekick 95 Calendar, 286–288
in Sidekick 95 Cardfile, 291
in WordPerfect, 44–45
See also editing text; formatting text
Envoy 7 Driver Properties dialog box, 253–254
Envoy, 251–266
bookmarks, 260–261
closing documents, 266
copying or moving between documents, 259
deleting pages, 259
highlighting items, 257
hypertext, 261–264
navigating pages, 256
overview, 11–12
printing documents, 266
publishing or printing to Envoy, 251–254
QuickNotes, 258–259
rearranging pages, 259
Runtime files, 253, 264–265
saving files, 265–266
sending files to others, 264–265
shutting down, 266
starting, 254
viewing documents, 254–255
equations. *See* formulas
erasing. *See* deleting
errors
correcting automatically as you type, 69–71
ERR or NA message in Quattro Pro, 171
missing parentheses in formulas, 166
See also troubleshooting

.EVY file extension, 253–254
.EXE file extension, 253
executing. *See* starting
Exit command, 18
exiting. *See* shutting down
expense records in Sidekick 95, 297
Experts
  Chart Expert, 192, 193–194
  in WordPerfect, 51
exponentiation operator, 162, 165

• F •

file extensions
  for Envoy files, 253
  for newsgroup and mail messages, 280
  overview, 56
  Presentations slide show files, 311
  for Quattro Pro files, 144
file formats, changing, 56
File menu
  Exit command, 18
  Publish to Envoy command, 252
File menu (Presentations)
  Cancel Bitmap command, 234
  Close Bitmap Editor command, 234
  New command, 223
  Open command, 223
  Print command, 248
File menu (Quattro Pro)
  Exit command, 135
  New command, 141
  Open command, 142
  Print command, 203, 212
  Save As command, 145
  Save command, 143–144
File menu (WordPerfect)
  Close command, 54
  New command, 50–51
  Open command, 52
  Print command, 58–60
  Save As command, 56
  Save command, 54–55
File Transfer Protocol (FTP), 268
files
  detailed information about, 53
  naming rules, 56
  pathnames, 60
  Runtime files, 246–247
  sound files, 243
  See also documents; spreadsheets
Files Preferences dialog box, 57
fills
  defined, 112
  page layout, 113
  pattern fills for text, 238
Find and Replace Text dialog box, 124–126
finding. *See* searching
First Line Indent option, 81, 86, 88
fitting on pages
  Envoy documents, 255
  spreadsheets, 216
  text in WordPerfect, 93–94
floppy disks, installing from, 344
flyout menus, 300
folders
  for e-mail, 275
  for newsgroups, 278
  overview, 53
  pathnames, 60
Font dialog box, 75–76
fonts, 74–78
  default, 74, 76
  finding and replacing, 125–126
  how WordPerfect applies changes, 75, 77
  in Presentations, 237
  in Quattro Pro, 154–155, 216
  selecting or changing, 74–76
  serif versus sans serif, 75
  See also type size; type style
footers
  in Quattro Pro, 216
  in WordPerfect, 104–107
Format menu (Quattro Pro)
  Block command, 154–155, 182, 208, 210
  Page command, 137, 208
  SpeedFormat command, 206–207
Format menu (WordPerfect)
  Border/Fill command, 113
  Columns command, 108
  Drop Cap, 320
  Font command, 75–76
  Header/Footer command, 104, 106
  Justification command, 90
  Line command, 82
  Make It Fit command, 93
  Margins command, 79
  Page Numbering command, 99
  Paragraph command, 86, 93

(continued)

Format menu (WordPerfect) *(continued)*
QuickFormat command, 122–123
Styles command, 119
Watermark command, 324
format of files, changing, 56
formatting spreadsheet data, 154–158
deleting cell contents and, 176
deleting cell formatting, 176
fonts, 154–155
numeric format, 154
SpeedFormat, 206–207
text alignment, 155–158
type size, 155
type style, 155
See also editing spreadsheets
formatting text, 73–94
after copying or moving, 66
automatically with QuickCorrect, 70–71
centering text on the page, 93
copying formats, 122–123
in CorelFLOW, 306
fitting text on pages, 93–94
fonts, 74–78
indenting, 85–89
justification (alignment), 89–91
page layout, 95–114
page margins, 79–80
page size and orientation, 78–79
QuickFormat, 73
in slides, 237–239
spacing between lines and paragraphs, 91–93
tab settings, 80–85
troubleshooting, 75
See also editing text; page layout
formulas, 159–171
copying, 184
for counting days, 326–327
creating, 159–163
ERR or NA messages, 171
functions, 159, 166–169
operators, 162
order of preference in calculations, 163–166
overview, 159
printing, 217
using cell addresses, 160–163
See also values
FTP protocol, 268
full justification, 89–90
functions
average, 168
current date, 169
median, 169
overview, 159, 166
table of, 169
using in formulas, 167–168
See also formulas

• G •

Go menu, 271–272
Go To box (WordPerfect), 46
graphics
adding to presentations, 229–235
bitmap images, 234
borders, 112–113
copying between Envoy documents, 259
creating with Presentations, 231–234
displaying as icons in Netscape Navigator, 274
drawing on charts, 200
editing in Presentations, 234–235
editing in WordPerfect, 111–112
fills, 112–113
images on CD-ROM, 13
inserting on WordPerfect pages, 110–111
lines, 112, 114
moving between Envoy documents, 259
printing, 60
Smart Libraries, 301–302
TextArt, 13, 322–324
watermarks, 324–325
See also charts; text-based graphics
Graphics menu (Quattro Pro), 192
Graphics menu (WordPerfect)
Horizontal Line command, 114
Image command, 110–112
TextArt command, 13, 322–324
Vertical Line command, 114
Graphicsland program, 249
grayed out commands on menus, 20
grayed out options on dialog boxes, 26
green parentheses in Quattro Pro, 166
gridlines of spreadsheets, 208, 217
Guidelines command, 79
gutter, 109

• H •

hanging indent, 86, 89
hard page breaks, 211
hard returns. *See* paragraph breaks
headers
  in Quattro Pro, 216
  in WordPerfect, 104–107
Headers/Footers dialog box, 105
Help, 29–35
  drawbacks of on-screen Help, 29
  Help Topics dialog box, 33–34
  keeping Help windows on top, 35
  keyboard shortcut, 334
  navigating Help windows, 34–35
  online, 34, 339
  PerfectExpert, 30–31
  printing Help screens, 35
  question mark buttons, 26, 34
  QuickTasks, 32–33
  QuickTips, 22, 24, 34
  reading this book, 340
  Reference Center, 35
  Show Me features, 31–32
  technical support, 339
  Upgrade Help, 34
Help Topics dialog box, 33–34
hidden codes in WordPerfect, 66, 75, 120–121
hidden symbols in WordPerfect, 85
hiding
  bars, 23
  customizing WordPerfect display, 41–44
  hypertext buttons, 263
  margin guidelines when previewing spreadsheets, 214
  spreadsheet columns or rows, 211–212
  See also displaying
highlighter
  Envoy, 257
  Presentations, 246
highlighting. *See* selecting
Home key
  in Quattro Pro, 141
  in WordPerfect, 47
Horizontal Line command, 114
hotkeys, 19
HTML (HyperText Markup Language), 269
HTTP protocol, 268
hypertext
  in Envoy, 261–264
  Internet links, 268, 280
HyperText Markup Language (HTML), 269
Hypertext Properties dialog box, 263–264
HyperText Transfer Protocol (HTTP), 268

• I •

icons
  for e-mail messages, 275
  in margins of this book, 5
  for newsgroup messages, 278
  for QuickNotes, 259
  QuickSpot, 41, 87, 90, 96–97
  tab icon, 83
images. *See* graphics
Inbox folder, 275
indenting text, 85–89
  displaying and hiding indent markers, 42
  double indent, 86, 88
  entire paragraphs, 86–89
  first line of paragraphs, 81, 85–86, 88
  hanging indent, 86, 89
  options and shortcuts, 88–89
  tabs versus, 81, 83
  in WordPerfect, 44
  See also tabs
Input line, 136
Insert Block dialog box, 180–182
Insert Image dialog box, 110–111
Insert menu (Presentations)
  Bitmap command, 234
  QuickArt command, 229
Insert menu (Quattro Pro), 179–180
Insert menu (WordPerfect)
  Character command, 103–104
  Date command, 101–102
  Sound command, 328
Insert mode, 45
  Tab key in, 83
inserting
  Address Book addresses in WordPerfect, 285
  bullets in WordPerfect, 96–97
  callouts on charts, 200
  current date and time in WordPerfect, 101–102
  Envoy items, 259
  graphics in WordPerfect, 110–111

(continued)

inserting *(continued)*
  items to numbered lists, 99
  line breaks in WordPerfect, 81, 97, 98
  numbers for lists in WordPerfect, 98–99
  page breaks in Quattro Pro, 211
  page breaks in WordPerfect, 44
  Smart Library objects in CorelFLOW, 302
  sound clips in WordPerfect, 328–330
  special characters in WordPerfect, 102–104
  spreadsheet columns or rows, 179
  spreadsheet pages, 180–181
  See also entering spreadsheet data; entering text
insertion marker in WordPerfect, 40, 45
installing Corel WordPerfect Suite 7, 341–344
interface
  customizing, 23–24
  defined, 24
Internet
  service providers, 269
  terminology, 268–269
  See also Netscape Navigator; World Wide Web
Internet For Dummies, The, 267
inventory tracking, 134
italics, 77, 334

• J •

joining newsgroups, 278–279
justifying text
  in Quattro Pro, 155–156
  in WordPerfect, 89–91

• K •

keyboard shortcuts
  for bullets, 97
  for closing documents, 332
  for creating documents, 332
  for cutting, copying, and pasting, 65, 333
  for dates, 102
  for dialog boxes, 26
  for Help, 334
  hotkeys, 19
  for indenting text, 88–89
  for justifying text, 90–91
  navigating documents and dialog boxes, 330
  for navigating in Quattro Pro, 141
  for navigating in WordPerfect, 47
  for opening documents, 332
  overview, 19–20
  for printing, 333
  for saving your work, 333
  for selecting text, 62–63
  for shutting down programs, 18, 334
  for symbols, 104
  for type styles, 77, 334
  underlined letters, 6, 19
  for undoing, 333–334

• L •

labels
  defined, 149
  entering, 150–153
  printing multiple-page spreadsheets, 217
  too long for cells, 151
  values versus, 151–152
launching. *See* starting
layers of slides, 223
Layout layer, 223
Layout menu, 237
leading, 92
left indent, 88
left justification, 89–91
left mouse button, 19
Left tab stop type, 84
letter templates in Sidekick 95, 294
line breaks
  in bulleted lists, 97
  in numbered lists, 98
  paragraph breaks versus, 81
lines (graphic)
  drawing on charts, 200
  drawing on spreadsheets, 207–209
  page layout, 112, 114
  See also borders
lines of text
  justifying, 89–91
  line breaks versus paragraph breaks, 81
  spacing between, 91–92
linking. *See* hypertext; Object Linking and Embedding (OLE)
Links command, 312–313
loading. *See* opening; starting
loan refinancing, 326
logging in, 268

• M •

Mail window, 275–276
Make It Fit dialog box, 93–94
manually advancing slides, 242, 246
margins. *See* page margins
marking Cardfile cards, 291
Master Gallery dialog box, 224–225
Match menu, 125–126
Maximize/Restore button, 22
@MEDIAN function, 169
Memo Expert, 51
menu bar, 20
menus
  conventions in this book, 6
  on dialog boxes, 25–26
  Find and Replace dialog box, 125–126
  flyout menus, 300
  grayed out commands, 20
  overview, 20
  saving time, 335–336
  underlined letters, 6, 19
  See also QuickMenus; *specific menus*
messages
  e-mail, 275–277
  newsgroups, 278–280
MIDI files, 243, 330
Minimize button, 22
minus sign (-) operator, 162, 165
mistakes. *See* errors; troubleshooting
modem
  dialing using Address Book, 285
  dialing using Cardfile, 293
  sending slides to Graphicsland, 249
  See also Netscape Navigator
modes of text-entry, 45
mouse
  advancing slides, 242, 246
  basics, 18–19
  copying and moving text, 65, 67
  entering cell addresses using, 162–163
  highlighter for slide shows, 246
  QuickMenus, 20
  selecting text, 62
moving around. *See* navigating
moving objects
  between Envoy documents, 259
  charts, 201–202
  in CorelFLOW, 306
  graphics in WordPerfect, 112
  keyboard shortcuts, 65, 333
  margins in WordPerfect, 40
  in Presentations, 239
  spreadsheet data, 187–188
  text in WordPerfect, 63–67
  toolbars, 24
  windows, 22
Multiple Pages option, 59
multiplication operator, 162, 165

• N •

Name option box, 55–56
names
  cell address, 136
  Envoy bookmarks, 260–261
  pathnames, 60
  rules for naming files, 56
  saving documents under different name, 56
  of spreadsheet pages, 139
  See also file extensions
navigating
  dialog boxes, 25–26
  Envoy documents, 256
  Help windows, 34–35
  keyboard shortcuts, 330
  mouse basics, 18–19
  Quattro Pro spreadsheets, 139–141
  scrolling, 22
  spreadsheets, 137
  switching between programs, 26
  switching between windows, 27
  WordPerfect documents, 46–47
Net, the. *See* Internet
Netscape and the World Wide Web For Dummies, 267
Netscape Navigator, 267–280
  address book, 277
  bookmarks, 273–274
  browser window elements, 270–271
  e-mail, 275–277
  finding Web sites, 273–274
  Internet service providers, 269
  Internet terminology, 268–269
  newsgroups, 269, 278–280
  overview, 12
  printing items, 280
  saving online time, 274–275
  saving Web pages to disk, 280
  using hypertext links, 271–272
  using URLs, 272

New Slide Show dialog box, 224–225
newsgroups, 268, 278–280
  displaying messages, 278–280
  icons after sender's name, 278
  joining, 278–279
  posting messages, 280
  printing messages, 280
newspaper columns. *See* columns of text
Newspaper columns option, 108
notebooks and notebook pages. *See* spreadsheets
Novell PerfectOffice, 2
numbering
  lists in WordPerfect, 98–99
  pages in WordPerfect, 99–101
  QuickFilling spreadsheet cells, 152–153
numeric data (Quattro Pro). *See* values

• O •

Object Animation Properties dialog box, 244
Object Linking and Embedding (OLE)
  advantages, 308–309, 338
  dragging and dropping between programs, 315–316
  editing OLE objects, 316–317
  embedding copies, 313–314
  embedding on the fly, 314–315
  embedding versus linking, 309–310
  entire documents, 316
  linking using automatic updates, 310–312
  linking using manual updates, 312–313
  OLE objects, 309
  overview, 308–309
  sharing data without OLE, 317–318
Objects page
  getting to and from, 137
  overview, 135
OLE. *See* Object Linking and Embedding (OLE)
OLE clients, 309
OLE servers, 309
one-and-a-half spacing, 92
online Help, 34, 339
on-screen Help. *See* Help
Open dialog box, 52–53
Open File dialog box, 142–143
opening
  Cardfile in Sidekick 95, 288
  copies of documents, 53
  Envoy documents, 254
  existing documents, 52–53, 332
  existing presentation documents, 223
  existing spreadsheets, 142–143
  new documents, 50–52, 332
  new presentation documents, 223
  new spreadsheets, 141–142
  PerfectExpert, 30
  See also starting
operators
  mathematical, 162
  order of preference, 165
option boxes, 25
Options menu, 126
orientation
  of pages in WordPerfect, 78–79
  of spreadsheets when printing, 215
  of text in Quattro Pro, 158
Outliner view, 240
outlining text in Presentations, 238
overruling QuickCorrect, 71

• P •

Page Advance setting, 218
page breaks
  in Quattro Pro, 211, 216
  in WordPerfect, 44
page definition, 78
Page Down key
  in Quattro Pro, 141
  in WordPerfect, 47
page icons in WordPerfect, 41
page layout, 95–114
  bulleted lists, 96–97
  columns of text, 107–110
  headers and footers, 104–107
  inserting graphics, 110–112
  inserting special characters, 102–104
  inserting the date and time, 101–102
  numbered lists, 98–99
  numbering pages, 99–101
  professional programs, 95
page margins
  guidelines in WordPerfect, 40, 79
  setting in Quattro Pro, 214
  setting in WordPerfect, 40, 79–80
Page Range option boxes, 59
page setup for spreadsheets, 215–216
page size, 78–79

Page Size dialog box, 79
Page Up key
  in Quattro Pro, 141
  in WordPerfect, 47
pages (Envoy), adding, deleting, and rearranging, 259
pages, notebook. *See* spreadsheets
pages (WordPerfect)
  borders and fills, 113
  creating new pages manually, 44
  headers and footers, 104–107
  numbering, 99–101
  page layout, 95–114
  printing specific pages, 58–59
  See also page layout
paper size for spreadsheets, 215
paperless office, 251
Paragraph Border/Fill dialog box, 113
paragraph breaks
  displaying and hiding, 42
  line breaks versus, 81
Paragraph Format dialog box, 86, 93
paragraph styles. *See* styles
paragraphs
  borders and fills, 113
  in bulletted lists, 97
  copying formatting, 122–123
  indenting entirely, 86–89
  indenting first line, 81, 85–86, 88
  in numbered lists, 98
  spacing between, 91, 92–93
  See also QuickSpot
parallel columns. *See* columns of text
Parallel columns option, 108
Parallel w/Block Protect columns option, 108
parentheses
  for function arguments, 167
  order of preference for calculations, 165–166
Paste command
  keyboard shortcuts, 65, 333
  in Quattro Pro, 185, 188
  in WordPerfect, 65
Paste Special command, 311–312
pathnames, 60
pattern fills for text, 238
percent sign (%) operator, 162
PerfectExpert
  overview, 30–31
  Show Me features, 31–32
performance. *See* speed
PgDn key
  in Quattro Pro, 141
  in WordPerfect, 47
PgUp key
  in Quattro Pro, 141
  in WordPerfect, 47
Phone Dialer dialog box, 293
pick lists, 25
pictures. *See* graphics
pins (CorelFLOW), 302–304
Play Slide Show dialog box, 245–246
playing slide shows, 245–246
  on other computers, 246–247
plus sign (+)
  formula indicator, 160
  operator, 162, 165
points (CorelFLOW), 302–304
points (fonts), 77
pop-up menus, 25
Position button in WordPerfect, 41, 46
posting newsgroup messages, 280
Power Bars
  Align button, 156
  custom, 336–337
  defined, 21
  hiding, 23
  Justification button, 90
  Line Spacing button, 92
  QuickFonts button, 76, 78
  QuickFormat styles, 123
  Styles button, 117
  Zoom button, 24
  See also toolbars
Preferences
  automatic saving, 57, 145
  overview, 23–24
  in Quattro Pro, 145
  in WordPerfect, 41–43
Presentations, 221–249
  3-D objects, 328
  adding slides, 228–229
  adding titles and text, 225–228
  choosing a Master, 223–225
  choosing a slide template, 225
  closing drawings or presentations, 223
  creating bitmap images, 234
  creating graphics, 231–234
  deleting slides, 240
  deleting text blocks or graphics, 239
  drawing tools, 232–233

(continued)

Presentations *(continued)*
editing graphics, 234–235
editing slides, 235–240
layers of slides, 223
opening documents, 223
overview, 11
playing slide shows, 245–247
printing to Envoy, 251–254
QuickArt, 229–231
QuickTasks, 32–33
Runtime files, 246–247
saving slide shows and drawings, 248
Show Me features, 31–32
shutting down, 223
special effects, 240–244, 327–328
starting, 221–222
undoing actions, 239
Upgrade Help, 34
viewing modes, 240
when to use, 13
previewing
CorelFLOW diagrams, 306
graphics, 111
spreadsheets, 213–215
Print dialog box, 58–59, 248–249
Print in Reverse Order option, 58
printing
Address Book addresses, 285
charts without spreadsheets, 203
in CorelFLOW, 306
documents, 58–60
documents without opening, 60
drawings, 249
e-mail messages, 280
to Envoy, 251–254
Envoy documents, 265
Help screens, 35
keyboard shortcuts, 333
newsgroup messages, 280
page margins and, 80
page size and, 79
in reverse order, 58
in Sidekick 95, 295–296
slides, 248–249
specific pages, 59
spreadsheet formulas, 217
spreadsheets, 212–218
transparencies, 225
Web pages, 280
profit and loss analysis, 134
programs
adding, 344
deleting, 344
dragging and dropping between, 67
installing, 341–344
running in background, 26
same button or command in different programs, 14
sharing data without OLE, 317–318
shutting down, 18
starting, 18
starting using DAD, 24
switching between, 26
uses for each program, 13
using together, 307–318
See also Corel WordPerfect Suite 7; Object Linking and Embedding (OLE)
protocol, 268
publishing to Envoy, 251–254

Quattro Pro
building spreadsheets, 147–149
charts, 191–203
closing spreadsheets, 143
customizing, 137–139
drawing tools, 200
editing spreadsheets, 173–189
entering data, 149–153
ERR or NA messages, 171
formatting data, 154–158, 206–207
navigating, 139–141
opening existing spreadsheets, 142–143
opening new spreadsheets, 141–142
overview, 11, 133–134
page breaks, 211, 216
previewing spreadsheets, 213–215
printing spreadsheets, 212–218
printing to Envoy, 251–254
QuickFill, 152–153
QuickSum, 170
QuickTasks, 32–33
refinancing loans, 326
saving spreadsheets, 143–145
shutting down, 135
SpeedFormat, 206–207
spreadsheet elements, 135–137
starting, 135

undoing actions, 176–177
when to use, 13
question mark buttons, 26, 34
QuickArt, 229–231
QuickChart, 192, 194–195
QuickCorrect, 45, 69–71, 337
adding words, 70–71
overruling unwanted corrections, 71
replacing abbreviations automatically, 70
symbols and special characters inserted by, 103–104
QuickCorrect dialog box, 70
QuickCorrect Options dialog box, 71
QuickFill, 152–153
QuickFonts, 76, 78
QuickFormat, 73, 122–123
QuickLaunch panel (Dashboard), 298
QuickLetter, 294
QuickMenus
copying and moving text, 64–65
deleting text, 63
editing charts, 196, 197, 199
for graphics, 112
highlighting in Envoy, 257
right-clicking for, 20
selecting text, 62
QuickNotes, 258–259
QuickSpot
bullets, 96–97
indenting text, 87
justifying text, 90
overview, 41
QuickStyle dialog box, 117–118
QuickSum, 170
QuickTasks, 32–33, 330, 337
QuickTips, 22, 24, 34
in Quattro Pro, 137
quitting. *See* shutting down
quotation marks and QuickCorrect, 103

• R •

radio buttons, 25
ragged left, 90
ragged right, 90
rearranging Envoy pages, 259
red
parentheses in Quattro Pro, 166
underlines in WordPerfect, 45
Redo command
in Quattro Pro, 176–177
in WordPerfect, 68–69
See also Undo command
Reference Center, 35
refinancing loans, 326
relative cell addresses, 164
relative tabs, 82
REMEMBER icon, 5
Reminders (Sidekick 95), 297
removing. *See* deleting
Replace menu, 126
replacing in WordPerfect, 123–126
resizing
charts, 202
CorelFLOW objects, 306
graphics in Presentations, 239
graphics in WordPerfect, 112
spreadsheet columns and rows, 181–183
windows, 22
See also size
Reveal Codes command, 66, 75
Reveal Codes window, 66
deleting styles, 120–121
right indent, 88
right justification, 89–91
right mouse button, 19
Right tab stop type, 84
right-clicking, 19
See also QuickMenus
rows in charts, exchanging with columns, 201
rows in spreadsheets
deleting, 179–180
hiding, 211–212
inserting, 179
overview, 136
QuickSum, 170
resizing, 181–183
selecting, 178
transposing to columns, 188–189
rows on toolbar, increasing, 23, 43–44
Ruler Bar
setting margins using, 79–80
setting tab stops using, 82
turning on, 82
running. *See* starting
Runtime files
Envoy, 253, 264–265
Presentations, 246–247

• S •

sales tracking, 134
sans serif fonts, 75
Save As dialog box, 55–56
Save File dialog box, 143–144
Save In drop-down menu, 54, 56
saving
  automatic, 57, 145, 338
  CorelFLOW diagrams, 306
  documents under different name, 56
  Envoy documents, 266
  files with different format, 56
  keyboard shortcuts, 333
  Presentations slide shows and drawings, 248
  Runtime files, 246–247, 264–265
  spreadsheets, 143–145
  Web pages to disk, 280
  WordPerfect documents, 54–57
screen
  customizing, 23–24
  See also customizing; windows
screen savers, 325–326
scroll arrows, 22
scroll bars, 22, 137
scroll box, 22, 137
scrolling, 22
  in Quattro Pro, 137, 139
  in WordPerfect, 41, 46
  See also navigating
searching
  in Address Book, 284
  in Cardfile, 292
  finding and replacing in WordPerfect, 123–126
  in WordPerfect, 123–126
Select Cardfile Template dialog box, 289–290
Select New Document dialog box, 50, 51
Select Page Numbering Format dialog box, 99–101
selecting
  Cardfile cards, 291
  Cardfile template, 289–290
  CorelFLOW objects, 305
  fonts, 74–76
  hypertext items and links, 262–263
  spreadsheet cells, 154, 177–178
  tab stop types, 84–85
  text, 62–63
selection handles
  for charts, 195
  for WordPerfect graphics, 111
sending
  e-mail, 276–277
  Envoy files to others, 264–265
  newsgroup messages, 280
  slides to Graphicsland, 249
sequential data, QuickFilling, 152–153
serif fonts, 75
service providers for the Internet, 269
shadow cursor in WordPerfect, 40
sheets. *See* spreadsheets
shortcuts. *See* keyboard shortcuts
Show Me features
  Do It for Me option, 33
  overview, 31–32
showing. *See* displaying
shutting down
  Desktop Application Director (DAD), 24
  Envoy, 266
  keyboard shortcuts, 18, 334
  Presentations, 223
  programs, 18
  Quattro Pro, 135
  See also closing; turning off
.SHW file extension, 311
Sidekick 95, 285–297
  Calendar view, 286–288
  call lists, 287–288
  Cardfile view, 288–293
  other tools, 296–297
  overview, 12, 286–287
  printing, 295–296
  recording appointments, 286–287
  To Do lists, 287–288
  Viewport, 295
  when to use, 13
  Write view, 293–294
sites (Internet), 268
size
  of files, 53
  of pages in WordPerfect, 78–79
  paper size for spreadsheets, 215
  type size in Quattro Pro, 155
  type size in WordPerfect, 74, 77–78
  width of text columns, 109
  See also resizing
Skip Slide option, 242

slash (/) operator, 162, 165
Slide Editor view, 240
Slide layer, 223
Slide List view, 240
Slide menu
  Apply Template command, 236
  Background Layer command, 235
  Layout Layer command, 237
  Make Runtime command, 246
  Object Animation command, 244
  Play Slide Show command, 245
  Slide Transition command, 241–242
  Sound command, 242
slide shows. *See* Presentations
Slide Sorter view, 240
slide templates, 225, 236–237
Slide Transition and Sound Properties dialog box, 241–243
Smart Libraries in CorelFLOW, 301–302
soft page breaks, 211
Sort Cardfile dialog box, 292
sounds
  in Presentations, 242–243
  in WordPerfect, 328–330
spaces
  between bullets and text, 97
  between header/footer and text, 106
  between lines, 91–92
  between paragraphs, 91, 92–93
  between text and graphics, 112
  column spacing, 109
  tabs versus, 80–81
  underlining across, 78
special characters
  inserting in WordPerfect, 102–104
  in spreadsheet cells, 152
special effects, 240–244
  advance modes, 242
  animation, 244
  for bitmap images, 327–328
  for bulleted lists, 244, 245
  sounds, 242–243
  transitions, 241–242
speed
  Netscape Navigator timesaving tips, 274–275
  printing graphics, 60
  timesaving tips, 335–340
SpeedFormat, 206–207
Spell Checker, 127–129
Spell-As-You-Go feature, 45
Spreadsheet Page Setup dialog box, 215–216
Spreadsheet Print dialog box, 212–213
Spreadsheet Print Options dialog box, 217–218
spreadsheets
  3-D spreadsheets, 140
  automatic saving, 145
  borders, 207–209
  building, 147–149
  charts, 191–203
  closing, 143
  customizing display, 137–139
  editing, 173–189
  entering data, 149–153
  ERR or NA messages, 171
  formatting data, 154–158, 206–207
  inserting pages, 180–181
  lines on, 207–209
  naming pages, 139
  navigating, 137, 139–141
  opening existing spreadsheets, 142–143
  opening new spreadsheets, 141–142
  overview, 135–137, 147–149
  page breaks, 211, 216
  page margins, 214
  page setup, 215–216
  previewing, 213–215
  printing, 212–218
  QuickFill, 152–153
  QuickSum, 170
  saving, 143–145
  text alignment, 155–158
  turning off gridlines, 208
  undoing actions, 176–177
  uses for, 134
  See also charts; editing spreadsheets; formatting spreadsheet data
standard installation, 342–343
starting
  Desktop Application Director (DAD), 24
  Envoy, 254
  Presentations, 221–222
  programs, 18
  programs using DAD, 24
  Quattro Pro, 135
  QuickCorrect feature, 71
  Spell-As-You-Go feature, 45
  WordPerfect, 39
  See also opening

status bar
hiding, 23
overview, 21
Position button in WordPerfect, 41
stopping. *See* shutting down
straight quotes, 103
Style List dialog box, 118
style, type. *See* type style
styles, 115–121
applying, 118
creating, 117–118
deleting, 120–121
editing, 119–120
overview, 115–116, 337–338
in Quattro Pro, 154
reusing, 118
types of styles, 116–117
Styles Editor dialog box, 119–120
submenus, 20
See also menus
subscribing to newsgroups, 278–279
subscripts, 77
subtraction operator, 162, 165
SUITE 7 icon, 5
superscripts, 77
switching
between programs, 26
between windows, 27
symbols
inserting in WordPerfect, 102–104
in spreadsheet cells, 152
Symbols tab of WordPerfect Display Preferences, 42

• T •

tab bar, 83
Tab Set dialog box, 82–84
tabbed dialog boxes, 25–26
tables. *See* charts; spreadsheets
tabs
back tabbing, 81
default, 81, 83
deleting, 83
displaying and hiding markers, 42
dot leaders for, 85
indenting versus, 81, 83
relative versus absolute, 82
setting, 80–85
spaces versus, 80–81
Typeover versus Insert mode, 83
types of tab stops, 84–85
underlining across, 78
See also indenting text
taskbar, 21
TECHNICAL STUFF icon, 5
technical support, 339
templates
Cardfile, 289–290
letters (Sidekick 95), 294
Presentations slide templates, 225, 236–237
WordPerfect, 51–52
text. *See* editing text; entering text; formatting text; text-based graphics
text boxes on charts, 200
TextArt, 13, 322–324
text-based graphics programs, 13–14
threaded messages, 278
Thumbnails (Envoy), viewing, 254–255
time
inserting the current time, 101–102
Netscape Navigator timesaving tips, 274–275
printing graphics, 60
timesaving tips, 335–340
TIP icon, 5
title bar, 20
titles
of charts, 100
printing for columns and rows, 217
for slides, 225–228
To Do lists (Sidekick 95), 287–288
@TODAY function, 169
toolbars
customizing, 23, 336–337
defined, 21
displaying more rows, 23, 43–44
hiding, 23
moving, 24
Presentations drawing tools, 232–233
Quattro Pro drawing tools, 200
See also Power Bars
Tools menu (Envoy), 261
Tools menu (Quattro Pro), 193
Tools menu (WordPerfect)
Address Book command, 282
QuickCorrect command, 70–71
Spell Check command, 127

trademark symbol, 103–104
transitions for slides, 241–242
transparencies, printing, 225
Transpose Cells dialog box, 188–189
troubleshooting
  formatting changes after copying or moving, 66
  formatting gives unexpected results, 75
turning off
  QuickCorrect feature, 71
  Spell-As-You-Go feature, 45
  spreadsheet gridlines, 208
  See also closing; shutting down
turning on. *See* starting
.TXT file extension, 280
Type menu, 125
type size
  changing, 77–78
  defined, 74
  in Presentations, 237
  in Quattro Pro, 155
type style
  changing, 77–78
  defined, 74
  finding and replacing, 126
  keyboard shortcuts, 334
  in Presentations, 238
  In Quattro Pro, 155
typefaces. *See* fonts
Typeover mode, 45
  Tab key in, 83
typewriters versus WordPerfect, 44–45, 61
typing. *See* entering spreadsheet data; entering text

• U •

Undelete command, 63, 67–68
underlining
  applying to fonts, 77, 334
  red in WordPerfect, 45
  spaces between underlined words, 78
  underlined letters in menus, 6, 19
  underlined words in Help, 34
Undo command
  changing number of undo items, 69
  Find and Replace feature and, 125
  keyboard shortcuts, 333–334
  in Presentations, 239
  in Quattro Pro, 176–177
  in WordPerfect, 68–69
Uniform Resource Locators (URLs), 268, 272
updating linked copies
  automatically, 310–312
  manually, 312–313
Upgrade Help, 34
URLs (Uniform Resource Locators), 268, 272

• V •

values
  defined, 149
  entering, 150–153
  formatting numeric data, 154
  formulas, 159–171
  labels versus, 151–152
  See also formulas
vector drawings, 234
vertical alignment in spreadsheet cells, 157
Vertical Line command, 114
View menu (Envoy), 254
View menu (Presentations), 240
View menu (Quattro Pro), 137
View menu (WordPerfect)
  Guidelines command, 79
  Reveal Codes command, 66, 75
  Toolbars/Ruler command, 43, 79, 82
View/Zoom tab of WordPerfect Display Preferences, 42
viewing. *See* displaying
Viewport (Sidekick 95), 295

• W •

WARNING! icon, 5
watermarks, 324–325
.WAV files, 243, 330
.WB3 file extension, 144
Web After Work For Dummies, The, 274
Web browsers, 268
  See also Netscape Navigator; World Wide Web
Web, the. *See* World Wide Web
What Do You Want to Know? box, 31
width of text columns, 109

Windows 3.1 program versions, 2
Windows 3.x Runtime files, 247
Windows 95
  clip art as screen saver, 325–326
  file naming rules, 56
  Runtime files, 247
windows
  closing, 22
  CorelFLOW window elements, 300–301
  Dashboard window elements, 298–299
  defined, 20
  maximizing or minimizing, 22
  moving, 22
  Netscape browser window elements, 270–271
  overview, 20–22
  Presentations window elements, 222
  Quattro Pro spreadsheet elements, 135–137
  resizing, 22
  switching between, 27
  WordPerfect window elements, 40–41
  See also customizing
Word Forms option, 125
word processor. *See* WordPerfect
WordPerfect
  closing documents, 54
  customizing, 41–44
  deleting text, 63
  drop caps, 321–322
  editing text, 60–71
  entering text, 44–45
  Experts, 51
  finding and replacing text, 123–126
  formatting text, 73–94
  inserting Address Book addresses, 285
  keyboard shortcuts, 47
  navigating documents, 46–47
  opening existing documents, 52–53
  opening new documents, 50–52
  overview, 10–12
  page layout, 95–114
  printing, 57–60
  printing Address Book addresses, 285
  printing to Envoy, 251–254
  QuickCorrect, 45, 69–71
  QuickFormat, 73, 122–123
  QuickTasks, 32–33
  saving documents, 54–57
  selecting text, 62–63
  Show Me features, 31–32
  sound clips in, 328–330
  Spell Checker, 127–129
  starting, 39
  styles, 115–121
  templates, 51–52
  TextArt, 13, 322–324
  Upgrade Help, 34
  watermarks, 324–325
  when to use, 13
  window elements, 40–41
WordPerfect for Windows For Dummies, 66, 75
WordPerfect Suite 7. *See* Corel WordPerfect Suite 7
WordPerfect Suite 7 For Dummies
  conventions, 6
  icons in margins, 5
  as last resort, 340
  organization, 3–5
  programs covered, 2
worksheets. *See* spreadsheets
World Wide Web
  Corel Web site, 274
  finding sites, 273–274
  online Help, 34, 339
  overview, 268
  printing pages, 280
  saving pages to disk, 280
  See also Netscape Navigator
wrapping text
  in Quattro Pro, 157
  in WordPerfect, 81
Write view (Sidekick 95), 293–294

• X, Y •

X (Close) button, 22, 54

• Z •

zooming, 24
  in CorelFLOW, 301
  in Envoy, 255
  previewing spreadsheets, 213–214
  in Quattro Pro, 135
  in WordPerfect, 42

IDG BOOKS WORLDWIDE REGISTRATION CARD

RETURN THIS REGISTRATION CARD FOR FREE CATALOG

Title of this book: WordPerfect® Suite 7 For Dummies®

My overall rating of this book: ❑ Very good [1] ❑ Good [2] ❑ Satisfactory [3] ❑ Fair [4] ❑ Poor [5]

How I first heard about this book:

❑ Found in bookstore; name: [6] ❑ Book review: [7]

❑ Advertisement: [8] ❑ Catalog: [9]

❑ Word of mouth; heard about book from friend, co-worker, etc.: [10] ❑ Other: [11]

What I liked most about this book:

What I would change, add, delete, etc., in future editions of this book:

Other comments:

Number of computer books I purchase in a year: ❑ 1 [12] ❑ 2-5 [13] ❑ 6-10 [14] ❑ More than 10 [15]

I would characterize my computer skills as: ❑ Beginner [16] ❑ Intermediate [17] ❑ Advanced [18] ❑ Professional [19]

I use ❑ DOS [20] ❑ Windows [21] ❑ OS/2 [22] ❑ Unix [23] ❑ Macintosh [24] ❑ Other: [25] ____________ (please specify)

I would be interested in new books on the following subjects:
(please check all that apply, and use the spaces provided to identify specific software)

❑ Word processing: [26] ❑ Spreadsheets: [27]

❑ Data bases: [28] ❑ Desktop publishing: [29]

❑ File Utilities: [30] ❑ Money management: [31]

❑ Networking: [32] ❑ Programming languages: [33]

❑ Other: [34]

I use a PC at (please check all that apply): ❑ home [35] ❑ work [36] ❑ school [37] ❑ other: [38] ____________

The disks I prefer to use are ❑ 5.25 [39] ❑ 3.5 [40] ❑ other: [41] ____________

I have a CD ROM: ❑ yes [42] ❑ no [43]

I plan to buy or upgrade computer hardware this year: ❑ yes [44] ❑ no [45]

I plan to buy or upgrade computer software this year: ❑ yes [46] ❑ no [47]

Name: Business title: [48] Type of Business: [49]

Address (❑ home [50] ❑ work [51]/Company name:)

Street/Suite#

City [52]/State [53]/Zipcode [54]: Country [55]

❑ **I liked this book!** You may quote me by name in future IDG Books Worldwide promotional materials.

My daytime phone number is ____________

IDG BOOKS
THE WORLD OF COMPUTER KNOWLEDGE

YES!

Please keep me informed about IDG's World of Computer Knowledge. Send me the latest IDG Books catalog.

NO POSTAGE
NECESSARY
IF MAILED
IN THE
UNITED STATES

BUSINESS REPLY MAIL

FIRST CLASS MAIL PERMIT NO. 2605 FOSTER CITY, CALIFORNIA

IDG Books Worldwide
919 E Hillsdale Blvd, STE 400
Foster City, CA 94404-9691